Bless.ed
One

Bless•ed One

One

*From a shantytown in Kabwé, Zambia,
to the first Black African
in the U.S. Open*

JAMES
ROTH

This Moment
Publications

Published by This Moment Publications, LLC

ISBN 978-1-7379830-2-6 (hardback)
ISBN 978-1-7379830-0-2 (paperback)
ISBN 978-1-7379830-1-9 (eBook)

Cover Design by Ida Fia Sveningsson

Book Design by Kory Kirby
SET IN GARAMOND PREMIERE PRO

Printed in the United States of America

For the men who most impacted my life but
were unable to share this moment:
Lyle James Roth, Claude Faure,
and Peter Muthiya.

And for the women that I am blessed to still have with me:
My wife, Stacey, our daughter, Aveline,
and my mom, Janet.

Contents

Foreword

As FAR AS I CAN vividly recall, the first golf lesson I received from my father as a six-year-old was not centered around golf mechanics, posture or the set-up of the golf ball. Neither was it him standing behind me with his hands covering mine to demonstrate proper grip or the dangers of a downhill putt. Suffice to say, mechanics were secondary.

Before we stepped foot on the golf course, he punctuated his most fundamental and non-negotiable rule: always apply the rules of the game and demonstrate proper demeanor and etiquette whilst on the course. A violation of this core tenet meant putting my clubs away for a period of time and perhaps a good dose of corporal punishment. His emphasis on decorum was about more than his personal belief in sportsmanship or his respect for the dignity and traditions of the game—both of which he had.

A student of history, he knew that each swing of a golf club or step down a fairway was a gift that few Africans before me ever received. Africa is rich in culture and tradition. Sadly, many of our ancient civilizations and cherished ways of life were destroyed over centuries by slavery, colonialism, war, corruption, miseducation and disease. Consumed by daily fights for survival, most Africans knew nothing about golf nor had they seen it. Even fewer could conceive of paying for an education and earning a living by playing a game. "Remember," my father would say, "generations of people just like you could never dream of this opportunity, including many alive today." As much as my own love of golf, these people became my inspiration and a core reason I strive to become a better person in victory and defeat.

The ability to control my emotions was critical as my eyes opened to the sobering reality that playing in tournaments did not put me on equal footing. Competitive high-level golf is an exclusive club that requires money. Throughout my childhood I was often the only Black player at an event and the only golfer having never received formal coaching. The uncomfortable stares at my secondhand clubs, worn shoes—and my Black presence—were blunt reminders that I was an oddity in a world where money mattered and centuries-old perceptions still lingered.

Guided by my father's words, I share the details of my personal journey with a great deal of humility and a clear sense for what I hope it achieves. If readers view Jayme's moving and well-researched work as nothing more than the struggles and achievements of one family—and one man—then the more fundamental messages have been missed. This book carries a larger purpose for me, far more important than shining a spotlight on a single golfer.

The following pages reveal a bond that was formed between people from vastly different ethnic and cultural backgrounds. Oceans apart. Zambian and American. Black and White. Initially a forced merger that no one asked for—or wanted—over time each began filling a void in the others' lives. During a time of racial division, my aspiration is that the evolution of this unlikely union will inspire readers toward greater openness to new and unexpected relationships, and perhaps even a broader definition of "family."

Secondly, people should view this story less as a cause to celebrate my life and more as inspiration for their own. Revealing the personal details of my journey is done to serve as an example for men, women and children around the world—regardless of race—who stand bravely in the face of daunting challenges and fear the mountain to climb is too high. My hope is they finish this story emboldened with a new sense of power to overcome their current situation, limited only by the strength of their work ethic and the power of their dreams, thinking, *If he can do it, so can I.*

Most important to me is that people are not left feeling completely content. The lasting impact of this story should be more than simply reading about the first Black African to reach golf's grandest stage and the first to play on several professional tours despite the financial barriers standing in the way. This book should raise a nagging and uncomfortable question that lingers after turning the final page: Why did it take so long?

Golf is a by-product of a strong economy and a healthy middle class. Nearly all the world's great golfers come from countries that enjoy both, or they are born into families that occupy a privileged place. At the opposite end of the spectrum stand billions of people trapped by extreme poverty. The largest percentage of those people live in sub-Saharan Africa. In Zambia, well more than half of the population survives on less than $2 a day.

But poverty is not limited to Africa. In the United States, Europe, Latin America and Asia, huge numbers of people go to bed hungry. Children are malnourished and cannot afford school. For those who believe it is just something seen on TV, or is somebody else's problem, poverty and wealth inequality will increasingly fuel political instability, spread contagious diseases and foster other global crises that impact us all.

For me, personal fulfillment will come if people finish this book with a greater awareness of the world, a deeper sense of empathy and a belief that leaders must do more to address basic human needs. I am compelled to use my voice out of deep respect and appreciation for the unimaginably difficult journey endured by my parents and grandparents and because of the role they played in my life. I can hear my father's voice reminding me that credit for my achievements does not rest with me alone. Generations of people have carried me.

—MADALITSO MUTHIYA

Preface

No one seemed to realize that history was being made right before their eyes when Madalitso Muthiya, a wiry, unassuming twenty-three-year-old from Kitwe, Zambia, strode to the first tee at the legendary Winged Foot Country Club just outside New York City in June of 2006. There were no photographers, video cameras or adoring fans. He was not the most accomplished golfer, nor the most watched. But his journey here was the most improbable. And revolutionary.

As he waited to tee off, Madalitso's breath was not bated. No butterflies fluttered in his stomach. His heart was not in his mouth. It beat slow and steady. He looked relaxed and ready, like a battle-tested veteran instead of a young golfer 7,000 miles from home, from a continent whose indigenous people were never before represented in one of the world's most famous sporting events.

His face showed the same cool, calm, collected confidence that I saw eight years earlier in a hotel lobby halfway around the world where I first came face-to-face with the soft-spoken, stone-faced teenage golf prodigy and his astute-looking father, Peter.

Peter Muthiya grew up in a mud hut, a Black child of colonial Africa in the 1950s who fell madly in love with a game invented by some of the whitest men on earth: the Scottish. And they brought to Africa by British colonialists as a White man's game, where Peter and his kind were not welcome. But Peter wouldn't let that get in the way of his love. He foraged for balls in the deadly, snake-infested brush edging the unlikely golf course near his home in Zambia. He was desperate to learn how to drive and putt, but the equipment was ridiculously expensive, available to only the well-heeled ruling class. When you don't know where your next meal is coming from, spending as much money on a set of Titleists as your family made in a year is unthinkable, no matter how deep your love for the game.

So Peter whittled homemade golf clubs from carefully curated sticks and played with his scavenged balls. He loved to play golf. Smacking the ball, watching it fly, and trying to figure out how to construct a swing that would make the ball go exactly where he wanted. He was consumed by proper club grip and body stance, correct form and strategy. He relished the history of golf and its great champions, time-honored etiquette, sportsmanship and traditions.

As Peter grew, his love affair with golf ripened and deepened, becoming more than a passionate pastime. It offered escape from a life of extreme poverty, where people survived on less than a dollar a day, the average life expectancy was thirty-seven and contracting AIDS or malaria was more likely than going to college. A few hours with his lovingly carved clubs was a calming balm that let him forget the crippled economy, the often insane, inhumane government policies and the systemic corruption that kept him and millions of his people in a perpetual struggle. He could also ignore the occasional pang of regret for the choice he made—one he wanted his son to avoid. He vowed that his son would have it better than he did, so hitting golf balls became his refuge, his sanctuary, his asylum.

But if you watched Madalitso approach his tee shot with his big, shiny Cleveland driver on that June day, you'd never have guessed that his father learned to play with whittled branches and scraps of wood. Or that he'd spent most of his life surrounded by disease, poverty and the looming legacy of oppression. While his father had passed on his encyclopedic knowledge of golf's history—the good, the bad and the ugly—he knew he was doing something no man had ever done. But he did not buckle with the weight of his people, his country and his father on his back. He never believed the widely accepted notion that a Black African golfer, without the benefit of coaching, access to world-class courses or proper equipment, could not compete on the grandest stage of world golf. His father wouldn't let him.

Standing there in the tee box of this famous, stately bastion of championship golf, he heard his father's voice in his head. His whole life, Peter Muthiya had told him that he was as good as anyone else and to measure himself not by what narrow minds thought or said about him, but by his faith, hard work, and determination. Those were things he had in abundance. He remembered his grandmother's words of wisdom: *Don't worry about the people around you. Just focus on what you need to do.*

Thus fortified, he planted his tee into the hallowed ground and nonchalantly yet meticulously placed his golf ball (brand-new and not scavenged from under a cobra!) on it.

Compared to staring down death, disease and a world where the deck was stacked against him, it didn't even seem like there was a deck—hitting a golf ball down the immaculate green fairway seemed like a walk in the park.

It didn't matter whether he dribbled the ball off the tee box or belted it 300 yards dead center. Just by hitting his tee shot, Madalitso Muthiya would become a historical figure, a living, breathing embodiment of breaking the yoke of racism and subjugation—of changing the world. With a driver, a nine-iron and a putter.

With a placid expression and easy grace, Madalitso prepared to tee off. The 400 yards of pristine green grass stretching in front of him was like an invitation. But I saw only the brown, patchy, unkempt course in a town that has since been erased from the map: Broken Hill. This is where his dad turned a childhood crush into a lifelong love affair that birthed "Mad," an award-winning golfer.

This is the story of how Madalitso Muthiya rewrote history. It all began in a rich, bountiful, beautiful country hardened and corrupted over centuries by the slave trade, apartheid and foreign oppression where men, women and children and homes, land and culture were destroyed.

In the heart of colonial Africa.

Bless.ed
One

PART I

I

WHEN HIS BIG BROTHER TOOK him to work at Broken Hill Golf Club in 1955, Peter Muthiya had no idea that at the ripe old age of five, he was about to start a love affair that would last the rest of his life. They came from a two-room mud hut that housed their entire family in a ramshackle shantytown on the edge of Broken Hill. Formerly known as *Mutwe Wa Nsofu* (Elephant's Head) by the local Africans, Broken Hill was created by White colonialists who flocked in droves after mineral riches were discovered long before Peter was born. Naturally, the rich White British transplants wanted a golf course. Thus, Broken Hill Golf Club was born.

Even at five years old, Peter was an optimistic skeptic who asked too many questions. He understood that his brother Patson's job as a caddie was to carry sticks that men used to hit small white balls into little holes in the ground. Peter grasped the concept of work for pay, but Patson's job seemed to serve no purpose. Why would these White men pay him to carry their sticks? And why would they want to hit small balls into little holes?

But when he laid eyes on the first fairway, with its vast sea of grass that seemed to reach the horizon, he had his answers. Peter was awestruck. He marveled as the first player teed off. He'd never seen anything that didn't have wings fly so far. He stood open-mouthed with a million questions on the tip of his little tongue. But his brother's stern glare was a clear signal to keep his mouth shut while the White players focused on the game.

Peter watched quietly as his brother handed clubs to the man hitting the balls. He was confused by how many clubs were in the bag. And that they all looked the same. He hated being confused. He wanted to understand the purpose of the bag and all those sticks and why these White men were so committed to getting their small balls into the little holes at the end of the green ocean.

Then he noticed something else. White men hit the balls. Black men carried the sticks. Around the clubhouse, Whites outnumbered Blacks three to one. When he thought back on it later, he realized it was the first time he felt like a minority in Africa.

Toward the end of the round, Peter saw a golf ball hiding under some brush along a fairway. He made sure there were no snakes lurking. Then, he reached under the thicket and picked it up. When he saw his brother, he proudly showed Patson the ball. His brother shook his head and gave him a sharp look. Peter quickly hid the ball in his pocket.

When the round was over, Patson collected his pay, and it was time to leave. Peter desperately wanted to see the inside of the clubhouse. But that was impossible.

No Blacks allowed.

DURING THEIR WALK home, Peter peppered his brother with questions.

What is the object of the game?

To get the ball into the hole with the fewest number of strokes.

What is par?

The number of strokes needed to complete the hole and the round.

So a golfer competes against the course *and* the other players?

Yes.

What if the player takes fewer strokes than par?

One stroke less than par is a birdie. Two is an eagle.

And more than par?

One more stroke is a bogey. Two is a double-bogey. Three is a triple. On and on.

Why are there so many sticks?

They're called "clubs," not "sticks." Each one is different, with slight variations in length and in the flat area that strikes the ball.

Why?

Each club is designed to achieve a different height or distance.

Peter's five-year-old brain chewed on and digested all valuable information.

Why were only White men playing?

Because only White men can play there. Africans are not allowed to play.

What would happen if we're caught playing?

We'd get thrown off the course or worse. Beaten. Arrested.

Peter thought again.

What if we played someplace else?

Where?

Anywhere.

Young Peter didn't care about the golf course. All he wanted was to smash that small white ball and then tap it into the little hole before the other players.

Peter remembered the golf ball in his pocket.

Can I keep it?

Yes.

Won't the owner miss it?

Are you kidding? Dozens of balls are lost on that course every day!

Dozens?

Yes.

What happens to them?

Nothing. A player hits a ball in the bushes, or out of bounds, he looks for a few minutes, and then gets a new one from his bag.

Peter's mind raced.

Can I come back tomorrow?

Do you promise not to ask questions while the men are playing?

I promise.

Patson sighed.

Okay.

And so began the childhood crush that would later become one of the true loves of his life: golf.

THE NEXT DAY at the Broken Hill Golf Course, Patson didn't see his little brother for hours. He was afraid Peter was dead in the rough, poisoned by a cobra, a common menace on Zambian golf courses.

Peter's disappearance was a distraction. Patson couldn't focus on the game and became more irritated by the minute. At the end of the round, his little brother reappeared. Patson unloaded on him. He couldn't waste his time worrying about Peter getting lost or hurt. How would he explain it to their mother if something terrible happened to him?

Peter shrugged, apologized and smiled.

Patson paused, puzzled, and demanded to know why Peter was smiling.

Peter revealed his overstuffed pockets, bulging with golf balls.

PETER HAD HIS balls. Now he needed clubs. He scoured the neighborhood for straight limbs, branches and sticks. He and his brother would grind, scrape and file down the end to create a flat surface to strike the ball. Occasionally, Patson brought home a damaged or discarded club they could repair.

On a rough patch of dirt, they made their own two-hole golf course. The boys teed off in one direction, holed out and played back the other way. They cleared away debris around the hole to make a putting "green." It was, in fact, brown. The fairway was strewn with rocks, sticks and patches of vegetation: built-in hazards, like the natural terrain on the ancient links near Scotland's coast. Moving the flag various distances meant they had a different course to play every day.

At five years old, Peter whaled on the ball, hitting it as far as possible. Then, he'd hit shorter shots, getting closer and closer to the brown green before tapping it into the hole. He didn't care about proper form or the number of strokes. He was giddy, having the time of his life with his new love.

Peter lived and breathed golf. He played every spare moment. And when he wasn't playing, he was dreaming (or daydreaming) about it. His friends didn't share his passion, since golf was so clearly a rich White man's game. But his mom let her sons play as much as they liked. *After* they finished chores and schoolwork.

Soon, his parents enrolled Peter in St. Mary's Primary School. Like most schools for African children, St. Mary's was founded by European missionaries. A few basic subjects were taught, including English.

His mother started getting complaints from Peter's teacher. He was disrupting the flow of class, questioning everything. It wasn't that he resented authority or needed attention; he just hated being confused. And he loved asking questions because he wanted to understand. Sometimes, his teacher indulged him, but it stopped the class from moving forward. Eventually, like Peter's brother, she got frustrated when the questions never ended.

His parents, Sandikonda and Kaliwé, were in a pickle. They believed in discipline and respect, but they refused to extinguish his desire to learn or his passion for asking questions.

Peter fell more in love with golf every day, as he easily completed his Sub A and Standard 1 at St. Mary's primary school.

Then his world turned upside down.

PETER'S UNCLE PAPSONJERE had a modest farm next to Fort Jameson in Eastern Province, where Sandikonda and Kaliwé were born. Fort Jameson offered Black children a chance to receive the best education available, a big step up from St. Mary's. Naviluli Primary School and Chizongwe Junior Secondary School were among the best schools for Black children in Northern Rhodesia, which would soon be called Zambia. By age eleven, many of those students were the only members of their family who could read, write and speak English.

Papsonjere talked passionately about these schools during family visits. Sandikonda and Kaliwé never gave it much thought until Peter began showing extraordinary ability and finished St. Mary's feeling bored and unchallenged. Initially, they couldn't imagine sending Peter away. The family had stayed together through mind-numbing poverty, traumatic forced relocations and body-depleting food shortages.

Peter's parents began to raise their voices at each other. His name was shouted in anger. He felt responsible.

Finally, Kaliwé sat her youngest son down. Peter looked into her red, swollen eyes and knew she had been crying. She put her arm around him and told him he was going to live with his uncle in Fort Jameson. Peter was devastated. She held him in her loving mother's embrace. Later, Peter realized what a terrible moment this was for her. But she was his rock. She never broke down. At least not in front of Peter.

The next day, his mother kissed him goodbye, and Peter began walking with his uncle to the Broken Hill bus station for the long trip to Fort Jameson. He took only what was most necessary.

One change of clothes. His little white golf balls. His precious homemade clubs.

Knowing he wouldn't see her for another year, he turned to his mother and waved goodbye. Leaving his parents at the tender age of seven was by far the hardest thing he had ever done. A few years later, when his mother believed he was old enough to understand, she offered a simple explanation.

Sometimes you have to love your children enough to send them away.

2

PETER'S HEART SANK WHEN THE bus pulled into Fort Jameson. It was slow and backward. It had no mines or money—which meant no hustle or bustle. No paved sidewalks, inviting storefronts or other amenities. No rumbling trains, groaning truck engines or daily flood of workers, like back home in Broken Hill. The small town center was essentially a glorified farmer's market. And he missed his parents, brothers and sisters so much it felt like a limb had been hacked off. It was hate at first sight.

It didn't help when they got to his new home. Turned out his uncle Papsonjere didn't have a wife. He had three. Nobody had three wives in Broken Hill. Or if they did, they kept it a secret. But when you're a child, even polygamy can get normal pretty quick.

THE GOOD NEWS: Peter's love affair with golf moved full steam ahead. Fort Jameson had much better terrain than Broken Hill, which was rocky, choppy, scarred, and chewed up with automobile and foot traffic. Fort Jameson was farm country, with wide-open spaces and rich fertile soil for grooming fairways and greens. And it was literally a breath of fresh air. In

Broken Hill, the filthy stink of billowing smoke hung so thick, you could practically chew the air.

Time passed, and Peter made a new golf course, complete with tee areas, fairways and flags festively sprouting from holes. And since he was, in addition to being architect and head groundskeeper, the superintendent and head pro of his golf course, he got to choose the number of strokes for par. A precocious ten-year-old with a good head for numbers, he decided pars were 8s, 9s and a couple of 10s for the really tough holes. Whatever it took to prevent a bogey.

Again, he snuck away to be with his love as often as possible. And slowly, he began to master the game of golf. By age twelve, his shots were longer and straighter. As he did in the classroom, Peter applied his sharp, analytical mind to distinguishing the subtle differences between good and bad swings, as well as solving the many riddles of the simple yet maddeningly complicated game, which Mark Twain once famously described as "a good walk spoiled." For Peter, it was the opposite. There was no walk that couldn't be improved with some clubs, a ball and a fairway.

Whenever he could, he visited Fort Jameson Golf Club, the oldest golf club in Northern Rhodesia. It had been there since wealthy White colonialists built it in 1902. Peter was not welcome in the front door. No Black man was, but he managed to sneak in and watch some good players. He studied their body positions and swings and tried to emulate them. How they blasted out of the sand. How they studied the greens and swung their putters. And of course, he went on golf ball safaris, tracking and bagging Titleists, Slazengers and the rare, exotic Hogan.

Peter found peace in the quiet open space of the little golf course oasis he'd made. The silence allowed him to reflect on golf, school and his parents back in Broken Hill.

He especially loved playing at twilight, when the sun set and the sky changed colors.

PETER'S SECOND LOVE was his new school. Instead of stifling Peter's inquisitive mind, his new teacher recognized his talent and desire. She saw his enthusiasm as a gift, rather than a nuisance. She gave him higher level work to perform quietly in his seat. Disengaged from classmates, he learned at an accelerated rate and spared the teacher his constant interruptions.

Peter quickly distanced himself from kids his age. He was doing advanced math and excelled in reading, writing and speaking English, often practicing with his teacher after class.

The government offered no accelerated learning programs for African children, and Peter's school could afford only basic supplies. Fortunately, his teacher had a calling, so she instructed an entire class *and* catered to the needs of one gifted child.

He was also getting a very different, but no less important, education in his new home.

UNCLE PAPSONJERE WASN'T tall, but his personality made him big. Peter loved his confidence, his huge smile and how he told his nephew the truth, even when it was hard. His uncle began teaching Peter the history of the Ngoni people. Uncle Papsonjere was a great storyteller who used vivid facial expressions and animated gestures to make his tales come to life. Peter particularly enjoyed the stories of Shaka, the great Zulu warrior—his revolutionary fighting techniques, advanced weaponry and vast conquests. Papsonjere's story transformed Shaka into a human deity in Peter's eyes. One day, Papsonjere revealed a shocking truth: Peter was a descendent of the great and powerful Shaka.

Papsonjere told how the Ngoni nation broke away from Shaka's *mfecane* ("the crushing"), conquering and incorporating tribes as they moved northward. Peter was in disbelief. The Ngoni had a complex system of government with chiefs and senior officials in charge of military, judicial, economic and administrative affairs. Peter only knew Blacks to be mine workers, laborers and farmers. But in truth, he was the descendent of chiefs, judges and great military leaders! He thought about himself in new ways. It laid the foundation for believing he and his children could achieve great things, change the world and be more than fodder for the White man's money-making empire, while living in disease, squalor and poverty.

As Peter grew older and learned more, he became confused. And he *hated* being confused. So Peter did what he always did. He asked questions.

How did the world described by his uncle evolve into the one where Peter was born? Why didn't Africans still control the army, the laws, the courts, the police, the health system, businesses and money? What happened?

Peter could see his uncle become visibly uncomfortable. But Peter was stubborn, tenacious and brilliant. A dangerous combination.

Finally, Papsonjere explained the arrival of Europeans, the broken treaties and the Ngoni defeat by a better equipped army. How White colonialists put a stranglehold on Africa by robbing Africans of their native lands, displacing them and using them in the industrial machine the invaders created to get rich, while severing Africans' historical ties to friends, family, home, language, customs and their cherished land. How they destroyed ethnic tribal pride, an ancient culture and a way of life. Peter realized his own parents, along with millions of other Africans, were thus abused in this well-orchestrated campaign. He heard for the first time how much suffering and persecution his people had endured.

Peter asked his uncle why he was able to remain in his home. Uncle Papsonjere told him that across Northern Rhodesia, small numbers of Africans found ways to pay colonial taxes and remain on native land with their people, retaining customs and passing down history to the next generation. It was hard, and he had to fight every step of the way, but Uncle Papsonjere was one of those few Africans in Northern Rhodesia who managed to keep what was his.

But no matter how it was explained, Peter still couldn't answer the burning question:

Why?

Papsonjere tried to explain the British unquenchable lust for wealth. But Peter questioned why Blacks and Whites couldn't dig the mines *and* share the money. After all, it was African land. Worked by African people. Wasn't there enough for everyone?

Finally, Uncle Papsonjere revealed the source of Peter's parents' poverty, the reason they left Fort Jameson, and the economic, political and social inequality between Blacks and Whites. Why African towns and African children had English names. Why if you were Black in Africa, you always ended up at the wrong end of an uneven deal. Why he, and all his Black brothers and sisters, were excluded from Broken Hill Golf Club.

The answer was black and white. The color of their skin. The color of the invaders' skin.

Peter had a chilling realization. Before this moment, he'd innocently accepted his world. He knew nothing of colonialism or apartheid. He believed Europeans in Africa was a good thing. After all, the Whites he met were mostly pleasant. His father's boss, Mr. Holton, was kind, occasionally giving their family used clothing.

Peter now saw the cold hard reality of his world. He understood that cordial exchanges or individual acts of generosity were not the way to judge people. Sometimes the benchmark is a person's willing participation in a system that harms others while benefiting themselves.

Years later, he would reflect on his loss of innocence as he increasingly viewed others with resentment and distrust.

But it would help him prepare his son to take on the world, defy history and smash through walls built by prejudice and oppression.

As PETER BECAME a teenager, he connected his uncle's history lessons with the civil unrest taking place in Northern Rhodesia and elsewhere in Africa. Tensions ratcheted up in the late 1950s when Europeans poured into the country to enjoy the privileges of a segregated society while Africans were thrown out of work due to falling copper prices.

Peter became political, engaged in raging debates, and tried to figure out ways of protesting. He was thrilled when Kenneth Kaunda, President of the

United National Independence Party (UNIP), vowed in 1961 to "strike at the very roots of the British Government in this country." Kaunda's fervor brought widespread enthusiasm and hope for Blacks in Northern Rhodesia.

Peter was brimming with hope, exhilarated and a little overwhelmed when he went to his first freedom rally in 1962. He loved seeing his people full of passion and conviction, marching, chanting, standing up to oppression and fighting for their rights.

His exhilaration turned to fear when agents of the "cha-cha-cha" revolutionary movement detonated an explosive device. Northern Rhodesian security forces responded with tear gas and gunfire. It was a chaotic scene. He heard shots and shouts as panicked people began running. More than a war of words and ideas, this was a life-and-death struggle. Some were not going to make it out of this revolution alive.

As he ran through the pandemonium, the angry screams and the wails of pain, he heard someone from a passing car yell, *"Kaffir!"*

This was Africa's version of the N-word. Peter caught the angry eye of a passing White motorist and realized, to his horror, that the hateful racist epithet was directed at him.

Europeans were nervous. Africans no longer averted their eyes or glanced downward deferentially to White people. Peter was a member of the new generation who stood their ground and looked the White man in the face.

A child's naïveté evolved into an adolescent's passion, burgeoning pride and desire to make the world a better place than he found it. Peter was encouraged by what he saw in his people's faces: anger, desire, courage, resolve and resistance.

FALLING IN LOVE with being an activist didn't dampen Peter's love affair with golf. He continued to play his DIY course. Slowly but surely, his whittled sticks were replaced with real golf clubs that players had abandoned at Fort Jameson Golf Club for one reason or another, and he had them repaired.

Little by little, Peter was learning. Bend the knees. Keep the left arm straight. Focus on the ball. Swing with a smooth but powerful rhythm. As he got older, he hit the ball longer and straighter. And fell more hopelessly in love.

Occasionally, Peter coaxed Uncle Papsonjere into hitting a few balls. But the elder Muthiya hated anything even remotely associated with colonialism, so he had little interest in what he viewed as a White man's game. But Peter had no qualms about loving something that originated in Great Britain. He thought it was just plain wrong to blame clubs, balls and holes for the slave trade or colonialism.

Peter couldn't seem to get his uncle to understand the deep peace he felt with a club in his hand, staring down at that little ball and trying to figure out how to make it do exactly what he wanted. His worries vanished. Life was reduced to a simple yet incredibly difficult task. Swing the club. Hit the ball. When he made that sweet connection, his body reverberated as the ball flew off his club, soaring like it had wings. It was pure joy watching the ball land softly, with the right spin so it followed the contour of the land and rolled slowly toward the hole. Sinking a putt and watching his small ball fall into that little hole. Peter could never quite explain to his uncle how lovely that was.

With mounting pressures of school and his nation's roiling turmoil, golf became a haven, a refuge and a great alleviator of stress.

A love into whose arms he could always fall.

PETER DECIDED, WITH the help of teachers who believed in him, that he would become the first member of his family to go to college. Of course, he didn't really know what college was or the mountain he would have to climb to make that happen.

In the early 1960s, only one secondary school in the colony prepared African students for college: Munali. Its faculty held degrees from good universities in Africa and England, and its alumni list was remarkable. The school enjoyed international recognition by staying true to its core principle: *Only the best is good enough for Munali.*

For Peter to have even a slim chance of going to college, he would have to be accepted to Munali. There was about as much chance of that as there was of his son becoming the first Black African to play in the U.S. Open. Although Fort Jameson was once the administrative center of Northern Rhodesia, it was fast becoming a remote backwater town, clear out in Eastern Province, far from the new epicenters of business and politics in Northern Rhodesia. Even with Peter's stellar academic record, it was hard to imagine a kid who grew up in a mud hut, and who now hailed from far-off Fort Jameson, would be good enough to be "the best."

And of course, as it is everywhere in the world, it's not what you know, it's who you know. Despite Peter's remarkable academic records and achievements, the Muthiyas were still displaced migrant workers. They did not rub elbows with the influential movers and shakers or the intelligentsia that dominated the small but growing world of educated and successful Africans in Northern Rhodesia.

Then, there was the bottom line. Money. The thing that makes the world go round. Even if Peter somehow miraculously managed to get admitted to the prestigious institution, his family couldn't even remotely afford tuition. Peter would need a full scholarship.

Peter approached his fourteenth birthday as the Chizongwe staff worked overtime to prepare his case for the Munali admissions board. When the materials were completed and dispatched to Lusaka, student and teachers were sure they had done their best.

Peter knew at this point it was in God's hands.

1964 WAS A memorable year for Northern Rhodesia—and for Peter Muthiya.

The campaign of universal adult suffrage, entitled "one-man one-vote," became a reality, and with it came real democratic elections. Secession talks with Britain accelerated.

On October 23, the Union Jack was lowered at 11:58 p.m. as the British National Anthem played for the last time. At midnight, a single light illuminated the green, red, black and orange Zambian flag. A huge multi-racial crowd chanted *"Kwatcha"* (the Dawn) while a copper torch burned over the city.

On October 24, 1964, Northern Rhodesia died, and the Republic of Zambia was born.

Peter was in Chipata, hundreds of miles from the ceremony, but he felt like he was there. There was dancing in the streets, big smiles, cheering, shouting and singing, celebrating the end of an era of slavery, subjugation, oppression, disease, displacement and misery.

Peter couldn't quite wrap his mind around what it all meant. No longer would the country's wealth benefit foreign interests. No longer would the few benefit at the expense of the many. He overflowed with optimism. The world had changed. He and his people would determine their own fates for the first time, leading their beautiful country into a future of abundance, prosperity, health and education. A place where anything was possible.

In the weeks that followed, Peter read in newspapers like the *New York Times* that Zambia was glowing with potential. Their mineral wealth made the odds for economic success better than those of other new nations that were springing up across Africa. He loved watching maps become outdated as English names were removed and replaced. Fort Jameson was now Chipata. Broken Hill became Kabwé.

A second landmark event of 1964 garnered no international press. No ceremonies. No national celebrations.

One morning, Peter was unexpectedly called to the headmaster's office where he was surrounded by Chizongwe's faculty, looking very stern. He was sure he was in trouble. The headmaster handed him an open envelope postmarked Lusaka. Peter reached inside, removed the letter and read the news as the room erupted in wild applause.

Peter and his beloved golf clubs were going to Munali Secondary School on full scholarship.

3

PETER LOOKED AROUND ON HIS first day at Munali and realized he was different. Even though the other students were African, many of their fathers were educated, held senior positions in the new Zambian government or were members of a small Black upper-class. They weren't millionaires, but they had far more money than the Muthiyas would ever see.

Peter's parents were uneducated migrant laborers, living on the lowest rung of Zambia's economic ladder. Few children with his background attended Munali, and he wondered if he really belonged with all these kids of the upper crust. He confessed as much to his parents.

Kaliwé would have none of it: She told him that they were who they were, and he was who he was. They were both there, so they both belonged. He should ignore their money. *Just focus on what you need to do.*

Those words would stay with him the rest of his life.

Peter's mother reminded him that Munali was a blessing. He was fifteen, an age when most Zambians were already toiling away in the mines or eking out a living through subsistence farming.

In Lusaka, Peter missed his parents in Kabwé and Uncle Papsonjere in Chipata. But he thrived. He enjoyed all his subjects. But he had two favorites. For the first time he got to work with real lab equipment, making science a hands-on experience. Peter loved rolling up his sleeves and digging in. The other subject was no surprise. He devoured every history book in the Munali library.

But not everything he learned was on campus.

Mr. Clifford Little, an Oxford-educated Englishman, played a key role in transforming Munali into the foremost secondary school in Southern Africa in the 1950s. He regularly opened his home to friends of all races and welcomed readers into his extensive library. Many benefited from his generosity, including the young Peter Muthiya.

Peter would find a quiet corner among the stacks of books in Mr. Little's private collection. He spent hours reading everything. He loved any book that chronicled the important people and events that shaped the world.

Munali also helped change the way Peter thought about himself, other people and his country. The school employed an integrated staff. White and Black teachers taught side by side in adjoining classrooms, and many lived next to each other. In Peter's world, the Whites played golf, and the Blacks carried the clubs.

His own personal experiences and his parents' suffering had given him preconceptions about race, color, money, exploitation and privilege that stayed with him well into adulthood. But Munali challenged his thinking. The school's faculty, regardless of race, cared for the welfare of their students...*all* of them.

One thing Munali did *not* change was Peter's love affair with golf. He adored the sport more than ever. But Munali's urban location provided little space for a makeshift golf course or driving range. Playing at Lusaka Golf Club cost money, so he was relegated to hitting balls on Munali's soccer field or putting in his dormitory.

He got lots of odd looks.

PETER'S LAST YEAR of secondary school was the final chapter of a stellar academic career at Munali. His grades were among the highest in his class, though he downplayed his achievements. Instead of focusing on grades, he tried to enjoy the process of learning. And knowing how lucky he was to even be at Munali made the experience all the more rewarding.

Peter credited each subject with playing a role in his personal development. Science satisfied his insatiable urge to question. Math his need for logic. English allowed him to express himself more fully. He *loved* to talk. History helped show him how he, and the world, got to be what they were.

Peter was the only student in his class to receive an academic distinction in history.

4

Peter Muthiya was eighteen, a proud young man from a proud young country. Now a Munali graduate, he'd soaked up four years of education from worldly, diverse teachers and rubbed elbows with classmates from upper-crest families. His eyes were opened, and the naive boy from Eastern Province was gone. For the first time in history, universities in England and the United States finally opened their doors to Black African students. And a growing number of universities were springing up across the sub-continent. He knew he had a vast choice of colleges.

Peter agonized over what he thought was the most important decision of his life. But not which university to attend. Whether he should go at all. He was carrying a boulder of guilt on his shoulders. While he matured and flourished in the rarefied air of Munali, his parents still lived in the same mud hut, surviving day-to-day, hand-to-mouth. As long as he could remember, Sandikonda and Kaliwé had known hardship and sacrifice. Yet they kept their family together and instilled their children with love, pride, toughness and an unflinching work ethic. Life had punished Sandikonda and Kaliwé Muthiya. Their youngest son wanted with all his heart to reward their hard work and ease their pain.

Peter dreamed of giving them running water, electricity, decent food and a better home. As a Munali graduate he was more qualified than most Zambians and could easily find work. Bright young minds and able young bodies were needed to fill skilled labor positions in the copper mines and in government ministries. Already the first in his family to complete secondary school, he loved the idea of being the first to attend college. But he loved the idea of helping his family more. His teachers thought he was crazy for even *considering* not going to college. But they didn't know how his parents suffered.

Deciding to meet his dilemma head on, Peter visited his family in Kabwé. That evening, Kaliwé asked which university he had selected. Choosing his words carefully, Peter explained with the earnest thick-headedness only an eighteen-year-old can muster that he thought it was more important to get a job and help his parents lead a better life.

Kaliwé exploded. They had made the most painful decision imaginable to send their beloved seven-year-old son away to Chipata because they wanted him to go as far as he could with his education and have the best life possible! Why was he insulting them by quitting now, after all their sacrifice and all his hard work? So he could go work in the mines? Had they raised a fool? Had he learned nothing at school? Why was he talking such nonsense?!

Peter was shocked into silence. He was trying to do the right thing by being a good, loving son. Looking back later, he would laugh. He should have seen it coming a mile away. This was Kaliwé's way. She was kind, wise, passionate, but unafraid to speak the truth, even when it was hard. And woe be unto you if you crossed her!

What he didn't expect was his father's reaction. Sandikonda rarely inserted himself into family squabbles. That was his wife's domain. He was the quiet one. It took a lot to get him riled up. But Peter had succeeded in doing just that.

Sandikonda addressed his eldest son with flat indignation. They didn't need Peter's help. He'd been ripped from his home by colonialists, forced to pay outrageous oppressive taxes and given a pittance for painful work with inhuman conditions and hours, but he still provided food and shelter for his family. Always! With steely, stern, paternal pride, he told Peter in no uncertain terms that his son didn't take care of him. He took care of his son.

Peter was devastated. He realized that he'd unintentionally diminished his father as patriarch—a terrible insult to an African man. He walked it back as fast as he could, carefully clarifying that he was so grateful for everything they had done for him. He simply wanted them to be more comfortable as they got older.

Sandikonda raised an eyebrow, clearly even more offended, and asked why Peter thought his dad was a feeble old man.

Everything that came from his mouth was wrong, and Peter kept digging himself into a deeper and deeper hole.

Sandikonda and Kaliwé brought a quick and merciful end to what had become an agonizing discussion for Peter. His mother made it clear that he was going to college. His father bluntly reminded Peter that he was the man of the house, and Peter was the boy. Who was going to college.

Peter had never gotten such a verbal bludgeoning. It was something he would never forget. And he would be sure to pass these lessons of pride, sacrifice and family to his son, who would one day use them to make history.

PETER KNEW THAT universities and colleges in Zambia offered far fewer programs and less world-class faculties than schools in the United States, Europe or other parts of Africa, but he was possessed by a young man's passion. He was driven to commit to something bigger than himself. The newly independent Zambia had ignited a spark that burned hot inside Peter. He was filled with an unbridled optimism and a deep sense of loyalty to his new nation. In 1969, as young Americans were trying to bring forth their own revolution, Peter saw himself as part of a generation that was going to throw off the yoke of a system that had throttled his people for generations. They were going to grow their own economy with a higher standard of living and make a better country for their people in the heart of Africa. None of this could happen if Zambia's best and brightest left the country. Peter believed with all his heart that educated, hardworking, forward-thinking Black African youth needed to stay and build their own brave new world.

Sandikonda and Kaliwé encouraged him to go where his heart took him. Peter loved them for that. And now he knew that they would be fine without him.

But his country would not, and he knew that, too.

Peter saw his friends and classmates from Munali leave to lead exciting new lives in Paris, New York City and London. He wondered what his life would be like if he left his homeland in Central Africa. What kind of amazing professors would teach him? What wonders of the world would he see? What incredible opportunities would he have? How many beautiful women would he meet? What riches would he accumulate?

The more soul-searching he did, the more he knew that he wanted to help make Zambia a great nation. He was, after all, a descendent of Shaka, the great Zulu warrior and leader of perhaps the greatest civilization in the history of southern Africa. It was his duty. It was his passion.

Peter Muthiya decided he had no choice. He had to stay.

PETER FELT LUCKY—AND excited—that a brand-new university had just opened in Lusaka, a town he came to know from his time at Munali. The University of Zambia was well staffed with impressive professors, had excellent resources and attracted the kind of students Peter wanted to mix minds with. He decided to dive into his favorite subject, science, and he took as many history courses as his schedule would permit. By the time he was twenty, he'd read every history book in Lusaka he could get his hands on, but he was hungry for more.

Peter loved being on a campus brimming with young Zambians who beamed with pride as they scurried around the new university. The liberating thrill of learning, forbidden by colonialists for generations, flowed through classes and spread with music, writing and passionate discussions everywhere you looked. Black youths carried books rather than copper, reveling in being the first in the history of their nation to be endowed with this gift. The name itself seemed the stuff of revolution and evolution, a symbol for a better world to come. The University of *Zambia*.

But Peter hadn't forgotten his first love. Despite a crazy schedule, he squeezed in a round of golf whenever he could. Luckily, he had a professor who played at Lusaka Golf Club, and it was pure joy when he got invited to play on a golf course, where a generation earlier, he would have only been allowed to caddie like his big brother. He loved losing himself in the peace of the rolling grass, the softly undulating greens. He loved how the club felt in his hand, the smooth beautiful motion of the swing, the little white ball sailing off into the sunset. There was still nothing like it. He tried not to be a pest about it, but whenever he saw his professor, it was all he could do not to plead for a chance to go out and smack the ball around.

One day when Peter's professor took him out to play, everything was working just right. His drives were long and true, his approach shots sweet and pure, and his putts found the bottom of the hole. His professor was impressed. He asked where Peter had gotten lessons. He was stunned when Peter told him that he had learned by playing with sticks he whittled into clubs, and the only instruction he'd gotten was watching other people who played better than he did.

His professor thought Peter was pulling his leg.

PETER MUTHIYA—A BLACK child, the son of uneducated laborers who was born in a mud hut under colonial rule—graduated from college with a degree in biochemistry, his grades among the highest in his class. He was happy, relieved and proud. But he was not overcome with emotion. He was excited to take the next step in his life—and take Zambia to the next step of hers.

Sandikonda and Kaliwé didn't quite know what to make of graduation. His mom chatted with everyone and fidgeted with Peter's hair and robe.

His father stayed stoic. Every once in a while, he flashed a slight smile. As usual, they balanced each other.

Peter strode across the stage with the vigor and confidence of a new generation of a new country ready to change the world. He allowed himself his own little smile when he grabbed his diploma. When he looked at his parents, they were smiling that same little smile. They had done it. Their son was a college graduate.

Diploma in hand, Peter saw a future as bright as the African sun. With Zambia's wealth now staying at home instead of being siphoned off to England or South Africa, he was certain that economic growth was inevitable. There would be more jobs, better housing, more food, better education. He was sure the people in charge were capable of fulfilling their precious mandate, guiding their fledgling nation from poverty into prosperity.

Initially he enjoyed the good fortune of being in the first generation of young, educated Black professionals in sub-Saharan Africa. Job offers poured in, his network of contacts expanded, and he could already envision a life far better than any Muthiya had ever experienced.

But the naïve optimism of youth often obscures the cold, hard reality of how difficult it is to change a whole nation. Just when everything was running smoothly, the floor dropped out from under him. Peter's faith was suddenly and terribly tested.

5

AFTER THE RUSH OF GRADUATION, reality reared its ugly head. Peter chose to work for a state-owned company, where he soon learned he was just another anonymous cog in a big machine, despite his initial hopes. Most definitely NOT helping transform Zambia into a shiny new world of prosperity and opportunity. For most educated Zambians of his generation, there was no alternative.

Zambia's independence from Britain did not liberate the economy. Often it meant that instead of key industries being controlled by foreign government, they were now controlled by outside business interests. All the money kept going to rich White people in Britain and South Africa. What was promised as the golden age of upwardly mobile Zambian youth turned out to be depressingly same-old, same-old. There was little chance for advancement or control of their own destiny.

The new Zambian government's remedy for wrestling control of the economy away from foreigners offered little hope for a young and ambitious professional like Peter Muthiya: nationalization. The government seized ownership and control of private enterprises, creating companies that they managed. Everything from manufacturing plants to sawmills to financial services were suddenly owned by the Zambian government. This included the biggest prize: mining. The two companies controlling Zambia's copper mines were consolidated into one behemoth: Zambia Consolidated Copper Mines (ZCCM). Peter's dreams of his government making sweeping changes to create a dynamic economy that eradicated poverty, fostered entrepreneurism and created prosperity were dashed.

After spending three increasingly frustrating years as a scientist on the bureaucratic hamster wheel at one of these state-owned entities, Zambia's National Council for Scientific Research, Peter found his true calling. Insurance. Placing a monetary value on risk piqued his interest. He thought it might be a way to provide for his family and help make the lives of the people in his new country better. He accepted a position with the state-owned Zambia National Insurance Brokers (ZNIB).

After quickly learning the business, he became an insurance officer with ZCCM, now the most important economic engine in the entire country. Peter and his team received briefings on the company's financial health. He groaned and gnashed his teeth in meetings when he saw that the government was making key decisions that made no business sense. Resource allocations were ridiculously inefficient. The government treated ZCCM as a welfare agency rather than a business. Peter thought it was noble to provide jobs and deliver social services, but focusing solely on these objectives would inevitably bankrupt and cripple ZCCM. Disaster for everyone.

Peter was powerless to stop the madness infecting his new country. He often found himself swimming upstream against a cadre of bureaucrats who lacked his drive for building a business—and an economy—based on efficiency, innovation and profitability. He always viewed nationalization as a temporary policy to wrest control away from the old colonial interests. Never as a long-term solution.

Peter saw clearly that this path led to ruin. He wasn't living in a mud hut anymore, but he often felt every bit as small and ineffectual, unable to stop the large forces working against him to make sure his fellow countrymen would not have a chance to prosper.

AS ALWAYS, IN times of trouble, Peter turned to his first true love: golf. While playing golf regularly was still prohibitive due to time and money, he discovered other ways to enjoy the game. Owning a television was still too expensive, but he managed to find one when golf tournaments were televised.

Peter loved watching Tom Watson shoot 9 under par at Royal Birkdale to win his third British Open Championship. He studied Watson relentlessly. His remarkable chipping and putting. He dissected the swing so he could understand how the man drove the ball to an approach to the green. Perhaps most, he admired Tom's easygoing manner and friendly sportsmanship. But the more he watched, the more he realized that this affable exterior disguised his steely competitiveness. Watching the best players in the world and hearing commentators' analysis was Peter's masterclass in the art of golf. He had no idea that his son would someday use the wisdom Peter imparted to play in the same tournaments as his favorite champion, Tom Watson.

And of course, Peter always wanted to know how and why it all worked. He applied the inquisitive mind that turned him into a scientist and broke down the technical aspects of the game of golf. As a boy, he learned fundamentals by watching players on the segregated golf courses in Kabwé and Chipata. Now he studied how tiny changes in grip, stance, rotation and torque could make the difference between a birdie and a double bogey. Players constantly battled Mother Nature as well. The way the grass on the green was cut. Whether it was damp or dry. How the wind gusted on the ground and at the top of the trees. ow the sun was shinig.How the sun shined and the clouds moved. The more he studied, the more he realized that golf was as much math and science as it was a sport.

Whenever he got the chance, he soaked in the moments of standing out in a fairway, under the big African sky, using all his tricks and skills, clearing his head and opening his heart and doing what he had been doing since he was a kid.

Swing the club. Hit the ball.

1978 BROUGHT PETER face-to-face with the tragedy of mortality. His father died. Everyone in the family knew that once Sandikonda was gone from their lives, Kaliwé would follow. Sure enough, Peter's mom passed soon thereafter. Through his haze of grief, Peter knew it was just their time. After seventy years of relentless labor, hard work and poverty, their bodies gave out. At least, he thought, they were together again in eternity.

As Peter returned to the humble mud hut in Kabwé, he saw his father's life in a new way. His dad never lamented his position in life, even with the deck so clearly stacked against him. He never cursed the sky for his place on this earth. Peter saw how much his father had taught him. Not with words, but with deeds. By example. He watched his father rise daily, bone tired when life was beating him down, and trudge off to work so he could provide for his family without complaint. Peter could finally see that this was the best education he ever received.

Just as his father was the source of Peter's resilience, his mother was the source of his spirit. She was nurturing, but she always stood her ground. He realized that his penchant for endless questions in the classroom, his ever-inquisitive tenacity—it came from his mom.

Sandikonda and Kaliwé were the bedrock of Peter's life and the source of everything he achieved. And yet, when they died, he felt no anger, resentment or bitterness that so often consumes people who have lived entitled lives where hardship is unfamiliar. In Peter's mind, God decided it was time for his parents to go. That was good enough for him.

And he knew in his heart that as long as he followed their example, they would always be there.

He vowed to keep them alive by someday passing on their work ethic, perseverance and devotion to his own children. When Peter's son eventually went where no man like him had ever gone, he took his grandparents with him.

PETER WAS NEVER a partier. But he did like going out and having a beer or three with friends, swapping stories, reliving old glories and dreaming of triumphs ahead. He knew a man who worked at the country's largest beer maker, Zambia Breweries. Every Friday the company hosted an after-work party, and Peter had a standing invitation.

One night he was hoisting a brew when a young woman caught his eye and refused to give it back. She had a big bright smile and shining eyes, and she knew how to talk. Edith Nakamba hailed from Northern Province. She had finished school at Evelyn Hone College and landed a job with Zambia Breweries. Edith went from being charmed to smitten by this young man who was so smart and full of jokes, confident but never arrogant. She felt good around him. He had a way of making everybody laugh.

Peter put on a full-frontal charm assault to woo Edith. Eventually he saw that she reminded him of someone. She had the same sharp wit and strong personality as his mother.

As one door closes, another opens. His parents were gone. But now he had the love of his life.

In 1980, they were married in a simple ceremony filled with friends, joy and the promise of building a new family.

Peter was ready to create the first generation in his family to be born Zambian.

And he was hoping they would all be golfers.

WONGANI PETER MUTHIYA came into the world on August 20, 1981, at Nkana Mine Hospital.

For years, the ruling White minority frowned upon traditional names for Black Africans. They found it to be an effective method of destroying a culture. African parents believed that if English names could make their children's lives even a *little* easier, it was worth it.

Peter and his generation wanted to break the shackles confining their ancestors in every way. And this meant giving their children traditional African names. He knew why his parents gave him an English name. Peter knew that to understand a man, you must first understand his history. And he understood history.

So when it came to naming his firstborn, Peter declared that the boy would have an African name. End of discussion. "Wongani" means "Thank you." Peter thought that sounded right.

On February 8, 1983, Edith delivered their second child. Afterwards, when talk turned to naming their new son, friends and family filled the room with suggestions. It seemed like the baby was the only one not shouting out names.

Peter's younger sister, Mary, noticed the tiny bundle of serene peace amidst the raucous conversation and laughter and uttered:

"Madalitso."

Not everyone heard Mary, but Peter did. "Madalitso" means "Blessings" or "One who is blessed." Peter gave his sister a little smile that revealed his enthusiasm for the name. Then he asked why she thought this child was blessed.

Mary told Peter to look at his baby. No crying or fussing. Only blessed calm. "It's like he knows something we don't," Mary said.

Peter believed that after birth, a name is the first gift from parents to their child. Peter and Edith could think of no more accurate description of their feelings and no better gift for their son than an eternal reminder that he is blessed.

Peter and Edith welcomed their third and final child on October 6, 1985, as the boys were given a baby sister—Ivwananji.

Wongani's and Madalitso's names were taken from the Ngoni language, Peter's native tribe. "Not this time," Edith said with a laugh. "Ivwananji is from my tribe, the Namwanga of Northern Province. 'To get along' is the closest translation," she explained.

YES, PETER WAS frustrated by the glacial pace of change in Zambia and the government's ridiculous incompetence and downright inept policies and practices. But he had a career as promising as any Zambian in his mid-thirties. He owned a house and car, his family was clothed and fed and his children attended school. He sometimes longed to live in the United States or Europe where his chances of rising to the top of his chosen field would be so much greater. Too many people with less intelligence, skill and ambition enjoyed a higher standard of living simply by virtue of their birthplace and their family name.

One of the fruits of his station in life was that he could continue his love affair with golf. As cruel as it might be sometimes, golf was proving to be a very rewarding love. Peter joined Lusaka Golf Club in 1985 and bought his first real set of golf clubs. They were used and inexpensive, but he finally owned clubs with straight shafts and properly angled heads. Never again tagging along as a guest, borrowing somebody else's equipment or trying to make do with his sad, mismatched, stuck-together-with-tape-and-glue clubs. Peter had his own complete set. And he was a proud member of the best golf club in Zambia.

No longer was he the poor Black African watching with longing eyes from the outside as the White colonialists got to enjoy the forbidden pleasures of golf. Now he was on the inside. And the pleasures were no longer forbidden. He had finally arrived.

Peter spent as much time as he could on the course or at the driving range. Around the clubhouse, he was his usual jovial self. But on the course, he was a fierce competitor and a shrewd analyst of the game.

Decades of acute observation, studying the best players in the world competing in world-class tournaments, reading golf guides and literature and applying his own analytical skills had turned Peter into something of an expert. He dissected the game with clinical, surgical precision. Stance, grip, swing and proper club selection. People soon started asking him for tips.

At five years old, he had chosen golf. Or golf had chosen him. It was simply a fun game to play. Later, golf became a mental exercise, involving math, science and history, which he enjoyed studying. Peter learned the game's ancient traditions and could rattle off its great champions. He knew from its earliest days that golf was a pastime for royalty and the upper class where some people simply did not belong. With televised tournaments, it became entertainment. It was also instruction. His sharp mind—still as inquisitive as it was at five years old—enjoyed soaking up information and doling it out.

Golf remained an oasis of serenity. Later, it also became an escape from the demands of being an adult. And a great stress reliever. On the course, there was no talk of business or providing for a family in a crippled and poorly managed economy. No reminders of his untapped potential or what his life might have been if he'd attended college in the United States or Europe. Golf was his retreat from pressures and frustrations. His escape valve, his self-help and his therapy.

But the game's role in his life was about to change once again. Very soon, golf would mean more to Peter Muthiya than he could ever imagine.

All thanks to a broken window.

6

SHARDS OF GLASS GREETED PETER on a spring afternoon in 1989. When he arrived home from work, he walked through the front door and was met by guilty faces. He glared past his two sons at the fist-sized hole in the kitchen window surrounded by a spider's web of cracked glass.

Channeling his dad, he asked what happened with a stoic, blank face.

The confession was short, not sweet. Ignoring stern warnings, Wongani and Madalitso had given in to temptation when they peeked into their parents' closet and saw the bright metal shafts sticking out of the tall colorful bag. All consequences were forgotten. They had to swing those clubs.

Madalitso owned up to it. He'd broken the window by smashing a golf ball through it. As far as Peter was concerned, it didn't matter. They were both guilty.

Peter led the boys outside, calmly asking why they hit balls so close to the house. He'd quite forgotten to ask why, against strict orders, they took his clubs in the first place. With raised voices and waving arms, the boys talked over each other, professing that they took the clubs to a place where the house was far out of range. Or so they thought.

Peter demanded to be shown the spot where Madalitso hit the ball. A few steps away from the house, he expected them to stop. They didn't. They walked and walked, until they crossed over their property line and onto a vacant patch of rocky land dotted with small shrubs.

Still they walked. After several meters, Peter suspected this was an attempt to avoid punishment by taking him so far away from the house. Irritated, he demanded to know why they were trying to play him for a fool. He ordered them to show him exactly where they hit the ball from.

The brothers swore they were telling the truth. It was just a little further ahead.

At last, they stopped and pointed to the ground. And there it was—a divot. Mouth agape, Peter stared at the house. Then the divot. He tried to maintain his composure. It was at least 100 meters. As long as an American football field. Madalitso had just turned six. It seemed humanly impossible that a boy so young had hit a ball that far.

Peter was silent. Wongani and Madalitso felt the heat of his glare and braced themselves. The boys knew their father had inherited his very firm views on child discipline from his own strict dad. He believed in traditional methods. He was old school. They had broken a rule and damaged the family home. They prepared for the worst.

But more powerful feelings prevailed that day. Pride wrestled with discipline in Peter. His sons were following his lead. They, too, were falling in love with golf. He was excited to discover their interest, thrilled by the promise of a new talent and overjoyed at the chance to teach something he loved to his children.

While all these thoughts raced through Peter's head, one stood out. He remembered another little boy whose infatuation with golf had led to playing on an equally neglected patch of dirt in Broken Hill. When Zambia was still Northern Rhodesia.

Wongani and Madalitso breathed a sigh of relief as fear of harsh punishment vanished with Peter's next words.

"So, you want to play golf."

THE FIRST ORDER of business was purchasing golf clubs for the boys. Peter was excited to teach Wongani and Madalitso. But there was no way he'd sacrifice his own set, so he bought a used set of ladies' clubs, shorter and lighter than his own. The boys didn't care that the clubs were pink. They were just like their father when he was a kid. All they wanted to do was hit that little white ball as high and as hard and as far as they could.

Peter stood silently behind the boys on their first trip to Lusaka Golf Club's driving range, observing their stance and swings before starting to teach the fundamentals. Madalitso quickly proved the broken window was no fluke. Actually, both boys hit the ball well. The only difference was attitude. You could close your eyes and tell how Wongani hit the ball just by listening. Like Peter, Wongani groaned after he hit a bad shot. He was a more exaggerated version of his dad.

Madalitso was different. He rarely made a sound after a bad shot. Or a good shot. He had inherited his grandfather's stoicism. He was peaceful and quiet. Just as he was the day he came into the world.

Peter and his sons became regulars on the driving range, putting green and practice bunkers. Peter never grew tired of demonstrating proper stances, grip or swing motions.

Playing on the course was still a few years away. It wasn't because Peter first wanted his sons to become proficient ball strikers. Through his intense study of golf, Peter Muthiya was schooled in the game's history, culture and traditions. He firmly believed that etiquette and respect said as much, if not *more,* about a player than distance off the tee. Peter's message was clear: Madalitso and Wongani would first learn the mores, behavior and customs of golf or they wouldn't play on the course. End of discussion.

Peter stood them at attention while he played the role of drill sergeant. He made them stay silent and stand away when others hit the ball. They were instructed to walk at a brisk pace so others didn't have to wait on them. Repair all divots and ball marks. Be careful to look around before you swing. Etc., etc., etc.

Despite Peter's constant lecturing, sometimes Wongani and Madalitso had to learn the hard way. More than once, Wongani stood too close as his younger brother was swinging, and WHACK! Wongani was smacked in the head by Madalitso's backswing.

As Wongani gasped and grasped his head in agony, Madalitso would calmly tell his brother to watch where he was standing. Wongani's fiery personality would ignite, and they'd both throw down their clubs and start fighting. Peter found himself in between the flying fists and feet of his six- and seven-year-old.

But despite the occasional fisticuffs, Peter cherished every second of sharing his love of golf with his boys.

MADALITSO FELL AS hard for golf as his dad did. He simply loved the game, whether he was playing or not. He studied players at Lusaka Golf Club's driving range, and he devoured golf tournaments on TV. Peter was pleasantly surprised that he now had a companion to join him on the couch and watch the great players of the day trying to win a major, dissecting the minutiae of rhythm, tempo, reading the greens, judging the weather conditions, managing the course and playing the field. Knowing when to take a risk and when to play it safe. Knowing how to grab a lead and hold on until you had the trophy in your hand.

One day, Madalitso mustered the courage to ask if he could watch his father play, fully aware that Peter treasured his private time at Lusaka Golf Club.

Peter flatly refused. He loved his family, but he needed the peace, solace and solitude of the game that had nourished and nurtured him since he was a child. Besides, he reasoned, he was already spending lots of time with the boys at the driving range.

But then he remembered his older brother allowed to watch him caddie at Broken Hill Golf Club. Walking those fairways fueled his interest and knowledge of the game. How could he deny the same experience to his own son?

As a young boy, Peter had always been antsy and full of questions. It was always a mighty struggle to keep his mouth shut.

Madalitso was content to just watch. At first, Peter thought he might be tired or bored. He was wrong. Mad, as he was then called by those near and dear to him, loved watching his dad play with friends. He observed, studied and took mental notes, trying to absorb everything.

In those early days, Peter learned a lot about Madalitso as he sat quietly and watched. He was in tune with everything going on around him. He just didn't talk about it.

Of course, Peter didn't know it at the time, but Mad was accumulating the knowledge, skills and training that would lead him to break a huge barrier in the world of golf.

The temperament, the steely even keel, the quiet confidence were already there.

Madalitso was born with that.

7

IN 1964, WHEN PETER CELEBRATED Zambia declaring independence from Great Britain, it was one of the most prosperous countries
in sub-Saharan Africa. By 1990, thanks to government mismanagement
and corruption, Peter watched in despair as it descended into one of the
poorest. He was aghast as he read World Bank statistics showing that since
1973 the average Zambian's income steadily declined to a mere $290 per
year, while inflation rose from 35 percent in 1986 to 64 percent in 1988,
and soared then to 154 percent in 1989. He felt impotent as the country
experienced shortages of food and other essentials that left 70 percent of
Zambian households without basic needs. Starving and furious citizens
rioted, resulting in chaos, mayhem and sometimes death.

Peter, along with many of his countrymen, had high hopes when President
Kaunda's United National Independence Party led the way to freedom. But
that led to a single-party system, which now represented the single biggest
roadblock to moving the nation forward. People wanted a choice. Peter was
beyond frustrated, desperately wanting to help his country move forward.

In 1990, his hope revived when President Kaunda allowed the creation
of other political parties. A coalition of intellectuals, labor organizations
and politicians joined in creating the Movement for Multiparty Democracy

(MMD). The new party chose Frederick Jacob Titus Chiluba, a trade unionist, as its leader.

Peter was thrilled by the first multiparty election since the 1960s, which was held on October 31, 1991. In voting that was deemed free and fair by international monitors, including former U.S. President Jimmy Carter, MMD won in a landslide. The new party captured 125 out of 150 seats in the National Assembly. Peter celebrated as Chiluba became Zambia's second president.

Chiluba rode to power promising economic reforms that Peter hoped would help turn his country around. Privatization. Foreign investment. Entrepreneurship. But part of him was afraid to believe. His country had dashed his hopes too many times with ill-advised and shortsighted decision-making. Still, he felt more excitement and optimism than he had since independence nearly three decades earlier.

Peter was ready to seize opportunity when it came. Businesses, whether large or small, foreign or domestic, needed insurance. Now was his time, and he was going to grab it by whatever means necessary.

In 1992, less than a year after Chiluba and the MMD came to power, Peter Muthiya opened his own insurance brokerage called Excess Insurance Agency. A short time later, the aspiring entrepreneur affixed his own initials to the company letterhead.

P.M. Insurance Brokers was born.

WONGANI AND MADALITSO shared Peter's excitement over the changes in Zambia's government and the opportunities that resulted from their father's new business. But for them, 1992 was the most exciting year in their lives for a very different reason: golf. Peter finally let them play on a real live course.

Driving to Lusaka Golf Club, Peter emphasized his lessons about rules and etiquette. Their father reminded his sons that playing on the course was a privilege that could be taken away. They were to be on their best behavior, and he would watch them. Closely.

When they had proven they were ready, Peter entered the boys in Lusaka Golf Club's adult-child competition. A member of the club was paired with a child. The lowest scoring duo were crowned champion.

Peter arranged for Wongani and Madalitso to play with other club members. He chose to wait in the clubhouse. He was the anti–helicopter parent. He was always preparing them to make it on their own, pushing them to be self-sufficient. And what better way to build independence? After hours of tutoring, it was time to see if the boys remembered what they were taught. Peter fidgeted and paced back and forth as the boys warmed up. Were they ready?

Mad was partnered with a pleasant and easygoing member, Ms. Monde Lisula. This was a bit of a surprise. There were a few avid women golfers in Zambia, but men far outnumbered their female counterparts on golf club membership lists.

As the boys got ready to tee off, Peter shrugged his shoulders and strolled into the clubhouse to enjoy a beer with friends. A couple of hours later, players began trickling in.

Peter spotted Ms. Monde walking in briskly with an odd look on her face. He asked her what had happened. And where was Madalitso?

She replied that he was just behind her, talking with some people.

Peter asked her why she looked so unsettled. Her answer was something Peter would never forget.

She shook her head in astonishment and told him that his son was a great player.

Peter did a poor job concealing his grin as he asked her to elaborate.

She told him that throughout the round, he kept making spectacular shots. Hitting the ball long and straight. Putting himself in great positions on nearly every hole. And he comported himself like he was born to be a golfer. Breathlessly, she recounted how he had driven his tee shot straight down the fairway on the second hole, a par 4. Much to the astonishment of everyone who witnessed, his second shot actually hit the pin. The ball plopped down next to the cup. Mad tapped in for an easy birdie.

Madalitso finally joined them as Ms. Monde motioned enthusiastically, vividly recounting a slew of outstanding shots made by her nine-year-old teammate.

Peter tried to hide his excitement, not wanting to show anybody up or give his son a big head. So he just smiled, nodded and said "ah-ha" a few times. She was so exuberant, common courtesy demanded that he have *some* response.

Madalitso's reaction was far different. In fact, it was basically nonexistent. Peter watched as his son just stood and listened, offering only an occasional shrug and grin while making as little eye contact as possible. Peter was slightly puzzled by his son's lack of reaction. Mad wasn't shy or lacking in confidence. He just took everything in stride. Never too high or too low. He was able to block out distractions and prevent extraneous noise from fazing him. Whatever the situation, he never seemed to let the moment get too big. It was Peter's first glimpse into a personality trait that would help his son down the road.

Madalitso wasn't the only golfer in the family. Wongani would not let his younger brother outdo him. He played with a carefree, almost fearless attitude, gladly choosing an outrageous shot rather than playing it safe and steady like his younger brother. On this day, it worked as he turned in a better score than Madalitso.

A trend was started that continued for years as the brothers good-naturedly battled to see who was best.

PETER HAD MADALITSO and his brother compete in the adult-child competitions and other informal events for a couple of years. Eventually these became stale, and the boys wanted more. So did Peter. Although thoughts of golf becoming a real pursuit was still years away, Peter wanted to test his sons' interest in the game he loved. And he wanted to test their maturity. So, he decided to enter his sons into Zambia's premier junior tournament, the Chick of the North Championship. It was a thirty-six-hole affair, governed by official rules. Mad had just celebrated his tenth birthday, and Wongani was still a few months shy of twelve. It was the first time they would compete as individuals. A sponsor was paying to transport players to the chaperoned tournament in Ndola via airplane.

As he drove them to the airport, Peter noticed the boys were relaxed but excited about competing in their first big tournament. They were also psyched about their first flight on an airplane. As usual, Wongani chattered away, while Madalitso sat in the backseat, watching and taking everything in.

Peter and Edith seemed much more nervous as they sent their ten- and eleven-year-old sons on a plane ride and overnight stay alone. But Peter was insistent, as always, that he wanted his children to be independent. His philosophy was to teach self-reliance. He believed with all his heart that this was essential to help children mature and prepare not just to survive, but to thrive on their own. Too many times had he seen children in Africa forced to grow up way too soon. And all of this was colored, of course, by the most painful chapter of his own childhood: when he was forced to leave his parents at a young age. Yes, it hurt, but it also made him a better, stronger, more self-sufficient man.

Zambia at that time had a population of almost eight million people, almost 99 percent of them Black. The remaining 1 percent were mostly White expatriates from Europe or South Africa, and first- or second-generation immigrants from South Asia, predominantly India.

In Madalitso and Wongani's world, they were surrounded predominantly by Black Africans. The tournament was a real eye-opener for the two brothers. They couldn't quite believe their eyes when they looked around at their fellow competitors. If you guessed the racial makeup of Zambia by the children who competed in those junior tournaments, you'd have thought that the country was half White and half Indian. For the first time, the boys grasped fully where they stood in the food chain of Zambia. At the bottom. It was a rude awakening to realize that their competitors were all boys of the small upper class. They had better clothes, fancier haircuts and a sense of entitled ease that comes with being raised with money. And of course, their families could afford club memberships, coaching in golf camps abroad, and cool spiked shoes for gripping the turf. Plus, of course, they had the best clubs money could buy in Zambia. This alone was one of the most essential elements of succeeding at golf.

Wongani and Madalitso saw very quickly that they were oddities. Their involvement in golf was a result of their father's obsessive love of the game and the middle-class life he had achieved. Not because they had been groomed to play the sports of the elites. Polo, cricket and golf.

But their father was always very direct with them. He had always told them in no uncertain terms that they were as good as anyone else, and if they worked hard and made good decisions, success would follow. The only difference between them and other players was their score and whether they conducted themselves with honor on the golf course. Nothing else. The true mark of a man was not whether he had expensive golf clubs but what he did with them.

The words of Peter's beloved mother rang in her grandsons' ears, passed on countless times by Peter: *Don't worry about the people around you. Just focus on what you need to do.*

That being said, Peter and Edith had their boys looking as sharp as budget would allow, decked out in Peter's best golf shirts, even if they were too big. Pleated wool pants were a must, despite the occasional stifling heat of sub-Saharan Africa.

Peter had drilled it into his sons' heads. Pants could not hang low off their waists, shirts tucked in, hats on straight. His father made it very clear. They had to be on their very best behavior. It was their duty to represent themselves and the family in a way that would make Peter proud, and that was in keeping with the rich traditions of the game.

When it came time to tee off, the boys took one last look around. And then at each other. Quietly, they knew what the other was thinking: would simply "ignoring others" and "focusing on themselves" be enough to counter the centuries of Black Africans being slaves, servants and subservient, a culture that made them the only Black kids at a golf tournament in the middle of Africa? Their father said this moment would come. But now it was actually here, no longer just part of his regular tutorials on golf and life. The emotions roiled around inside them, as they wondered if they were good enough, if they would be welcomed, if they would ever belong. It was a lot for two young boys to process.

Madalitso could feel the stares when he and his odd, oversized shirt and unspiked shoes finally stepped into the tee box in his first big tournament. He could hear whispers around him. Strangers had never taken an interest in him before, and it made him uncomfortable and self-conscious. He knew his father wasn't there to offer encouraging words or even a quick reassuring nod. So, instead of people, he made eye contact with his ball and slid his tee into the ground and carefully balanced it on top.

People stopped talking, and the tension spiked. The crowd was clearly curious what the slightly built Black youngster in the inexpensive, ill-fitting clothing moving into position was going to do with his opening drive. Peter wasn't there for the first life-changing golf shot of Madalitso's life—the drive that broke the kitchen window—and he wasn't there for this one. But that was the way Peter wanted it. Independence. Self-reliance. Standing on your own two feet.

Madalitso did what his dad had trained him to do. He focused on his ball, on his swing, on the rhythm, the feel of the club in his hand, the target in the fairway where he wanted the ball to land.

Slowly, the stares, the whispers, and the nagging doubts all faded until there was nothing but the ball, the club, the target and himself.

He let out a deep breath and swung the club back, as he had thousands of times before. The backswing was smooth and easy. The club reached perpendicular, and the easy weight transfer carried the club in a clean line so the clubhead was flush when it hit the ball with a louder-than-normal *THWACK*. The follow-through was effortless, like he was swinging the club in his backyard.

As the ball screamed off his clubhead, the spectators gasped, exclaimed and let out low whistles of appreciation. Clearly, they'd just witnessed something special. This kid was different. He had that thing had separates good from great.

His tee shot rocketed straight and true down the fairway of the lengthy par 5. The crowd gawked as Mad's drive just kept going and going and going, his ball soaring past where every other player had landed.

He was overjoyed with his first golf shot in his first important tournament. People's reaction only fueled his adrenaline. But while Mad heard and appreciated the applause and "WOWs" that echoed around the tee box, he remembered his father's advice not to let himself be affected by others. So his face registered nothing of what his heart felt as he picked up his tee, put his secondhand driver back in his beat-up bag, hoisted it onto his shoulders, and in true workmanlike fashion, headed off down the fairway, already planning his attack on the next shot.

Madalitso was like a teen golfing machine throughout the Chick of the North. Good shots, bad shots, they all sparked the same reaction—none. He just kept moving forward, focused on the only things he could control. The club, the ball, the target and himself. He could feel he was being watched. Evaluated. He could hear bits and pieces of conversations. He kept coming back to Peter's oft-repeated words: *Don't worry about others. Just focus on what you need to do.*

Both boys were closely scrutinized and widely discussed by the other golfers, who were mostly White and Indian and mostly upper class. But after a few holes, Mad and his brother weren't being judged by the color of their skin. It was because they were distancing themselves from everyone else. Players and spectators were also struck by Wongani's loud and colorful personality as much as his ball-striking ability. After a bad tee shot on the par 4 ninth hole, Wongani scolded and threatened both the ball and his golf club. "You bastards better get your act together or else you'll end up in the trash can." After a good recovery with the next couple shots, another player observed, "I guess your ball and clubs got the message."

Shot after shot, Wongani and Madalitso demonstrated a knowledge and skill for the game far greater than their competitors. And why not? They probably had the best teacher in the entire country.

Two days later, Peter and Edith received a telephone call from Patson, Peter's older brother, who had watched the boys compete in the Chick of the North. "Your sons were remarkable," he told Peter. "Wongani won the thirteen and under competition, and Madalitso was runner-up. The boys unquestionably outplayed others in their age group."

FLUSH WITH THE remarkable success at Ndola, Peter was overjoyed that his sons had not only inherited his passion for golf but they were actually good at it. It was frustrating to watch his country flounder. But he could see right before his eyes that Zambia was actually changing. In one generation, his sons had opportunities that he never even dreamed of. To compete in real tournaments against White and Indian kids, to be part of the ancient tradition of golf and to blaze their own traditions in his new country of Zambia. To remake a world where Peter had been on the outside looking in.

Of course, he was still Sandikonda's son. No gushing or gloating. But in his own way, Peter quietly showed them how proud he was. Then he showed them in a very public way. Much to their delight, he entered the boys in the Lusaka Golf Club's weekly junior tournament.

Even though money was still tight, Peter made an important decision. If they were going to do this seriously, the boys would have caddies. If you want to be a champion, you must act like one. Champions have caddies. Caddies are also an important tradition of the game, so it was an opportunity to further his sons' education. Plus, it was a way to help others. Peter had a bittersweet flash of being a small boy and watching his brother hand over the money he made from caddying to their mother to help pay for food. He was sad for his brother. And happy for his sons.

The boys teed off, and Peter made his way to the clubhouse, per usual. He wanted them to make their own way. To figure things out for themselves. Another demonstration of the philosophy he believed in so deeply. To make his sons independent and self-sufficient. While sipping his second Budweiser, Peter spotted an unsettling sight. Wongani's caddie was sitting outside. He left his beer, walked outside and asked the man what he was doing there.

The caddie shrugged his shoulders. Wongani had fired him.

Peter was flabbergasted. He asked the caddie what happened.

The caddie rolled his world-weary eyes. He explained that Wongani had hit a couple of bad shots and lost his temper. He shouted. He yelled. He blamed the caddie for giving bad advice, even though he only made a club recommendation. The caddie had even offered to carry the bag without speaking. But Wongani was so furious that he claimed even the presence of the caddie would bring him bad luck. He said that he would rather carry his own bag. Wongani told the caddie that he was fired and that he should leave immediately.

Peter was livid. He had spent months teaching his sons proper etiquette and manners on the golf course. In fact, their whole lives had been an exercise in learning how to comport themselves in the world and make the family proud. Wongani's behavior had disgraced him and the whole Muthiya family. Even more, it was an insult to the game that Peter had loved and respected since he was a boy. As the boys finished their round, Peter seethed in the clubhouse, trying to figure out what punishment would fit this heinous crime.

Luckily for Wongani, they were in a public place, so he got a quiet but intense earful about right and wrong, respect and tradition, honor and family.

Anyone watching father greet son after the competition would never have known that Wongani won the tournament. To Peter, it was irrelevant. Wongani had tarnished the victory. The way he conducted himself was much, much more important than the number on his scorecard. And he had failed miserably in that regard.

Wongani was ashamed. He knew his dad was right. But he had a terrible time controlling his temper. It was deflating to go from winning the competition to being the brunt of his father's wrath, as Peter continued scolding him in the car, even before they pulled out of the parking space. He could already feel the sting in his backside. And the worst part was that he knew he deserved it. But Lady Luck shined down upon him. Madalitso saved the day.

Mad, as was his custom, watched and listened, taking in his father's tirade, silently soaking in the lesson that his brother was learning the hard way. But during a silence in his dad's angry monologue, choppy little nasal bursts of constrained laughter filled the car. They were coming from the back seat.

Peter glared at Madalitso in the rearview mirror. Mad did not want to be on the receiving end of the scolding his brother was enduring, so he apologized as fast as humanly possible. He explained that he was in the group ahead of Wongani. Just as they teed off, they heard shouts and turned around. Wongani was on the previous green, yelling and screaming, his arms flailing, pointing all over the place like he had escaped from an insane asylum. It was hilarious, and naturally, everyone started laughing. Madalitso barely hid his smile as he described the scene.

Now it was Peter's turn to try to hide his smile. Yes, he had to remain firm. Wongani and Madalitso both needed a clear and unforgettable message about how unacceptable this terrible behavior was. But hearing it from Mad's point of view gave Peter new perspective. He couldn't help visualizing his eleven-year-old son going crazy and firing a grown man. Even he had to admit, it was funny.

By the time they got home, a strong dose of corporal punishment seemed inappropriate. It was clear that the boys got the point. Madalitso learned several valuable lessons that day. Discipline is necessary and important. But it's also important to see the humor in life.

No matter how well you play, you will ultimately be judged by something much more important than how hard and well you hit that little white ball. What mattered most was how you acted on the course. For a Black boy playing the game of White royalty, Peter knew society would hold his sons to a higher standard.

It was a lesson that would stick with Madalitso for the rest of his life.

8

1996. ZAMBIA. PEOPLE WERE SUFFERING. Peter felt betrayed. All the high hopes and great expectations of a better tomorrow seemed dead. It would have been funny to think how naïve they had been if it wasn't so depressing. The great dream of President Chiluba had turned into an even greater nightmare. Hundreds of state companies were rapidly sold off to the powerful and well-connected, often below value. Millions of dollars were never accounted for. It was a feeding frenzy. And as usual, the people at the bottom of the food chain suffered.

Even though Peter knew more about insurance and pricing risk in Zambia than anyone, he found himself competing against giant foreign companies with enormous resources and the ability to underbid him. Most companies in the new Zambia would not even let him vie for their business. Edith, like thousands of others, lost her job. Local businesses died on the vine. Banks collapsed. Unemployment was rampant. Incomes fell. Fewer children were being educated. Families were starving.

Worse yet, many of the injustices of the colonial machine were now being perpetuated by the very leaders who vowed to do away with them.

Peter was beside himself, exasperated and clueless about how to fix his broken country.

Despite the mismanagement and corruption, President Chiluba won a second term in 1996. But if the 1991 election celebrated how far our democracy had come, 1996 showed how far it still needed to go as elections were viewed as unfair and lacking in transparency.

Catastrophic governmental failure was greatly exacerbated by a darker plague creeping across Africa. By the mid-1990s, one quarter to one third of the urban population was infected with AIDS. Nearly one hundred thousand people died of the disease in 1999.

And, as always, children paid for the sins of adults. Households headed by AIDS orphans grew from a quarter of a million to 650,000 in just three years. In Zambia, AIDS orphans were often left to survive as beggars, thieves and prostitutes, selling their young bodies to buy food for themselves and their younger siblings.

Peter was livid. And again, infuriated by the fact that there was so little he could do to help. Year after year, he watched as Zambia ignored AIDS. The stigma of openly identifying AIDS as a national pandemic was too great.

Because there was no education or information, *mis*information took its place. Rumors spread that an infected male could cure himself of AIDS by having sex with a virgin. Horrifying cases of sexual abuse of children became commonplace, which begot further tragedy as more and more younger and younger Africans became infected with this disease for which there was no cure. Miserable, lingering death was everywhere.

Wongani, Madalitso and Ivwananji were given a specific route to take home from school. Peter and Edith lectured their children on stranger-danger. Classrooms were filled every day with more empty seats from children dying or having to leave school because their parents were gone.

Peter and Edith wanted their kids to understand the tragedy eating their country alive, so they began driving the boys through depressed parts of Lusaka. Maybe Wongani and Madalitso had to occasionally share clothes, but outside the car were children with no clothes. Mothers clutching sick and dying kids. People having the life sucked out of them by the plague.

Peter also wanted his children to recognize their good fortune, to feel compassion for others and to give thanks. Decades later, Mad still remembered the humility and empathy he learned on those drives.

But there was something else Peter looked for. He wanted to hear their reactions. Wongani sat in the front seat, wearing his heart on his sleeve as usual. His sadness was peppered with anger and righteous indignation—at the government mainly, but occasionally at people who failed to help themselves.

Madalitso was different. He rarely spoke. Driving along, Peter listened for any reaction coming from him, even a murmur or sigh. Nothing. Even though Madalitso was taking it all in, he told Peter how bad he felt for people that were suffering only when he felt like it. Until then, not a sound. Peter didn't think it was his job to make Madalitso talk. Or to make Wongani be quiet. His job was to make them think. Make them feel. Make them learn. Get them ready for the world. And to get the world ready for them.

As Peter looked around during those drives, he went back and forth between rage, bewilderment, disillusionment and resignation. After independence, his country needed educated and ambitious young entrepreneurs to stay home, so he had put aside his dreams of a fortune overseas and answered the call. He spent years learning the insurance industry inside and out and then opened a business of his own. How had he been repaid? By shortsighted policies that stymied growth, discouraged local business and caused economic decline. By shocking corruption, greed, ignorance and downright stupidity. While the economy was being flushed down the toilet, the people were being ravaged by a silent, crippling killer.

But Peter Muthiya was an optimist. He loved life. Each day he thanked God for his many blessings. For his beautiful wife and his beloved children. He just knew he needed a win so he could see it wasn't all for naught, so he turned to his twin pillars: God and golf.

Little did he know, they would both soon reward him.

9

IN 1996, THE ZAMBIA GOLF Union needed a player to represent the country at the World Junior Championship at Blackpool North Shore Golf Club in England. The trip included a visit to Royal Lytham & St. Annes Golf Club, the site of that year's British Open and the place Bobby Jones won his first British Open in 1926. With his interest in golf history, Peter considered trying to pass himself off as a fourteen-year-old. Since that wouldn't work, an idea started growing in his head. He had two talented, able-bodied, golf-loving sons. Maybe they could earn a trip to the hallowed golf grounds.

But as the ZGU prepared to hold a qualifying tournament, a more fundamental question arose. Should Zambia even send a representative to England? People wondered if a Zambian junior could really compete with players from developed countries. Peter wanted his sons to have an opportunity he never had. To compete with the best in the world. Ultimately the powers-that-be decided to move forward and at least *try* to find a young golfer worthy of playing in a world championship.

Wongani asked to play in the qualifier despite the long drive to Nchanga Golf Club in Chingola. He'd recently declined an opportunity to play in the Mufulira Open because it was too far from home. And, frankly, he was losing interest in golf. But the World Junior Open qualifier was different. It was a trip to England, a chance to see the world! And meet girls!

The boys would play in different groupings. Going into the qualifier, Madalitso had never beaten Wongani. He knew Mad was improving, but Wongani was still confident he could beat his little brother.

Wongani began with a good opening drive and after just three holes had a sizeable lead over the others in his group. He was playing well. Nothing spectacular, just consistent.

Peter didn't follow Wongani's group down the first fairway. He waited several minutes at the first tee for Madalitso, recalling his youngest son's last competitive event, the Mufulira Open. Unlike his brother, Madalitso did travel to Mufulira, with high hopes of success in an area drenched in racist brutality, exploitation and oppression.

Much like Peter's hometown of Kabwé, Mufulira was a community built on White colonial theft. Copper was discovered in the 1930s, the town was built around it, and the golf course came soon after. Copper exports enriched Whites in Mufulira and England for decades, and the golf club became a place to celebrate their success. African minerals. African land. African labor. But no Blacks allowed. In management and ownership. And in the golf club.

Mufulira is near the Congo border, an arbitrary line drawn by colonial empires that separated African tribes and families. Growing up in this part of Africa meant hearing stories about the horrors that occurred in Congo under Belgian's King Leopold II. Africans were enslaved, murdered, beaten and mutilated, all for natural resource extraction. If production levels were deemed too low, White men would cut the hands and feet off of Black African children.

Madalitso arrived having heard from his dad the stories of Mufulira and the atrocities just over the border. Peter was as candid in discussing the past with his children as Uncle Papsonjere was with him. For years, the Mufulira Open was a stop on the now-defunct Safari Tour, and the clubhouse had a list of champions. All were White Europeans. And cutting right through the golf course was an abandoned railway line, a visual reminder of the Black people who were forced labor shipped in like cattle—and the mineral riches that were shipped out.

History hung in the air like a bad stench as Madalitso prepared to tee off. Despite his youth, he had already shown an ability to ignore external pressures, judgments and distractions. But playing in this environment? Against grown men? Even though he never admitted it, he wasn't sure if he was up to the challenge.

He placed his tee in the ground and took a couple practice swings. People stopped talking, and a thick tension crackled in the air as all eyes turned to the slender adolescent in the oversized golf shirt.

Madalitso tried with all his might to focus on ball, club and target, but the weight of this world rested heavy on his shoulders. He went through his swing routine. Carefully measured his club to the ball, calmly executed his easy yet powerful backswing and swung through.

Instantly, he let go of his club with one hand and slumped his shoulders as the ball careened off the right side of the fairway and into some trees. His trademark taciturn reaction was gone. He didn't quite feel in control. His body language screamed "disappointment" as he snatched up his tee. Minutes later, he and his caddie were searching outside the fairway, ever careful of lurking snakes. At last, he found his ball. There was no danger of wild animals, but there was also no shot at the green. He checked his frustration, chipped back onto the fairway and swallowed the bitter pill of a bogey on the first hole.

Madalitso had never really dealt with this level of failure during a tournament round. But he found himself haunted by the tragic story of this region. He tried to focus on his father's voice. Peter had counseled him on moments like this. *When things aren't going well, don't get discouraged. Clear your mind and rely on your fundamentals.*

It had always been the right formula before. But just as we all have bad days, every golfer has tournaments where nothing goes right and the strategy for mitigating damage also doesn't work.

In the tee box at the twelfth hole, a par 3, Madalitso closed his eyes and inhaled, trying to center himself and be in the moment. He had taken more deep, calming breaths during this tournament than he cared to remember. "Okay," he whispered. "Fundamentals." He pinpointed the target he was aiming for, carefully found his grip on the club and settled into the same stance he had countless times before in his young career. Eye on the ball. Left arm straight. After a brief pause and a methodical backswing, the ball shot from his club.

It was headed right for the hole. But slowly, it hooked left. "Come on," he quietly implored as his frustration poured out. "Not again!" But it was clear that the ball was not responding to his pleas, as it kept sailing left. A few agonizing seconds later, it buried into one of the greenside bunkers.

He was so fed up with himself that he simply put his club back in his bag and stared down the fairway, stone-faced and speechless. One of the grown players in his group offered a word of encouragement. Madalitso managed a weak smile and thanked him.

Minutes later, he was surrounded by sand, facing a bunker shot no different than hundreds he'd made while practicing at Lusaka Golf Club. With eight feet to the elevated green, he did everything correctly, firmly planting his feet into the sand with a slightly wider-than-normal stance, ball positioned forward, and a strike point targeted a few inches behind. Perfect. Or so he thought.

He paused a few seconds with his wedge extended in front of him, eyes laser focused. His backswing and follow-through sent a sandstorm into the air, with the ball in the middle. But the flight was woefully brief. The ball landed inches above the lip of the bunker and rolled back into the sand.

It was a perfect metaphor for his whole day. Take a nice swing, hit the ball well, and it ends up back at his feet as he moved one step closer to failure.

What is going on? He was focusing on fundamentals. He was staying competitive. Shot after shot and hole after hole, he was never able to get everything to click, couldn't put two good shots together and always found himself scrambling to avoid a bogey instead of surging toward a birdie. He never even entertained the idea of giving up and just going through the motions to finish out the tournament. He was his father's son after all. And he hadn't descended to banging his precious secondhand clubs against the ground or screaming at his driver as his brother famously had. He kept his calm composure, but inside he was in a desperate fight with despair. *So why is this happening?!* he asked himself over and over. He never got an answer.

From the moment his ball smashed through the kitchen window, Madalitso dreamed of big things. He pictured himself playing in tournaments he and his dad watched on TV. Teeing off in the U.S. Open. For a young boy taught that good things happen when you believe in yourself and focus, Mufulira was a calamity. It made no sense. And it shook him to the core.

By the final few holes, the ghosts of this bloody place began to take root inside him. It felt as if the demons of Mufulira's White colonialists, the past golf club members, and even King Leopold and his brutal mercenaries were taunting him. *You think you belong in this sport?* the demons laughed. *You think you can play in golf's biggest tournaments?*

Madalitso finished second-to-last at the Mufulira Open. He forced himself to smile and shake hands around the eighteenth green, having been drilled in good sportsmanship by his father. But Peter saw the expression on his son's face. He knew Madalitso couldn't wait to get into the car and drive home.

Neither said a word as they rushed out of the parking lot and cruised down the road as soon as they could. Peter broke the ice with an open-ended question about the day.

Madalitso said that he never felt at ease or comfortable on *that* course. He could never find a rhythm. He was always one step behind, playing catch-up, not quite in his own body.

Peter comforted his son as best he could. But he cautioned Madalitso that there would always be places that seemed strange, awkward and uncomfortable. Becoming a great player meant battling through these feelings. Mufulira showed what happened when you focused on external forces like history, geography, comparing yourself to others and paying attention to people staring, whispering, making you feel small, weak and like you didn't belong, weren't good enough or rich enough or didn't have the right shoes. Whether it was the ghosts that hovered around Mufulira and the surrounding region, or just a bad day on the course, Mad learned a powerful lesson. *Just focus on what you need to do.*

Madalitso told his dad that he'd done everything the way he'd been taught. And still nothing worked.

Peter let Madalitso's words sink in. Then he sighed and somberly agreed. Yes, sometimes in life, you do everything right, but you still fail. Peter Muthiya knew from his own history.

He quickly caught himself, snapped back to the present and pulled the car to the side of the road. Staring intensely into his son's eyes, Peter raised his voice and stressed that such moments are the exception to the rule. On most days, when you have faith and just focus on your task, on what you can control, it pays off!

Mufulira shook Madalitso. But he woke up the next morning from a good night's sleep feeling better, and each passing day provided more distance and perspective. He believed everything his dad said on the drive back. But more than that, Madalitso had found his life's mission, and it would take a lot more than one tournament to knock him off course. His father made sure he understood that all the skill in the world was nothing without perseverance and faith in yourself. Mad couldn't wait to compete in the qualifier for the World Junior Open in England.

As for the demons that taunted him in Mufulira, Madalitso would get his chance for revenge less than a year later. And he would do so on a colonial-era golf course with much deeper and more personal meaning to the Muthiya family.

Peter thought Mufulira was nothing more than a bad day. In a strange way, he was almost pleased that Madalitso suffered the experience. It was a lesson only life could teach. Even though Madalitso didn't score well, Peter thought the tournament was a great success because Mad's demeanor on the golf course was so impressive. Mufulira was an event for amateurs of *all* ages, including a couple of Zambia's best adult golfers. Peter was proud that his son never got down, lost his temper or displayed frustration. And for Madalitso to succeed in this sport, battling history would be unavoidable.

Peter knew better performances would come.

PETER STOOD MOTIONLESS as Madalitso finally arrived at the first tee at the World Junior Open qualifier, positioned his ball and assumed the stance Peter helped him carefully construct. Eyes on the ball. Left arm straight. Smooth backswing. Full extension and release. Good follow-through. The ball flew true and landed well beyond the others in his group. Peter was unsure whether his son would represent their country in England, but with one swing, he knew that day would be different than Mufulira. He smiled and made his way to the clubhouse and the beer waiting for him.

Madalitso was used to this. His father never coached him during tournaments. In fact, he often wasn't even there. Mad knew his dad wanted him to learn how to stand on his own, to solve his own problems. At the time, Madalitso found it frustrating. There were many moments during his early days as a competitive golfer when he wanted to ask his father a question. But Peter was nowhere to be found. One day, after much failure and even more success, Madalitso would understand.

After the round, the two brothers described their performances as almost mirror images of each other. *Keep the ball in the fairway. Put myself in position to score well. Make smart decisions.* Both ground out steady rounds, avoiding killer mistakes.

By the tenth hole, the competition had developed into a fraternal horse race between two brothers—Wongani and Madalitso. The closest competitors were several strokes back. Peter's son would travel to Royal Lytham in England. But which one?

Peter strolled to the eighteenth green in time to watch Wongani finish his round. Wongani smiled, happy as he told his dad what a good score he shot. Peter was pleased and proud that his eldest son had played so well. The two stood chatting until Madalitso's group made its way up the fairway. Mad's approach shot landed soft as a feather on the green, stopping about six feet from the hole.

Things became golf-silent at the eighteenth green. Informed of his brother's score, Madalitso knew this putt meant everything. But as Peter watched his boy intently, he saw no signs of nerves. Mad didn't appear flustered or even concerned by the magnitude of what he was about to attempt. As he studied the green, he carefully went through his checklist. With the grain or against it? Breaking left or right? Rolling fast or slow? When he had methodically processed all the information, just as Peter had taught him, just as he'd done hundreds of times himself, just as he'd watched the best professionals in the world do on TV, he lined up what appeared to be a straight putt. His breathing slowed as he looked back and forth between the ball and hole. He let out a final exhale.

As if he were out for a fun round on a Sunday afternoon, Madalitso executed an easy, rhythmic, textbook stroke.

Zambians wanting a representative in England held their breath as the ball rolled toward the hole.

Tension filled the spectators as it got nearer and nearer.

Shouts and cheers exploded as the ball gently plopped into the cup.

Madalitso didn't pump his fist. He didn't throw a cap into the air. He didn't scream, shout or holler. He bent down, picked his ball up out of the hole and allowed himself the luxury of a little grin. After shaking hands with his group, Mad joined his father and revealed his score.

He and Wongani had tied. Little brother had caught up.

Peter had envisioned many scenarios for how the tournament might end. This was certainly not one of them. As he recovered from the shock of having not one, but two sons qualify for the World Junior Championship, a representative from the ZGU walked over and said there would be no playoff.

Peter had to pick which son would represent Zambia on the world stage in England.

He was now faced with a parent's nightmare. How could he select one son over the other? He loved them both, heart and soul. Suddenly his proudest moment turned into a decision which would affect all of their lives.

Another father might have suffered paralysis. Not Peter. Not in Zambia. He made a decision and the boys accepted it without argument. And in the end, it wasn't even that hard. It was obvious at this point that Madalitso's passion was golf. He loved competing, practicing, watching, studying, even *talking* about the game. The World Junior Championship mattered more than anything to him, and it would enhance his development. Wongani was a good player, but his interest was passive. Madalitso was going to England.

As much as Wongani wanted this great adventure, he agreed with his father. He knew he was a fine player and he certainly had fun playing golf, but it wasn't something he thought about much. It was, on the other hand, Madalitso's passion, his calling, his everything. Wongani knew that his father had made the right choice. He was happy for Madalitso, never harboring any resentment or jealousy toward his younger brother's triumph. Mature beyond his fourteen years, Wongani knew he would get his chance to shine, and his father would support him completely.

Peter was much prouder of his son for the way he loved and supported his brother than he was for the great score Wongani had posted. It did his soul good to watch his eldest demonstrate the values that he and his wife tried to instill in all of their children.

And so it was that Zambia named its representative to the 1996 World Junior Championship.

Madalitso Muthiya would travel to one of golf's most celebrated and storied venues.

ZAMBIA'S QUALIFIER WAS held weeks prior to the World Junior Open. Rather than sitting idle, Peter felt strongly that it was important to continue playing, competing and improving. In June, Peter entered Madalitso in the Chainama Open, which always drew a large and competitive field.

The thirty-six-hole event welcomed amateurs of all ages. The best players in the country, stars like Kevin Phiri and Mohammed Zulu—as well as other top amateurs—were all trying to take home the trophy. This was the second time that Madalitso competed against adults. The first was still fresh in Peter's mind, the Mufulira Open, where Madalitso played so poorly.

Peter didn't know why Madalitso had underperformed. His son was always a hard person to read. He began to have second thoughts about

Chainama. After a strong performance in the World Junior Open Qualifier, he did not want Madalitso's confidence to suffer if he stumbled against the stiffest competition in Zambia. Especially with the trip to England coming up so quickly. But Peter's philosophy was to always help Madalitso face challenges. Not avoid them.

Driving to the course and during warm-ups, Peter looked for signs of jitters. There were none. Madalitso didn't say much. But then again, he never did.

After his name was announced, he went through his normal pre-shot routine with what seemed like casual nonchalance. He planted the tee and ball into the ground, assumed his stance and found a good grip on the club. He looked down the fairway at his target one last time. With arms extended, he measured his distance to the ball.

These are one of the hardest times for any parent. And Peter was no exception. There was nothing he could do anymore. He had imparted all his wisdom, shown his son everything he could and prepared him in the best way he knew how. Now, the only thing he could do was take a deep breath and say a quick prayer to the golf gods.

A sweet swing and smooth, powerful follow-through produced solid contact, and when the club whacked the ball, it made a satisfying, resounding *SMACK!* The ball launched as if it were shot from a rocket. Peter knew it was good. Sure enough, Madalitso's drive was long and straight, plopping down in the middle of the fairway.

That day, Peter didn't immediately retreat to the clubhouse. He stuck around for a couple of holes to watch his progress. Madalitso parred the first hole, birdied the next and parred the third. Peter wondered when the steady play would stop.

It never did. Drivers, irons, wedges—everything seemed automatic. At the end of the first round, Madalitso sat only a few shots behind the leader. Peter could see his confidence growing, and the momentum of his excellent day flowed into the second round.

More and more onlookers began following the group led by the freakishly calm, prodigiously talented thirteen-year-old. Each fantastic shot brought smiles, oohs and aahs and applause. Later, when asked about the unexpected attention, Madalitso showed what was becoming his trademark modesty and laser focus: "I really didn't notice."

Peter smiled when he saw himself in his son. His smile got even bigger when he realized that at thirteen, his son was a greater golfer than he would ever be.

Scores remained tight as excited spectators ran back and forth between groups to see if the young boy would catch the country's top amateurs. The suspense ratcheted from high to higher when Madalitso made his putt on seventeen and found himself in a four-way tie for second place. To catch Kevin Phiri, he would need to birdie Chainama's eighteenth hole, a par 4.

His flowing, powerful, seemingly effortless tee shot drew more appreciative applause from the growing pack of enthusiastic onlookers. It was even more impressive given the fact that Madalitso was thirteen, stood 5'4" and weighed 130 pounds soaking wet.

The ball hurled off his driver and landed nearly 250 yards down the middle of the fairway. Only a casual nine-iron stood between him and history. The pin was placed near the edge of the green where only the most daring players would aim. Madalitso, true to his nature, chose a more conservative approach. He aimed for the heart of the green, playing the percentages, opting to rely on his excellent putting stroke.

The ball landed in a perfect spot but hit the putting surface with a little too much speed and rolled into the short rough on the edge of the green. It would take a world-class chip-and-roll to catch Phiri now. Madalitso took his time, pacing the twenty feet between the hole and his ball, surveying the green like a seasoned veteran. Such a mature, calm and deliberate approach by a thirteen-year-old made heads shake in appreciation and smiles bloom on many faces in the gallery.

He lined up his shot, swung the club like a pendulum in perfect rhythm and followed through like his dad's idol Tom Watson. The ball landed in an ideal spot on the green. The silent crowd roared, trying to will it in, as it rolled on a perfect line toward the hole.

The noise got louder and louder as it became clear that Madalitso hit a perfect shot. It was going, going...

And stopped inches from the hole, before it reached the lip of the cup.

Madalitso made his putt and finished in a miraculous three-way tie for second place. A sudden death playoff awaited him on the eighteenth hole, against the two players who shared his score. Both were full-grown men. He was still barely a teenager.

One of them stared down Madalitso as they waited for sudden death to begin. Finally, with a stern stony face, he asked his young opponent how old he was.

Madalitso, utterly unfazed, replied that he was thirteen.

"You're only thirteen years old?!" his opponent shouted in a high-pitched tone, eyes bugging out from his skull. Laughter erupted from the crowd. Even Mad had to laugh.

Only three holes were needed to decide sole possession of second place. On a par 3, Madalitso watched the grown-ups hit errant tee shots. He methodically went through his routine, took a deep breath and hit a gorgeous three-iron that landed gracefully on the green. He easily two-putted. The playoff was over.

Madalitso was the most unexpected runner-up. He finished just behind Kevin Phiri on the leaderboard, but ahead of everyone else, including a familiar champion, Mohammed Zulu. He also beat Peter Armstrong, a Zambian-born golfer who had played professionally throughout Africa and Europe.

The *Times of Zambia* captured the feeling of those who witnessed Madalitso's performance:

"13-year-old Madalitso Muthiya stunned 86 golfers by scooping the runner-up position of the Chainama Golf Club Championship in Lusaka."

Peter was ecstatic by how well Madalitso had played. But he was even more impressed by Madalitso's demeanor, how he carried himself with such grace and composure in the face of ridiculous pressure from the best players in Zambia, men twice his age who had won countless big events. Mad never looked out of place or in over his head; he just took everything in stride. He knew that people were tracking his scores hole by hole. He knew it was close. But still, he remained even keel.

To the outside world, Madalitso amassed victories humbly and quietly, but inside, his confidence grew. The game was starting to make sense. With each passing tournament, more shots and more situations looked familiar to him, and he was learning from past mistakes. Figuring out how to block external forces, as well nagging doubts from inside. Many thirteen-year-olds struggle with their own insecurity, and Madalitso was certainly not immune from a typical adolescent's occasional feelings of awkwardness. But he was starting to feel like he did belong, like he could compete with the moneyed rich kids decked out in their expensive finery, with their glistening new golf bags, shiny new shoes and state-of-the-art clubs. His foundation of family and faith made it possible for golf to be the tool by which Madalitso was building internal fortitude and resiliency. Two qualities he'd need as he stepped up to the international stage, where there would be more scrutiny, more judgment and more pressure.

Peter was proud of his son. He knew Madalitso was ready for England.

IO

THE WORLD JUNIOR OPEN CHAMPIONSHIP was Madalitso's first trip off the African continent, a journey from one of the poorest countries to one of the wealthiest. And he did it alone, flying solo, unaccompanied by coach, friends or family. Many thirteen-year-olds would have been intimidated by traveling from one culture and continent to the other. But Peter made sure Madalitso was prepared. He had already traveled by himself to tournaments. He'd played his whole life without a coach or parent hovering over his shoulder. He'd learned how to navigate a golf course without any help, much as he was learning to navigate life by himself.

As was his way, Madalitso took it all in stride. He was immediately impressed by Gatwick Airport. It was so much nicer and more modern than anything he'd seen in Zambia. And there were much better roads. In Lusaka, the streets were paved, but rough. And there were many dirt roads. There were no dirt roads around Blackpool and certainly none in London. But he was surprised by how old the buildings were. He expected a gleaming, modern city with tall, shiny skyscrapers and crisscrossed highways. It was all new and nice, just not what he expected.

But this trip also opened his eyes in unexpected ways.

Blackpool North Shore Golf Club held an introductory reception for players the day after he arrived. Madalitso's first glimpse of the entire group came as everybody found their seats. Something seemed odd. As his eyes scanned the room, it suddenly dawned on him. He wasn't in Zambia anymore.

Madalitso was the only Black player. He was shocked. Players from all over the world were there, so he assumed there would at least be a few Black golfers. As Madalitso processed this realization, he was struck in a new way by where he now stood. In an elite golf club. A storied venue. A building his father almost certainly would have been barred from entering when he was a boy. And he was about to compete against some of the best golfers on the planet in a game that his father was forced to play with sticks on vacant land.

But unlike a colonial golf course in the hinterlands of the British Empire, this was England. The empire that viciously exploited his people to extract blood money for generations. The complex system that subjugated Blacks was designed here.

Beyond the history he learned in school, there were the deeply personal stories passed down from Uncle Papsonjere. He had a flash of his grandparents Kaliwé and Sandikonda being forced by White colonialists from their land and into a mud hut. The place where his father would begin his steep and seemingly insurmountable climb out of poverty.

It was yet another moment where Madalitso was not just confronting history. He was at risk of being overwhelmed by it. The last time history cast a shadow over a tournament, it seemed the universe turned against him. Peter knew there would be many such moments. How would it affect him this time?

Ms. Sonia Copeland Bloom, the tournament organizer, confirmed Madalitso's observations of the tournament field. The World Junior Open was her personal project before it became sponsored by the United Kingdom's governing body for golf: the overwhelmingly White Royal & Ancient.

Bloom designed the tournament program containing player photographs and biographical information. Over thirty countries sent players to the 1996 World Junior Open. But only one sent a Black player: Zambia. Kenya and Zimbabwe also sent players. The Kenyan was of Indian descent. The Zimbabwean was White.

Growing up, Mad's parents stressed that he was as good as anyone else. If you work hard and make good decisions, you will succeed. Here was yet another chance to prove it.

When Madalitso walked into the clubhouse in Blackpool, his blank face did not betray how overwhelmed he felt. He was like a little boy at a PGA facility. Everywhere he looked, he saw the latest state-of-the-art clubs, brand-new shiny shoes and beautiful, glossy golf bags. Many of the players seemed to know each other, casually chatting with aristocratic ease about their private golf clubs and expensive instructors in their home countries.

Madalitso stood in the heart of privilege with his secondhand shoes and a set of mismatched clubs painstakingly pieced together over time by Peter, who slowly but surely accumulated a used driver and some repaired and salvaged wedges and irons, along with a very experienced putter. When he had a little extra money, he inched Mad closer and closer to a complete set. The only private instructor he had was his father, an insurance broker. As if that weren't enough, he was also one of the shorter players competing. The tournament was for ages sixteen and below. Mad was only thirteen at the time, a lightweight at 130, barely five and a half feet tall. Some of the sixteen-year-olds looked like grown men.

Scanning the faces of the adults and children around him, he thought their stares meant they thought he was out of place. That he did not belong. That the color of his skin made him inferior. Excluded him from this world of wealth, privilege and status.

But the more he looked at all those White faces looking at him, the more he wasn't sure how much of that was coming from them and how much was coming from internalizing the message he'd been getting from the world since before he was even born. The message his dad was always helping him fight by telling him that the blackness of his skin didn't determine his worth and value. As a golfer. Or as a man.

But he quickly shook his head, deciding that he could not let the weight of history—whether his country or his own family—consume him. And he would not concern himself with the outdated views of people he didn't even know. *Get on with the job,* as Peter would say. He was there to play golf. He'd been taught that the only way black and white applied to him was that he was a Black boy hitting the same kind of white ball as all the White boys. Skin color, equipment, training, height and age never really bothered him. Nor did the opinions of others. He knew it would all be settled on the golf course. He heard his dad's voice in his head, reminding him that if he was there and they were there, they both belonged. Kaliwé's words about Peter's first days at Munali found new meaning. *Just focus on what you need to do.*

BLACKPOOL'S FIRST HOLE is a 430-yard par 4. The last of his group to tee off, Madalitso slowly pulled his secondhand driver from his golf bag. Just as he noticed their clubs, they surely noticed his. Players and spectators stood silent as the slightly built, untrained, poorly shoed and underequipped thirteen-year-old got into position. Their eyes scanned him from head to toe while he stared down the fairway, found his grip and eyed the ball. Any sympathy for the Zambian, or doubt that he belonged, quickly faded as he unwound his rhythmic backswing, made solid contact with the sweet spot, and flowed into a smooth follow-through. His ball sailed long and straight down the fairway, landing well past his competitors'.

Spectators clapped enthusiastically. One of the other players even asked to see Madalitso's driver, as if the well-worn club had anything to do with it.

Blackpool is a traditional links course—open and sparsely vegetated with windswept grass. For many, it was a first-time experience. Stiff seaside breezes, tall dunes and deep bunkers provided a cruel education that few expected or enjoyed. The wind played havoc with everyone, as consistent accuracy eluded all the boys, including Madalitso. Weather and course conditions on the British coast were chilly, tempestuous and volatile, drastically different from the big open skies and heat of landlocked southern Africa.

But his distance off the tee was a delight to spectators and the envy of his competitors, particularly on Blackpool's three long par 5s. Each is over 500 yards in length. Madalitso smoked his drives way past his older, more seasoned playing partners on both days of the competition. However, anyone assuming he was just a long ball specialist was mistaken. Madalitso's short game was tested on Blackpool's eighteenth hole when his second shot flew straight into one of the notorious greenside pot bunkers, which have spoiled the rounds of many a grown man. He stepped into the sand and found himself face-to-face with an impossibly steep wall. He had to back out of the bunker and stand on his toes *just* to see the flag location. He had to give up all hope of going close to the hole. His objective was just to somehow get out of the deep pit he was standing in.

Madalitso pulled his most lofted old wedge from his battered bag, assumed a wide-open stance and dug in with his feet. He took a couple of mock swings to simulate the swing he would need to hit his half-buried ball straight up and onto a green that was over his head and out of sight. As far as he remembered—clear back to when he started playing golf at the age of five—he had never hit a shot like this.

A short backswing and textbook acceleration through the shot sent a cloud of sand exploding into the air. Out of this sandstorm, a white ball emerged, flying up, up, up and out of the bunker. Madalitso immediately knew he had the right upward trajectory, but standing down in the bunker with sand in his eyes, he had no idea where it landed. Applause gave him some hope. He scrambled around the edge of the bunker and up to the green to see where his ball landed. He was pleasantly surprised to find it resting a few feet from the cup. Later he would confess that there was some luck involved with that one.

But that's what happens when you work hard, focus on what you need to do, believe in yourself and the golf gods are watching.

OVER THE NEXT two days, boys from around the world ate, slept and played golf together. They compared favorite movies and music, shared family stories and talked of their homes. They were very different from each other, and yet very similar. As often happens, sports and youth broke down barriers.

It was Madalitso's first time interacting with people from around the world with such clear cultural and economic differences. All of those kids had more money than him, but he was surprised how much everyone had in common. They all liked the same things and laughed at the same jokes. His parents had always told him that he was no better and no worse than anyone else. He assumed they were right. But it was reassuring to get proof.

Madalitso matched his better equipped competitors, shot for shot and hole for hole. By the end everyone had long forgotten his inferior clubs, shoes and training.

Remembering his father's emphasis on etiquette, Madalitso was appalled by some of the behavior he witnessed. Players lost their temper, banging their clubs on the ground and cursing. Even guys who were playing well would curse up a blue streak. For all their money and privilege, a few seemed to lack class, manners and sportsmanship.

Madalitso was stoic by nature. And thanks to Peter's consistent haranguing, proper behavior on the golf course was ingrained. He simply knew no other way. At Blackpool, he never lost his cool, never used foul language and never changed his demeanor. Not once.

Sonia Copeland Bloom was duly impressed. She remembered Madalitso being a very diligent, quietly determined boy. She was impressed that he was a model of decorum and was always well-mannered.

Madalitso finished with the lowest score of all the non-European players at the 1996 World Junior Open and tied for fifth overall. Equally important, at least to his father, Madalitso made his family proud, and honored the sport of golf with his exemplary behavior.

News travels fast. Before he arrived home, *Zambia Daily Mail* reported:

"[T]hirteen year-old sensational junior golfer Madalitso Muthiya scooped the Special Junior Open World-wide trophy for participants from outside Europe at the just-ended scholar tournament in England."

Zambia Golf Union President Alex Moshano called Madalitso's performance "a great achievement." He emphasized that it was "an encouraging result especially that it was the first time that Zambia had been represented at such a big competition. The young man did Zambia a lot of pride."

Madalitso eased into his seat for the return flight from London to Lusaka with a greater understanding of other people and himself. For his entire life, he only knew Zambia. While television and books had provided images of the outside world, it was still a vast mystery.

No more. Boys from Europe, the United States, Asia and elsewhere might look and talk differently, but these were small distinctions. Madalitso learned they were mostly just like him. Their interests, hobbies and music tastes were familiar. He enjoyed their company, and they enjoyed his.

They were certainly no better at golf than him. Madalitso may not have won the tournament, but no player consistently played better than him or made shots he was unable to make. Centuries of history put these boys in different countries and at different places on the economic spectrum. Madalitso perceived the unevenness up close but now saw it as nothing insurmountable.

Madalitso's grandmother Kaliwé once told Peter that the differences in wealth he perceived at Munali Secondary School were irrelevant. They were who they are, and he was who he was. They were both there, so they both belonged. He should ignore their money. *Just focus on what you need to do.* Madalitso now believed those words applied to him. On any golf course, in any tournament and in any clubhouse in the world, he belonged.

As for Peter, he thought Madalitso looked older and more mature when he returned from England even though he was only gone for a week. And he was certainly a more confident player. Peter was proud and pleased that his son had left Zambia, his comfort zone, to compete against a talented international field and never wilted. Such a drastic step up in competition so far from home could have broken lesser boys and men. But Peter knew a good performance would raise his son's confidence in ways not possible through any junior tournament in Zambia. His strong showing against better trained and better equipped players changed him. From then on, Zambia seemed a little bit smaller.

Both Madalitso and Peter knew he was ready for more.

THE FINAL UNDERAGE event of the year was the Chick of the North, the biggest and most celebrated junior tournament in Zambia, hosted by Ndola Golf Club. Like so many others, Ndola Golf Club was built by poor Black people for rich White people with mining revenues during colonialism. In 1972, Ndola was the venue for the inaugural Zambia Open—still an important stop on Southern Africa's Sunshine Tour.

Today, Ndola remains one of Zambia's finest courses, rivaling Lusaka Golf Club in popularity and quality. Golfers play on manicured fairways lined with big, beautiful trees. Despite the rough greens, golfers can score well on the relatively short par 72. Provided, of course, they successfully navigate Ndola Golf Club's most notorious challenge: anthills. Golfers must battle with over 300 anthills scattered throughout the course, some over nine feet tall. Visiting players have unknowingly followed their golf balls into ant-infested areas. It's not uncommon to see golfers emerge screaming and flailing as African ants—the piranhas of the ant world, known for their ability to devour any living creature on the continent—sink their teeth into the players' flesh, thus giving a whole new meaning to the word "hazard."

As the Muthiyas arrived at Ndola, the previous year's Chick of the North remained fresh in their minds. Wongani had won the under-13 age group, beating his brother in the process. Though Wongani's interest in golf had waned somewhat, sibling rivalries die hard. He was determined to defend his title and, perhaps more importantly, beat his little brother who was now making headlines in the paper for being Zambia's budding new star and youngest athletic hero.

But even in warm-ups, Wongani noticed a change. Madalitso swung his clubs with authority, and he'd learned a new putting style. He moved around the driving range and practice green like a pro. Wongani had a sinking feeling. Maybe it wouldn't be so easy to beat Madalitso this time.

He was right. It was soon clear that the younger brother he routinely beat no longer existed. Madalitso shot out of the gates on fire. He birdied two of the first three holes to secure an early lead, which he never relinquished. Even when a bad shot left him vulnerable, he rebounded without batting an eye.

A prime example was the errant shot that Madalitso hit on Ndola's sixth hole, a par 5 with dreaded anthills on either side of the fairway. Madalitso's drive strayed out of bounds. From the tee box, it was unclear exactly where his ball landed, but the closer he got, the worse it looked.

He stopped dead in his tracks when he saw where his ball was lying—on the backside of an anthill. A couple of quiet gasps and a few "oh no"s, including one from his caddie, came out of the onlookers. The only person who didn't seem perturbed was Mad.

He took a deep breath, contemplating his next move. First, he carefully inspected the ground around his ball to make sure it wasn't moving or that he might lose a foot to the killer ants. Sensing no imminent danger, he asked his caddie for the sand wedge. He inched forward, still looking for any of the tiny razor-toothed carnivores that lived in the giant monstrosity standing between his ball and the green. His caddie, the spectators and even a tournament official remained safely on the fairway, breath bated, waiting to see whether the young, slender, unflappable golfer was going to flop.

He took a few casual steps to peer around the anthill, gauge the direction of the hole and find his target. He came back and addressed his ball, positioning his body to give himself the best chance of recovering from what could easily be a catastrophe. Of course, it had to make it over the anthill first. Otherwise, he risked a bogey and possibly an all-out, flesh-eating ant assault. He bent his knees to get the most elevation on his ball. He closed his eyes and took a deep breath, trying to focus on his shot instead of the colony of predators whose home he had invaded. A slow and careful backswing, then a smooth, powerful follow-through launched his ball high into the air. He looked up to see it easily clear the anthill. Knowing he had just disturbed an angry army ant barracks, he quickly scooted back to the fairway. His caddie, the spectators and fellow players applauded. He spotted his ball sitting with a clear shot to the green. His caddie told him that he'd been the only person who didn't look stressed. Madalitso just smiled.

Madalitso's play was the talk of the tournament. Buzz was already sweeping golf aficionados and fans because of his great success in England. Everybody wanted to take a look at this new and unprecedented phenom. Onlookers and competitors, some of whom were five years older than he was, couldn't stop talking about how well the young prodigy was playing. Lively chatter erupted as his approach shots and chips landed within striking distance of the cup. But the liveliest response came at the tee box. The ever-growing gallery crowded around with breathless anticipation. When the slightly built youngster would smite his ball with an audible crack, it would fly like a tiny white cannonball hundreds of yards down the fairway. And the peanut gallery would erupt into rapturous applause.

Wongani played well at the 1996 Chick of the North, finishing third behind Madalitso and another boy. But his lasting memory was how much his younger brother had improved. He knew Madalitso loved the game. How his brother had studied other golfers and played whenever he could. It really showed. He was a different player. Young Mad looked like a champion. Wongani could not have been prouder.

For Madalitso, the day finally came. He had wanted to beat his older brother for as long as he could remember. "Stealing" their father's clubs and breaking a kitchen window not only sparked a passion for golf, it also launched a sibling rivalry that fueled intense battles every time the boys practiced at Lusaka Golf Club or simply putted in their backyard. Wongani's boisterous personality only hardened Madalitso's resolve.

With the sibling rivalry now put to rest—at least when it came to golf—Mad didn't taunt or point fingers. Despite years of heated competitions, Wongani's sincere joy in his brother's success would've made that seem petty and mean-spirited. During the awards ceremony, the boys made eye contact and smiled at each other as onlookers applauded Madalitso. The drive home was full of fun and laughter as they shared stories from the tournament. Both knew the baton had been passed. Wongani suspected he would never beat his brother again. He was right.

The *Times of Zambia* called Madalitso the "[G]olfing whiz-kid" who "scooped the Chick O' North golf championship." The *Times* added that he "displayed fantastic play and stunned several of the junior competitors with his brilliant drives and hard-hitting skills."

Although one would never have known it by looking at him, Madalitso was pleased.

But now that he'd tasted international success again, he wanted more. So did Peter.

AUTUMN OF 1996, Peter wanted to build his son's growing self-confidence. And he wanted to test him against the best of the best. He knew Madalitso needed to keep playing, but there were no junior tournaments until the next year. Too much idle time.

So he entered Madalitso in the Champion of Champions, a thirty-six-hole amateur competition. Winners of other tournaments were invited, along with top amateurs of *all* ages. Madalitso would again face adult players, including local superstars Kevin Phiri and Mohammed Zulu.

Ndola Golf Club and all of its anthills hosted the 1996 Champion of Champions.

The tournament had added meaning thanks to a certain spectator: Madalitso's mother. Edith rarely visited golf courses, but after hearing of her son's feats, she had to see what all the fuss was about.

Edith enjoyed watching Madalitso warm up on the range and work his way around the practice green. She was slightly amazed when she watched him smash the majestic opening drive on the par 5 first hole. She smiled when spectators—complete strangers—applauded her son. And how humble and focused he was. Not wanting to disrupt the established routine, she joined her husband in the clubhouse. On the one hand, Mad wasn't totally surprised to see his dad disappear. He was used to it. His dad left him to his own devices during tournaments.

Mom was different. She was the family nurturer, the comforter, the emotional supporter, the one who made his dinners, picked him up after falling down and kissed his boo-boos. On the golf course, Peter was the drill sergeant who focused on teaching the physical and mental skills needed to succeed at golf, the independence to work through problems alone and the toughness to compete against any odds. Madalitso expected his father to disappear into the clubhouse.

But not Mom! Edith was different. When she announced her plans to attend the tournament, a small part of Madalitso hoped she would be there for a kiss on the cheek or at least some encouraging words after a bad shot. When she followed her husband into the clubhouse, it became even more difficult for him to focus and rely on himself. Exactly what Peter wanted.

The '96 Champion of Champions, like all tournaments that pitted him against adults, produced an added challenge. Raised in a traditional household, his parents always taught him to approach adults with respect and deference. Politeness, manners and courtesy were required. With both Peter and Edith attending the tournament, part of him felt compelled to treat Phiri and Zulu like two of his parents' friends who had come over for dinner.

But this was a competition, requiring an attitude that he was just as good—and even better—than any other player. He needed to beat these adults. Worrying about their feelings was not even a consideration. As he prepared to tee off, he realized the only sensible approach to this tournament was simply to block out all of the mixed feelings: his mom's presence, the grown men he would soon confront and the excitement the Zambian golfing community had for its young prodigy. Just play golf.

Madalitso's opening blast set the tone for his performance. He was near the top of the leaderboard throughout both rounds. Not every shot reached its intended target, but he kept himself in contention with his short game, chipping and putting with the cool nerves and deadly skill of a player twice his age.

On the arduous fourth hole, arguably the most difficult hole of the course, Madalitso winced ever so slightly as his tee shot sailed into the left rough. Keeping the ball in the fairway is a must, as landing anywhere else almost certainly means a bogey or worse.

Madalitso found his ball lying in sparse tall grass right next to a few trees. He was short of the green and well off the fairway. The worst place he could be. His caddie advised him to simply hack the ball back onto the fairway, take his lumps and move on. Shooting for the green could easily turn a minor mistake into a major disaster.

Madalitso heard his caddie but said nothing. Slowly, he paced back and forth behind his ball, examining the next shot from different angles and working out the calculations with cool analytic resolve. Finally, he walked over to his clubs and paused for a moment. After taking one last look at his ball, he pulled his seven-iron from his bag. The caddie frowned, confused and concerned as Madalitso moved to address the ball. It was clear he was not looking to just "get out of trouble." He was going for broke, trying to land this impossible shot on the green. He'd have to power his ball through the tall grass, bend it around the tree trunks and keep it under the branches. There was only one way to hit this shot right. And a million ways to hit it wrong and turn a bogey into a round-ruining 7 or 8. It was a shot that would only be attempted by a seasoned professional—or a young rash teenager who hadn't learned enough hard lessons on the golf course. Mad was young, but he was never rash.

He calmly went through his pre-shot ritual, seeing the exact line he would have to travel. After a few practice swings, he addressed the ball and took a deep breath. He moved forward so the ball was further back in his stance, to make sure it stayed low. But the lost elevation meant he'd need more power.

He took his usual, sweet, rhythmic backswing. But his weight shift, follow-through and shoulder rotation were fierce yet controlled, generating all of the force his thirteen-year-old body could muster.

The clubface hit the ball crisp and pure. It rocketed off in a low line drive, exploding out of the trees and straight toward the hole.

Madalitso emerged from behind the obstructions just in time to see his ball stop on the edge of the green.

His caddie, relieved and slightly incredulous, slapped him on the back and applauded.

He allowed himself the smallest grin, where his brother would have whooped and hollered and gone crazy. But inside, he was exhilarated.

Salvaging this hole became a snapshot of his tournament, frequently needing a miraculous shot out of the weeds to make birdie or par.

On the thirty-sixth and final hole of the tournament, to everyone's amazement but his own, Madalitso found himself one shot behind Mohammed Zulu and Aaron Simfukwe, two grown champions with dozens of tournament victories between them. He needed to birdie the last hole, a par 4, in order to join them in a three-way playoff.

The gallery was now formidable, building as the tension mounted with hundreds of eyes staring at the small boy with the big driver. The air was electric; Zambians waited with bated breath to see if all the hype was real. When he needed it most, could the budding star produce? Was he a contender or a pretender?

Madalitso found his grip and took a few casual practice swings, trying to mentally shrug off the errant shot on the fourth hole and a few others that caused him headaches throughout the day. Settling into his stance, he didn't even notice the hushed crowd holding its breath, eager to see whether the thirteen-year-old would tie the heralded champions Zulu and Simfukwe.

He took a large, calm breath and began his swing like he'd done tens of thousands of times before. It was his same perfect, sweeping backswing until the club was parallel to the ground. Then the easy, deceptively powerful shift of weight as the undersized hips began to rotate. The club picking up tremendous speed, culminating in a satisfying *THWACK!* And finishing with the sweet easy follow-through as he posed after his fluid, powerful and effortless stroke. The fact that this small package generated such force, torque and power brought smiles to faces, kudos to lips and shouts of exultation pouring out of mouths as the crowd applauded.

Before the club recoiled from around his body, he knew it was a good shot. The ball sped straight down the fairway. He couldn't have done much better if he'd walked down and placed the ball where it landed. He had a perfect approach to the green. Now all he had to do was hit an easy iron to a spot below the hole where he'd have a makeable putt. Otherwise, there would be no chance for a spot in the playoff. He could do this on the practice range practically blindfolded. But could he do it when the championship was on the line?

He pulled his trusty, beat-up nine-iron from his bag and focused on a safe place near the pin, away from potential dangers. Just like Peter taught him. He stood over the ball as a crowd encircled the green, waiting to see if the much-heralded wunderkind could deliver the goods under pressure.

Peter and Edith emerged from the clubhouse but stayed camouflaged among the other spectators to avoid being a distraction to their son. By looking at them, you wouldn't have known that their hearts were in their mouths, beating so hard they were afraid Mad might hear it.

Mad did what he'd been training nearly his whole life to do. He made another beautiful fluid swing and clicked a sweet little chip straight at the hole. The ball landed soft on the green. Voices rose as it rolled straight at the pin. It looked for a moment like it actually might go in. But it didn't quite have enough juice. The gallery sighed and moaned a little, disappointed that they wouldn't see a miraculous eagle. Madalitso was left with an 8-foot putt for birdie. Not impossible, but certainly no gimme. Especially with what felt like the whole world watching.

Madalitso strolled onto the green like a boy without a care in the world. He surveyed the landscape for subtle clues as to which way the ball would break and how hard he had to hit it. Just like Peter had told him to do. Just like Tom Watson did. He viewed it as a fairly straightforward putt. All he had to do was get the speed right.

Madalitso assumed his stance and took a few practice strokes. He breathed, exhaled and stepped over the ball.

The entire Zambian golfing community seemed to hold its breath.

Silence. Backswing. Contact.

As soon as he hit it, he knew he had left the putt short. One of the cardinal sins in pressure putting. Never leave it short. He was surprised. Mad had tried to hit the ball through the hole, so he wouldn't leave it short.

It rolled true, though, straight at the heart of the hole, and never wavered. Mad's eyes went wide when the ball dropped, plopping down into the cup. Birdie. Playoff.

As the gallery went wild, erupting in raucous celebration, he heard the ball rattle around the bottom of the cup. Turned out it wasn't short at all. In fact, it went in so hard, for a moment he was afraid it might jump back out.

Not a chance. Madalitso was going to the playoff.

Not that he would've done much celebrating anyway, but there was no time to revel in his amazing achievement. He quickly but politely shook hands with the players in his group and marched over to the tenth tee box, the first playoff hole. Zulu and Simfukwe were already there, quietly talking to each other when Madalitso walked up.

The two men ceased their conversation, turned their heads and stared at the child who had forced them into a three-way playoff. An introvert by nature, Mad's inclination was to avoid eye contact and stand by himself. But Peter and Edith taught him that when meeting adults, it was polite to smile and shake hands. And so, Madalitso set aside his shyness, approached and extended his right hand. The gesture seemed to disarm Zulu and Simfukwe as both smiled back and returned his greeting. It was a simple act, but its effect was significant. Friendly conversation with two men more than twice his age washed away any chance that he would ever again feel intimidated or deferential to an adult player.

Zulu and Madalitso opened with good drives. Simfukwe put himself in a difficult position and could not recover. The 1996 Champion of Champions was down to two players: Zulu and Madalitso. Heralded, battle-hardened champion versus brash, young newcomer.

Madalitso was thrilled to have come this far, but he wasn't satisfied. He smelled victory, and even though he never showed it, he desperately wanted this win for himself, his dad and his family.

If Mad felt the pressure, no one could tell. If you didn't know one player was thirteen and the other was in his thirties, you would have never guessed it by the serene yet intense way they both stepped up to their balls and ripped pressure-packed shot after shot.

Both parred the tenth and eleventh holes and proceeded to the eighteenth. They mimicked each other down the eighteenth fairway, each playing within himself while waiting for the other to make a mistake. Both chipped to within a few feet of the cup. Madalitso's ball was furthest away, so he would go first.

He channeled his father's voice and got down to business, blocking out everything except what he could control: the green, the ball and his trusty old putter. Six feet separated him from victory, another playoff hole or defeat. He knelt down, walked around his ball and the hole and knelt down again, studying the green intently and seeking out the correct line.

Peter watched, admiring Madalitso's cool, calm concentration, marveling at how his boy was becoming a man right in front of his eyes. He'd watched his son make pressure shots when he had to, regardless of the stakes and distractions. Mad just focused on his technique, his form, his game. Edith, on the other hand, was a bundle of raw nerves. She could hardly watch. But she couldn't look away. Again, pride surged through Peter. If only his father could see his grandson dominating in this White man's game in a world that had been forbidden to both of them. Madalitso acted like he belonged there. Because he did. One part of Peter could hardly believe that his son was one stroke away from beating one of the best and most famous players in Zambia. But one part of him was not surprised at all. After all, the boy had been blessed since the day he was born.

After finding his line, he got into his stance and took a few easy practice strokes.

Dead silence fell on the nervous crowd gathered around the green.

Mad couldn't hear the silence. His whole being was focused on ball, putter and hole.

A slow steady exhale was followed by a slow steady backswing and smooth follow-through.

Again, Madalitso knew he had the perfect line, but Zambia's greens can be unpredictable.

But this time, the speed looked just right. Inch by inch the ball rolled, never deviating from the path he'd visualized and the stroke he'd executed with such precise aplomb.

The ball dove off the green and disappeared down the hole.

The crowd went berserk, screaming and cheering for the miraculous kid who'd become such a crowd favorite, staring down men twice his age all tournament.

Edith was more relieved than happy, as she breathed for what felt like the first time in hours.

Peter was ecstatic. He tried to hide it. But was not successful.

All eyes turned to the legendary champion, Mohammed Zulu. Would he extend the tournament to a fourth playoff hole? Or would Madalitso, the young prodigy, make 1996 even more earth-shattering for the Muthiya family?

Zulu was laser-focused as he completed his pre-shot routine and stepped over his ball.

Mad moved off to the side, as etiquette dictated, but made sure he found a spot where he could watch every second.

Zulu stroked the ball well. Mad was sure he'd hit the perfect putt. After all, he'd been making these kinds of putts before Madalitso was even born.

But the greens were unpredictable, and the shot rolled just past the hole.

The crowd let out a collective groan. Zulu tapped in just to finish out.

Madalitso didn't fall to his knees. He didn't throw his ball. He didn't pump his fist. He just stood for a moment and took it all in. The crowd going wild applauding him. Zulu and Simfukwe shaking his hand and congratulating him. He told Simfukwe and Zulu that he was grateful for the chance to play such accomplished golfers. It was the perfect sign of respect—and perhaps a little sensitivity for how they must have felt getting beaten by somebody still years away from his driver's license.

His caddie slapped his back excitedly, overjoyed at their triumph. Mad simply accepted the congratulations with a modest smile and a quiet "Thank you."

And so it was that thirteen-year-old Madalitso Muthiya beat the best amateur golfers in Zambia to become the youngest winner of the Champion of Champions.

Edith had to stop herself from running and screaming in glee and throwing her arms around her baby boy who had grown into a champion. In an unfamiliar place surrounded by strangers, she stood with her hands clasped in front of her. But the wide smile on her beaming face revealed that she was overflowing with giddy excitement and joy over her young son's victory. When Madalitso finally finished and made his way through the swarm of well-wishers, he approached his mom. With a brief but firm hug and a quick kiss on the cheek she said how proud she was of him.

Madalitso was so glad she'd been there for this life-changing moment. She'd been there every step of the way, giving him love and support.

Peter couldn't stop a huge grin from overtaking his face. But that was enough. Father and son communicated a lifetime of love, sacrifice, hard work, satisfaction and elation without saying a word.

On the drive home, Peter and Madalitso skipped the usual in-depth post-tournament deconstruction, debriefing and analysis. Instead, Madalitso gave his mom a funny play-by-play tutorial. He broke down critical holes, key shots and club selection, stopping occasionally to make sure she understood the difference between a driver and a putter, a bunker and a green. Madalitso loved golf, and he was over the moon about winning the tournament, but seeing his mother added an extra layer on his cake of joy.

Peter drove the car without saying a word, enjoying his son's enthusiasm and his wife's smile, which hadn't left her face since Madalitso sank his last putt. He was also pleased that his latest curveball—elevating Madalitso's excitement by bringing his mother and then promptly removing her from the course when play began—did not faze Madalitso.

The *Times of Zambia* quoted Madalitso as crediting the victory to his "focus" and "confidence." The headline read "Golf whiz-kid blessed with victory."

Peter joked that it was a clever reference to Madalitso's name.

He gave the reporter the benefit of the doubt.

IN 1996, MADALITSO added a new component to his training, an activity that greatly enhanced his knowledge of the game and would eventually become his trademark: watching television. Peter brought home a documentary on the history of the Ryder Cup. It followed the evolution of the tournament back to the first unofficial matches between American and British golfers at Gleneagles, Scotland, in 1921.

Mad enjoyed the history, but he loved studying clips of legendary players. Jack Nicklaus, Nick Faldo, Tom Kite, Seve Ballesteros, Colin Montgomerie, Jose Maria Olazabal. And especially, Peter's (and now his) favorite—Tom Watson. Every cut, fade and draw. Every drive, iron, chip and putt was analyzed. This became his golf classroom, and he was the most studious student. He watched frame by frame and soaked in the commentators describing width of stance, closed or open grip, rotation of shoulders and hips, shifting of weight, using the arms to get full extension. Over and over, Madalitso would pause the VCR, go outside and reenact the minutiae of a swing. Just as Peter had found invigorating peace in his love for golf, his son would lose himself for hours on end, getting totally pumped watching the greats of yesteryear, then using those lessons to hone his craft.

Peter got great pleasure bonding with Madalitso as they studied the tapes of golf greats. They would deconstruct the strengths and weaknesses of legendary swings. Many a day, he'd arrive home to find Mad outside the house mimicking something from a Ryder Cup. His only worry was that his son might wear the tape out. But it only ever became a problem when no one else could get a crack at the television.

Peter collected other golf tapes and occasionally a live tournament was televised. Whatever the program, whatever the tournament, Madalitso was right there, breaking down the swings of PGA players and imitating everything down to the last detail.

Peter didn't have access to watching this extraordinary library of golf legends. He had to learn the rules of golf and the fundamentals of a good swing by watching White men on local segregated golf courses. It was important to him that Madalitso not only got to study the greatest swings of golf's past, but that he saw himself competing against anyone, anywhere, regardless of race, creed or color. And since he couldn't afford to give his son the best private coaches money could buy, he was determined to help Mad learn the game by watching the world's best players and applying these principles to his game.

Peter had always had a passion for history, reading and rereading every book within his grasp. He believed we could only understand the world, the future and ourselves by understanding the past, where we came from and who our ancestors were. Watching Mad study past Ryder Cups, Peter saw himself in his son. It was one of his favorite parts of being a dad.

Peter already knew that his boy had talent and loved the game. But he was proud of Madalitso's determination to squeeze every last bit of knowledge from those precious tapes.

He loved that Mad was becoming a real student of the game's history.

Little did he know that his son would one day become *part* of the game's history.

1996 MARKED A turning point. Amateur golf tournaments in Zambia were no longer just competitions. They were opportunities for the country's youngest sports star to showcase his skills to a growing fan base. Zambia was hungry for one of their own to show the world that they were as good as any other country. Many of them saw Madalitso as the answer to their prayers.

His emergence as a singular sensation became national news.

He was awarded Zambia's most coveted prizes in junior athletics.

Madalitso Muthiya was crowned Rothman's "Junior Sportsman of the Year."

11

MADALITSO'S JOURNEY TO HIS MOST important tournament of 1997 began with father and son climbing into the car for a long drive north to Peter's birthplace. The town was renamed Kabwé over thirty years ago, but the old colonial name, Broken Hill, was still etched in Peter's mind.

As the miles passed in slow motion, Madalitso was irritated, wondering again why they were driving all this way to play in the Kabwé Open, a one-day, thirty-six-hole event, against mediocre competition at a course that was obscure and poorly maintained. But instinct and the mood in the car told Madalitso not to ask. Peter was stone-faced, barely saying a word. Inside, he was still haunted by vivid and painful images from his own life: sweat-drenched Black children under the hot African sun carrying heavy bags for the pleasure of White men who opposed their education while enriching themselves from African forced labor and African mineral wealth. Peter was determined not to put that weight on his son's shoulders before a tournament. He remembered how the dark history of Mufulira had hung over Madalitso like a cloud just a year earlier and made it difficult to play up to his usual high standards. Peter knew Madalitso was baffled by his insistence that he play in this tournament, but he decided that sharing the reasons would come later.

Pulling into the parking lot, Madalitso was even more confused. The clubhouse was old and run-down. Unlike Lusaka Golf Club, people clearly stopped caring about this golf course shortly after the colonialists left.

Normally when they arrived at a golf course, Madalitso would remove his clubs from the trunk, and he and his dad would proceed to the clubhouse together. Not today.

Unlike his son, seeing Kabwé's clubhouse stirred emotions in Peter. His heart rate quickened as he took off toward the door, forcing Madalitso to carry his bag at a brisk pace. His son didn't realize that the last time Peter was there, he wasn't allowed inside.

As he burst through the door, people looked over abruptly, surprised by how forcefully this stranger was entering the quiet, run-down, neglected clubhouse. Peter quickly realized what a scene he just made. Later he smiled when recalling all those shocked faces. But none of them knew Peter's story. And if they did, they would've understood. Walking into the clubhouse where he'd been forbidden because of his skin color was long overdue, an important and symbolic moment in his evolution. From the boy who lived in a mud shack to the father of a championship golfer. But entering Kabwé's clubhouse was not the purpose of this journey.

Well...not the *sole* purpose.

Madalitso began his first round with a long and well-placed opening drive. He walked down the fairway and saw his father with a few spectators. Usually, Peter would already be enjoying his first Budweiser. But this tournament was too important.

Peter's presence had no effect. Madalitso just played like Madalitso. He started strong. *Very* strong. By the fourth hole, he held a firm lead. The few spectators who bothered to attend this marginal event gathered to watch the fourteen-year-old. News of the rising sports star had even reached remote golfing venues like Kabwé.

Madalitso had become used to playing much better golf courses. Lusaka and Ndola golf clubs had bumpier greens and less pampered fairways than courses in the United States or Europe, but they were better than this. Madalitso slogged his way through the unkempt course and dealt with choppy greens. By the end of the first round, the outcome was a foregone conclusion. Barring some monumental collapse, Madalitso would win the 1997 Kabwé Open.

This was no surprise. The few players in Zambia who could challenge Madalitso were not there. And he knew they wouldn't be there. The champion's trophy was not the prize Peter was seeking.

Well...not the *ultimate* prize.

Madalitso began the second round just like the first. He kept the ball in play, and his short game positioned him for birdies and pars on every hole. In what was becoming a common scene, a growing gallery basked in the joy of watching the young, studious boy who was the very model of humility, showing monster driving skills, pure iron play and a deft touch around the greens, all executed with confidence, skill and maturity well beyond his fourteen years.

Peter stood near the eighteenth green as the first players finished. He casually chatted with spectators and thanked those who complimented his son's performance. Outwardly, he appeared calm and carefree. It was all smoke and mirrors. His insides were churning. He wanted his son to become champion of the place that banned him. He wanted it so badly, he could almost taste it.

He watched his son walk up the fairway and hit a gorgeous approach shot that nestled four feet from the cup. Madalitso sank his putt and applause erupted from the thirty or so spectators encircling the green. He shook hands with the other players and strolled over to his father. He shared his score. In that moment, Peter saw why destiny had demanded that he bring his son here.

Madalitso had broken the course record.

"Teenage Golfer Muthiya scoops Kabwé Open" was the headline in the *Zambia Daily Mail*. Though his victories were no longer a surprise, the *Daily Mail* still reported the "[S]ensational teenage golfer" had "stunned the veterans by winning the Kabwé Open Golf Championship."

To Madalitso, the 1997 Kabwé Open was another victory on his growing résumé. To Peter, it was much more.

When he grew old enough to understand his world, this golf course represented so much that Peter hated. There were far more egregious examples of racial injustice and subjugation during the colonial era. And he had seen them: forced labor, copper mines, unequal schools and the outflow of money to England and apartheid-led South Africa. Dire poverty, rampant ignorance, ravaging diseases.

But this golf course was *his* personal link to colonialism. It was the first place that excluded him. It was the first place that told him he was not good enough, that he was—just because he had dark skin—inferior. Racial superiority was the foundation upon which it was created and the underlying tenet of its rules. Its existence was owed to the misery inflicted on innocent people, including his parents, who had worked themselves to the bone to feed the machine that was crushing them.

It didn't matter that Broken Hill Golf Club was now Kabwé Golf Club. Still standing was the clubhouse that Peter and his brother could not enter and the course they could not play. Every fairway, every bunker and every hole sparked reminders of an era long since passed but whose impact was still evident throughout Zambia and sub-Saharan Africa.

But there was something else. This golf course also represented so much that he loved.

Broken Hill Golf Club was where he first fell in love with what became his lifelong passion. As a young boy, watching club members compete was what drove him to scrounge for balls and grind sticks into clubs. Before he knew it as a symbol of apartheid, this place produced some of his earliest and fondest memories, memories that only later were clouded by dark bloody history.

As he stood back and looked at Kabwé Golf Club, he wondered if one place had ever been so loved and so hated by one person.

Only one thing could reconcile these two competing emotions. He needed to discredit the theory of racial superiority upon which this golf club was built and managed for years. It was an open sore that he was compelled to cleanse and to heal. He wanted to exorcise its demons. To save its soul. Peter couldn't erase the history of Kabwé Golf Club, so he wanted to provide it with a new history, a better history. And in so doing, some form of salvation. When Madalitso sank his final putt to break the course record, the purpose of this trip had been fulfilled.

Although Sandikonda and Kaliwé were his parents, in many ways, Peter Muthiya was the child of Broken Hill Golf Club. This place gave birth to a boy who did not exist before he walked its fairways. In the world of golf, Kabwé Golf Club is an infinitesimal speck. A distant outpost. And yet this neglected and almost forgotten relic of a bygone era gave a child of colonialism two of his most identifiable traits: his passion for golf and his determination to defy the way the world looked down upon and abused him and his people.

When Peter looked back on his life, he couldn't think of a single place that had a larger role in defining him than Kabwé Golf Club.

And now, whenever someone reads the names on the walls in this colonialist-built clubhouse, they will see that of all the men—regardless of race—who ever played at Broken Hill Golf Club *or* Kabwé Golf Club, the greatest was a fourteen-year-old Black kid.

Madalitso Muthiya. Peter Muthiya's son.

1997 WAS SPECIAL for another reason: Madalitso took his first trip to the United States. His performance at the World Junior Open the previous year earned him a week at the David Leadbetter Golf Academy in Bradenton, Florida.

After playing professionally, Leadbetter became one of the game's most famous and influential teachers. He has worked with many Tour players, and today, he and his team of experts instruct players of all abilities.

Senior Instructor Larry Marshall completed the Leadbetter Academy's instructor certification program in a record eight months. He was in his fourth year at the Leadbetter academy when a group of boys arrived for a week of instruction, including a teenager from Africa who had become a champion despite never receiving a lesson from a professional coach.

Madalitso had previously traveled great distances to play golf, but only in tournaments against teenagers. Never for the sole purpose of playing under the watchful eye of a professional coach and certainly not one of the best coaches on the planet.

Well, it was bound to happen, Mad thought to himself skeptically. It was only a matter of time before he'd play in front of somebody who was paid to analyze golf swings, dissect flaws in mechanics and then teach properly. At tournaments, Madalitso answered the doubters and nay-sayers by beating them or matching them stroke for stroke.

This was different. Madalitso was not playing against Larry Marshall. He was playing *for* him. Putting himself under a microscope so a scientist could conduct an examination and tear apart his swing and find fault with his game. Would Marshall call him "unorthodox," "unconventional" or some other dog-whistle description to suggest Madalitso's success was dumb luck, and his swing subpar? And of course say that he was the one who could "fix" Mad's homemade swing? Would Marshall insist that Madalitso's game was fine for Zambia, but wouldn't pass muster in a country that hosts three of the four majors, including the U.S. Open? Would Marshall become another distraction that Madalitso would have to block out?

Answers to these and other questions were unequivocal. Madalitso spent only one week at the Leadbetter Academy, but ten years later, Larry Marshall still remembered him.

Marshall saw right away that the kid had an excellent golf swing and good rhythm. But the more he studied Mad, the more shocked he was that Madalitso had never received a professional lesson in his life. He explained it like this: "What makes golf seem so easy is precisely why it is so hard. Neither the player nor the ball is moving. Everything starts from a static position. Hitting the ball properly requires precise control of several moving parts. That's why so much time is spent studying the game and so much effort goes into instruction.

"It's very unusual for somebody to play on Madalitso's level without formal training. Players today have the advantage of video cameras and other high-tech equipment. They learn from experienced coaches. To have such a natural swing...it certainly *can* happen. But it's very rare."

The group spent a week on the golf course, driving range and putting green. Marshall remarked that a week-long session is hardly enough time for an instructor to change the mechanics of any player. And with Madalitso, there was no need to try. If it ain't broke, don't fix it.

Madalitso confirmed as much. "I knew Mr. Marshall was an exceptional coach," he said. "I enjoyed spending time with him. But he didn't really teach me anything new. I think Mr. Marshall thought that my swing was fine. He just encouraged me to keep working."

Madalitso loved state-of-the-art equipment that he could only dream of in Zambia. He relentlessly watched and rewatched footage of his swing frame by frame in the golf performance studio to ferret out the tiniest flaws and visited the flexibility and fitness studio. But he was careful to avoid fixing a problem that didn't exist.

The experience at Leadbetter turned out to be the next logical step in his growth as a golfer. He'd beaten the best youth, then adult players in Zambia. He'd excelled against a top international field in England. Now the week at Leadbetter practicing and playing side by side with great golfers his own age from all over the world had proven to him and everyone else that he did indeed belong with the best and the brightest. Now his golf swing was given the stamp of approval from a celebrated golf instructor at arguably the most influential golf training school in the world.

Grandma Kaliwé was validated once again: *If they are there and you are there, you both belong.*

Madalitso had taken his first step into America and toward becoming a groundbreaking part of golf history.

He returned to Zambia more confident in his game and in himself. Growing up in southern Africa without the means to travel, the world he saw on TV seemed vast and intimidating. But with each experience, the walls of mystery began to crumble and so did the belief that every player in the developed world was great. With each chapter in his evolution, Madalitso increasingly believed that he could play with anyone. Anywhere. It was courage and fortitude that he would need in a few years at tournaments that would determine the rest of his life.

MADALITSO RETURNED HOME and immediately built on his impressive résumé. He took second place at the Chainama Open just a couple of shots behind an adult player, Oliver Seno, prompting *Zambia Daily Mail* to hail him as the "Lusaka Golf Club wonder boy."

Soon after, he won another all-ages event, the Lusaka Golf Club Championship. By the third round, he was playing the course, not the other golfers. He focused on navigating every fairway and avoiding every tree, bunker and bush. Occasionally, an opening drive would go astray, but this just allowed him to attack a familiar hole from a different angle, try a new club or perfect a new approach shot. This was Madalitso's home course, and he played like it.

Next on his schedule was the Junior Club Championship. After dominating a strong field of golfers of all ages, he was now competing against other kids. Peter quietly wondered if there would be a letdown. Would his son be lulled into a lackluster performance and play down to his competition?

Hardly. Madalitso put on a clinic for the spectators and other players.

But all of these competitions were tune-ups for Zambia's premier junior event. Madalitso arrived at the 1997 Chick of the North with all the buzz of a celebrity. Ndola Golf Club was anxious to see the young man generating excitement in the Zambian sporting community.

Of course, golf fans in Zambia were few in number because so few could afford to play. But Madalitso was beginning to transcend the sport. People who never played golf—and even those who barely understood the game—were showing up at tournaments to watch Zambia's first golfing star, young Madalitso Muthiya.

Peter was blown away. From the time they arrived at Ndola until the time they left, people wanted to speak with Mad about his game, his trips to England and the United States and his growing number of tournament victories. It seemed his only respite from answering questions and shaking hands was when he was actually playing.

Peter was meticulous, and he thought he had everything covered. When Madalitso showed an ability and passion for golf, Peter designed a curriculum that would prepare his prodigy son for whatever golf or the world threw at him. Or so he thought. He'd gone over how to handle every conceivable scenario on the golf course. Hitting out of a deep sand trap. A long putt from the rough. Bad luck, bad weather, a bad playing partner. He'd also prepared Mad for being the least trained and most poorly equipped player in tournaments full of rich players with shiny new clubs and shoes. For being one of the few Black players. Or the *only* one. And perhaps most importantly for an African golfer, what to do when a snake is impeding your lie in the rough.

But fame? How to react to seeing his name in the paper? How to feel when reading superlatives about his play on the golf course? How to respond to complete strangers who know his name and want to ask him questions? Peter had not thought to plan for his shy, quiet son becoming a star.

Ready or not, the media train was barreling right at Madalitso, and Peter didn't want his boy to look like a deer in the headlights. So Peter knew he had to prepare Mad, particularly after a conversation he overheard earlier that week. Wongani was reading the *Zambia Daily Mail* out loud to Madalitso, emphasizing in a funny way each and every kind word that was printed about his kid brother. The two were laughing their heads off. Peter listened to the banter but stayed out of the room. However, the moment stuck in Peter's head. He waited for the right time to address it and get his son ready for the onslaught of jaded reporters that could twist his words into anything they wanted.

A few days before the Chick of the North, Peter and Madalitso were on the driving range at Lusaka Golf Club. Peter hit a shot and was positioning his next ball when, without looking at his son, he casually asked what he thought of the recent news stories about his victories.

Madalitso, surprised, tried to catch his dad's eye. But Peter was preparing to hit another ball. "It's nice, I guess," he replied.

Peter lined his shot up and drove one deep. After watching his ball bounce and roll to a stop, he replied, "Yes, it's nice."

Madalitso knew more was coming, so he watched and waited while his dad casually placed another ball on the tee.

"How is it different from the compliments you receive from strangers or the rude stares and whispers you notice from others?" Peter asked.

"I don't know." Mad was puzzled, unsure sure where his dad was going with this.

As Peter lined up to hit his next shot, he asked, "What do you think the newspapers would say about you if you played terrible?"

Madalitso thought for a moment. "Something negative, I guess. Or they would say nothing about me at all."

Peter connected with the ball and turned toward his son, not watching where it landed. "That's right," he said, punctuating his remarks with a steely look that pierced Mad. "The newspapers would print something bad about you or ignore you. And what have we said about insults or compliments that are conditional upon you winning?"

"They're extraneous," Madalitso answered, finally understanding the point his father was making. "They don't matter."

So Mad tried to look at the gushing and fawning as fool's gold. Pretty to look at, but false, and in the end, without value. Madalitso had always been an introvert who let his game speak for him. If it was up to him, he would've ignored reporters who peppered him with questions. Having microphones and cameras shoved in his face was annoying, but his parents demanded that he be respectful and courteous to everyone, even reporters who were simply doing their jobs.

As Madalitso got used to the media and built his interview muscles, he actually enjoyed the media coverage sometimes. Even Peter thought the news stories and the photographs were good fun—but he never let his son see that. He didn't want Mad to become attached to the empty praise from fair-weather fans and journalists. And so, the kind words became more background noise, like the intrusive stares at his shabby shoes or his shoddy clubs, the dog-whistle doubters and the snide haters.

As the commotion grew and the crowd of reporters got bigger, Madalitso remembered his father's advice and took the whole media circus with several grains of salt.

THE FLOCK OF media and spectators who came to the Chick of the North to see if Madalitso had the right stuff didn't have to wait long for their answer. After parring the first hole, Madalitso felt good as he arrived at the second tee box and decided to take an aggressive approach. A straight 385-meter par 4, Madalitso saw it as a birdie hole. For fans and spectators, it was a chance to see the teenaged long ball hitter grip it and rip it.

Madalitso took out his trusty old driver, slid his tee into the ground, then balanced his ball on top. After a couple of easy practice swings, he peered down the fairway at the green and locked in on his target. With calm aplomb, he addressed his ball, bent his knees and extended his clubhead to make sure the distance was right.

All conversation stopped as Mad slowed his breathing. His eyes laser-focused on the ball, and everything else faded away. He swung the club back with fluid smooth grace. Just like Peter had taught him.

Then, with a fast-torquing force that belied his shy demeanor and skinny frame, Madalitso shifted his weight and whipped the clubhead forward with controlled power until it completely wrapped around his body.

The sound of his driver smacking his ball was different from the other competitors', a propulsive *THWACK* that broke the enthralled silence.

The ball hurtled off his club and sped down Ndola's second fairway like it had been shot out of a cannon, soaring toward the green.

"OOHHHs" and "AHHHHs" rose out of the dozens of spectators, as mouths dropped open and eyes widened, revealing amazed admiration and joy at the muscular clout generated by the pint-sized lad with the funky driver and discount weathered cleats.

After what seemed like an eternity, the ball finally crash-landed in the middle of the fairway, less than 100 meters to the green and a safe distance from Ndola's notorious and deadly anthills.

Madalitso gave a polite little grin, acknowledging the applause and praise. It was clear from the deferential nods and surprised expressions of begrudging appreciation from the other players that the battle for this tournament was probably going to be for second place.

Madalitso would have to land his next shot on a sloping green. It required finesse, not power, just the right loft and distance. Many wondered if he had the finesse and touch to complement his raw power.

He pulled his nine-iron and identified the exact spot that would make the ball cozy up to the cup. He positioned himself over his ball and took one last breath as spectators scrambled for a good place to see if Mad could back up his length with a feathery shot that would give him a chance at a birdie or leave him scrambling for a bogey.

The contact was crisp and clean. Grass and dirt followed his ball into the air.

It was a sweet, high-arching shot that Madalitso knew would land on the green. But where would it stop? Would the slope make it hop and roll instead of landing soft and gentle in one spot?

His eyes followed the ball as it soared. It landed softly on the spot he targeted, and then began its slow, downhill roll. Briskly, he walked toward the green, just as the ball proceeded leisurely straight toward the hole.

A roar rose, and smiles bloomed on the faces of the crowd, getting louder and bigger with each passing second as the ball moseyed closer to the cup.

Finally, it ran out of steam and decided to rest a foot from the flag.

The crowd went crazy, applauding, cheering, whistling and hooting.

It was clear something special was happening. A star was being born.

He casually tapped in for birdie and gave a nonchalant nod to the crowd, so as not to be rude.

You'd never have known it by looking at him, but Madalitso was excited to be that deep in the zone.

Madalitso used that birdie as a springboard and poured it on, slamming drives and delivering subtle elegance around the greens. He took the lead and left the pack in the dust. By the second round, the outcome of the tournament seemed a foregone conclusion. Some players even began asking him for advice. On the tricky tenth hole, a 350-yard par 4 with a wicked dogleg right, his awestruck playing partner asked Madalitso whether he should try to cut the dogleg or lay up short.

"Well," Mad advised, "if you can safely drive the ball three hundred meters, go ahead and cut the dogleg. But if your ball falls short, you'll miss the fairway and end up next to an anthill."

Having seen the boy play, Madalitso knew he could not drive the ball 300 yards, but he was too polite to say so.

The boy's eyes grew wide as he muttered his appreciation. "Well...I...I think I'll play it safe."

Madalitso watched the boy opt for safety and hit the ball 200 yards down the middle of the fairway, just before the dogleg.

Madalitso was adjusting his glove when the boy approached. "What are you going to do?"

Smiling politely, Madalitso looked the boy in the eye as he walked into the tee box. "Cut the dogleg."

Madalitso completed his pre-swing routine with two easy practice strokes before moving toward the ball and planting his feet. He loosened his shoulders, found just the right grip and relaxed his breathing. With textbook form, he swung the club back, knees bent, left arm straight and eyes locked on his ball.

In the blink of an eye, his clubhead flashed forward and whipped through the ball, sending it soaring high and mighty over the trees and rough on the right side of the fairway.

Congratulations filled the air when his ball eventually descended, clearly avoiding the nastiness of the rough. Of course, he wouldn't see the final landing spot until he walked past the fairway. But he knew he'd hit a good shot.

He arrived on the other side of the dogleg to find that indeed his ball easily made it past the trees and anthills but landed in a bunker guarding the green. Sand wedge in hand, he stood above the bunker looking back and forth from his ball to the hole, sizing up the danger, measuring distance and analyzing green slope and wind speed.

Spectators gathered around the putting surface, wondering if the wonder-kid could dig himself out of this dicey jam.

After scrutinizing the green with a thorough maturity that seemed well beyond his years, Madalitso trudged down into the deep bunker and stood next to his ball. He recalled his father's tutorials and the PGA tournament videos he'd studied so closely. He knew they'd provided the formula necessary to get his ball out of this devilish sand pit and give him a chance to salvage par. With a wide base and open stance, he positioned himself so his sand wedge would hit the sand before striking the ball. The open club face would—if he executed the shot correctly—get his ball up out of the sand and land it softly onto the green.

After a few mock swings, Madalitso turned and twisted his heels to imbed himself deeper in the sand. He paused and locked his eyes on the ball. With an abbreviated backswing and a forceful follow-through, he sent a sandstorm flying into the air. His ball emerged from the blizzard of grit. Climbing at a steep trajectory, the ball eventually flopped straight down onto the green.

It rolled slowly toward the hole as the crowd gasped. Finally, it stopped eighteen inches from the cup.

Madalitso thought he'd hit it well, and he was encouraged by the crowd's excited reaction. But as he climbed out of the bunker and walked onto the green, even the unshockable Mad was shocked. He lifted his hand in appreciation for the love the crowd was showering him with.

The other players were a mix of wonder, respect and frustration, wondering how in the world they could beat a player who managed to turn his bad shots into miraculous birdies.

They invited him to tap in for birdie. He was happy to oblige in the humblest way imaginable.

Madalitso would birdie three of his final eight holes, cruising to victory in the Chick of the North. Throughout the day, he carried himself with a level of focus and confidence that almost made him seem out of place. Applying the knowledge he gained in Britain and the U.S., Madalitso navigated the course less like a local teenager and more like a seasoned professional visiting from overseas.

Times of Zambia proclaimed:

"MUTHIYA ROMPS HOME!"

Zambia Daily Mail declared:

"MUTHIYA STILL CHAMP!"

Recapping his sensational season, the *Times* added:

"This was Muthiya's fifth title this year..." and that he was "enjoying support from a number of fans..."

As 1997 DREW to a close, Peter and Madalitso began seeing Zambia's junior events in a new way.

For Madalitso, they became less about the other players and more about improving his own game. They were chances to master new golf courses, lengthen his drives, improve his irons and wedges, gain experience with new putting surfaces and grow comfortable playing in front of others. He had his eye on bigger prizes. And the only way to get there was to become better and better. Every day in every way. As a golfer. But also as a human being.

As Madalitso's talent surfaced, Peter prepared him for the day when other Zambian juniors could no longer challenge him. He trained Madalitso to ignore other players in a tournament. Ignore their good shots and their bad ones. Disregard their superior equipment. Tune out the cheers or groans from the crowd. Focus only on *his* game. *His* mental preparation. *His* next shot. If a golfer brings that approach to every tournament, good scores, victories and everything else will take care of themselves. Make your goal being your personal best, then you will bring everything you have to the contest.

But it was not just golf lessons that Peter was teaching. These lessons applied to everything. Focus on your own performance and success will come, regardless of others around you.

Peter began viewing golf tournaments as serving a more fundamental purpose. His life's journey had been defined by certain milestones. They had names like St. Mary's, Naviluli, Chizongwe and Munali. These schools were his stepping-stones to something better.

He'd never expected his son to play like this. But as time passed, he believed that Madalitso's stepping-stones could be Chick of the North, Chainama, Mufulira and Champion of Champions. These golf tournaments might evolve into more than just stories for his grandchildren. They could change his life.

He had no idea how right he was.

12

"Președinte Chiluba wants to see Madalitso and you in his office tomorrow."

Peter, a man of many words, sat in stunned silence. He managed to mutter, "Uh... Okay," then he hung up, falling back into his chair as if dazed. It was early 1998. He sat at his desk trying to figure out why the President of Zambia wanted an audience with him and his son.

That evening, he and Madalitso sat together on the living room sofa. They agreed it obviously had something to do with golf. But what? Did President Chiluba simply want to congratulate Madalitso on his success? Did he want to take a photo? Was the President looking for a Youth Golf Ambassador? Maybe he wanted to play a round of golf with them.

Peter couldn't stop the possibilities from racing through his head that evening, and he was too keyed up to sleep that night. What in heaven's name did the President want from his kid? As for Madalitso, concentrating at school the following day was basically impossible. An upcoming golf tournament never distracted from classes. Tournaments were familiar. He knew what to expect because he prepared. Diligently. Relentlessly.

But this was different. He was walking into a completely unfamiliar place to speak with the most powerful man in the country. And he had no idea why.

The next day, both still puzzled, Peter picked up Madalitso from school, and they arrived at State House.

Anticipation grew as an attendant parked their car and they were escorted inside and down a long corridor. As they sat waiting in a room behind a very heavy-looking door, the air was thick with nervous tension. Peter wracked his brain to think if he or Mad had done anything wrong that they might be in trouble for. After a few anxiety-drenched minutes, the door opened, and they entered President Chiluba's personal office.

The President rose from his desk and shook hands with Peter and Madalitso. Chiluba stood just over five feet tall. Madalitso was surprised that the President, who seemed so big on TV, was one of the few adults shorter than him. But like many leaders, his presence was far more commanding than his physical stature.

With a broad, warm smile that washed away any nervousness, he invited his guests to "please sit down." Then he looked at Madalitso. "How are you?"

The shy, polite fourteen-year-old smiled and gave his usual three-word answer: "Fine, thank you." As Peter expected, President Chiluba congratulated Madalitso on his performances. The President explained that he'd been following Madalitso's progress through the newspapers and from the personal reports of people at Ndola and Lusaka Golf Clubs. Chiluba also complimented Peter on mentoring his son.

Peter was secretly relieved. They weren't in trouble. As suspected, the President just wanted to offer some kind words and encouragement.

Wrong! Grinning, Chiluba leaned forward and looked Madalitso square in the eye. "How can I help you?"

Madalitso was dumbfounded. In fact, both father and son were caught off guard. They smiled but had no answer. Finally, to break the silence Madalitso answered, "Mr. President, any assistance would be appreciated."

The President relaxed in his chair and spoke with his eloquent verbosity for several minutes on the importance of helping talented young people achieve their goals. Zambia, he told them, didn't have many resources to assist promising young people, but that didn't mean they couldn't help a few.

"The nation as a whole," Chiluba declared, "benefits from making such investments. There is no way to measure the pride and self-respect of people who see greatness achieved by one of their own, particularly on the world stage. Madalitso, you would benefit, and so would Zambia. While the world may see Zambia and sub-Saharan Africa for all of its problems, the accomplishments of a single person can go a long way in changing perceptions."

The President finished his thoughts, rose from his seat and thanked Peter and Madalitso for coming.

Peter and Mad smiled like they knew what had just happened. In fact, they had no idea. And with that, father and son were escorted away.

The meeting was an unexpected splash of cold water to the face. How could the President help Madalitso move forward?

Peter firmly believed his son could someday play in golf's biggest tournaments. He had watched enough golf in his life to know what separates good players. But as certain as Peter was in his son's talent and where it could take him, he was less certain of the strategy for getting there.

The ultimate destination was known. The path to get there was not.

But having the President in their corner couldn't hurt. Could it?

AT THE AGE of fifteen, Madalitso Muthiya had produced a hurricane, winning every major junior and amateur tournament in Zambia. He excelled at an international event in the United Kingdom and was a recognized sports figure in his country. He traveled to a celebrated golf academy in the United States where a renowned instructor could only admire and compliment his skills. Newspaper clippings were filling the family scrapbook, and strangers were coming to watch him play. Now the President of the Republic was meeting privately with father and son at State House.

To Peter, a man with a logical explanation for everything, his son's feats were a mystery. No matter how many times he tried to wrap his big brain around it, he couldn't understand. Growing up, he'd learned fundamentals by watching and imitating the White men in Broken Hill and applying his knowledge of mathematics to choose clubs and identify angles. But this couldn't explain Madalitso's success. Yes, he knew more than most golfers in Zambia. But compared to highly trained instructors in the United States or Europe? No way.

In developing countries, superior athletes usually emerge in sports like football (soccer), where all you need is a ball (or even a grapefruit, like Pele!). Or running, where all you need is a couple of legs and feet. People can excel at these things without a great deal of expensive equipment, country club–caliber courses or technical training. Speed and agility alone won't turn anyone into a world-class golfer. The technical difficulty of golf is off the charts. Every part of a person's body must be positioned properly. Every minute movement of the swing has to be performed in perfect synchronicity. And then there's club selection and course management. Plus, the ball is so small! Huge sums of money are spent on advanced equipment and instruction. Professional coaches devote their careers to learning and teaching the game. They had no such people in Zambia. And Peter knew he certainly didn't qualify.

No matter how long or hard he pondered, Peter always came to the same conclusion. God had given Madalitso a gift. A blessing.

MADALITSO PLOWED THROUGH the first half of 1998 like the most taciturn steamroller in history. The victories mounted—the Ndola Junior Stroke Play Championship, the Chilanga Junior Open and the Chainama Open. His appearance at tournaments now attracted more than devoted parents. Tee boxes and greens were surrounded by Zambians who normally found little interest in watching teenagers and didn't know a driver from a bogey. They came to see Madalitso, the young African superstar, the Great Black Hope, tear up the course and destroy his opponents in his methodical, deadpan way. They were not disappointed.

In every facet of the game, he stood out. He pounded the ball farther than anyone. His irons were struck with surgical precision, landing softly in just the right spot. His chipping and putting were clean and meticulous, always in or near the hole. He had a clear but quiet confidence. Never rushed, hurried or flustered. He was like a young golf monk, and you got the feeling watching him that nothing could knock him off his game. A spectator need only watch a few holes before concluding that there was Madalitso Muthiya, and then there was everybody else.

Mad himself remained unfazed by his success and the increasingly relentless attention it brought. Amidst the ongoing chatter, constant staring and pointing, all the cameras and media attention, he simply remembered his father's words:

Just focus on what you need to do.

Halfway through the 1998 season, the only issue troubling him was his meeting at State House. President Chiluba's question still lingered: *How can I help you?*

Madalitso wanted to play golf all over the world against the best of the best. But there was a painful reality. The Muthiyas couldn't afford the expenses of a professional golfer.

And then there was college. Peter often lectured his children. The world is a jungle full of lions and snakes, he'd say. To survive, you must get an education. Since meeting with the President, Madalitso struggled over which to pursue—college or golf. Soon, he realized that he didn't have to choose.

He was watching television one day and turned to a sports station that was televising the United States' college golf championships. Something called the NCAA. Until then, Mad didn't even know that colleges in the United States had sports teams, never mind that it was a multibillion-dollar industry. Or that students could earn a degree *and* participate in athletics. His jaw dropped when he discovered that top college athletes actually had their expenses paid for by the school!

The more he thought about it, the more he realized that intercollegiate golf would give him so many more golfing *and* career opportunities than he could ever find in Zambia.

Of course, he'd be oceans away from his parents in a country where he knew no one.

He thought about leaving his family. Being alone. Leaving would be heartbreaking.

ALL OF THIS was put on the back burner while Madalitso focused on a more immediate task: his second trip to England for the World Junior Open Championship. Much had changed since Blackpool just two years earlier when he was a largely untested neophyte at the upper echelons of competitive golf, when he was still worried about his mismatched clubs and their proper usage. And whether he really belonged with all these upper-crust country club prodigies.

Not anymore. Madalitso was now a champion. Young Sportsman of the Year. He had a better grasp of the game, his equipment and his own abilities. And he walked with a maturity and confidence that blossomed from his sustained success.

The 1998 World Junior Open was held at Formby Golf Club in Merseyside. It was a different venue, but Mad now knew what to expect from an English links course. He remembered the intimidating walls that rose straight up from Blackpool's deep steep bunkers, the fairways lined with wispy grasses and surprisingly tough rough, the constantly shifting seaside breezes that smelled of salt water and could make your approach shot land short, or fly the green. And this time, he was prepared for something else: a tribe of young White players with better equipment, professional training and wealthier families.

There would be no surprises. Well...except for one.

Cold. For a young African golf warrior, it was freezing. It never got too hot or too cold in Zambia. The frigid temperatures at Formby were unlike anything he'd experienced. It was a cold that lived in your bones.

But when it came time to tee it up, Madalitso gave the chilly weather the same treatment that he gave the crowds, the noise, the media, the hoity-toity clothes, shoes and clubs and the pedigree of his opponents. He ignored it.

Whenever the players gathered, Madalitso was once again surrounded by people who looked different than him. Once again, there were long stares at his patchwork clubs and worn-out golf shoes. And once again he didn't care. Because he'd seen the stares before and because he was trained by his father not to care about those things. And because he was, well...Madalitso.

As always, his underwhelming equipment would soon be forgotten due to his overwhelming game. Standing at the first tee, he wondered whether the morning cold and wind would negate his length off the tee on this relatively straight 435-yard par 4. He remembered tournaments on television where players adjusted their swings in cold and windy conditions. But in Africa, there was no cold wind. Just snakes and killer ants, and he had those covered. The commentators had explained how players would modify their swings to keep the ball low, under the radar and beneath the wind. But Madalitso knew it was risky to try something this new and unfamiliar, especially mid-tournament. He decided to play his game until the golf gods told him otherwise.

He took a few more practice swings than normal to get the blood flowing in his shivering body. Planting his feet and finding his grip, he eyed an area down the left side of the fairway, away from the trees and the deep fairway bunkers. One last pause for a deep breath and to make sure he focused on the ball and not his frozen fingers.

His backswing felt loose and easy, as did his follow-through.

The frigid wind seemed to have no effect on his titanic blast down Formby's first fairway.

Watching his drive sail down the left side well past the others in his group, Madalitso breathed a sigh of relief. It was cold, but everything was working so far. Madalitso hoisted his bag and began walking down the fairway. A couple boys enthusiastically joined him. They complimented his swing and his drive. Suddenly the cultural, racial and economic differences separating them melted away as the universal language of golf bonded them.

He stood in the middle of Formby's rolling fairway, staring down a 150-yard shot to the hole. The danger was clearly the formidable bunkers pinching the green from both sides—one on the right and two on the left. The obvious (and safest) strategy was to land deep into the green, well beyond the bunkers. Yes, it would leave a long, difficult putt back toward the hole for a birdie, but the risk of the bunker far outweighed the reward of a shorter birdie putt. Watching another player's ball land in one of the deep sand pits confirmed Mad's decision.

The wind kicked up and slapped him in the face, as if it was warning Madalitso not to forget how mean and dangerous it was. But he decided to roll the dice a little and put some loft on the ball so it would land soft and not roll off the green. He grabbed his seven-iron, loosened his arms and walked around briskly to warm his blood while he waited for others to hit.

When it was his turn, he took his usual stance and took one last look at the green before launching his fluid backswing and driving up under the ball. It shot up at a steep trajectory. He knew it had the right height and direction. But he was unsure of the distance.

He stood stock-still, holding his breath as he uttered a quiet plea to the ball. "Come on, a good start. Come on."

The other boys in his group were mesmerized, wondering if the long ball hitter from Zambia would be able to navigate the blustery British gusts and follow his tee shot with a good approach.

His ball landed softly at the rear of the green, stopped and yanked a few inches backward. Mad finally breathed again as another player hollered, "Good shot!"

It was a long putt for birdie, but at least he wasn't sandy.

This is going to be a lag putt, Madalitso thought to himself before he even set his bag down.

The first of Formby's notorious and dauntingly undulating greens, Mad faced a 30-foot putt that was uphill to the hole with gradual (and often hidden) ebbs and flows along the way.

No matter how much he walked back and forth from his ball to the hole, or how many times he analyzed the speed, flow and angles, he could not find a definitive line.

But he knew that parring this hole would be a fantastic way to start this tournament, both for himself and for anyone viewing him with a skeptical eye. The maturing golfer in him was mindful that he was playing the course and not the other players, and he reminded himself not to be concerned with whatever anyone else was thinking. Peter had drilled this into his head so many times it was now second nature. But the steely competitor in Madalitso had other ideas. He wanted to let this course know who the Zulu boss was right from the first hole.

Finally settling on the best path he could find, he set his feet into the ground and took his customary crouch over his ball. One last look up the incline and over a couple of ridges. Then, he pulled his clubhead back and, like a pendulum, firmly and smoothly stroked the ball forward.

His ball darted forward, easily climbing the smooth grassy elevation. Halfway to the hole, he saw his ball slowing down, and he knew there was no danger of rolling past the hole into the short rough.

Still crouched over, he saw the uneven green and deceleration make his ball move from left to right. He willed it forward as it moved slower and slower with each passing inch. "Come on," he whispered. "Keep going."

It seemed to hear and respond, as his ball curled lazily and came to rest a few feet from the cup. An excellent lag putt leaving par within easy reach.

Crisis averted.

He placed his marker and moved away so the other teenagers could face the mind-bending trial-by-fire of Formby's first green in the chill of this early morn.

As he studied his 6-foot par putt, Madalitso was relieved. Every angle suggested his ball would veer slightly from left to right. He stood over his ball. He took a deep breath and pushed aside fear of failure and paralysis by analysis, paused a moment, then cranked up his sweet simple putting stroke.

The ball did just what it was supposed to do. It rolled forward and—just as the landscape had whispered to him—broke slightly to the right. Then, it obeyed his orders and fell into the hole.

Madalitso parred his first hole at Formby.

Reassured by this early success, his jitters were put to bed, and Mad proceeded to play his game on Formby's front nine, noting the wind but not letting it get in his head.

He arrived at the ninth hole, knowing full well it was perhaps the toughest on the course. There was little margin for error, and the gusts just made it that much more insidious.

He navigated his opening drive successfully and landed in the middle of the fairway, avoiding the two ball-eating fairway bunkers. One shot down, one to go.

Madalitso stood behind his ball, 200 yards from the green. It wasn't the distance that gave him pause. He could get there with power to spare. It was the vicious wind. *Again.* All morning, gusts had bent the trees and made them gyrate, sending waves crashing through the grass.

But he decided that since he'd made it this far by playing his normal game, why fix what ain't broke?

He grabbed his six-iron and took a few easy practice swings, per usual. Determined not to second-guess, he found his grip and addressed the ball. His acceleration forward and contact with the ball both felt good. He watched it climb. It felt good. It looked good. He figured he'd have at least a shot at a decent birdie putt.

Then, trouble.

His ball was headed toward the heart of the green. But just as it reached its peak, the wicked wind grabbed it and took it dead left.

Whaaaat? he thought. *How could this be?*

Shock and fear filled him as he watched it continue off-course and get pushed further and further left. His mouth hung open and his club dropped as the ball finally buried in a greenside bunker. The *only* greenside bunker on the dreaded ninth.

Madalitso knew he had ignored the weather one too many times. And the golf gods had made him pay.

Seeing the stunned look on Mad's usually implacable face, another player uttered three simple words: "This wind sucks."

Madalitso began walking to the pot bunker that had swallowed his ball and eaten it for lunch. He reached two conclusions. First, he *had* to get out of this bunker. Second, he had to respect the power of the mighty wind, not ignore it.

He stepped into the bunker and faced the wall towering over his ball. They didn't make pot bunkers like this in Africa, with their imposing walls and terrifying height. The only good news was that the flag was on that side of the green, so just getting out of the bunker would probably put him in a good position for a save.

Mad plucked his super lofted wedge from his bag and took a deep, calming breath. He needed this. Failing to make it out of this hole would likely mean another shot requiring an even steeper angle. One wrong move could turn this into an 8, the dreaded snowman which would pretty much ruin his day—and possibly his whole tournament.

Quietly and methodically, he went through each step of his pre-shot routine, and this made his focus sharpen and the foreboding fade. Open the face head. Find his grip. Widen his stance. Place weight on lead leg. Swing hard and down into the sand. Execute.

The ball shot up through a windswept cloud of sand, easily clearing the lip, landing on the green. He heard a round of applause as he scrambled out of the tomb of the deepest bunker he'd ever had the misfortune to land in. He hoped and prayed that the golf gods would smile on him this time.

He emerged just in time to watch it roll to within about ten feet of the hole. For a player of his caliber, it was absolutely a makeable putt to save par. Breathing a sigh of relief, he grabbed his battered putter and stalked the putt.

He studied the slight incline. It was a straightforward putt with a mild right to left break.

The other players, having already holed out, watched with rapt attention.

Madalitso had been playing a dangerous game. He'd been daring Mother Nature herself, not bending to the wind, even as he felt its bite. Defiantly, he'd refused to alter his swing or club selection. But now, he worried the wind might break him. Saving par on the ninth hole after landing in the bunker would be golf's equivalent to standing on a landmine and surviving the explosion unscathed. If he could escape this potential catastrophe, he'd begin the back nine with a clean slate, a hard life lesson learned.

Crouching over his ball, he found his grip and eyed the hole one last time. Deep breath. A rhythmic backswing and pendulum swing forward shot the ball straight ahead. It followed the right-leaning line he'd carefully chose. As it got closer, he silently begged it to break left. The ball obeyed, curling the last few inches toward the hole and catching the right edge of the cup then lipping out.

He closed his eyes for a moment and thanked the golf gods before plodding over to the hole, barely hearing the accolades pouring over him. As he tapped in for bogey, he saw that thumbing his nose at the wind had cost him a stroke. And it could have ruined his round. His tournament. By the time he got to the tenth tee, he figured it was a small price to pay for wisdom.

Madalitso would have done anything to hit the pause button, go back to the driving range, and practice hitting low line drives. But the only magic in golf is created by the player. It was time to tee off again and make his own magic.

The tenth hole at Formby is a 215-yard par 3. The challenge is not distance. It's accuracy. The green is guarded by brutal bunkers left, right and center. And right behind the green? Rough so deep it hurt to look at it. The green is an island surrounded by monsters waiting to devour the meek, weak or incompetent. And once your blood pressure is raised to the breaking point, you're faced with a warning from club management to "pay attention to the wind when selecting your club." The howling, blustering wind was ready to smash Mad to bits all over again.

Madalitso was a changed man-child. He scrutinized the trees and grass as they swayed. Nothing in his memory bank could help him; he was a rank novice when it came to cold and wind.

Then, he flashed back to watching the British Open with his dad. How the greatest players had "clubbed down" and pushed the ball to keep it under the wind. He put his seven-iron back in his bag and grabbed his six-iron, knowing his ball would get walloped by the wind.

He put his ball further back in his stance so the clubhead would strike the ball on a downward angle and produce a line drive instead of a fly ball. He choked up slightly on the grip to control distance. He put more weight on his front leg so he could drive through lower.

Madalitso searched his brain with calm desperation. *Is there anything else?*

All eyes were upon him, waiting for him to strike. A good shot would kickstart his back nine. But another windblown disaster would make him and his confidence tumble down the leaderboard, a recipe for failure.

A short backswing, a punched delivery and a low follow-through shot his ball forward. Not up. He felt brief relief as he saw it had the right trajectory. Now, direction and distance. Like a cannon shot, his ball blasted straight ahead. With each yard it remained on course, streaking toward the heart of the green and completely unfazed by the wind, his optimism grew. As it descended, it safely cleared the front bunker. At this angle and speed, there'd be lots of roll. He visualized the thick jungle rough behind the green and gritted his teeth. *Okay, get down,* he begged. *Get down!*

The ball plopped on the front of the green, rolled fast past the flag and checked up at the back, stopping well short of the ball-eating rough.

"Good shot!" another player said.

Mad let out a huge sigh of relief. Two putts and a par later, he was revitalized. He'd navigated the frozen wind. He'd made peace with Mother Nature and played nice with the golf gods, adjusting himself and his game mid-tournament with no help from anyone. By controlling the only thing he could control. Himself. Just as his dad had taught him ad infinitum. He couldn't wait to tell his dad about this moment in their post-tourney debriefing. Pride filled him and morphed into confidence.

Madalitso went toe-to-toe with great junior players from around the world. Although he remembered his experience at Blackpool two years earlier, the wind, the cold and a few other challenges proved he was still new to the unique quirks of English links courses. About this experience, Peter would advise him later that countless strange and unexpected challenges lay ahead, but Madalitso showed that his mind was capable of developing strategies on the fly and that his body could execute them.

While other players at Formby had more experience in northern venues, Madalitso used his prodigious distance off the tee, his skill around the greens and his unflappable demeanor to level the playing field.

Madalitso finished the 1998 World Junior Open in fifth place. He retained the African Trophy which he won two years earlier. Additionally, he received the award for "Best Competitor," given to the player who most displayed sportsmanship, decorum and treated others with courtesy and respect.

The *Zambia Daily Mail* broke the news. Alongside a photo of Madalitso swinging a club was the caption: "Mechanical precision. Sensational golf whiz-kid Madalitso Muthiya follows his shot during the World Junior Championship at Formby Golf Club in the United Kingdom where he successfully defended his African title for the second time."

True to form, Peter tried to temper his enthusiasm. Madalitso had just competed in the United Kingdom, the birthplace of golf where the game acquired its White royal heritage, and he received an award for upholding the dignity and traditions of the game. Peter somehow managed to confine his reactions to three short words:

"I am proud."

PLAYING IN THE 1998 World Junior Open was memorable for Madalitso, but his experiences *off* the course made it life changing.

Shortly after the players arrived, an American approached Madalitso, stuck out his hand, and with a big smile said, "Hi, I'm Michael."

Madalitso shook the boy's hand. A friendship was born. Soon they were chatting about golf, friends back home, their countries and normal stuff that teenaged boys discuss. The two sat together at meetings, meals and any other time players assembled.

Meanwhile, word spread that this year's World Junior Scholarship Tournament included the sons of two golfing legends—Tom Watson and Greg Norman. Mad pulled Michael aside. "Did you hear that Watson and Norman's sons are here? That's pretty cool."

Michael just smiled and replied, "Yeah, I heard that."

Later on, players were summoned to the clubhouse for a rules meeting. One of the tournament organizers asked the sons of Tom Watson and Greg Norman to stand.

Madalitso sat in stunned silence as Michael rose to his feet. All the time they spent together, he never told Mad his last name—Watson. Madalitso was very impressed that Michael was so humble. "He just wanted to be liked for himself," Mad recalled, "not because he was Tom Watson's son."

After the tournament, players and parents gathered for an awards ceremony. Madalitso was named Best Competitor. The room burst into applause, clear evidence that the award was much deserved. After the ceremony, he was chatting with others when he suddenly felt two hands on his shoulders. He turned around and found himself standing face-to-face with Greg Norman.

Mr. Norman congratulated Madalitso on his performance and sportsmanship. Norman was so nice, Mad was taken aback. Looking back on this important moment in his life, Mad remembered, "It says something that Mr. Norman took the time to come over and compliment me. He didn't have to do that." Madalitso soaked it all in. More clues how to carry oneself like a true champion.

With the tournament behind them, players prepared for one of the perks of playing in the World Junior Open: a ticket to the British Open. In 1998, the British Open was played at Birkdale. Junior players were given access to watch the practice rounds and stay through the entire weekend.

During a practice round, Madalitso positioned himself along one of the fairways. Soon he saw a familiar face walking toward him. It was Michael Watson, with his father, one of Madalitso's idols, the great champion Tom Watson.

The Watsons came close enough for Madalitso to give a quick, shy, "Hey, Michael." Michael responded in kind. "Then something happened," Madalitso recalled. "Michael whispered to his father as they walked past me. Mr. Watson walked another few feet, turned around and looked straight at me. He then smiled and motioned for me to come over. Initially, I was afraid to jump the rope, but I figured Mr. Watson would stop me from getting in too much trouble," Madalitso laughed.

Mad spent the next couple of hours walking with Tom Watson during his practice round for the 1998 British Open.

To this day, it is one of Madalitso's most treasured golf memories.

13

PETER AND EDITH KEPT MADALITSO on a tight schedule when he returned from England. Peter knew that if Madalitso wanted to earn a college degree and play golf, he needed a taste of what was in store. With little rest, Madalitso prepared to play at a course that received far less attention and care than Formby but whose history was more important, at least to the Muthiyas—Kabwé.

It was Madalitso's second Kabwé Open in as many years. Despite Peter never fully sharing its significance, Mad was beginning to understand the importance of this tournament to his dad and their family. But it was difficult to grasp as a fifteen-year-old who hadn't lived Peter's life of deprivation, hardship and subjugation.

Madalitso never really thought about playing for somebody else, or even for himself. He just enjoyed playing golf, figuring out shots in his head and then executing them, a beautiful symbiosis of the body and the mind. This tournament was different. He'd never forget the big bright smile on his father's face when he broke the course record at the very venue where Peter *first* found his love of golf and *first* faced the exclusion, debasement and hate of racial discrimination. Peter had drilled into him the importance of focusing only on things he could control and ignore anything extraneous. But Madalitso carried his dad in his head and heart at the Kabwé Open.

Madalitso stepped up to the first tee box, inserted his tee in the ground, placed his ball on top and backed away for a few practice swings. Then he did something he'd never done before.

He looked right at his dad. Father and son made eye contact and stared into each other. Peter was caught off guard. He furrowed his brow and nodded forward sternly. *Come on, man! Don't look at me. Get on with the job!*

Madalitso was struck hard in the best sense. There was no time or room for sentiment or deeper meaning now. It was time to play golf. Conquer the course and himself.

He turned away and faced his future. His fate. His destiny. He adjusted his glove and his mind.

After a few more casual practice swings, he stared down the fairway at Kabwé's 400-yard par 4. The Kabwé Open, as usual, attracted few great players, mostly marginal has-beens or never-would-bes. Crowds were sparse, mostly local curiosity seekers here to check out the country's hot, new, young sports star.

Quiet shrouded the crowd as Mad addressed the ball.

Combining his hard-earned perfect form and DNA-supplied natural athleticism, Madalitso flowed through his silky backswing and effortlessly whipped his clubhead forward and boomed his ball dead center down Kabwé's first fairway. The ball finally stopped over 300 yards away, leaving him with an open invitation to an early birdie.

Madalitso quickly looked for his father to exchange a moment of satisfaction. Dad was already gone. After a moment of disappointment, Mad smiled. Another lesson imparted by his father. There would be time for satisfaction after the job was done. Right now, it was time to take care of business.

"I knew at Kabwé I was more of a distraction than at other tournaments," Peter recalled. "Sharing our family history and my personal connection with that golf club had, unintentionally, put an added burden on Madalitso. He needed to play golf, not worry about anything else. Especially me."

Madalitso was only seventy-five meters to the green. An easy pitch and putt away from the fast start he wanted. He grabbed his pitching wedge and analyzed the green, looking for the sweet spot to land his ball. He knew Kabwé was not as manicured as most of the courses he played, so he didn't want to risk an odd bounce or a wonky roll. He opened his stance to get the right loft and minimize the chance of an unexpected ricochet. With a crisp compact swing, his clubhead struck under the ball, sending it skying, along with a chunk of grass and dirt, up off the fairway.

Seconds later, it plopped softly in the middle of the green. A slow roll made his ball stop sooner than he'd hoped, leaving him with a tricky 10-footer instead of a tap-in from five feet.

Putting at Kabwé is often an adventure because the greens were...well... nasty. Flat stick in hand, Madalitso stalked the putt, reading the green like a poorly written book, making note of bumps, chunks and bare patches that would impede his ball from the hole.

After he had all the equations worked out in his head, he stood over his ball. Knees bent and arms locked, he rolled the ball on the path he'd chosen with extra firmness. Contact was good, speed seemed just right. As expected, the ball hopped over little bumps that sent it left and right. But the muscle he'd added kept it on line. Voices rose as the ball eased toward the hole.

Madalitso's body unconsciously twisted and bent, his body language speaking volumes. With few inches left, players and spectators—Madalitso included—held their breath, expecting a tiny pebble or bald patch of grass to push the ball sideways.

The muted, knifelike tension erupted into applause when the ball stayed true and tumbled into the cup.

Madalitso had drawn first blood, notching a birdie on the first hole of the tournament.

Tone set, Mad was ready to conquer Kabwé. Naturally, there were glitches, hitches and bad bounces. On the par 3 twelfth hole, after an approach that was nearly a hole-in-one, Madalitso was primed for another birdie with a 3-foot no-brainer putt. He sent the ball on its merry way, and everything was going according to plan...until the last second. With no warning, the ball jumped left like an invisible demon had kicked it and glided just over the rim of the cup. He resisted the urge to scream at the golf gods, knowing it would only make things worse. He accepted his par and moved on.

Only a few golfers in the whole country of Zambia could challenge Madalitso at this point. And the Kabwé Open didn't attract any of them. The crop of mostly locals were there because they liked playing and wanted to see Madalitso in action. Staying focused was a challenge as Kabwé residents constantly wanted to shake hands and share how they knew his family.

Patchy uneven fairways, bumpy greens and the old friends he had never met could not stop Madalitso from the swift completion of his appointed rounds.

Once again, the name etched on the list of Kabwé Open Champions was Madalitso Muthiya.

Peter saw Madalitso's record-breaking performance at the 1997 Kabwé Open the previous year as a loud, proud statement that was both public and personal. The victory, the press coverage and the name "Muthiya" hanging on the wall disproved ancient lies, blew up flawed ignorant beliefs and vanquished ghosts as Zambia watched in admiration. It was deeply healing for a man who was brutalized by the cruel systemic injustices inflicted on himself and his family.

The 1998 Kabwé Open was different. As satisfying as it would be for Madalitso to win this tournament and set new course records for the next fifty years, Peter knew that he and his son had done their part to disprove history and right wrongs. That box was now checked.

As father and son left Kabwé's clubhouse and got in the car, Madalitso was ready to have a deep conversation about the Muthiya family's dark and epic journey from Eastern Province to Broken Hill and the years of impoverished hateful deprivation they'd endured in Kabwé. His love for his dad was so big that he wanted to hear how they had—*once again*—claimed victory against those who believed his father and his uncle were good enough to be subservient caddies but not good enough to enter the clubhouse as equals. He wanted to hear how they'd slayed the dragon once again.

But Peter had other ideas. He decided against revisiting the history lesson from the previous year. Underscoring the importance of this tournament and the impact of this golf course on his own life was unnecessary. Their eye contact at the first hole was proof that Madalitso was aware...perhaps *too* aware. As they began talking, Peter decided to reference the Kabwé Open as nothing more than part of maintaining a steady pace to prevent any rust from growing on his game.

The *Zambia Daily Mail* simply wrote: "Golf Champ bags another medal." This brief and understated headline was fine with Peter.

Madalitso celebrated his victory with a late drive back home so he wouldn't miss Monday's classes, a week of grinding away on the books in school, racing over to practice at Lusaka Golf Club until dark, then back home to do homework, eat and pass out. Finally, on the day of the next tournament, an exhausted Mad stuffed his golf bag into the trunk for the long drive to the Chibuluma Open. "Chibuluma" is a native term meaning "roaring lion." Like Kabwé, Ndola, and so many other towns on the Copperbelt, it was an old mining community established during the colonial era. Also like the others, it wasn't the most carefully manicured course in the world—such is the life of a golfer in Zambia. One notable difference was that Chibuluma is a nine-hole course, so players must play holes twice to complete a round, crisscrossing each other along the way.

Peter wanted his son's name on the wall of this former Whites-only golf establishment. So did Madalitso.

Mad had to jump out of the car and warm up as soon as they arrived. There was no break. Peter intentionally made it that way. He wanted to test his son's endurance and his ability to perform under adverse conditions and sleep deprivation. He was training a champion. Madalitso admitted later that he was mentally and physically exhausted. Peter had his son right where he wanted him. Now, how would the boy react? The only problem was that Peter was also so tired he could barely keep his eyes open.

At Chibuluma, holes one through four are par 4s. The fairways run parallel, like fingers on a hand, the lone exception being the fourth hole, which doglegs slightly left. The design is almost like a race where players try to be the first to hole out before turning and playing back the other way.

Starting with four long fairways gave Madalitso a decided advantage.

He could outdrive the competition and start his round ahead of the field. And he knew it. Shaking off the cobwebs and getting loose after a long car ride in the middle of a demanding tournament schedule, his blood pumped. Now more than ever, with his body fatigued and his mind weary, Madalitso knew that all of his attention had be razor sharp. But knowing his day began with four long par 4s, he smiled ever so slightly and thought, *By the time I get to the fifth hole, this tournament will be over.*

The usual deafening silence descended among the onlookers as Madalitso prepared to tee off. He drove as he had driven 10,000 times before. On contact, he knew it was a good shot.

The ball split the heart of the first fairway.

Shouts of "Whoa!" and "Good shot!" flew out from the sparse but enthusiastic gallery as his drive stopped within easy range of the green. Hands were still clapping as the next player moved into the tee box with a wide-eyed facial expression that was both *Wow* and *How am I going to top that?*

Minutes later, he found himself standing over his ball sitting with just over 100 meters to the flag. He knew the greens were fast and bumpy. With the flag planted near the back of the green, he wanted his ball to land softly in front of the flag and roll close for an easy birdie.

Madalitso replayed moments from the PGA tournament tapes that he'd memorized over the years. And of course, the thousands of hours spent on the golf course with his dad where every scenario was hashed, rehashed and *re*-rehashed. He steadied his breathing while the other players and tournament spectators looked on, curious to see if he could match his power with finesse. His swing was less aggressive, keeping his body slightly behind the ball rather than driving through it and finishing higher than normal.

Mad got the loft he wanted. He knew the distance and direction would be good, but the landing and the roll would determine whether he'd be dancing with a birdie chance or scrambling to save par.

It landed nice and soft on the green with no erratic ricochet. Madalitso held his breath as the ball slowly rolled toward the pin. He waited for it to stop. It didn't. As it crawled ever closer, an audible hum from the onlookers grew louder. Shouts of *"Come on!"* came from the excited spectators.

It looked like an elusive eagle. But no. The ball ran out of steam two feet from the cup. Still unsure how to handle applause and adulation, Madalitso forced a smile onto his face and gave a light wave. After a tap-in, he was one under after the first hole.

Madalitso played steady-as-she-goes all morning but hadn't yet grabbed the round by the throat and throttled it into submission.

And then came Chibuluma's fifteenth hole. At just under 400 meters, the distance wasn't daunting. But the green was barricaded by three nasty bunkers and clumps of trees and bushes, making the green a tiny oasis surrounded by man-eating sharks.

After an uncharacteristically bad tee shot landed him in the short rough, Madalitso had just over 100 meters to the flag. It was a tough spot at a make-or-break moment in the round and the tournament. His plan was to launch a high arcing shot just over the front bunker and let the ball roll, much like he did on the first hole.

After zeroing in on his target, he looked down at the ball and took one last deep breath. His swing seemed sound. But at contact, he knew it was off. The ball leaked right and headed straight for a side bunker. No amount of body English would help. He let out a little groan as the ball buried in the bunker.

Two poor shots in a row, with three more holes in this round and the entire second round to complete, he knew he was in trouble. Thirty feet from the hole, deep in a pit of sand and misery, his A-game suddenly MIA. Other players seeking an opening, and spectators looking for a place where the teenage star might stumble, waited to see if this young star had the right stuff or would crumble under the strain of adversity. He'd faced many challenges already in his nascent career and dug himself out of jams before. But hype, reputation and prior successes meant nothing now. Golf, like life, is about your *next* move, not your last.

Madalitso stood above the bunker where he could survey his ball and the hole. After seeing all he could see, he grabbed his lobbing weapon and stepped into the hellhole. A hush fell over Chibuluma as people took up position around the green to witness this turning point.

Many couldn't even see what was going on deep inside the bunker.

Suddenly, a cloud of sand shot into the air, and rocketing out of the haze was his ball. Heads moved in unison as it peaked above the green before gravity pulled it back to earth. Madalitso knew it was a good shot. But *how* good it was depended on what happened after it landed.

The ball seemed to pause and think for a moment before starting its roll. While the crowd watched with rapt intensity, Madalitso scrambled out of the quarry so he could see his destiny either fulfilled or denied.

The ball's journey seemed to be following a sweeping arc that would lead it straight toward the cup. Anticipation mounted as it moved ever closer. Madalitso had a feeling this wouldn't be a narrow miss, a lip out or a ball that tantalizingly stopped short.

A tiny smile crept onto his face just before it dropped into the hole. Birdie. Escape. Disaster turned into triumph.

And this is how champions are forged.

The small crowd erupted. Madalitso raised a hand. One player shook his head in what appeared to be a stark realization—even when you thought Madalitso Muthiya was giving you an opening, he wasn't. A shot from a bunker, from the rough, or from behind an anthill was merely an opportunity for him to demonstrate his ability. Madalitso didn't *try* to hit his ball into the right-side bunker on Chibuluma's fifteenth hole. Forcing himself to make a 30-foot shot from the bunker for birdie wasn't part of the plan. But the result was the same: any feeling of hope by other players was smashed.

In the end, fatigue, the long drive, none of it mattered. Madalitso humbly accepted another trophy, crushing the entire field in Chibuluma and winning the tournament going away.

Peter shook his head and allowed himself a small, private smile. He had no idea how Mad had kept it together, considering the breakneck pace Peter had kept him on since England. But he had a remarkable ability to block out everything and focus on what was important: playing his best golf and being his best self on the course.

Peter was more than proud. He was impressed. He marveled at his son's resilience and basked in the fact that his son's name was now atop yet another colonialist symbol.

Madalitso, on the other hand, couldn't wait to take his trophy and hop back into the car. He later quipped, "It was the only place I could sleep."

He needed all the rest he could get because he and his father were driving to yet another tournament—the DC Sharma Memorial in Ndola.

Stopping the car didn't wake him. Neither did turning off the engine. Peter had to shake Madalitso awake when they got to Ndola Golf Club.

Madalitso pried open his eyes, rolled out of the passenger's seat and hauled his golf bag out of the trunk. With the bag hanging off his slumped shoulders, he slogged to the clubhouse, half-asleep. Along the way were some familiar friendly foes, including a few adults who had previously beaten him. Tournaments at Ndola Golf Club attracted the best amateurs. The 1998 DC Sharma would be no different. It was stacked with not just players, but Players. Champions. Best of the Best.

Madalitso felt like he was underwater. Everything was a struggle. Even lacing up his golf shoes was exhausting.

Peter could see Madalitso was completely wiped out, almost asleep on his feet. By now, Peter was usually sipping his first beer. Not this time. He wanted to study his son's first swing, to see how he would handle all the adversity he handed Mad, so he remained near the first tee while carefully staying out of sight. He honestly had no idea what to expect. Mad was running on empty. Would he crash and burn? Or rise to the challenge?

Peter was shocked by what he saw. Suddenly, it was as if somebody flicked on the power. Madalitso sent a rocket down the first fairway that drew applause from the onlookers. He lifted his bag with his usual authority, threw it over his shoulder and marched forward like he woke up from a refreshing power nap.

Smiling, Peter retreated to the clubhouse with the peace of knowing what would happen: Madalitso was going to conquer this course and leave everyone else in the rearview mirror.

The beer tasted especially good that day.

THE MEDIA SEEMED to fall in love with Madalitso as it chronicled his triumphant march through the golf season. The headline in the *Zambia Daily Mail* simply read:

"JUNIOR GOLFER UNEQUALED"

"Sensational junior golf champion Madalitso Muthiya at the weekend completed a double where he won the Sharma Memorial and Chibuluma Open golf championships...Muthiya, who is Africa junior champion was at his best when he took the Sharma title in Ndola on one-under par over 18 holes to register his second win in less than a week. The junior golfer, who had scooped the Kabwé Open the previous weekend, never rested and was on the road the next day... He has take[n] the lead on the Zambia Golf Union (ZGU) Order of Merit list."

The Order of Merit is the ZGU's national point standing. He was, at that moment, the best amateur golfer competing in Zambia. And he was still only a skinny kid who hoped to be shaving regularly soon.

Again, Peter decided there would be no rest. Madalitso faced a full week of studying, reading, taking tests and attending school every day with his dad's eagle eye over his shoulder to make sure i's were dotted and t's were crossed.

Awaiting him at week's end was the Lusaka Open.

Occasionally, Peter questioned his foot on the accelerator. But only to himself. He never asked Madalitso whether he needed a break from golf, and he never gave permission to miss a day of school. He had faith in his son and was convinced that Madalitso would let him know if he reached his limit.

Only once during this time did the train veer off track. Peter called the house one afternoon to speak with Madalitso. He was driving home from the office to take Madalitso to Lusaka Golf Club for a practice round. Peter instructed Mad to be ready. He was in no mood to wait around.

When Peter got home, Madalitso was not ready and waiting outside. His son was lounging on the couch, barefoot. Seeing his father's anger, Madalitso dashed to get his shoes and golf clubs. He returned to the front door seconds later, only to find Peter's taillights growing smaller in the distance. Practice was canceled.

Aside from this lone blip, there was no letup. And the results were staggering. The courses and tournaments had different names, but the stories were the same. Intrigue and suspense were gone. In 1998, amateur golf in Zambia was no longer competitive.

He won the Lusaka Open.

He won the Lusaka Junior Club Championship (second year in a row).

He won the Chick of the North Championship (second year in a row).

He won the Champion of Champions (second time in three years), the final amateur tournament of the year.

The long, grueling season now blessedly in the rearview mirror and Madalitso's golf clubs—along with another trophy—safely in the trunk, Peter slid into the driver's seat, pulled out of the parking lot and glanced quickly back at the clubhouse. "I am proud of you, son," he said. "The last few weeks have been mentally and physically exhausting. A breakneck pace. I hope you understand; I want you to get a sense for the challenges you will confront in college: a full course load, practices and workouts every day and a demanding tournament schedule. This is what you have waiting for you. So I pushed you."

"Dad, it's okay." Madalitso paused for a moment, preparing to share something with his father for the first time. "I am a little worn out, but it's no big deal. I put all of this in perspective."

"What do you mean?" Peter asked.

"Sometimes I think about what our family has been through," Madalitso began. "Grandpa Sandikonda and Grandma Kaliwé struggled against colonialism every day just to stay together. Just to survive. You had to fight to get an education, leaving home as a young child and then being by yourself at Munali. All of this struggle simply to have a better life and to provide a better life for me. How can I complain about being tired? From playing golf?"

Madalitso finished, reclined the passenger's seat and closed his eyes.

A smile made its way onto Peter's face. But he said nothing. His youngest son usually kept such deeply personal feelings to himself, and Peter was not about to interrupt the moment. Besides, what could he say after that?

A few minutes later, Madalitso was asleep in the passenger's seat.

But Peter kept on smiling.

Madalitso was at the height of his game. His mind, body and equipment were all working in unison. He was in a zone, steamrolling the competition in Zambia and nothing could be done about it.

Madalitso was the very model of humility and took it all in stride. Yes, he had a good year. But somebody better would always come along. Records are set and surpassed. That's the way it's supposed to be.

Peter's reflection on the year was further proof that modesty was a family trait. He acknowledged that Madalitso worked very hard. But he also saw how very fortunate his son was. In the end, Peter would say, "It's all in God's hands."

But Peter also loved those long hours on the road, traveling to tournaments, just the two of them. They talked about everything. Not just golf. Family, history, dreams of the future and stories of the past. Looking back, after all the unexpected success, the stunning string of victories and the shocking championships, spending that time together with his son was what he cherished most.

With the amateur season complete, the Zambia Golf Union performed its annual tabulation and easily determined that Madalitso had won the Order of Merit, finishing the year with the highest point total in the entire country.

Madalitso could finally take a break. But he and his father agreed that one more tournament remained.

The most prestigious golf tournament in Zambia is the Zambia Open.

Its origins trace back to before Zambia's independence. Today, the Zambia Open is part of the Sunshine Tour, one of several tours that comprise the International Federation of PGA Tours. Drawing elite players from Africa and Europe, its past winners include former Masters Champion Ian Woosnam and many European Ryder Cup players.

Despite a home course advantage, Zambians almost never beat the best players from countries where golf is a far more developed sport.

Madalitso needed permission to miss school so he could play on Thursday and Friday. The headmaster at Lake Road PTA appreciated Madalitso's excellent attendance considering all the golf he played that year. And it certainly didn't hurt that Madalitso competing in the most famous tournament in Zambia would make the school look good. He was very cooperative.

Lusaka Golf Club was completely transformed for the Zambia Open. TV cameras were strategically positioned around the course. Journalists lurked about, looking for players to interview. Tents were erected to handle tournament business. Spectator ropes lined the fairways and greens. The Zambia Open had all the features of a PGA tournament—including fans. Zambians love their sports and turned out to watch the best pool of international talent that assembled in their country for *any* sporting event.

Madalitso was unfazed by the pomp and circumstance, having already played on some big stages.

Tournament organizers also transformed the course at Lusaka Golf Club to make sure it was hard to shoot a low score. Tees were moved far back. Par 5s became par 4s. Pins were tucked into the most difficult parts of the greens. And Zambia's rainy season meant that longer and nastier rough lined the fairways and punished mistakes.

Lusaka Golf Club was Madalitso's home course. Having grown up playing there, he could have brazenly charged into his first round believing he could take chances that others could not.

But Mad quickly saw this was not the course he knew and loved. Again displaying maturity and discipline beyond his age, he opted to treat Lusaka Golf Club as if it were new and unfamiliar.

But Lusaka Golf Club certainly didn't treat him as new and unfamiliar.

The partisan crowd, which had politely clapped for each player who teed off, suddenly erupted when the local teenage sensation stepped up to hit his opening drive. So raucous was the reception that Madalitso took extra time to ease his breathing, slow his adrenaline and refocus his mind. It was almost as if the entire city of Lusaka lifted him off his feet and gave him a giant bear hug and a kiss on the cheek.

Eventually, the golf-savvy crowd ceased their applause and quieted their voices out of respect for their hero. Madalitso waited before taking one last, deep breath and stepping forward. With a calm yet serious expression on his face, Mad peered down the first fairway of his home golf course. He planted his feet and found his grip, all the while reminding himself that the cameras, fans and expectations were outside his control. *Just this shot.*

In what appeared to be almost religious adherence to fundamentals, Mad carefully completed his backswing. With the entire Zambian sporting community holding its breath, he drove through the ball with a swing that was honed exactly where he was standing.

Heads turned in unison as the ball rocketed down the first fairway. Club still coiled around his body, Mad joined his fellow Zambians in watching the flight of his first drive. While others waited anxiously to see where it landed, Madalitso already knew. It was excellent. The ball came to rest in the center-right of the fairway, approximately 100 yards to the pin. More applause.

Madalitso took it in stride with a casual smile and wave, while inside, he was almost relieved to exit the first stage and play golf.

As he proceeded through his opening round, the strategy of taking nothing for granted was working. He was steady, though not spectacular. His drives left him in a good position to reach the green, and his approach shots landed in safe areas. His putting was adequate, but he knew he could do better.

His first-round score was 72, one over par. The low round of the day was a jaw-dropping 63 by South Africa's Hennie Otto. Most contenders shot between 69 and 73, which meant that Madalitso didn't put himself near the leaders, but he didn't shoot himself in the foot either. While he was in a good position heading into Friday, he needed another steady performance to make the weekend cut.

Friday was almost a mirror image of the day before. Madalitso was satisfied with his drives and irons, but once again, there were too many missed putts.

Another 72 was turned in at the scorer's table. It wasn't spectacular. But checking the leaderboard brought a smile to his face. He easily made the cut. With consecutive rounds of 72, Madalitso was in striking distance of the leaders. He was playing consistently, with no blazes of glory, but no tournament-ending mistakes. Which was his plan all along.

Madalitso stood in thirty-second place on Friday evening. Quite an achievement considering seventy-two players survived the cut. The real competition would begin the next morning.

As expected, South Africans dominated the event with some Zimbabwean and European players scattered throughout. Most were tour professionals, grown men who played for money. This was very different from every amateur tournament Madalitso had played. The men around him were playing for their livelihoods.

Excitement and tension grew as Saturday morning dawned and brought a larger crowd, most of whom wondered if the local fifteen-year-old local-legend-in-the-making could continue hanging with the big dogs.

They got their answer immediately. Madalitso parred the first eight holes, cruising along, focused and in a zone.

And then trouble.

On the par 3 ninth hole, his tee shot veered hard right and disappeared in the gnarly rough. Sighs arose from the pro-Zambian gallery as Mad grumbled.

He found his ball resting on a scabby patch of dirt directly behind a large tree. He could see a glimmer of the green, but his view was obstructed by branches. The spectators couldn't see it, but he groaned slightly, just loud enough for his caddie to hear.

He circled the impossible shot and came to the unmistakable conclusion that he had two options. Bad and none. Bad meant lofting the ball over the tree, driving it through the branches or hitting it sideways back onto the fairway. He decided on a flop shot, which would require skying his ball over the tree. Worst-case scenario: the ball would hit the tree, and he'd end up right back where he started, staring a double bogey—or worse—straight in its evil eyes.

Onlookers encircling the green waited, hoping to see the ball fall from the sky.

Madalitso hit the ball fat, snubbing the hard dirt. The ball went straight into the branches. He closed his eyes, and his heart sank as he heard the ball smacking leaves and wood before falling straight down toward the base of the tree.

He gathered himself, put the past in the past, and managed to chip the ball onto the green, leaving him with a knee-knocking 10-foot putt. As he studied it meticulously, it looked like a straightforward putt, although the irrational nature of Zambia's greens meant that no putt was really what it seemed.

He looked back and forth between his ball and the pin. Ball, pin. Ball, pin. Ball, pin. He took his position, took a breath and stroked the ball. It felt good. It looked good. Mad held his breath, waiting, inch by inch, for the inevitable bad hop or wayward roll. Against all odds, the ball stayed on course and fell in. A miraculous bogey.

He picked up his ball and raised his hand to acknowledge the muted, perfunctory applause that comes from courtesy, not enthusiasm for a sloppy hole.

Mad moved to the tenth hole, a par 5 with a slight dogleg to the left. With Mad's length, it should be a birdie hole—and a chance to erase his mistake and get back in the running.

Loosening his shoulders, he calmly breathed in and out and repeated his father's mantra: *The most important shot is the next one.*

Madalitso was determined to get every ounce of distance off the tee by cutting the dogleg, shortening the hole considerably. He took his stance, breathing easy, eyes focused.

Peter often said, "I taught him many things on the golf course, but his swing is inherent." Madalitso seemed to be born with a smooth, effortlessly efficient backswing, or the foundation upon which a great golf swing is built. The weight shift, the rapid acceleration through the strike area and the sweeping follow-through all seemed instinctive to the boy who could smash a ball 200 yards when he didn't even know how to grip the club "properly." His swing was textbook. Even though he'd never read a word of the text.

Here on the pivotal tenth hole, his desire, his drive, the thing that makes good athletes into champions, provided him with an extra oomph.

The ball soared toward the trees and rough it needed to clear to cut the dogleg and reach the fairway on the other side. Madalitso knew his margin of error was tiny, but he didn't know how tiny until he watched his ball climb higher...*much* higher than he intended. His eyes slowly closed, realizing that his need to reach the green in two strokes made him bring too much muscle to the party. The ball flew over the trees, over the fairway, and into the nastiness on the far side.

"Ahhh!" he exclaimed.

This was like a raging scream for a young man who never showed his emotions, especially on the golf course. *What is going on?* he asked himself. He looked down at the ground, unmoored, then pulled himself together and trudged off the tee box.

He didn't make eye contact with anyone, but he could feel the sad stares of the spectators who were rooting for this young man, their native son, to succeed.

The next four shots were a fever dream nightmare. Madalitso, master of control, could no longer do what he was born to do, what he could do with the best in the land: control himself or his ball. It refused to find the fairway, leapfrogging the smooth green grass, getting sucked into shrubs, knocking off rocks and skittering away from the green.

With each ill-fated swing, the voices inside his head screamed louder and louder.

What's happening here? followed by *Forget it. Move on. Next shot is all that matters.*

After he hit his fifth shot on this birdie-friendly—and very familiar—par 5, he was left with a 20-foot putt...for *bogey*. The way he'd been playing, a three-putt seemed almost inevitable. An 8, a triple bogey, a dreaded snow-man, would mean 4 OVER par in the last two holes. It would be virtually impossible to come back from that. His tournament would, for all intents and purposes, be over.

But he was Madalitso Muthiya, so he pushed failure to the side and focused on what he'd been relentlessly taught he could control. Himself and the ball. He went back to basics.

Calmly, he went through his familiar, comforting pre-shot routine, walking back and forth between his ball and the hole, studying the putt from every angle.

At last, he lined up to send his ball across twenty feet of unpredictable green, hopefully bringing the misery of this hole to an end. With a firm, smooth stroke, he sent it on its long journey. For several feet, the speed was good and the line he chose was accurate. He'd salvaged another bogey. Or so he thought.

Halfway to the hole, the golf gods frowned upon him, and his ball bounced up, slowing it considerably.

It stopped three feet from the cup.

Deafening silence from the hometown fans greeted him as he mercifully put himself and the hole out of their misery and tapped in. Madalitso had just bogeyed the ninth and doubled the tenth, even par to three over in what seemed like the blink of an eye. He was freefalling down the leaderboard.

After all his success that seemed to come so easily, he was being tested by a firestorm of failure. His nerves were frayed. His mind clouded with doubt. Was he resilient? Could he conquer adversity? Did he have the heart of a Zulu warrior? Or was he just another pretender?

And along with the reconfiguration of Lusaka Golf Club, something else was unfamiliar: the expectations of a nation now rested on his teenaged shoulders. Zambians had been coming to watch him play for a while now, but it was just to meet and watch the young star who was already becoming a legend. This was different. The Zambia Open was a professional event with an international field of top competitors. It was in his home country, and he was the only Zambian.

For the first time, he felt the weight of expectations from a hometown crowd. He could see it on their faces, hear it in their cheers and feel their groans in his bones. It began to feel like if he played well, their lives would somehow be better. It was pressure he'd never expected. Playing for Zambia filled his heart with pride, but having his performance disappoint or sadden people rose bile in his stomach.

Between shots, he tried to process the strange new position he was in. Naturally, his dad was not around for counsel and advice, but he heard his dad's voice in his head. *Others' expectations are beyond your control. It is not something you can worry about. Just focus on what you need to do.*

This may have been the first time that Madalitso confronted a huge and unexpected challenge as a rising sports star and tried to figure it out without his dad. He had been trained for independence. And he came from a long line of ancestors who had faced much worse than this. What, after all, is golf, compared to fighting for your life? What does failing at a tournament mean next to having your home and culture stolen, to facing starvation and death?

Zambia breathed a little easier when Madalitso righted his ship and parred the eleventh and twelfth, with good opening drives and solid putts. Then, he strode to the thirteenth hole. Despite a nice recovery on eleven and twelve, his bogey and double-bogey on nine and ten were enough to rattle the confidence of any seasoned professional, let alone a fifteen-year-old boy. Of course, Madalitso's face and body language gave away nothing as he pulled out his driver and stared stone-faced down Lusaka Golf Club's thirteenth fairway.

Twenty-four holes were left to play in the Zambia Open. Twenty-four opportunities to put an exclamation point on the end of a historic year and show that he belonged with accomplished professionals. Twenty-four chances to build on his stellar record of achievement in a country that had no business producing a golf star. Twenty-four steps away from further entrenching himself as the most promising young athlete in Zambia and a national hero.

Or showing his country, and his dad, that he wasn't just another flash in the pan.

14

MADALITSO BLASTED HIS TEE SHOT straight down the heart of Lusaka Golf Club's thirteenth fairway. His distance drew "OOHS" from onlookers and congratulations from other players. It was a par 5, so a decent approach meant a good chance for birdie.

Madalitso pulled an iron from his bag, methodically went through his pre-shot routine and moved into position. The partisan crowd, desperately wanting their native son to succeed, held their breath. After a long pause, Mad let it fly.

His shot wasn't decent or even good. It was spectacular. From his angle, he couldn't see exactly where the ball stopped, but the crowd's reaction told him it must be close to the pin. Turned out it was *very close*. Seven feet to be exact.

His putter had been balky all day, and a pressure-packed seven-footer was no gimme. There was a strange, humpbacked ridge between his ball and the hole. Very tricky. After looking at the shot from every angle, he settled on a strategy that would at least leave him with an easy shot at a birdie. He took some practice strokes before stepping into position. His eyes moved slowly back and forth from his ball to the hole before focusing in. The crowd silenced just before his backswing. He made perfect contact and watched the ball as it followed the *exact* trajectory he wanted.

Eagle!

The thirteenth green gallery erupted in wild cheers and rowdy applause from people who were begging for this. When Madalitso picked up his ball, you couldn't tell if he'd gained two strokes or lost them. Only his quick acknowledgment to the crowd gave any inkling that he had done the near-impossible as he headed to the fourteenth tee.

He finished his third round with another birdie, a bogey and three pars. Rebounding beautifully after holes nine and ten, he finished the day with another 72. A solid turnaround. More importantly, he demonstrated an ability to maintain composure and come back from near failure.

This is the stuff from which champions are made.

MADALITSO AWOKE ON the final day of the 1998 Zambia Open feeling no nervousness. No anxiety. It was just another round of golf to enjoy. Peter drove him to Lusaka Golf Club like it was a practice round. Mad went through his standard warm-up routine. He didn't hit his usual booming drive. Zambia groaned as he bogeyed the first hole, a putt that simply deviated at the last second and lipped out.

Strangely, it didn't bother him. Mad had arrived that morning confident, mentally alert and filled with adrenaline. He was determined to show the visiting players that this was *his* home course. Suffice to say, disappointment over his initial bogey didn't last.

Madalitso went on an absolute tear.

He birdied the second hole.

He parred the third.

He birdied the fourth.

He parred the fifth.

And then he birdied the sixth, seventh *and* eighth holes.

He birdied five of the first nine holes.

Madalitso was shredding the course. His spectators increased exponentially, as did their enthusiasm. He was the youngest, lightest, least accomplished player in the field with the worst equipment. He had no chance of winning. But it didn't matter. This was a Zambian teenager proving that he belonged with professionals from much wealthier countries. Proving that Zambia belonged.

Although his last nine holes were less sensational than the first, it couldn't dampen the buzz. This was a mind-boggling performance by a teenage boy who should have been a mere footnote in this tournament. Instead, he duked it out toe-to-toe with grizzled veterans and seasoned professionals.

Peter was gob-smacked when he saw Madalitso walk up the eighteenth fairway to the loudest applause enjoyed by any player. They made eye contact before he putted in for par, and Peter could tell that despite Mad's stoic exterior, the round was good. Then, his son told him the news: 69.

Madalitso finished in twenty-second place out of 112 players who entered the tournament. His score of 285 was tenth best overall and just twelve shots behind the winner.

The *Times of Zambia* featured a story on Madalitso's triumphant performance. The front page of the sports section featured a huge photo of the fifteen-year-old turning toward the camera with a broad smile. Underneath, the caption read:

"Zambian sensational: Madalitso Muthiya, the best-placed local after finishing 22nd in the Zambia Open Golf championships at Lusaka yesterday."

The *Times* reporter captured the excitement in the air:

"The loudest plaudits belonged to Zambian youngster, Madalitso Muthiya, who finished the day with an impressive 69, two-under par... five birdies on the front nine, which he finished with a 31..."

Even Peter was recognized. "Muthiya, whose father is the Captain at the Lusaka Golf Club, thanked his family and the crowd of fans that willed him on throughout the championship."

Sunshine Tour veterans gave the *Times* their own assessment of the local boy: "The two professionals who played with him were full of praise for the teenager... 'He's very solid. He's got a helluva short game. A very, very good putter,' said John Nelson of South Africa."

Madalitso Muthiya was the pride of Lusaka and the entire country. No longer would Zambians assume that good players had to come from South Africa, Europe or the United States. Zambia's poverty and lack of resources made it harder to compete.

But a fifteen-year-old proved it could be done.

PETER KNEW THE landscape had changed when he and Madalitso pulled into the driveway on Monday afternoon to find a stranger standing by the front door. The man shook their hands and told them he had come to bring Madalitso to State House for a meeting with President Chiluba.

Neither Peter nor Madalitso asked *why* the President wanted to speak with his son. As Peter deadpanned later, "When you're summoned by the President, you go."

Peter knew that this was different from their last meeting. He didn't accompany Madalitso this time. It was another opportunity for his son to stand alone. The same as playing in tournaments. Peter had always believed that the only way your children become comfortable speaking with important people is to teach them and then let them do it themselves.

Madalitso climbed inside, and the driver whisked him to State House. He was led down the same hallway and waited just as before. Finally, the same woman opened the door to President Chiluba's office and gestured for Madalitso to enter. Meeting the President always warrants some level of deference and produces a few butterflies, but this time, Madalitso entered the room knowing what he wanted to achieve with this meeting.

President Chiluba stood from behind his desk. "How are you, Madalitso? Please sit down."

The shy teenager responded with a succinct but polite, "Fine. Thank you, Mr. President."

The President offered warm congratulations, declaring how proud he was to see a Zambian's name among the leaders at such a celebrated professional tournament, particularly a player of Madalitso's age.

"By every conceivable measure," Chiluba asserted, "Zambia cannot compete with South Africa or Europe in terms of resources to develop young golfers. Not even close. But you matched players with more experience, better equipment and years of expert training."

"Thank you, President Chiluba. I was inspired and humbled to have so many Zambians supporting me," Madalitso said shyly.

The President shifted the conversation from the Zambia Open to the real purpose of this meeting: advancing the career of Zambia's brightest young star. He asked Madalitso again. "What can we do to help you?"

The President had offered his assistance once before. But neither father nor son responded. This time, Madalitso was prepared. He leaned forward and looked the President in the eye. "I want to attend college and play golf in the United States."

There was a pause. The President kept listening.

"American colleges have teams that compete against each other," Madalitso explained. "I saw it on TV. The team members play golf and attend classes like other students. I will need financial assistance. Some players receive money from the college they attend. It is called a scholarship. My family cannot afford an education in America."

President Chiluba stared at his young guest for a few seconds. Madalitso could tell the President of Zambia was thinking hard about what he said. Which was cool. And a little uncomfortable.

Finally, Chiluba broke the silence. "I will ask the Zambia Golf Union to work on this. Through its contacts, the ZGU is best placed to find potential sponsorships for you." He paused for a moment.

Madalitso understood the first part of the President's answer. The second part of the strategy was more confusing.

"Our government is working with a man in the United States. He might be able to help. We will arrange for you and your father to meet him." The President did not identify this "man in the United States" and provided no further explanation. Madalitso simply thanked the President, and the meeting ended.

True to his word, Chiluba immediately took action. A headline in the

Times of Zambia publicly revealed the President's wish: "Help Muthiya become champ."

The story included excerpts of a speech written by the President and delivered by his Minister of Sport, Youth and Child Development.

The speech opened with a tribute to Madalitso's "tremendous" talent. The President then "urge[d] the ZGU chairman and the Zambia Open and the minister responsible for sports to harness his potential and afford him the opportunity of becoming Zambian Golf champion." Chiluba called on the ZGU to help Madalitso secure a golf scholarship to advance his golf career and his education. The President summed it up like this: "[G]oing to the U.S. would be the best for him."

Peter, as his nature dictated, was skeptical. He did not think the ZGU could help much. They organized and secured sponsorships for golf tournaments in Zambia and developed relationships with other governing bodies. President Chiluba was asking them to complete a task that was completely outside of their expertise. The ZGU had plenty of contacts in the business community, but locating financial support for a single amateur golfer? Securing an athletic scholarship to an American university?

He could almost hear a collective groan from ZGU leadership.

MADALITSO'S WHOLE WORLD changed, and everything shifted into high gear. On Sunday afternoon, he was being lauded and applauded as he walked up the eighteenth fairway at the Zambia Open. A few days later the President boldly proclaimed his future to be a national priority. ZGU was being pressed into action. And now some "man in the United States" whom the Muthiyas had never met held the key to the future. It seemed as though every man, woman and child in Zambia was ready to take action. Except one.

Peter.

The previous week his son's hope of leaving Zambia to attend an American college was little more than a fun topic at the dinner table. The subject was almost an abstract, unreal impossibility in the immediate future.

Not anymore. The whole country, it seemed, was being tasked by President Chiluba to find Madalitso a golf scholarship to play and go to school in America.

On the day of the President's proclamation, Peter tried to insulate himself from the constant buzz. He sat by himself and read *that* article a hundred times. Had they really considered everything before asking the President to unleash this avalanche? He was so conflicted. By that evening, he was in the middle of a shouting match inside his own head that continued for days.

Breaking up the family was out of the question! The Muthiyas drew strength from each other. Peter would not allow President Chiluba, the ZGU or some *"man in the United States"* to separate his son from the rest of the family. The time they spent together could not be duplicated by anything else. Certainly not the opportunity to play American golf.

Madalitso could build his career closer to home by playing on the African Sunshine Tour. The purses were more than enough to support a professional golfer, including the occasional trips to the U.S. and Europe.

Peter was proud of his son's desire to pursue a college degree, but he could do so at home. The University of Zambia allowed Peter to escape the abject poverty that gripped most Africans. Madalitso could easily follow in his father's footsteps by attending the hometown school. Or any of the fine institutions of higher learning in Southern Africa. Traveling to the United States was unnecessary! And it was soooooo far away!

Peter also questioned whether Madalitso was ready to stand on his own. Peter and Edith were their son's foundation and support. Moving to the United States meant that in an instant, they would be absent. Madalitso would be alone, with no one he knew, ten thousand miles from home. Remaining in Africa would make his transition to independence more gradual.

At that point, Peter took a deep breath and forced himself to calm down.

If it were true that Madalitso was unable to stand on his own, then he and Edith had failed. Why had they made their sons travel alone to tournaments when the boys were barely taller than their golf bags? Why did Peter refuse to coach Madalitso when he competed? Why did he allow Madalitso to meet with President Chiluba by himself? Underneath it all was the tragic reality that African children often must become adults much, much sooner than children elsewhere.

Although Peter loved his alma mater, the painful truth was that the University of Zambia had declined since the late 1960s. Dwindling government support brought serious budget problems. And honestly, universities in Africa had nothing comparable to the NCAA that allowed student athletes to compete in top-level sports and pursue an excellent education at the same time.

Madalitso certainly *could* earn a decent living by playing on the Sunshine Tour. But playing amateur golf in the United States was a rare gift. And Peter knew it.

Peter also had to consider non-golf realities. In 1998, Zambia was at the bottom of the world's economic ladder. Corruption was a crippling problem. Peter wanted to spare his children from the lack of opportunity and the seething frustration he felt for most of his life.

Lastly, there was "breaking up the family." Peter shook his head at himself. How could he think, even for a moment, that the Muthiyas' bond could be weakened by geography? Scattering the family around the world would never shake their love for each other. The values that Peter and Edith instilled in their children could not be worn away, despite the oceans separating them.

But Peter's stomach churned when he thought of loading Madalitso's suitcase into the car and driving to the airport. It would be the end of so much that had become beautifully routine: going over strategies on the golf course, long road trips to tournaments on the Copperbelt, meeting on the eighteenth green at the end of a final round and seeing the smile on his son's face after another stellar performance.

And there were the days when father and son sat down to watch golf's major tournaments. Soon, Peter would find himself alone in front of the TV. As a young man, Peter would have gladly given up food for golf. And yet his passion for golf *before* Madalitso started playing was dwarfed by what the sport meant to him afterward.

Peter finally realized that was it. He would miss his son. He finally admitted the source of his hesitation. It wasn't as though the naysayers in his head lacked good arguments. But the opportunities at an American university simply could not be matched in Zambia. It was an unfortunate truth. But it was the truth.

It was late at night when Peter finally confessed the true nature of his reservations. The debate raging inside his head over the past few days gradually died down. Reluctantly, he decided to meet the man from the United States that the President mentioned.

And then he remembered being in this same situation once before. Only he had been the son, listening to his mother make the hardest choice of her life.

At that moment, a voice he hadn't heard in years suddenly emerged and repeated a message he had almost forgotten.

Sometimes you have to love your children enough to send them away.

PART II

15

THERE I WAS, A WHITE American sitting across from the leader of Zambia, President Chiluba, listening as he informed me that I was the "man in the United States" that he mentioned to some teenager I'd never met. He stared directly into my eyes, waiting for my answer to his question. Would I help a young African golf prodigy get a scholarship to a United States university?

I didn't make a sound. I couldn't. A clenched throat, dry mouth and a rush of perspiration kept me from speaking. I was so confused. *Did I misunderstand him? Did he really just ask me that? Is this an assignment that the President—the most powerful person in the country—actually expects me to carry out?*

These and a hundred other questions raced through my mind as he focused on me. It got hotter and hotter in the room, sweat rolling down my back as his senior advisors turned their heads in my direction. I knew almost nothing about golf. I barely even played the game. How did he expect me to find a university to accept a kid I had never met, that they'd never even heard of? Despite (or maybe because of, I still don't know) all of this, my mouth seemed to have a mind of its own. It opened, and I heard these horrifying words come out.

"Yes, Mr. President."

Fate called my name. I answered. I didn't really want to. But I did.

When President Chiluba had gotten what he wanted, the meeting was over and it was time to leave. After shaking the President's hand, a few of us were escorted outside and into a car that would take us to our hotel. One of my contacts on the President's staff walked out with me. Seeing the stunned look on my face, he smiled and threw an arm around my shoulder. "That doesn't seem so hard, Jayme."

I forced a return smile. "Yeah."

As our driver wound through the streets of Lusaka, I rubbed my throbbing temples and asked myself, *What have I gotten myself into?*

My work in Washington investigating the genocide in Rwanda and helping secure passage of the African Growth and Opportunity Act had caught the attention of several African countries. President Frederick Chiluba was particularly keen on strengthening economic and political ties between the United States and the Republic of Zambia. He directed some of his key people to enlist my help in accessing government agencies and building relations with the U.S. private sector.

I knew it was a terrible idea for me, a young professional on Capitol Hill, earning a steady paycheck while trying to build my résumé brick by brick. These were the years I needed to carefully chart my future.

But Peter wasn't the only one with an ancestor whispering in his brain. As the deadline for my answer approached, I kept hearing one of my mother's own personal proverbs: *Good things always come from hard work...but not always right away.*

The more I thought about it, the worse the idea sounded. So naturally, I said, "Yes."

The only time I second-guessed my decision was at the doctor's office. I was there to purchase a bottle of malaria pills and receive the six (yes, 6!) immunizations necessary for this trip. In the exam room, I removed my shirt as a nurse walked in carrying a tray of hypodermic needles that were lined up one after another. She set them down on a table next to me. "The doctor will be in shortly," she said on her way out.

The door closed. For five of the longest minutes in my life, I stared at all those needles ready to pierce my skin. I took several deep breaths. *This is it.* For reasons I can't explain, allowing myself to be injected seemed a more fundamental and *personal* commitment to this journey. More than quitting my job, this was my point of no return.

My anxiety grew until I thought my head would explode as I asked myself over and over:

What am I doing? This is CRAZY! It's not too late to back out.

I almost decided to jump ship and abandon the whole idea.

Just then, the doctor entered the room and looked at me. "Ready?"

I wasn't ready. Not at all. So naturally, I said, "Yes, Doctor."

MY WORK IN Congress required a great deal of research into sub-Saharan Africa. But no briefing memos or statistical data could have prepared me for my first trip there. For most of my life, my idea of African people was a mix of Nelson Mandela's strength, smiling bright-eyed children and ancient tribal cultures—whether the Maasai of Kenya or the Zulu of South Africa. And of course, graphic news footage of extreme poverty, violence and disease often compelled me to change the television channel.

We touched down at Lusaka International Airport, and the flight attendant opened the door. Moving toward the exit, I saw the inside of the airplane as the final outpost of everything I knew.

When my turn came to step through the door, I felt the kind of adrenaline rush that only comes from holding your breath, stepping off a ledge and dropping into complete uncertainty.

I knew my life was going to change.

But I had no visions of helping a young man and his dad change history.

THE AIRPORT LOOKED like it had fallen into a coma in 1964 and never woke up. It was clean but impossibly outdated. After being smacked in the face by a blast of African heat, I walked down the portable staircase and across the baking tarmac (there were no elevated Jetways). I was led into a private reception room where several Zambian Government officials were waiting, including the men who'd talked me into taking the job in the first place.

"How was your flight?" one of them asked. "A long trip, eh?"

"Not at all, the United States and Zambia are practically neighbors." They laughed. Truthfully, I was beyond exhausted, and it took all my energy to smile and be charming after the twenty-plus-hour journey. But these were my hosts *and* my clients. "I reviewed all of President Chiluba's priorities and wonder if we should go over some potential strategies I prepared."

"Don't worry about that right now," one of them said. "You are visiting our country for the first time. Tonight, we celebrate your arrival."

I took a deep breath. "Yes, but tomorrow we meet with the President. I want to make sure..."

One of them put a friendly hand on my shoulder. "Jayme, relax. President Chiluba is very affable. He is looking forward to meeting you. There is nothing to worry about."

I nodded and smiled. Chiluba was surely "affable," but the cause of my twinge wasn't the President of Zambia. It was me. I had spent many hours developing plans to confront Zambia's problems and had no shortage of confidence. Still, it was an official meeting with a head-of-state, and he was looking to *me*, a man less than five years removed from his law school commencement, to help advance some of his country's top priorities. Frankly, I was scared he wouldn't think I was up for the job. I wish, looking back, that I'd had just a smidge of Madalitso's unshakeable confidence.

We collected our bags, exited the terminal and boarded a van. My first ground-level view of Africa consisted of some green landscape and a steady stream of pedestrians flowing on the road as we sped by. Some carried food or other belongings. Many just walked. It took a moment to process that these people were walking on the road. Not on a sidewalk. *On the road!* While cars whizzed past them just a few feet away. I was surprised that there weren't multiple fatalities every day.

My face pressed against the window, I studied the Africans' faces. They were unfazed by 2,000-pound vehicles speeding by, sometimes inches away. I studied my companions inside the van. They were equally nonchalant. I was, not for the last time, keenly aware of my own naiveté.

Dinner, dancing and jet lag kept me from getting my full night's beauty sleep, but it didn't matter. My adrenaline kicked in as we reached the gates of State House the next day.

We were escorted into an open-air waiting area that was filled with exquisite plants and flowers. Behind the building were a variety of birds and animals—and a golf course.

A small team of President Chiluba's advisors appeared, and we were led down a corridor into an outer office, then through a door into a grand suite.

President Chiluba gave a hearty "welcome" and shook everyone's hand. When it was my turn, he flashed a warm, sincere smile. "Mr. Roth, it's good to meet you. I am pleased that you are in Zambia." His charm put everyone at ease. "Please sit down."

When everyone was settled, he began. "Zambia stands in a unique position. We are a landlocked country, and some of our neighbors do not share our democratic ideals or our interest in being an attractive destination for foreign investment. But this gives us an opportunity to set a positive example in the heart of Africa." Chiluba spoke and moved with unwavering confidence, sure of everything he was saying. It was easy to understand how this small man had such a big job.

President Chiluba went through his list of global, regional and domestic problems his country faced. In his view, "...each could be aided by strengthening Zambia's relationship with the United States, and *this* is the team that would make it happen!"

Possessed with youthful invincibility, I was sure I had all the answers to what ailed a poor country of over eleven million people. *No problem. I got this.*

The room was silent. Just as I began wondering if he would invite comments from the group, he uttered the words that caused me to revisit how I got here...how I arrived in a strange country halfway around the world and into this situation.

"Oh, one more vital issue that I hope Mr. Roth can help us with." I was taken aback. It was the first time since initial handshakes that he called any of us by name.

President Chiluba turned and looked directly into my eyes: "We have a young boy in our country who is an accomplished golfer. His family has little money, and Zambia is not a place where his talents can be fully realized. We hope that you can help him secure a scholarship to play golf at a university in the United States."

My face maintained its confident smile. But inside, I cried, *No way in hell I got this!*

I WAS COMPLETELY deflated by the time my car arrived back at the hotel. Just thinking about it made me groan and rub my temples.

Part of me was embarrassed by my attitude. I was asked to help a poor and talented young man pursue his dream, and all I could do was pout. *Shame on you and your first world problem.*

I was sure the kid would be better off with somebody else. Working with the Zambian Government energized me because their needs suited my strengths. I knew how to access Congress, government agencies and businesses—all were within reach of my office in Washington, DC.

This was completely different. President Chiluba was asking me to somehow convince a university to offer an athletic scholarship to a golfer from Zambia. I didn't even know where to start. I was sure of only one thing: I would fail. Epically. And when I did, the Zambians would cancel my contract. Word of my disaster would spread, and a cloud would hang over every future job interview. I'd gambled with my career because I understood and knew I could do what was being asked of me. I shook my head and collapsed into myself.

This is not what I signed up for! How do I get out of this mess?

16

PETER MUTHIYA GOT A CALL from State House, asking him to bring his son to meet "an American we're working with." He reluctantly agreed and spent the next forty-eight hours wondering who this American was that President Chiluba had selected to help chart his son's future. He never doubted the President's interest in helping Madalitso or that he would select somebody that he believed was qualified. But Peter was dubious. And he had a million questions. He was, after all, Peter Muthiya, and this was his nature. He was bound and determined to make his own assessment.

I scanned the lobby of the Intercontinental Hotel, but nobody fit the description of the two people I was scheduled to meet. I waited. Two minutes later, a man entered the lobby with a teenage boy in tow.

I walked straight up to the man and extended my hand. "Mr. Muthiya and Madalitso? I'm James Roth."

Peter projected an air of chilly suspicion as he nodded his head and shook my hand. "Yes, nice to meet you." Madalitso did the same, although he seemed more curious than suspicious.

I guessed Peter to be around 5'7" and Madalitso about an inch shorter. Peter's medium-length Afro and wire-rimmed glasses reminded me of a college professor. He looked me straight in the eye. Madalitso looked at me, shyly turned away, and then looked back again.

We found a quiet corner and sat. Since I was tasked with helping their family, I thought that sharing a few personal details would help us get acquainted.

"So, Mr. Muthiya, where are you from?"

"You can call me Peter, Mr. Roth," he replied with a straight face.

"Thank you, Peter. Please call me Jayme." In business situations, I usually introduce myself as "James," but figured I would take the first step toward establishing a personal rapport.

"Thank you. I am from a city called Kabwé. It's on the Copperbelt." I waited, but he offered nothing other than a blank stare. He didn't ask where I was from. This was not going well. I felt like a fish out of water, flopping around in a hotel lobby 10,000 miles from home. I panicked a little as I mentally rummaged through my suddenly blank mind for a question that would break the ice on this hot African day. "So...what line of work are you in?"

"I own an insurance brokerage business," he answered like I was interrogating him and he was waiting for his lawyer to show up.

I paused, thinking that he might ask about me. I got back nothing. Zip. Zilch.

Madalitso remained silent.

My hopes of establishing a personal bond already dashed, I retrieved my notepad and turned the conversation toward the purpose of our meeting. "What is your handicap, Madalitso?" I had no idea what a good handicap in golf was. In fact, the only thing I knew about handicaps in this context was that I had two bad ones: I knew NOTHING about golf, and NO ONE who could help them. But I figured it was the first question that a college coach would ask.

"Plus 4," Peter responded, quick, hard and condensed.

"How many tournament victories in the past year?"

"Ten or eleven," Peter replied.

"Any other notable finishes, not victories necessarily, but impressive showings?"

Peter again answered. "Highest finishing amateur in the Zambia Open and fifth in the World Junior Amateur Open."

"Are these internationally recognized tournaments?"

"Yes," Peter answered. Even though I was *clearly* directing the questions at his son.

"For me to speak intelligently about Madalitso's accomplishments, I'll need a detailed tournament record, like a résumé. Along with a videotape of Madalitso playing golf. Since none of them have seen him."

"Obviously," Peter responded. "I will send everything to your office in Washington, DC."

I figured that Madalitso would need a validator, a seasoned instructor to help sway doubtful university coaches.

"How often does Madalitso work with a professional coach?" I asked.

"Madalitso doesn't have a coach," Peter said with flat brusqueness.

"Okay... Then how many years *did* Madalitso work with a coach?"

Peter flashed a subtle smile and stared at me for a moment like I was mentally slow. "Mr. Roth...Jayme, there are no professional golf coaches in Zambia. Few people here can afford such things."

"Well, Madalitso, how do you explain your ability to play golf?"

As Madalitso opened his mouth, I looked down, preparing to take notes.

"My dad taught me some basic fundamentals. I watch tournaments on television and imitate what I see."

I let out a brief laugh, thinking they were pulling my leg. I looked up from my notepad and saw two blank stares.

With that brilliant stroke of utter awkwardness, I reached the end of my questions, and our meeting was mercifully put out of its misery. A minimum of barely polite farewells was exchanged.

I headed toward the elevators groaning to myself and rubbing my temples again. *Never had a professional lesson? Learned from his dad? And watching TV?!* Although my knowledge of golf was limited to the fact that there were clubs, a ball and a bunch of holes, I understood that it's an extremely technical sport. And yet the source of this kid's knowledge is an insurance broker and television. I had visions of the Olympic Games where a last place African bobsledder is cheered for his effort while the winners are getting their medals.

How in the world was I going to succeed at President Chiluba's assignment of convincing a coach to give a scholarship to a kid he'd never seen, from one of the poorest nations on earth, with no formal coaching?

I was also frustrated that neither Peter nor Madalitso understood how impossible this was. I needed vital information, exhilarating stories, personal anecdotes—*anything* to grab the attention of college coaches.

Instead, all I got were two stone walls.

At least we agreed on one thing; none of us was happy with this situation. And yet, here we were.

LATER THAT EVENING back in my room, there was a message from Peter Muthiya.

I called. Peter asked to speak with me in person that evening. Half an hour later, we were sitting across from each other in the hotel bar.

"I'll have a Heineken," I said when the waiter came to our table.

"Excuse me, Jayme," Peter interjected. "Can I convince you to try Mosi? It's a local beer."

I'd heard a rumor that formaldehyde was an ingredient in Zambian beers. But this was the first civil word Peter had spoken to me. I was not about to turn down an olive branch. Especially when the olive branch was a beer. We ordered a couple of Mosis.

"Can I tell you something?" Peter asked. The cold bite of this afternoon had been replaced by a thoughtful, worldly ease.

"Sure."

"You remember earlier today when we met?"

"Of course."

"Well, I thought you were with the CIA."

"HA!" I burst out laughing. "Why is that?!"

"Well, you walked right up to Madalitso and me without hesitation. I thought that you must've seen photographs of us."

Now it all made sense. They thought I was an agent sent to spy on them. Or worse!

We laughed as we enjoyed our Mosis. It was a surprisingly tasty beer. When he realized his absurd mistake, Peter was his usual engaging, wise, funny self. As one beer turned into two, then three, we talked about sports and life, our homes and families, our pasts and our futures.

Eventually, we got to politics. After hearing that I'd worked in Congress, he asked a question that stunned me. "Do you think the Republican takeover of Congress in 1994 will be short-lived, or will it endure like the Democrats' takeover in the 1950s?"

Wow!

I was blown away by his being more knowledgeable than most Americans about our current events and history. We had a fascinating discussion about America, democracy and Africa. Peter was a brilliant conversationalist. Warm, polite and with a grand sense of humor, his opinions were logical and informed. But he was also understated and courteous, curious and inquisitive, showing genuine interest in what I had to say.

As we declined the bartender's offer of a fourth round of Mosi, Peter leaned forward in his chair. "Jayme, there is something I want to tell you before you leave Zambia. I know you think that my son's abilities are exaggerated, that he can't compete against American amateurs."

He was right. But I didn't want to rain on this wonderful man's parade, so I kept my mouth shut.

"It's a fair assumption. Madalitso has never owned top-notch golf clubs or received professional instruction like kids in America. And considering where we live and the competition that Madalitso faces here, skepticism is justified."

Again, I kept my skepticism to myself and let him continue.

"I've played golf and watched others play my entire life. I'm not a professional, but I understand the game. I assure you, right now, Madalitso can compete with any amateur in the world, including kids who play at American colleges. My son is that good." Peter spoke in a measured tone with unwavering conviction.

"Peter," I said, "I will do my very best."

"Good," he said, nodding his head.

"So, Peter," I began. "Does Madalitso have a favorite player?" I asked, trying to change the subject.

"Probably Tom Watson. Madalitso met him once. He is a very nice man."

"That's great. Are there any Zambian golfers that Madalitso enjoyed watching in major tournaments?"

"No," he said flatly. "Zambia has never produced a prominent golfer on the world stage. You see, South Africa and Zimbabwe, which have produced champions like Ernie Els and Nick Price, had larger White populations historically. More Europeans settled in those countries than in Zambia. Golf became more developed there."

"Has a Black golfer from *any* African country ever played in a major?"

"In the British Open, yes, but I think that was after a special qualifying event was held in Nigeria," he said.

"So no Black golfer from any African country has ever played in a major on U.S. soil?"

"No," Peter replied matter-of-factly.

"Not the U.S. Open, PGA Championship or the Masters?"

"No."

I shrugged my shoulders and shook my head. "I had no idea. That surprises me."

Then it happened.

Peter stared at me, his smile gone. His furrowed brows said he was confused and annoyed. After five of what are still to this day the most uncomfortable seconds in my life, Peter said in a dark, serious voice, "You're surprised? Do you know much about the history of Africa?" He wasn't loud, but his words contained a challenge. His eyes never left mine.

My mind raced, trying to think of a good answer while wondering how I had provoked him.

Just as I opened my mouth, unsure of what would come out, Peter launched another missile: "Do you know much about the history of golf?"

One thing was immediately clear: a man doesn't ask these pointed questions in such a confrontational tone unless *he* is an expert. "No, Peter. Not really."

His face lightened with a nice smile, and a relaxed look slipped back into his eyes. "Well, if you did, you wouldn't be so surprised."

I wondered what had sparked Peter's pointed questions and so drastically darkened his mood. What about my off-the-cuff remark touched a nerve that was so raw, sensitive and deep?

I wouldn't know how to answer these questions for years. But thankfully, Peter moved on, the dark cloud at our table lifted, and our carefree banter resumed. "You know, Peter," I said, "I think we should start a business importing Mosi into the United States."

He roared a big happy laugh.

Eventually, we rose from the table and walked toward the exit. "I will send you the videotape and golf résumé," Peter said.

"Great. I'll look into the SAT exam and any other hurdles." My dour prophesies of disaster were gone. Perhaps fueled by a few rounds of Mosi, I was suddenly energized to find a scholarship for Madalitso. And I could see a path toward becoming friends with Peter.

We shook hands. "It was a pleasure meeting you, Peter."

"Likewise, Jayme. I look forward to talking again." As Peter looked me in the eyes, I was struck by the depth and warmth I found there and the easygoing smile on his face. I flashed on his friendly manner in our conversation at the hotel bar. He'd clearly lived a life with suffering and deprivation. But there was never a hint of anxiety, self-pity or desperation.

Peter didn't have the resources to give his son what they both wanted; that was clear.

He and his son needed my help with this scholarship—we both knew that.

But his smile and steady demeanor revealed a man who'd overcome greater challenges and beat steeper odds. A man whose confidence would not be shaken, scholarship or no scholarship.

I was sure there was much more to this man than I knew.

That moment, I vowed to do everything in my power to help make their dream come true.

17

N OW ALL I HAD TO do was find Madalitso a scholarship at some top-tier golf college. When I got back to Washington, DC., I began researching the weird and mystifying world of serious intercollegiate golf. I wanted a school that struck the right balance between athletics and academics. Peter was well educated. I knew he'd want the same for his son.

As I began my research, I became convinced that Madalitso's unique background might be an advantage. Coaches are always looking for diamonds in the rough, a raw and undiscovered talent that can excel with the right training and guidance. And it might be a feather in some school's cap to have the first Zambian golfer in American history on their team.

In a couple of weeks, I had detailed notes on over fifty universities, with coaches' names and telephone numbers. I was pretty satisfied with my research. I kept reminding myself that we only needed a scholarship offer from one school. Thus buoyed, I called Peter.

"Hi, Jayme." It was nice to hear his warm, welcoming voice with its rich accent.

"How are you, Peter?"

"Fine. Doing fine."

"Sorry for the delay in calling you, Peter. Getting my office running has been hard."

"It's quite alright, Jayme," he said, relaxed and upbeat. "I remember the headaches of starting my own business."

"Peter, I've made a list of around fifty schools with successful golf programs, a healthy balance between athletics and academics and a location that allows golf to be played year-round."

Peter's casual "mmm-hmm" drifted across the wire.

"I can run through them if you'd like."

"No, Jayme, I'm sure your list makes sense. This is unfamiliar territory for us. We will make the final decision, but we trust you to manage the process."

Wow. "Thank you, Peter. Again, I will do my best."

"Yes, I know you will." His unexpected yet simple vote of confidence helped transform this project from something I had to do to something I *wanted* to do. And Peter's trust in such an important matter seemed like a sign of friendship.

He drafted his son's golf and academic résumé and arranged to send me a videotape.

Madalitso's contribution would come later, at the most important golf tournament of his life.

"SORRY, COACH IS OUT," a receptionist said. "I'll pass you to his voicemail."

This would become a source of increasing frustration as I started calling golf coaches.

"Uh...sure," I replied. Waiting for the beep, I realized I should have thought of what to say. "Hi, Coach. My name is James Roth. I'm an attorney in Washington, DC, and I'd like to discuss an excellent young golfer. In the meantime, I'm sending a videotape and résumé. Please call at your convenience."

My second call was to another eastern school.

"Sorry, Coach is out." This receptionist sounded like the last one's sister. "I'll pass you to his voicemail."

And so, *once again*, I left another charming message about an outstanding golfer.

Third call. Receptionist. Voice message.

Fourth call. Receptionist. Voice message.

Fifth call. Receptionist. Voice message.

And on and on, ad nauseum. Before the holidays, I worked my way across the country calling every school on my list. With every voice message, my delivery improved, and my frustration grew.

"Would you like to leave a message for Coach?"

"Well, sure...if Coach *returns* his calls."

The rare occasion when a living, breathing college golf coach actually picked up the phone shocked me so much that I tripped over my own words: "Ohh...hello, Coach, how are you?"

After my best sales pitch, the call always ended with a vague, unconvincing promise:

"It sounds interesting. Send the materials. I'll get back to you."

WEEKS PASSED. BY mid-winter as much as I dreaded it, I needed to speak with Peter. Telephone service in Zambia was unreliable, but eventually I got through.

"Hi, Peter."

"Hello, Jayme." He seemed so pleased to hear my voice. I dreaded disappointing him. "How are you? How was your New Year's?"

"It was good, Peter."

After exchanging holiday stories, I rubbed my temples, exhaled and turned to my embarrassing and humiliating lack of progress. "Peter, hardly any coaches have returned my calls or even confirmed receipt of Madalitso's information. Only three out of fifty have called back." The words sounded so awful that I tried to comfort him. "But...this is a slow time of year... Coaches are taking time off."

Peter just listened while I spoke, offering only the occasional "mmm-hmm." After a brief moment of silence, he replied, "Well, I wouldn't worry. Nothing worthwhile is easy."

Whew.

We were discussing his son's future, and yet he was calm and unruffled by my complete lack of success. It reminded me of the last time we met, when I first sensed there was something special about this man and his son. It was time to bring up the topic I *really* wanted to discuss.

"Peter?" I said, feeling a little uneasy.

"Yes."

"There is something else I want to talk about."

"Okay?"

There was no going back now. "I think Madalitso's story would appeal to people. It might help us."

"What do you mean?"

"Well...I've been thinking about our last conversation in Lusaka, about Madalitso and African golfers." I cleared my throat and swallowed. "*Black* African golfers."

There was no sound on the other end of the line.

"Peter...are you there?"

"Jayme, why would people care about a Black African kid that plays golf?" I could almost see him rolling his eyes.

"If you give me a minute, I'll explain," I said as sweat beaded on my forehead.

Silence.

I took a deep breath. "You said no Black Africans have really achieved anything in this sport. That is important, Peter—important enough for people to know." Peter's sharp reaction in Lusaka replayed in my head: *Do you know much about the history of Africa? Do you know much about the history of golf?* I was again poking under the surface at something deep and painful.

More silence.

"But Peter, you had a passion for golf before Madalitso came along. You taught him the game, so the story can't begin with Madalitso's life. It has to begin with yours."

I visualized Peter's face and knew he was more than a political enthusiast or history buff.

There was more here.

But this was a risk. A *big* risk. I was asking Peter to share his life with me—a man (and a White man at that!) he barely knew—then allow me to reveal intimate, personal things about him.

Finally, after a few long and excruciating seconds, he answered with a simple, "Sure, okay." I detected a smile in his voice, almost as if he was flattered by my interest in his life and intrigued that others might be as well.

What a relief!

"So," Peter said with a good-natured but teasing tone, "speaking of Africa and golf, did you start your history lessons yet?" He let out a sly laugh, ribbing me in the sweetest way for when I unintentionally chafed him in Lusaka.

"Uhh...no, Peter. But you sure got me thinking about it."

"Well, instead of thinking about it, you should read some books. In light of the project you are now taking on, I'd be interested in your thoughts— once *you're there*."

"Okay. Sounds good," I replied, determined not to let my new friend down.

Asking Peter to share his personal stories with me was a risk I was almost unwilling to take.

But considering how it transformed our relationship (and me), I thank God I did.

18

PETER AND I TALKED EVERY week over the phone. Naturally, we talked about golf scholarships and Madalitso. But as our unlikely friendship grew, he told me his stories, and I told him mine. And so, I met his long-gone parents, Sandikonda and Kaliwé, two people whose land, culture and heritage were stolen and who struggled every day to survive and stay together under the oppression of colonial rule. I pictured the two-room mud hut in Broken Hill/Kabwé where they raised their children, including their youngest, Peter, whose energy, drive and desire to learn forced them to make the selfless and gut-wrenching decision to send him away.

I heard the pleas of a five-year-old boy, begging to watch his older brother perform work he didn't understand at a living monument to rich White people's crimes against poor Black people. I learned that sticks can be ground into golf clubs and children can transform empty land into a golf course.

Peter revealed deep and personal insights into his life. He shared the significant and often tragic events that shaped him and his family. Listening to some of the details was hard. And they made me see my White American life very differently. Eventually, I found them transforming me. His stories were no longer just the subject of my writing. They were a gift. Each phone call renewed my faith in the human spirit, confirming the potential in others and in me. Peter soon became a source of personal inspiration, a man that I admired and a close friend, unlike any I'd ever had.

But Peter's openness came at a cost: he expected the same from me. Peter wanted to know who *I* was and the personal events that shaped *my* life. These conversations were often difficult and painful.

"Jayme, you regularly mention your mom. Tell me about your dad."

"He died when I was young."

"How did he die?"

"My dad served in the military during the 1960s, and like a lot of young men, he suffered exposure to toxic substances. Years later, he developed brain cancer and passed away in 1979. He was just thirty-four years old. I was ten."

Over the years, these sentences had become my boilerplate response to questions about my father's death, a tape recording I played more times than I care to remember. After a while, they became rote. There was no feeling behind the numb recitation of the hardest thing I'd ever endured, the tragedy that helped shape my life.

Peter knew it. He said nothing for a moment. Finally, he asked, "That's it? He just developed brain cancer and died? It was instantaneous?"

This was a first. After reciting my canned four sentences, it was always the other person who became uncomfortable and wanted to change the subject. Not Peter.

I took a breath. "Well...no. It lasted awhile. It...the illness...lasted awhile."

"I would like to know what happened, Jayme. Will you tell me?"

Sitting quietly, only more bland sentences came to mind, as a question grew louder in my head: *How can I hold back from a man that has shared so much with me?*

An uneasy, queasy feeling filled my stomach as I tried to collect my dark, troubling thoughts. "Uhh...okay." I realized that I'd never gone into such depth on the topic I most hated.

"My dad worked in construction after his military service. A few years later, he and my mom started their own business installing water and drainage pipes, sewers and underground utilities. We had a lot of equipment, a dump truck and backhoe. My dad wasted no time in teaching me to run it. Can you imagine? An eight-year-old operating a huge tractor?!"

Peter and I both laughed before I continued.

"His headaches started a year or so later. We thought it was just stress over the new business. But it got worse. He and my mom took a vacation to Hawaii to see if that would help. It didn't."

I paused, breathing in and out. "Tests revealed a tumor. This led to chemotherapy, radiation and his first operation. Then another. And another. Doctors called each surgery 'a success,' which brought smiles, hugs and tears. But each time...as the weeks passed...our hopes faded as we learned the cancer had returned and spread."

Pausing and clearing my throat, I wanted Peter to say something—*anything* to change the subject. He didn't. His silence traveled 10,000 miles as he waited for me to continue.

"My dad's health got worse, and the treatments continued. My mother fought the insurance company, but of course they still found a way to limit coverage. Our money soon ran out.

"We had to sell our equipment to pay medical expenses. One of my most painful memories was the day they took away our dump truck and backhoe while my dad watched." My voice cracked. I felt a rush of emotion, and my eyes welled up. "Peter, I can't talk about this anymore."

"That's fine, Jayme, just one more thing. What about you? What about your life during all of this? What were your days like?"

Peter's thoughtful, caring question let me breathe and collect myself. "My dad spent his last few months at home. A full night's sleep was rare because the pain was so bad it kept him awake, and my mom had to help him. Sometimes I stayed with relatives or friends, just to give me a break.

"On most days, I raced home from school to see how he was doing and to be there if he needed anything. At the end, when he couldn't make it to the bathroom, I helped my mom change the dirty bed linens. I was ten. My challenge was to grit my teeth and keep my stone-face on. My dad didn't need the burden of seeing his only son cry.

"During his last days, my mom would say that he'd already left. God had taken him. This man with the mood swings—yelling at me one moment, holding me and crying the next—was not the father I should remember. 'Dad is gone, Jayme. It's our job to care for the remaining pieces that cancer left behind.'"

SHARING MY PERSONAL stories with Peter made me very uncomfortable. After hearing the hardships he faced growing up and raising a family in sub-Saharan Africa, I was embarrassed. My own troubles seemed trivial.

But there was a much deeper reason. Unlike other young boys who grew up without a father figure to confide in, I never went looking. On the contrary, I ran from them. My dad's life was defined by hard work, honesty and love for my mom and me. When he died, any desire for an adult male confidant died with him. My mother was there, and that was enough.

Peter Muthiya, a man I barely knew, from a completely alien culture, was now pushing open doors that were slammed shut twenty years ago. At times, I actually felt physically sick. Which is probably how some of my questions made him feel.

Although we never discussed it, I knew Peter's insistence on an equal exchange was not about feeling uncomfortably exposed or some competitive need for reciprocation. Peter Muthiya harbored no such insecurities. Rather, he believed my writing was incidental and the true purpose of our phone calls was to build and strengthen our relationship. Peter believed that he, Madalitso and I were joined on a mission.

A journey that was bringing us together to make us better human beings.

"SO, JAYME. REGARDING your history lessons...are you getting there?" Before hanging up, Peter would always needle me about the subject that caused initial friction in our relationship. (Months later, I still wondered what I said to set him off.) Then came the "gotcha" laugh, letting me know that he had caught me unprepared and slightly embarrassed.

I always answered with a sheepish laugh of my own. "No, Peter. I'm not there yet."

Peter broached the subject good-naturedly, but he clearly wasn't letting it go. Part of me attributed it to Peter's love of history. But on a deeper level, I sensed that he saw my quest for Madalitso's scholarship as being part of a broader idea about his world, my world, how these worlds came to be and how we could make them one world. A better world.

I enjoy history, though it's a passive interest. Besides, every day my calendar was filled with urgent tasks. I often didn't even have time to enjoy friends, go to the gym or finish the half-completed household projects that silently mocked me. Studying African history or the origins of golf was far down on my to-do list.

But Peter's persistence made me determined that one day I'd pick up some books and get to the bottom of what Peter wanted me to know.

Then we would have a conversation. Someday. There would be time.

19

M Y LIST OF OVER FIFTY colleges was now covered in hundreds
of little notes indicating when I'd called, written or emailed each
coach. After six months of ever-increasing frustration, I had spoken with ten.

Four bluntly dismissed me and my idea, then explained why the other
forty or so coaches were ignoring me. First, amateur golf was dominated
by Americans. Every year from 1978 to 1998, the prestigious U.S. Amateur Championship was won by an American. The runner-up was also an
American. With the NCAA limit of five scholarships per team, universities
easily filled their rosters with local kids. Why consider an unknown from
halfway around the world?

But our biggest hurdle was pure skepticism. The very concern Peter had
tried to allay at the hotel bar. Coaches simply didn't believe that a teenager
from the heart of Africa could compete in America. It was the same tired
lament Peter had heard his whole golfing life. Expensive equipment, expert
training and travel. Money. Great golfers come from places with money.
Zambia didn't have nearly enough of it.

I told them that I understood. But wasn't it *possible* for a gifted player to
come from somewhere unexpected? Most coaches replied with a hard "NO!"

Updating the Muthiyas got harder and harder. Picking up the phone, I felt the weight of Peter's hope in his son's future and his faith in me. Lucky for me, he remained his usual calm, philosophical self. "Some things are hard, Jayme. Just keep pressing forward." We both were determined. Though his blood pressure seemed much lower than mine.

My conversations with Madalitso were far less frequent, mainly because Peter had the family's only cell phone. When we did speak, Madalitso never projected one iota of nervousness or frustration over my complete failure to find him a golf scholarship.

I was relieved, because most schools had zero interest in him. Most, but not all.

Six schools were in the running. Or rather, they didn't laugh in my ear and hang up. The best I got was a mild level of curiosity after viewing the videotape and written materials.

But there was one caveat: they needed to see him play. In a tournament. In the U.S.

Every time I heard that, my guts plummeted. Just thinking about the logistics made my brain hurt. I tried thinking of creative ways to get around it. But every coach who was even vaguely interested insisted on seeing Madalitso play in person. And they certainly weren't traveling to Zambia.

Fortunately, the Zambian Government had no objection to Mad traveling to America and was nice enough not to ask why I couldn't persuade coaches on my own.

There were lots of tournaments run by the American Junior Golf Association (AJGA). But the AJGA required membership in their organization *and* an entry fee into the specific tournament. I saw the price tag and almost swallowed my tongue. Yet another barrier to high-level golf that kept poor kids out.

Then there were passports and entry visas. Peter and Madalitso had traveled internationally before, so that seemed doable. Finally, there were airplane tickets, hotels, food and incidental expenses. This would be an expensive endeavor.

But I had bigger worries. Let's say I found a tournament for Mad, made all the arrangements and got the coaches to show up. What if Madalitso flew 10,000 miles *and didn't play well*? Everybody has bad days. What if the golf gods frowned upon us, and this was Madalitso's bad day? Coaches offer scholarships after watching athletes many times over a period of months, sometimes years. Madalitso would have *one* shot. *One* tournament.

With the clock ticking, the pressure mounting and so many mountains to move, I found myself thinking of the Muthiya family's journey. Colonialism stole their culture, language and land and forced them into a shantytown next to a lead mine where Peter was born. From his fascination with golf and his unlikely rise through Zambia's missionary schools, to Madalitso's emergence as a national figure, each chapter gave me faith and inspiration. If they could overcome so much, maybe I could, too.

These were inspiring stories of a family I hardly knew. They had nothing to do with me.

But as the obstacles mounted, I realized that I was now a character in their story. Madalitso had chosen a path for his future, and Peter and President Chiluba had somehow chosen me to help deliver their dream. The five-year-old boy in the mud hut and the six-year-old boy who broke his parents' window were no longer just tales I'd heard. The Muthiyas were part of me, and I was part of them.

The next chapter of this family had begun, and they were relying on me to help write it.

Each day, my mood was heavier.

THE NOLAN HENKE/PATTY Berg Junior Masters in Fort Myers, Florida. After months of research and wrangling, phone calls and internet searches, that seemed to be the best we were going to do. It was a three-day, fifty-four-hole event, named after ex–PGA professional Nolan Henke and the late Hall-of-Famer Patty Berg, a winner of fifteen majors and a founding member of LPGA.

That was basically all I got from the internet. I couldn't tell if the tournament was run by experienced professional officials. Was it a serious, well-regarded competition with talented juniors or just a fun event for kids? Madalitso would *not* travel all the way from Africa for a tournament that was merely an opportunity for rich kids to get participation trophies while their parents snapped photographs for the mantel.

I finally got tournament director Jeanne Rubado on the phone. She convinced me the Henke-Berg was indeed a respected, legitimate competition. When I explained the situation, I was delighted to hear her say that a player traveling all the way from Zambia—particularly one with Madalitso's résumé—would in fact bolster the image of the Henke-Berg.

I expected Peter to be excited. I was disappointed. As always, he took the news in stride. It was "just another step in the process." Reflecting on the long trip ahead, all the arrangements and the pressure of the tournament, he simply remarked that "nothing worthwhile is easy."

After I got over myself, I understood that Peter's way was better than my way. He never got too high and never got too low. It was a revelation. All I had to do was not stop. Keep doing what I was doing. Just focus on what I needed to do.

Peter then, matter-of-factly, delivered some great and unexpected news. "I am coming to Florida with Madalitso."

A huge smile came across my face. "That's great, Peter! It will be so good to see you!"

So much had happened since our first meetings in Lusaka. For months, we shared the highs and lows of pursuing a new future for Madalitso and the Muthiya family. And in revealing the personal stories of our lives, we'd become companions on a deeply personal journey that was changing both of us. Somewhere along the way, I started to believe that Madalitso earning a scholarship would be one of the most worthwhile things I would ever do. Over the past seven months, I'd become emotionally invested in this project and in them.

And now, Peter and Madalitso were coming to the United States. I couldn't wait to see them.

THAT WAS THE easy part. Now came the real work: convincing cynical, skeptical, overworked, in-high-demand college coaches to fly to Fort Myers to see some kid they never heard of from some place they didn't even know existed. A little part of me died when I found out that the Henke-Berg was overlapping with a big AJGA tournament that many coaches seemed to be attending. Every coach told me point-blank that I was forcing them to make an impossible choice. Watch 100 of the best young golfers in America. Or come see this Madalooctoe Moothalleessum, or whatever his name was.

My response was rooted in a basic sales technique. Exclusivity. They could see every player at the AJGA event again. But this was a once-in-a-lifetime opportunity. The Henke-Berg was their *only* chance to see Mad-a-lit-so Mu-thi-ya.

After a few days of heavy lobbying and many nervous minutes by the phone, we had our list. Joining Peter, Madalitso and me in Fort Myers were coaches from New Mexico, Florida, Florida State and the University of Washington. The head coach at Stanford sent a former player who lived in the area. University of Virginia's head coach was unable to attend but asked for daily updates.

All of the arrangements were made. Only one small detail remained.

Madalitso had to play.

20

THE 1999 HENKE-BERG WOULD BEGIN on Wednesday, August 4. Peter and Madalitso arrived in Fort Myers a few days early so Madalitso could practice on this new (to him) course and acclimate to the time change and weather. Contrary to popular belief, all of Africa is not a perpetual steam bath. Lusaka is dry and arid with a temperature that rarely reaches ninety degrees Fahrenheit. The August heat and humidity of Fort Myers was familiar to players from Florida and other southeastern states. For outsiders, the brutal sun and the strength-sapping humidity at the Henke-Berg would be a severe test.

"HAVE YOU SEEN two Africans, a father and son?" I asked the concierge at our hotel when I arrived on Monday night.

Her eyes widened and a big smile took over her face. "Peter and Madalitso?"

I chuckled. I should have known. They'd already charmed everyone here. "Uhh...yes."

"Well, sure. They're big celebrities around here. Everybody knows them." I thanked her with a laugh, walked to my room and dialed Peter's room.

"Welcome to America!" I proclaimed with my best red, white and blue enthusiasm.

"Welcome to Fort Myers," he replied with dry African drollness.

I burst out laughing. I was so happy to hear his voice, knowing he was now minutes away instead of continents.

We made plans to have dinner together.

I wondered how the three of us would react to seeing each other again. Our last face-to-face meeting was over a few beers in a hotel bar and a reluctant agreement to work together. Considering all that had happened since then, I hoped there would be no awkwardness.

"Jayme!" Peter called out with obvious glee when he saw me. "So good to see you!"

"Hi, Peter." I gave him an ear-to-ear grin. "Man, it's great seeing you! Hey, Madalitso!"

Madalitso let out a little laugh. "Hi, Jayme, good to see you too."

Smiles, warm handshakes and happy conversation of old friends followed. The new relationship forged through months of phone conversations clearly translated to real life in real time.

We woke up on Tuesday, ate a hearty American breakfast and headed to Cypress Lake for Madalitso's practice round. An official informed us that recent torrential rains had saturated the course. All practice rounds were canceled.

What?! Why were the golf gods raining on our parade (literally) after all we'd sacrificed to them?! This was Madalitso's one chance to get to know the course before the tournament. Many fellow competitors had played Cypress Lake, some several times.

I was stymied. But before I could even think of what to say, Peter stepped up. "Can we borrow a golf cart?"

Peter was given a key, and he and Madalitso jumped in. "Jayme, we'll be back."

Father and son sped off to do what they'd been doing Madalitso's whole life. They were going to talk golf. They would take all their years of reading, watching tape, discussing strategy and playing all over Zambia to design a game plan for attacking a course they'd never seen.

That evening, Peter and I waited outside of a players' meeting. When all of the young golfers from all over the region burst into the hall, Madalitso clearly stood out. Peter let out a quiet laugh.

"What is it?" I asked.

"Well, at so many events, my son is the only Black boy in the field."

I just smiled, unable to think of anything to say.

Peter may have laughed at the sight of Madalitso sticking out like the beautiful black onyx in a sea of white pearls, but his smile was a mask that hid his true feelings. Seeing his son standing with all these post-colonial White boys was a reminder of the centuries of cruel, brutal oppression and injustice that had led him and his prodigy son here to the heart of White privilege built on the blood and bones of their ancestors.

But there was more than that in Peter's smile. He was a competitor. He had fought his whole life against a system that didn't want him to get an education and achieve a decent life for his family. That was why he was standing at a golf club in Florida ready to watch his Black son play in arguably the Whitest, richest sport in the world. His smile said, *My son may be the only Black kid in the field. His equipment and training may be less than the others. But he belongs here. Let's just see what happens.*

For Madalitso, this was business as usual. Playing in England at the World Junior Championship had opened his eyes to see the White world of high-end golf, who plays it and why. At the Henke-Berg, he knew he was walking into a realm unlike anything in Zambia. He felt eyes on him. He heard whispers and caught suspicious stares at his shoddy shoes and cut-rate clubs. Did this mean they did *not* see him as one of them? That he did *not* belong? Yes, the boys he met seemed friendly and welcoming, but it was clear that he was the oddity, the misfit, the less-than.

Madalitso took a deep breath and told himself that these feelings of being on the outside looking in were only natural. And that they would only hold him back. If he bought into this fallacy, he would prove them right.

He knew in his heart that the quality of his clubs, shoes and instruction was irrelevant. Madalitso once again channeled the voice of his father. *If you are there and they are there, you both belong.*

In his mind's eye, he saw his Grandma Kaliwé, again imploring him to believe in himself, that all he had to do was hunker down and focus on what he needed to do.

He was getting used to this. Playing against grown men in Zambia, two international tournaments in England, a week at a golf academy in Florida, competing against seasoned professionals at the Zambia Open—all were important stages of development. All made him feel out of place. And all were moments that Peter had a hand in orchestrating. As awkward and painful as they were, each played a role in preparing him for this. The most important tournament of his life.

We ate dinner and returned to the hotel early. It would be a long three days.

That night, I tossed and turned in my bed, thinking about the tournament and Madalitso. Peter had assured me in Lusaka that his son was good. Madalitso's list of accomplishments was impressive. But trophies and news stories were not enough. I tried to visualize him ripping great tee shots, making long putts, the crowd going crazy for the new kid from Africa. But I also imagined Mad shanking tee shots, fluffing irons and putting like a kid with bad equipment, used shoes and no training.

I wasn't quite as bad as the college coaches. But I needed to see it for myself.

THE ALARM SOUNDED while it was still dark on Wednesday morning. We got to Cypress Lake before 7 a.m. so Madalitso could go through his typical warm-up. He hauled his clubs and shoes from the trunk, and we headed toward the practice area.

Peter turned into the clubhouse with a restaurant and bar, glancing quickly at me over his shoulder as he said: "See you in a while." It was my first time watching Madalitso compete, and I was completely unaware of their pre-tournament routine. I was confused. Peter, of course, believed that practice was their time together on the golf course. To teach. To strategize. To prepare. But Peter wanted Madalitso to stand alone on the course and rely on himself. Because someday that's the reality he'd face, both on the golf course and in life. It didn't matter that this was the most important tournament of his life. Peter was not about to change their proven formula. I paused, puzzled, just long enough to watch him disappear through the doorway. Then, I followed Madalitso to the driving range.

I stood with other spectators, recruiters, college coaches, parents, personal coaches and what seemed to be an odd sports psychologist as Madalitso found a vacant tee box. He set down his bag all by himself and changed into his golf shoes. He didn't look like the greatest young golfer Zambia had ever produced. He looked like a kid who didn't have enough money for nice new golf shoes, getting ready to play an early-bird special because he couldn't afford to play in prime time when the rates were higher.

I looked up and down the driving range. TITLEIST, TAYLORMADE, and CALLAWAY logos were stitched boldly onto big, shiny and glossy bags. And emerging majestically from the top of each bag was a matching set of new(ish), state-of-the-art clubs.

Madalitso's bag was ancient and tiny compared to those monoliths. The leather was worn, the shoulder straps were frayed at the edges and every club he pulled from his bag seemed to be a different brand, design or color than the one he put back. It was obviously a patchwork set pieced together over time. If it were a horse, they would put it out of its misery.

His shoes completed the picture. Cracks and deep creases marred the leather. The heels were worn, and in some places, it looked as if the sole was breaking away from the shoe. I wouldn't have been surprised if one of his toes suddenly poked out.

Other boys were decked out in the highest, finest, latest in golf fashion. Well-fitted shirts, creased new trousers and freshly shined golf shoes. I watched them warm up, chat with their parents and peers or confer with what appeared to be their private coaches surrounded by their top-of-the-line drivers and sparkling irons. They looked like they'd stepped out of a catalogue.

They stood a few feet from Madalitso, but their worlds could not be more different. These well-to-do lads had never faced down flesh-eating ants or coiled cobras on the golf course! They'd never had to make their own clubs, fix broken-down drivers or cobble together sets from the used equipment bin. They'd never been the only White boy in a locker room full of Black faces.

Madalitso was his usual meticulous, methodical, unflappable self. As he hit his first ball, I was approached by two men wearing golf shirts with university logos blazoned across the breast. I introduced myself to the coaches and thanked them for coming. No comments about Madalitso's equipment were made. But how could they not have noticed that Mad was playing with a set of clubs that looked like it was put together for a kid whose parents meant well but didn't have two nickels to rub together?

Madalitso was at the beginning of the most intense three-day trial of his life. Everything about him would be scrutinized and analyzed by men who could turn the dream of a college scholarship into a reality with the snap of their fingers. And of course, they were evaluating every other player too, trying to fill one of those precious slots that are always given to kids with shiny logos on their bags.

But for these kids, this tournament wasn't their one and only hope for attending college. I could practically see the expensive price tags on their outfits, their custom-fitted clubs and the late-model SUVs and sedans they climbed out of in the parking lot.

Madalitso was different. Ever since he'd watched the NCAA Championship on television as a kid in Zambia, it had been his goal, his driving force, to attend college in the United States and play golf. Now it all came down to one shot. One tournament. Three rounds of golf to convince a coach he'd never met that he was worthy of a precious scholarship. If he failed, his quest would be over, and he would be forced to return with his tail between his legs to Zambia. And figure out a Plan B for the rest of his life.

It was unimaginable pressure.

Later when I asked Madalitso how he handled it, he said he heard his father's voice: *Don't worry. Just focus on what you need to do. The next shot.*

Madalitso unleashed his smooth effortless swing, and the club hit the ball with a louder *THWACK!* than those of the other boys hitting their warm-up drives. And Mad's balls shot off the club faster, flew higher, longer and farther than any other player near him on the range, all the more surprising in that it erupted from such a small, unassuming cannon.

Suddenly, no one seemed to care what kind of clubs Madalitso was using when they saw him pummel the driving range balls into submission.

I looked over at the coaches beside me. They had gone from polite to surprised and impressed. As they often did wherever Mad played, spectators, admirers and even a few other coaches and players quickly migrated over to see the visitor from Africa punish golf balls. I didn't know it at the time, but word had already spread about the kid from Zambia. He was rapidly becoming the talk of the tournament.

I looked for Peter to share my excitement. But he was nowhere in sight. Leaving the course to search for him was not an option. I was host to a handful of collegiate golf coaches, most of whom were peppering me with questions about Madalitso. They all wanted to know about his background, high school grade point average and his character, trying to decide if he was worth a scholarship valued at thousands of dollars, not to mention the valuable assets and time that would be poured into these young men. Would Madalitso Muthiya be worth it? Would he represent their institution well? Would he help bring conference championships to their school? My job was to woo these coaches and report back to Peter and President Chiluba, who were waiting with bated breath to see if their dreams and ambitions would come to fruition.

As Madalitso made his way from the driving range to the practice green, I spotted the remaining coaches who'd told me they were going to be there. Thankfully, all were present and accounted for. One by one, I shook their hands and offered to answer any questions. They were all quite polite, but at this point, there was nothing to say. They already knew everything I could tell them about Madalitso. He looked good on the driving range. But lots of people look good on the driving range and have no idea how to win a golf tournament. They needed to see him play.

I wanted them to meet Peter, but there was a problem: still no sign of him.

Finally, it was time for Madalitso's group to gather at the first tee. The threesome shook hands and introduced themselves. The other two boys kept chatting while Madalitso moved away. He took some casual half swings and then paused, quiet and expressionless.

This is it, Madalitso said to himself. He took a moment at the tee box to breathe it all in. This was the fruit of thousands of practice sessions with his dad, hours watching and rewatching videos of PGA players and rushing outside to imitate them. Years of dull, endless travel on sparsely paved roads to slog his way through rinky-dink tournaments nobody here had heard of, in a country few of them could find on a map, brought him to this place. He told President Chiluba that he wanted this opportunity. He and his father put their faith in an American man they'd never met, just to get here, to get his one chance.

He quickly shut all that down. It was too big, too heavy, too much to process. He had to be loose, relaxed, like he was the nothing-to-lose kid playing in the hard-scrabbled backyard back home. Now more than ever, he needed all of his focus. All of his heart, body and soul. All of his energy needed to be geared toward one thing: *This shot. Nothing else. This shot.*

The first hole at Cypress Lake was a short par 4. As the preceding group reached the putting green, Madalitso's trio prepared for their opening drives. I scanned the area as Madalitso knelt over to insert his tee into the ground. For weeks, I'd looked forward to walking the course with Peter. So much depended on these three days it seemed only fitting that we experience the ups and downs together. He wasn't there, and I was disappointed. But by now I knew him. There had to be a good reason, so I focused on watching Madalitso and speaking with the coaches.

Madalitso's drive was effortless, long and true, easily outdistancing the others in his group. It landed in the fairway with a clear line to the flag. The bad news was that because the course was waterlogged, his ball torpedoed into the ground and submerged under two inches of mud.

It was an impossible lie. Again, it seemed like the golf gods were betraying us after we gave them so much.

Madalitso summoned an official. I stared anxiously as the man closely examined the ball. Madalitso's calm demeanor never changed. From the time he discovered his unplayable lie, through the seemingly endless analysis of ball and mud, he showed no angst or frustration. Nothing. Finally, the official determined that the ball could be lifted, cleaned and dropped without penalty.

Thank you, golf gods.

Madalitso drilled his next shot to the edge of the green, giving himself a good chance at birdie. He made a nice stroke, but his putt stopped just short of the hole. A tap-in par.

The perfect way to start the tournament that will determine the rest of your life.

One hole was all it took for me to forget Madalitso's shoddy equipment, lack of professional training and litany of disadvantages that I dwelled on far too much. His beautiful smooth swing, careful attention to form and calm, measured maturity told me all I needed to know.

For the other players, the 1999 Henke-Berg was an opportunity to compete and improve their golf games. For Madalitso, these three days would determine whether he went back to Africa or started a whole new life on a whole new continent.

You would have never known it by looking at his face.

"PETER CAME TO see how his son is doing. I'm here because somebody said there was whiskey on the course," Doc, an old grizzled man, announced as he pulled up in a golf cart with Peter riding shotgun. Madalitso's group was waiting to tee off at the tenth hole. It was the first I'd seen of Peter since he'd ducked out before Mad started warming up. At this point, I was way beyond being shocked by anything.

I introduced Peter to a couple of coaches. They shook his hand, praised Madalitso and complimented him on teaching the sport to his son.

I expected Peter, a textbook extrovert, to schmooze with his usual charm. But he seemed slightly uncomfortable. When the boys finally teed off, Peter and Doc disappeared.

As the day wore on, Madalitso outperformed the others in his group. His ball stayed on the fairway, his approach shots were well placed, his putting was good and his long drives sparked reactions from onlookers. He was settling in.

Madalitso's confidence increased with the temperature. The thermometer hovered around ninety degrees, and the humidity level was well over ninety percent. All of the players were guzzling water and sweating through their shirts. The sunscreen I applied in the morning was washed away by perspiration.

Madalitso was feeling the heat like everyone else, but outwardly, he seemed his usual cool-customer self. He was used to the heat. Literal and metaphorical.

The twelfth hole at Cypress Lake is a straight ahead 421-yard par 4 with water lining the final 100–150 yards on the left side. Seemed an ideal time for Madalitso to launch a rocket that would leave him an easy approach and a good shot at a bird.

But his swing had less speed and force than usual. The ball landed in a safe spot on the right side of fairway, protected from the water and with a clear view of the green. But it was no longer a pitch and a putt. It was more a full-blooded high iron, a more difficult shot.

Mad calmly grabbed an iron and took a nonchalant swing (even for him). The ball landed far away from trouble, but also well away from the flag.

Mad was playing it safe. But safe doesn't often win tournaments. Safe isn't what got him here.

Two putts later, Madalitso achieved par in what was obviously a textbook approach to a par 4 with a large water hazard. As he picked up his ball, my initial reaction was that this was a lost opportunity. But I quickly reminded myself that Madalitso knew far more about golf than me.

At the end of the first round, Madalitso learned he was in a dog fight. The tournament leader was a boy named Keith Harris, followed by Madalitso and another player named Brandon Smith—a three-man race.

BACK AT THE hotel, Madalitso and I jumped right into the pool. After a day in extreme heat and humidity, it was a glorious relief. We cooled off together. I was excited to get to know Mad better, to scratch the surface of this amazing enigma.

"So, does it ever get this hot in Zambia?" I asked him.

"No, never. People think Zambia gets hot because it's in Africa, but it never gets this hot."

Silence.

"What are you thinking about studying in college?"

"Probably economics. Business really interests me."

Silence.

"Besides golf, are there any sports you like watching on television?"

"Well, I don't really watch football, I mean American football or baseball. I like soccer and basketball," he replied.

His short answers and shy face were far different from my exchanges with his outgoing father. But I knew he was shy, and I didn't mind being the instigator. "You could have a second career playing poker," I ribbed him.

Peter laughed, relaxing on a lounge chair by the pool. He watched his son flail around in the deep end. "My son, you are a far better golfer than a swimmer!"

We joined Peter at a poolside bar, the Cabana. This would become our after-hours hangout. Peter and I would slowly turn one beer into two, then three. I was fourteen years older than Madalitso and eighteen years younger than Peter. So Madalitso and I talked about golf, girls and music, while my conversations with Peter often centered around politics or world affairs. When we got deep into the weeds of some thorny political discussion, Mad would lose interest and head back to his hotel room.

More comfortable with Peter and feeling the effects of a few beers, I asked the question that had been nagging me all day. "Peter, today I was hoping you would spend time speaking with the coaches and walking the course with them. I know Madalitso, but you can speak to his game far better than me. Where were you?"

I sensed Peter didn't appreciate the question. Slowly, he explained that their golf time was the hours of practice and breaking down PGA events on TV. The tournaments were where Madalitso had to stand by himself. To solve problems on his own—when to use a seven-iron and when to use a wedge. How to dig himself out of a bunker or from behind a tree. Peter would not always be there to help him, especially when Madalitso went away to college. Peter's philosophy was about more than golf. It was about life. He had always believed that self-sufficiency and the ability to solve his own problems would make Mad the master of his own destiny.

"Okay, Peter," I responded with a shrug.

Peter set down his beer and stared into my eyes. "Jayme, this is our routine. It works. It's been working for years. I will meet the coaches you invited. Don't worry." Then he raised an eyebrow and asked, "Look, is it more important that I socialize with coaches or that Madalitso win this tournament?"

Point taken, I shut up.

Those few days in Fort Myers brought us closer together and solidified the familial connection and bond we were forging.

Although we traveled here so Madalitso could play in a golf tournament, our evenings at the pool and Cabana are still my favorite memories of the trip.

THE SECOND ROUND mirrored the first. Madalitso struck the ball very well, but played carefully, avoiding harmful mistakes. There was lots of water on the course, and Madalitso took no unnecessary chances, meticulously analyzing every shot.

It was safe. But it was *too* safe. As I watched Madalitso compete on day two, I sensed a great deal of caution. Like he was playing not to lose. Instead of playing to win.

Temperatures approached ninety degrees with humidity levels at ninety-six percent. I was wilting, but Madalitso said nothing. But when the sun reached its peak, he started walking down the fairway with a wet towel draped over his head.

Peter made another impromptu appearance with Doc, who provided some comic relief for players and parents dealing with the sweltering heat: "Okay, which one of y'all has the booze?"

Madalitso reached the par 5 fourteenth hole, a 530-yard dogleg right. This was definitely the time for a classic Madalitso grip 'n' rip. To outdrive his opponents. To *finally* be aggressive.

The fourteenth is dissected by a creek as the fairway turns right toward the hole. Considering Madalitso's distance off the tee, he'd have no problem cutting the dogleg past the creek and landing within easy striking distance of the green. An excellent birdie opportunity. Maybe even an eagle.

Clutching his driver, Madalitso stared down the fairway while wiping the grip free of perspiration. In Zambia, he cut doglegs like this routinely, risking his ball landing in water, next to a ravenous band of ants. Or worse. But his mammoth driving distance made these shots almost routine.

There is so much riding on this tournament, he thought to himself. *What is the wisest course of action?*

Finally, he made his decision, stepped up and swung. But his swing seemed restrained. The ball flew straight down the fairway, rather than soaring over the trees and rough. Over 200 yards later, it came to rest just before the creek. Again, no risk. But no reward.

Madalitso ignored the few people who clapped. He didn't think the shot was anything to be proud of. He masked his emotions well, but if you knew what you were looking for, you could see disappointment and frustration etched on his face.

Rather than reach the green on his next shot, he chose to lay up short. His ball landed just in front of two bunkers guarding the right and left side. One chip shot and two putts later, he tapped in for par. Ho hum.

At the end of round two, Madalitso was still in second place, behind Keith Harris. The second day of the Henke-Berg was eerily similar to the first. I found myself waiting for something to happen. I wasn't alone.

Driving back to the hotel, Peter broke the silence. "So, how did it go out there?"

"Fine."

Peter let Madalitso's nonchalant tone hang in the air for a few seconds.

"Fine?" Peter's voice rose slightly at the end, framing his comment as a question and invoking a tone that almost suggested Madalitso's answer was lame. "Well, okay."

More silence.

"I hit good shots and managed to avoid mistakes. I could've been more aggressive, but decided to play it smart."

Silence. Peter was letting Madalitso hear and process his own words.

"Tomorrow I might do things a little differently."

"Sure. When in doubt, go for the pin."

I didn't quite understand it at the time, but looking back, I realize it was kind of a lesson in Parenting 101. Don't tell the kids what to do. Especially a teenager. Peter broke it all down for me later. "Force-feeding sixteen-year-olds doesn't always work. It's better to give some subtle guidance, let them reach a conclusion on their own, then make their plan accordingly."

That evening, we relaxed in the pool and Cabana bar. We engaged in idle chitchat, avoiding the foremost issue on our minds. Madalitso was playing well but had not distinguished himself. Tomorrow, he had one round to do it. Eighteen holes.

DAY THREE. FINAL eighteen holes. Make or break time for Madalitso.

That's what was going through my head anyway. Mad was his usual same-old, same-old self. It was reassuring. And slightly maddening. The only surprise was my companion: Peter. He decided to walk the final round with me. I tried to suppress my nerves so he wouldn't regret his decision.

Madalitso was grouped with Keith Harris and Brandon Smith. The top three scorers of the tournament thus far. All three started off playing well. Jeanne Rubado was right. Madalitso was not the only talented player in this tournament.

The players were on the fourth hole when the tense status quo was finally disrupted.

The blue sky was being covered by dark, fast-moving clouds. The light quickly disappeared, almost as if it were sunset. Everyone had one eye on the golf course and one on the sky.

The rain started falling just as the players reached the fourth green. The first drops were sporadic, but heavy and fat. By the time Madalitso and the others finished and walked to the fifth tee, the skies opened. It was a deluge, with a strong wind whipping right to left.

Peter and I huddled under an umbrella. Players, parents and tournament officials scrambled for cover. But it didn't matter. Everyone and everything was getting drenched. Eventually, every person was crouched under something.

Except one.

Madalitso stood upright in the tee box, club in hand, ball resting on the tee. As he stared down the fifth fairway, a short par 3, chest out and chin raised, it was clear that he was *not* waiting for the weather to pass. He was ready to tee off, stinging rain, high winds or hurricanes be damned.

Fearing disaster, I whispered to Peter. "What is he doing? The official will surely let him wait until things calm down..."

Without saying a word, Peter raised his hand to signal that he knew what I was thinking.

As Madalitso moved toward the ball, something else joined the rain and wind.

Thunder.

Please. Not this.

Tournament officials, particularly at the junior level, will postpone or cancel an event without hesitating if there's even the *slightest* danger to players.

But Madalitso knew he was in second place, so play *must* continue if he wanted any chance to win. Ending the tournament now would draw some pats on the back, but a full athletic scholarship? No way.

No tournament officials appeared, so Madalitso took a couple of mock swings. Battered by Biblical rain and wind, he found the proper grip and stepped to the tee. Expressionless, he extended his arms and club to the ball to ensure proper distance.

The only sounds were rain splattering on the earth, wind howling through the trees, the distant clapping of thunder and the internal pounding of my heart.

Madalitso's backswing and follow-through was powerful and smooth as usual. The ball launched upward and slightly to the right. But it immediately disappeared into the thunderstorm. Unable to track its flight, I looked toward the green. Time stood still as my stomach churned, and my brain visualized the ball landing in rough, in water, in TROUBLE!

Come on...where is it?!

Finally, out of the windswept tempest of a sky, the ball dropped slowly onto the green.

It stopped less than two feet from the cup.

My mouth dropped open as wild applause erupted all around us from the shocked, soaked onlookers. I leaned close to Peter, and over the wind, I said, "Go for the pin, eh?"

He just smiled.

It was only the fifth hole, but the 1999 Henke-Berg was over.

Madalitso tapped in for birdie. One of the other boys bogeyed the hole. The other lost his ball and took a penalty.

With one gutsy, impossible, dramatic shot, Madalitso had finally stopped constraining himself and broken free.

At the sixth tee, the wind stopped, and the sun peeked through the dispersing clouds.

Maybe the golf gods were smiling on him after all.

WHILE THE TOURNAMENT rolled toward its climax and the holes disappeared in the rearview mirror, the players were bathed in sweat and drenched after the deluge as tension ratcheted and nerves frayed. After hitting an errant shot, one of the other boys slammed his club on the ground and dropped an F-bomb. Peter turned toward me, shaking his head. "If that were my son, this tournament would be finished. I would take his clubs away."

Madalitso put on a clinic. He was a technician around the greens, showing you didn't need fancy clubs or expensive coaching to be a champion-caliber golfer. His long drives continued to draw oohs, ahhs and raucous applause.

The large crowd went nuts when he sank his final putt on the eighteenth hole. Just three hours earlier, he was languishing in second place before his now legendary shot into the storm on the fifth tee produced a dramatic turnaround. The final leaderboard was posted.

Madalitso won by six shots.

Ever gracious, he shook hands with Brandon Smith and Keith Harris, gathered his clubs and approached Peter. The two shook hands, Peter's left arm warmly grasping Madalitso's shoulder. It was the closest they'd come to a hug. In public anyway.

After watching Madalitso rise up in the face of life-altering pressure under the glare of coaches who held his dreams in their hands in a foreign country that has produced the greatest golfers the world has ever known and storms that would make even Noah seasick, I couldn't believe I'd actually questioned how good Madalitso really was. His performance was mind-boggling. Even a novice could see that Mad was not just an excellent player with uncommon talent.

Madalitso Muthiya was a champion.

The final leaderboard was a brief headline. The real story was that a sixteen-year-old from one of the poorest countries in the world flew to a strange place halfway around the world to take on players with vastly superior resources, equipment and training. While carrying the pressures of his future, his family and his country on his skinny shoulders.

One by one, the coaches congratulated Peter and expressed how impressed they were with Madalitso.

A few of them wanted a private word with Peter, Madalitso and me. They were encouraging, which was great. But they were vague, which was infuriating.

"Scholarships are scarce." "We have to crunch numbers to determine availability." "We'll definitely be in touch."

Pretty words, but nothing else.

Of course, we wanted an offer. But we certainly weren't discouraged. We were ecstatic over Madalitso's victory and satisfied that we'd done everything we could. Peter smiled. "The rest is in God's hands."

I agreed. His proclivity for taking things in stride was contagious. I had a faith I'd never had before. I owed it all to Peter. And Mad.

Glen Millican, the assistant coach at the University of New Mexico, made a real impression on father and son. Glen had a straightforward, no-nonsense delivery. During an era when college coaches were increasingly obsessed with "connecting" with young athletes, he didn't try too hard to be cool. On the contrary, he showed a keen sense of his audience, referring to Peter as "Mr. Muthiya" and frequently using "sir" when answering questions. Glen fit right in with the African tradition of showing respect to elders and valuing polite, civil discourse.

Nolan Henke and Patty Berg were guests of honor at the awards ceremony. All of the boys took photos with them. Madalitso received a trophy to wide applause along with words of congratulations from the other players. A smile and a "thank you" was his only response.

WE CELEBRATED BY partying our final night away at the pool. Madalitso was beyond exhausted from three tension-packed days of golf and enduring inhuman humidity, so he started fading pretty quickly and excused himself so he could pass out in his room. Peter and I moved to our old haunt, the Cabana, to rehash the tournament over many beers.

For the next couple hours, we laughed and talked over each other, reminiscing about everything from the fancy golf bags, to the Alpha-male coaches, to the sick heat, to the madness of the sudden thunderstorm.

"Peter," I asked, "how were you so relaxed at the fifth hole when Madalitso teed off into the rain and wind?!"

He just shrugged his shoulders and smiled. "Well, I had a feeling the boy knew what he was doing. But I thought you might need CPR, Jayme."

After surviving the battles of our first tournament together, I mustered the courage to share something I'd been meaning to tell him. "Peter, I want you to know that I admire you for the challenges you've faced and your many achievements. And I appreciate you sharing your stories with me. It's a pleasure knowing you."

"Thank you, Jayme. And I know that you struggle to talk about your dad, to share your life story. For an adolescent boy, a father's guidance is irreplaceable."

I avoided his eyes and stared down into my beer.

"Well, Peter, my mom has been great. She had to be mother and father. I wouldn't be where I am without her."

"Of course. But a father helps his son grow from boy to man by sharing his own life experiences."

"Peter, remember when you described your feelings after your parents died...that you could keep them alive if you followed their example?"

"Yes."

"Well," I said, still struggling to look at him, "sometimes I think about that."

Leaning forward in his chair, Peter tried making eye contact with me. "Jayme, you don't have to worry. I am a father. I have sons. Trust me—from what I have seen, you don't have to worry."

"Thank you."

For seven months, we'd been sharing our most personal, and often the most difficult stories. It was an exhausting internal battle, and I often struggled to get the words out. But I'd never asked for Peter's thoughts or opinions on what I revealed. Until now. Part of me was shocked to hear the words coming from my own mouth. But it was also a great relief. Like releasing a pressure cooker. Now it was clear what allowed me to do what I'd needed to do for so long. Our close friendship and my deep respect for this remarkable man.

Peter smiled and took a sip of beer as we relished the warm silence only true friends can share.

"So, Jayme, are you getting there?" Peter's eyes fixed on me.

Again, he managed to catch me off guard. Of course, I knew what he was talking about; it was our old tug-of-war. My ignorance of the history of Africans and golf.

I sighed, swallowed my beer with a smile and avoided his stare. "Peter, I have done no reading on the history of Africans or golf. Both sound interesting, but I just have not taken the time."

"But you have spent time learning about my life and Madalitso's life."

"Yes, I think everything you shared with me about your life, your interest in golf and Madalitso's success, it's fascinating and inspiring. I think a lot of people would enjoy it, particularly if Madalitso does something special in this sport."

Peter stared at me for a long moment. "I've been thinking about your interest in Madalitso and me...and golf. This whole thing. If Madalitso were to do something memorable—reach some new height or whatever—I don't know whether people would be interested. But what I do know is that a person cannot fully appreciate the significance an event, *any* event, unless he knows *why* it is significant. What has happened through the course of history that makes this event meaningful?" He paused and looked at me to make sure his words were sinking in.

I mostly agreed with him, but not completely. Peter's and Madalitso's lives can be appreciated without delving too much into the past. Was an understanding of African history and golf history *really* necessary? Africans are poor, and golf requires money. Was there much more to it?

He read my expression and seemed to know what I was thinking. *I had forever to do this. What's the rush? There would be time.*

"Jayme, understanding people is no different. To fully know a person, you need knowledge of his experiences. What he has been through. And a meaningful event cannot be fully appreciated by its witnesses unless they understand how history molded the institutions and players involved. This includes how history shaped people's views."

I said nothing.

He took another drink and smiled.

"Besides, I think you'd enjoy the reading, and I'd enjoy the discussion... once *you're there*."

21

EXCITEMENT KEPT ME AWAKE THAT night as the next morning Peter and Madalitso were flying with me to my hometown, Seattle. For months, my folks had listened to stories about the Zambian boy and his father, the strange and fateful assignment from President Chiluba, my fervent search for a scholarship and the crucial, impossible mission to Fort Myers. My mom had been on edge throughout the Henke-Berg. Picturing my birth family meeting my two new chosen family members filled me with joy.

My folks live in Mukilteo, a suburb outside Seattle, and run our restaurant, Charles at Smugglers Cove. My mom, Janet, manages the dining room. My stepfather, Claude, is the finest French chef in the Pacific Northwest.

After handshakes and introductions, there were smiles, laughter and lots of storytelling. My girlfriend joined us that evening as Claude prepared his usual *coup de maître*. Together, we sat on the second floor of Charles and enjoyed each other's company while the sun set majestically over Puget Sound.

We had a fantastic time showing Peter and Madalitso around Seattle. Peter was curious as always. He wanted to know about Seattle's history and was probably frustrated that I knew too little about my own birthplace. Madalitso eyed the skyscrapers and found the hip-hop stations on our car radio. We walked through Pike Place Market, though neither of them showed interest in tossing fish.

We took in a Mariners-Yankees game. New York beat Seattle 9–3 as Peter struggled to follow the action, and I tried in vain to explain the rules of baseball. I chuckled when he offered his expert analysis: "It has become clear to me that the boys from New York are more proficient at striking the ball than the Seattle club."

On Peter and Madalitso's last night, Claude prepared a five-course extravaganza at our home with some of our closest friends. Peter told a story that still makes us laugh. It began with Peter playing a round of golf one afternoon in Zambia with a friend.

"In the middle of the round, we walked onto a green. Coiled on one side of the hole was a cobra. I told my friend, 'That is it for me,' and I started walking away.

"'Wait,' said my friend. He approached the cobra, which stood up and spread its hood, ready to strike. My friend calmly leaned over and spat in the cobra's face. Startled, the cobra crawled away.

"Sometime later, the two of us were golfing with another man when *again* we found a cobra sunning itself on a green. We told our guest what happened before, and he insisted that he could perform the same trick as my friend. Despite our warnings, he was determined to try.

"The man set down his clubs and approached. As he leaned over the cobra suddenly lurched forward and bit him, and he died."

Peter stopped talking and took a bite of food. The room was silent. Everyone looked at Peter to finish the story, but that was it. None of us could quite believe a man had died playing golf in Africa from a cobra bite. But Peter kept calmly chewing his food. After a few uncomfortable seconds I blurted, "The man died?!"

"Yes," Peter answered matter-of-factly. "He died right there."

The same wide-eyed expression was on everyone's faces: *Holy crap! The guy friggin' died?!* A tragic story, but Peter's sudden dry ending left us struggling to restrain our laughter.

After dinner, we moved onto the deck for a glass of wine as the conversation turned to politics. Our friends offered their opinions while Peter waited patiently to speak. "If I lived in the U.S., I would probably be a Democrat."

"Why is that?" my mother asked.

"I grew up during our independence movement. I am aware of President Kennedy's efforts toward desegregation. In Zambia, we broke free of colonialism the same year as the U.S. Civil Rights Act, 1964. In watching U.S. politics, it has always been Democrats that have pushed for equal rights of all people. But as a small business owner, I would align myself with Democrats like President Clinton, who also prioritize economic growth."

I smiled as Peter spoke, remembering that he was a first-time visitor to the United States from one of the world's poorest countries. Although our Republican friends may have disagreed, there were nods of appreciation and a few looks of surprise.

Engaging Madalitso was a little different. *"Are you looking forward to college in the United States?" "How long have you been playing golf?" "What are your favorite subjects at school?"* These icebreakers were met with shy responses. Madalitso laughed and enjoyed everyone, but unlike Peter, he was not a natural raconteur.

Our post-dinner chat ended all too soon. Peter and Madalitso were leaving for Zambia early the next morning, so they booked a room near the airport.

Warm smiles were everywhere as my mom hugged our departing guests. "Your family is always welcome here, Peter, though I may put Madalitso to work at the restaurant."

"You have my permission to go up his backside if he slacks off!" Peter responded.

Claude promised to give Madalitso a cooking lesson on his next trip to Seattle. Warm words of friendship flowed, and new bonds were formed among people of different races, nationalities and life experiences. This was the best of America. The best of humanity.

I drove them to their hotel near the airport and hated saying goodbye. Handshakes would not suffice. Peter and I exchanged a hug. Though I admit it was I who initiated it. Clearly, I caught him off guard.

"Yes, well done. Well done," he said with a chuckle. Madalitso laughed but said nothing.

It had been quite a whirlwind. The storybook victory in Fort Myers, new relationships built in Seattle, bonding among the three of us and my private conversations with Peter. The past several days were life-changing. I had so much to say, I didn't know where to start. "Have a safe flight. We'll miss you," was all I could muster.

"Yeah, me too," Madalitso replied shyly.

Peter looked me in the eye and smiled. "We will talk soon, Jayme. We will talk soon."

DRIVING AWAY, I was overcome by a feeling that I had arrived somewhere unfamiliar—a new place where everything was right.

I brought Peter and Madalitso to Seattle with the hopes of joining two families together. The Muthiyas would be sending their youngest son halfway around the world to attend college. I wanted them to know that Madalitso would have more than a few acquaintances in the America. He would have a second family.

I thought of everyone comprising this picture and could not remember a time when I felt this content with the people in my life. "Family" suddenly had a new and bigger meaning for me.

All of this was swirling in my head as I merged onto I-5 North. It was August, the best time of year to be in Seattle. The evening temperature was still around seventy degrees. With the windows down, I recalled all of the hard work I'd put in the past several months and the hard work Peter and Madalitso had been putting in their whole lives to reach the extraordinary place where we now found ourselves. I was convinced that these were the good things my mother always talked about.

That drive from Sea-Tac Airport back to my folks' house was one of the happiest times of my life.

22

DESPITE GUSHING OVER MADALITSO AND his astounding victory, the college coaches who could offer full scholarships slowly faded away until there were only two left: the University of New Mexico and the University of Virginia. And even with them, it was all talk and no commitment.

With nothing new to report, calling Peter became painfully awkward. There were only so many times and ways I could say, "New Mexico and Virginia are still narrowing their list of recruits and deciding how to allocate their scholarship money." He could probably feel me rubbing my temples all the way from Africa.

President Chiluba's staff called me with increasingly relentless frequency. The Henke-Berg was a cause for celebration, and now a payoff was expected. *What else did the universities need to see? What was the point of traveling all that way if no scholarship was forthcoming?* I explained that winning the Henke-Berg was what gave Madalitso *the chance* for a scholarship. My explanations seemed to provide no comfort at State House.

The Muthiyas showed no signs of mental strain or anxiety, though it was surely there.

After I reported that both schools were still deliberating, Peter and I would catch up on each other's lives and continue sharing our personal stories. Over time, these exchanges became easier for both of us. Growing up without my father was finally something I could discuss, at least with him. And he always asked about my mom, Claude, my girlfriend and our family friends.

He also kept prodding me about my lagging history lessons. "Are you getting there, Jayme?"

"Peter, I...well...with everything going on, I have no time to casually read history books. But I'll get there...eventually." *There will be time.*

GLEN MILLICAN, UNM's assistant coach, requested a three-way call with him and Head Coach J.T. Higgins in Albuquerque, Peter and Madalitso in Lusaka, and me in DC. I stopped myself from asking if they'd reached a decision. Whatever the verdict, the Muthiyas should hear it first.

Immediately I rang Peter. As I waited for him to pick up, I tried to restrain my own cautious enthusiasm. *The coaches would never request this call just to deliver bad news...would they?*

Peter answered and listened to me summarize my conversation with Millican.

"Why do they want to speak with us?" he asked after a moment of silence.

"Well, I suspect New Mexico has made a final decision on a scholarship."

"I figured as much, Jayme!" His voice was filled with sarcasm and frustration. Clearly the pressure of all this was finally having an impact. "What do you think they will say?"

"I don't know, Peter. My hunch is they wouldn't bother telephoning if the answer is no."

"Okay."

After a moment of silence, we said goodbye and hung up. It was our shortest conversation. It would be a very long forty-eight hours.

On Monday, Coach Higgins, Coach Millican, Peter, Madalitso and I were finally on the phone together. The moment of truth was here. I was hoping for the best and expecting the worst.

In my role as consigliere, I remembered that Peter and Coach Higgins had never spoken, so I introduced them.

"Hello, Mr. Muthiya. It's a pleasure finally speaking with you." Higgins's upbeat tone fanned my optimism that good news was coming.

"Yes, it's good to speak with you as well, Coach Higgins," Peter responded, polite and tight.

"Please, call me J.T. I apologize for not being in Fort Myers at the Henke-Berg. Coach Millican gave me a thorough summary of Madalitso's outstanding performance. Unfortunately, the level of competition at the Henke-Berg was not as high as other tournaments, but our evaluation of a recruit can be done independent of other players."

Peter's "mmm-hmm" came faintly over the line. I wondered where this was going. I nervously waited for Higgins to continue, and I suspected that Peter and Madalitso were equally on edge.

"I watched the tapes that Jayme sent to my office. And I completely trust Glen's judgment. Both of us are convinced that Madalitso's best golf is ahead of him and that he would be an excellent representative of the golf team and the university..."

My heart surged.

"...so we are offering Madalitso a scholarship to the University of New Mexico."

I shot out of my chair, thrusting both of my clenched fists into the sky. But I didn't say a word.

Neither did Peter. I wondered if he and Mad were also doing a happy dance.

Higgins immediately added, "There is one issue, however."

The other shoe was about to drop, and I collapsed back into my chair. *Oh God. What!?*

"The first year's scholarship is only eighty-five percent. The next three years will be one hundred percent—a full ride. We have obligations to outgoing seniors, so the other fifteen percent goes to them."

Peter remained quiet. I pictured him trying to understand all of this. So I jumped in. "J.T., do you have a rough idea of how much money the Muthiyas would owe?"

"We don't have an exact figure, Jayme. Scholarships are divided between tuition and room and board. Maybe around fifteen hundred dollars per semester."

More silence from Peter.

The coaches further explained that Madalitso needed approval from the NCAA clearinghouse and to pass the SAT exam.

Peter still said nothing. I knew this meant he wanted to speak privately. "J.T. and Glen, can we think about it for a couple of days?" They agreed.

Peter and Madalitso thanked them and said goodbye.

I was elated. We were *just a fraction* away from our goal. We had to make this work.

"What do you think, Jayme?" Peter asked.

"Peter, New Mexico is our best and *only* option. And it's a GREAT option. You, Madalitso, Edith and the Zambian Government should be proud. New Mexico is a good school with an excellent golf program. Several UNM alumni are playing professionally."

"Well... Okay. Let's talk tomorrow, Jayme."

I was a little sad they didn't share my enthusiasm at this amazing turn of events. I reminded myself that this was their way.

Peter, Madalitso and I spoke a lot over the next couple of days. But it was the first time I felt that my words had no value to them. All of Madalitso's freshman year expenses would not be covered. Although $1,500 was a small amount to me, I was operating from my position of White privilege. I didn't understand their financial situation. And Peter was too proud to offer details. It was a dilemma the Muthiyas had to resolve on their own. But we needed a decision soon. College recruiting is a fast-moving process where scholarship offers can be extended and withdrawn in the blink of an eye.

I arranged another three-way call. Madalitso opened with a question. "Coach Higgins, what is a lobo?"

"A lobo is a wolf, a tough, independent and ferocious hunter."

"Well, Coach, I come from a land of lions and crocodiles. To us, a lobo is like a house pet."

Laughter erupted in Albuquerque.

I was glad that Peter let his son take center stage. It was great to hear Mad step up. "A lot of thought has gone into this," he told the coaches. "Thank you for the confidence you have shown in me. I know in the United States you have many good golfers to choose from. After speaking with my family and discussing it with Jayme, I have decided to accept your scholarship offer to New Mexico."

"All right! Fantastic! That's great!" J.T. and Glen shouted exclamations over each other.

I heard laughter coming from Peter and Madalitso.

Inside my head, my brain screamed:

WE DID IT! WE DID IT! WE DID IT!

My body did a silent dance of its own.

"CONGRATULATIONS, MADALITSO," I said when the coaches dropped off the line. "How do you feel?"

"Good," he said in his usual, understated tone. "Relieved."

He passed the phone to Peter. "You better not have another aspiring athlete in the family," I told him. "I don't have the energy."

"Neither do I," he snapped back with a wry chuckle.

There were still hurdles left to clear: the SAT, the NCAA clearinghouse and New Mexico's admissions department. Those battles would be fought another day. Now was a time to celebrate.

"We've come a long way," I told him. We looked back nostalgically at some of the key stops on our journey. Our first meeting in the Intercontinental Hotel lobby when they thought I was a CIA spy. Our second meeting in the hotel bar where we got half-drunk and bonded. Cypress Lake Country Club and the Cabana bar in Fort Myers. Bringing families together in Seattle. And of course, the endless phone calls that truly deepened our relationship.

"Thanks for the faith you placed in me, Peter. It's a real compliment, and I cherish it so much."

Peter took a few seconds to formulate his thoughts. "There is something I want to tell you, and I hope I'm not overstepping my bounds." As he paused again, I sensed that he was choosing his words carefully. "Everything you've done this past year...the scholarship and everything else. Your father would be proud."

I paused, choking up. I took a couple of deep breaths to compose myself. "Thank you."

"Do you remember," Peter continued, "when we first met at the Intercontinental Hotel with Madalitso?"

"Of course," I said.

"Well, my reticence had nothing to do with disinterest or a failure to grasp the challenge we faced. It was something else...a distaste for how this entire process was unfolding. A small group of people, most of whom I didn't know, were involved in a very private matter: the future of *my* son. President Chiluba, senior government officials and some American I'd never met were part of a plan that I did not create or control. The whole thing contradicted the very principles of independence and self-reliance that defined much of my life."

Peter paused to take a breath. I stayed silent.

"And...you know...this whole thing was a test for both of us. For you, it was about convincing universities to take an interest in Madalitso. For me, the challenge was letting go of old suspicions and setting aside unrelated issues. It was getting past myself and things I experienced from my earliest days as a young boy. But we have arrived at a good place together."

Peter said nothing else. He didn't have to. I knew what he meant, from the stories he told me about his life and the oppression endured by his family. I just needed to piece it together. As he told me in Fort Myers:

"You can't fully know a person without some knowledge of their experiences. What they've been through."

23

"THE PRESIDENT MUST BE TOLD about this right away!" My contact in President Chiluba's office was giddy with joy, practically hanging up before I finished telling him Madalitso had been awarded a scholarship at a leading American university. I was still surprised by how closely the President was keeping tabs.

A string of excited phone calls ensued, and within hours I was booked on a flight to Lusaka. Peter, Madalitso and I were scheduled to announce the scholarship at a press conference at Lusaka Golf Club, Peter and Madalitso's home course.

As my plane touched down in Zambia, there were far less nerves and anxiety than my first trip.

But visiting Africa will always evoke a sense of awe.

"WELL, HELLO THERE, old friend!" Peter stepped out of the car at the Lusaka Golf Club, smiling wide.

"Hello to you, old friend!" I replied with a laugh.

It was the morning of the press conference and we were all in various states of euphoria.

To my delight and surprise, both Peter and Madalitso greeted me with handshakes *and* hugs. "I guess a little bit of America rubbed off on me," Peter laughed.

"I'm glad," I replied, "because quite a bit of Africa has rubbed off on me. But don't worry, I will never spit in the face of a cobra!"

We must have looked half-crazy standing in the parking lot laughing our heads off.

Entering the clubhouse, we were greeted by the President of the Zambia Golf Union. The walls were decorated with names of past tournament champions. Etched in several places was: Madalitso Muthiya.

We walked outside to a podium that was jerry-rigged together by draping a tablecloth over a box on a folding card table. Behind the podium stood the captain of Lusaka Golf Club, the lady captain, the former and current heads of the Zambia Golf Union, Peter, Madalitso and me. Sportswriters, news reporters and TV cameras were spread out in front of us.

It was like being in a movie.

Surveying the scene, I looked back on our journey together. Just one year after a miserable first meeting in a hotel lobby, we were standing together in front of what seemed like the entire Zambian media and being hailed as heroes.

And it all happened because a son followed his father's advice to never be intimidated by people who had more than he did and who looked different than him. To focus only on himself and what he needed to do.

Even more, it was a celebration of Peter's life. A Black African child born under colonial rule to a family crammed inside a two-room mud hut where they slept on a dirt floor. From these impoverished beginnings, he climbed a ladder in a place where none existed, pulling himself up rung by rung. And now his son would attend a university in the United States of America on an athletic scholarship for a sport he had no business playing.

To me it seemed, and still seems, like a miracle.

Peter calmly stepped to the podium. With his trademark steady voice and warm smile, he welcomed members of the press to this "very momentous occasion...an event that has never taken place before. We are here to acknowledge what has happened over the past eight months.

"Jayme was tasked by our President to search for a place for a budding young golfer, Madalitso Muthiya. I wish to thank the President of the Republic, Mr. Chiluba." Peter also thanked the Zambia Golf Union for building junior talent despite financial constraints and Madalitso's school, Lake Road PTA, for allowing him to compete in "local and overseas competitions."

He then paused and looked down for a moment. "To Jayme, I don't know how to thank you. Having achieved all of this in record time. You've done a sterling job." His voice was crisp and unwavering. Only a person who knew Peter would understand that this was the most heartfelt expression of thanks and love that this very private man could give in a public forum.

Moved by Peter's gesture, I took my turn at the podium. "I have a prepared speech which I'll give in a minute, but first I'd like to say something to Peter and Madalitso. As Peter said, I was asked by President Chiluba to assist Madalitso. While initially I started this job as a favor to the President, I finished it because Peter and Madalitso have become part of my family."

I told of the first meeting with President Chiluba and why he gave me an assignment that I didn't want. *When there are young Zambians blessed with a talent—academics, the arts or athletics—it is incumbent on all Zambians from the President on down to assist these young people.*

"Credit for this occasion goes to three people: to Peter, for instilling in Madalitso the values of hard work, discipline and sportsmanship. Madalitso, for building his future with vision, hard work and confidence as his tools. And thank you, President Chiluba, for bringing us together.

"At some point a few years from now, Zambians all over the world will be watching their televisions. They will turn to the person next to them and say: 'Do you see that man, the one who sank the winning putt? He is my countryman. He is Zambian.'"

Stepping away from the podium, I glanced at Madalitso as he came forward, scanning his face for any signs of nerves. There were none. Whether he was teeing off in a rainstorm or speaking in front of television cameras, he seemed completely unfazed, essentially telling observers that these and other such moments were not what caused his blood pressure to rise or his voice to crack.

Madalitso never sought media attention, preferring to let his golf speak for him. But this was not a normal post-tournament interview. It was a celebration. Time to have fun. He saw his family, the Zambia Golf Union, government officials, members of the media and Zambian citizens all there to revel in the fact that one of their own had earned a scholarship to an American university to play *golf* of all things. It was a dream come true. A moment of history. And they all wanted to drink in every drop of it.

But it wasn't all about Madalitso Muthiya, at least not in his mind. Mostly, it was an opportunity to publicly thank his family, President Chiluba, the Golf Union, the Zambian people and "a man from the United States" in whom he placed his trust.

"Today is a very special day for me. The University of New Mexico offered me a scholarship to pursue my economics degree and participate in their golf program. Clearly this has not been an easy achievement." He thanked President Chiluba "for facilitating the search for my scholarship.

"My grateful thanks to Jayme Roth, who very ably marketed my talent in the United States. I'd like to say to you that I am indebted to you for giving me international exposure.

"To my family, I will always treasure the tremendous support you gave me and continue to give me. To my father, I'll always cherish the moments you walked with me on the golf course. To my mother, thank you for keeping me strong and healthy."

I kept a videotape of the press conference and still watch it from time to time. Years later, I am moved by Peter's closing remarks, words of advice to his son:

To Mad, my son,
The message is simple.
The road to success is often fraught with pitfalls.
It can be rough and tough.
But with the kind of discipline that you've shown,

you can achieve quite a lot.
So my message is, you cultivate between the virtues
of self-discipline and hard work.
Both at your academics and your game.

PETER AND MADALITSO had been honored guests of my family in Seattle. Now it was my turn. After the press conference, the Muthiyas asked me to join them for dinner. Peter had given me such vivid mental images of Edith, Wongani and Ivwananji that it was hard to believe I'd never met them.

From my hotel, we drove to a nearby restaurant. Edith's warm, lovely smile and friendly laugh welcomed me and made me feel right at home. Peter and Madalitso had told her all about our time together, so she asked about our restaurant and home in Mukilteo. "I would love to meet your mom and Claude."

Wongani and Madalitso were close in age, but their personalities were as different as night and day. Five seconds after meeting him, it was obvious that Wongani was the family comedian. Outgoing and animated, he was full of questions about the United States. And he wasn't shy about sharing his plans to start and grow his own business. If he were a stock, you'd be crazy not to invest in Wongani Muthiya.

We could have talked all night if not for work and school in the morning. Driving back to the hotel, I promised to navigate the University of New Mexico admissions department and send preparation materials for the SAT.

Suddenly, I was standing with Peter and Madalitso outside my hotel, saying another hard goodbye. "I guess next time we see each other will be in the United States when you're a Lobo."

Madalitso laughed. "That's right, Jayme. I'm looking forward to being a wolf!" We laughed. He took a moment to look in my eyes and said, "Thanks."

"You are welcome." I've never meant anything more in my life.

I turned to Peter. "Hopefully, thousands of miles and international phone calls are not always part of our friendship."

"It won't always be like that, Jayme. Besides, I like our telephone calls." Peter looked at me with the same warm, loving smile that he gifted me during our final exchange in Seattle.

My meetings ended a couple of days later, and I headed to the airport. Once again, my car zoomed past a steady stream of foot traffic. But this time, my reaction was different.

Regardless of whether Madalitso ever played golf professionally, he would graduate from an American university. His degree would enable a standard of living far above that of most Zambians, including the people outside my car.

I smiled, knowing one young Zambian would never have to travel this road by foot.

24

Zambia and the United States have different grading systems, so preparing Madalitso's transcripts was like trying to convert cobras into apples. Eventually we learned the required SAT score, and my first packet of study materials landed in Zambia. Each day, Madalitso went straight from school to a spare desk in Peter's office where he studied under the uncompromising eye of his father.

No music. No TV. No friends.

A few months and a few exam prep books into this regimen, my phone rang.

"How are you, Jayme?"

"Peter! I'm fine. How are you? How are Edith and the kids?" We caught up quickly, but I sensed a nervous, awkward tone in his voice.

"Jayme...I...can we chat for a minute about the exam...the SAT exam?"

"Sure."

"Well, uh...I—yes, uh..." Rather than continue stumbling, Peter paused.

"Does Madalitso need more study materials, Peter?" I offered.

"No, no. We're fine. It's just that, in Zambia the SAT is offered only once a year."

This had been a pebble in my shoe for some time. Students in the United

States can retake the exam every few months to achieve a desired score. Madalitso did not have that luxury.

"I know, Peter. I know."

"It's just that...if Madalitso doesn't achieve the required score, he cannot immediately enroll at New Mexico. His life would be on hold for another year."

Silence hung in the air.

"Well, what are you thinking?"

Nervously, I waited as Peter struggled to find his words.

"I think we would go the route of playing professionally."

It was a punch in the gut. "Peter, does this mean that Madalitso will not take the exam? I mean...have you already made this decision?!"

"No, no. I'm just saying it's possible. We need a fallback plan if the exam goes poorly."

"Okay...well...please give my encouragement to Madalitso."

"I will, Jayme. Thank you."

Still reeling, I hung up. Peter gave no hint of what prompted his warning. He simply told me that Madalitso was "working hard." For American kids, the SAT can be a strange and high-stress process because futures are made or broken, depending on the outcome. I could only imagine how it was viewed by an African. Especially when the African was Mad. His life was hanging once again on a thread, and only a great performance when the stakes and pressure couldn't be higher would make his dreams come true.

Nobody I knew valued education like Peter Muthiya. As a child, it was the thin rope he used to claw his way out of the abject poverty that his parents and the vast majority of Zambians lived with every day. Without question, he wanted the same for his children. He wanted Madalitso to get that SAT score.

I was sure that Peter hadn't shared his concerns with his son. Attending New Mexico was Madalitso's sole obsession. He had no interest in hearing or discussing other options.

Selfishly, I also thought of myself. The hard work and mental stress of our mission had brought Peter, Madalitso and me together. In the midst of our quest, we shared each other's secrets, lives and families. Plans were made for Madalitso to become a part of our home in Seattle over summer vacations and winter breaks.

Madalitso was fast becoming like a younger brother. And Peter was now my older male confidant, a role long missing from my life.

Now all of this was in jeopardy. In Peter's "fallback option," friendships would surely remain, but we had little chance of becoming permanent fixtures in each other's lives. It would be heartbreaking.

Madalitso's golf and Peter's stories had also given me a sacred mission: a chance to be part of something special, perhaps even historic. Although I could just hear Peter say that my scant knowledge of history kept me from "appreciating the significance" of such an event.

This would be a huge loss all around. My stomach churned. He *needed* to get that SAT score.

We worked for a year, telephoning coaches, sending emails, mailing résumés and videotapes, orchestrating trips to Fort Myers and Seattle and constantly reporting back to the Zambian Government. But mastering the SAT was Madalitso's job. All I could do was wait and try not to worry. Even as I worried and worried.

Madalitso studied like his life depended on it. Which, in some ways, it did. Watching footage of the NCAA championships years earlier instilled a sense of purpose uncommon in a boy who had barely reached adolescence. Now he was within arm's length of a goal that had seemed unreachable to that little boy. The only dragon left to kill was a three-letter standardized test.

I tossed and turned the night before Madalitso's exam. I wasn't this nervous before my *own* SAT. The next morning, I did anything to occupy my mind. Finally, I couldn't take it anymore, and I called the Muthiyas.

"It went okay, I guess." Madalitso didn't sound disappointed or shaken by the experience, but he didn't sound particularly hopeful or optimistic either. I reminded myself that this was just Mad being Mad. "I felt prepared. None of the material was new to me. But for many questions, there was more than one good answer."

Of course, the most important date was not the exam. It was one month later when the results were released. Peter asked me to retrieve the score. An official with the College Board told me to let four weeks pass before telephoning. I waited three.

Every afternoon, I dialed the College Board and waited in nervous agony to speak with a live person. I took a deep breath when placed on hold. It was almost a relief when somebody came on the line and uttered the same two words:

"Not yet."

I grew comfortable with this routine, content not having an answer.

But I knew the day of reckoning was coming.

It was late in Lusaka. I paused before dialing because Peter and Edith were probably asleep. But they deserved to know.

The phone rang a few times before a gruff sleepy voice answered. "Hello?"

"Peter, it's Jayme. I apologize for calling this late, but I have something to tell you."

"Oh...uhh...hi, Jayme. What is it? What's going on?"

He was clearly discombobulated, so I waited as he cleared his throat and collected himself.

"Peter...he did it. Madalitso passed the SAT. He got the score he needed. HE DID IT! HE DID IT! HE DID IT!"

"Oh." With a one-word whisper he seemed to release all of the anxiety and stress of the past several months. Of his whole life.

On my end, it was hard to keep still. Overflowing with excitement, I could have talked for hours. Then I remembered it was the middle of the night in Lusaka. We agreed to speak the next day and hung up, happy and exhausted.

I contacted Coach Glen Millican at UNM. Recently promoted to head coach after J.T. Higgins left for Texas A&M, Glen's commitment to Madalitso never wavered. "That's great, Jayme."

My final call was a celebration that I'll never forget: "Hey, Mom! Tell Claude a new family member is on the way!"

I dialed Peter the next morning, apologizing again for calling so late the night before.

"I didn't sleep a wink after we spoke, Jayme. I was too energized."

"I wish I could have seen Madalitso's reaction, Peter."

"He was extremely relieved. He got out of bed and sat with me in the kitchen. Then Wongani joined us. Soon the entire family was up, talking and laughing."

I smiled, picturing the scene. A family awake in the middle of the night, gathered together in their modest home in the heart of Africa celebrating the news that their youngest son would attend college in the United States.

"My mom and Claude send their congratulations, Peter."

"Oh, thank you. Please pass my regards to them."

"And tell my younger brother to expect his share of the housework."

"Don't worry. I'll tell him," Peter laughed.

For months, Peter had been calling me Madalitso's "big brother in America." These expressions of familial endearment became more and more common, milestones as our relationship grew and deepened.

Peter and I were laughing when I asked, "Wait a minute...if Madalitso is my younger brother, what does that make us?"

Peter answered without hesitation, in a tone that suggested my question was almost stupid. "What do you mean? You are my American son."

"Ah-ha! Then you need to send my allowance. I'm low on cash."

"Money?! I'm more inclined to go up your backside with my belt!"

25

As Madalitso prepared for the next phase of his life, I was also transitioning. My girlfriend and I had been headed toward marriage, but the relationship fell apart. Friends offered welcome support. But for advice I only turned to two sources: my folks and Peter.

"I just don't know if I'm doing the right thing, Peter. I'm going back and forth. Maybe I should've tried harder."

"Forget your heart for a minute," he said flatly. "What does your head tell you?"

I exhaled. "My head says this is the best thing."

"Well, there is your answer, Jayme. When both your head and heart are conflicted, the decision is more difficult."

I didn't respond.

"Marriage is *hard*," he emphasized. "It's serious. More than love, it's a partnership. You have to think rationally about whether this person is a good companion for life. Is there real compatibility? Big differences will only get worse over time."

I sighed hard and rubbed my temples harder. "Yeah...I guess."

"Let me tell you something," he continued. "I know about internal conflicts. There are times when you know the right decision. Just listening to you, it seems clear this is the best thing. I think you will see that clearly before long."

I welcomed Peter's input because he was smart and because he cared about me. More importantly, when Peter spoke, I was hearing the words of somebody born into a hard and unforgiving world.

Making tough decisions was how he climbed out. And how I was going to climb out.

TO KEEP THE rust off his game, Madalitso played in the 2000 Botswana Open, a three-day, fifty-four-hole professional tournament, part of Southern Africa's Sunshine Tour. Madalitso would face many accomplished South African and European professionals. But the quality of the field was irrelevant to him. "I am competing against the course and myself, not the other players." Just like his dad taught him.

The key difference between this Sunshine Tour event and the Zambia Open was the venue: Gaborone Golf Club. He was now on unfamiliar ground. But anyone wondering if Madalitso's performance at the Zambia Open was a result of home field advantage would soon know the truth.

"Guess what your younger brother did today," Peter teased.

"I don't know. What?"

"He shot an opening round sixty-five at the Botswana Open. He is in first place." Peter was calm, but the excitement traveled 10,000 miles over the phone lines.

"HOLY SHIT!" My officemate glared at me, and I apologized for my Not Suitable For Work outburst.

"Yes, that was my reaction too," Peter laughed. "He has two more rounds, and he feels good."

"That's fantastic, Peter," I said, keeping my voice down. "Please give him my best."

While Thursday's score of 65 was his best round of the tournament, Madalitso continued blowing up this strange new course. 65, 67 and 69.

Those were his scores over three rounds. He finished tied for fourth place. He was the only amateur to make the cut.

Print and television reporters were abuzz over the amateur going toe-to-toe with the pros. Spectators openly rooted for the Zambian teenager. The Zambia Open and the Botswana Open were the two most competitive events of his young career, and he performed incredibly well in both.

The NCAA awaited.

"IT'S HARD TO believe the day is finally here." Peter was somber, having just driven Madalitso to the airport. "The journey was too long to retrace. All the years of talk, planning and preparation...driving to tournaments for hours on unpaved roads. I can't believe it's been *twelve whole years* since that golf ball crashed through our kitchen window." I stayed silent at the other end of the line as Peter let his emotions surface. "I miss my son."

It was a familiar story to him, having left his parents as a young boy to live with his uncle. But now, on the other side, being the one who's left instead of leaving, his feelings were different. "It's much harder." Though it was still early in Zambia, Peter sounded tired and emotionally drained.

When I finally asked how he was feeling, he sighed. "How you might expect."

"MADALITSO!" I SHOUTED.

Spotting me in the crowd at Dulles Airport in Washington, DC, he flashed a big, bright smile that lit up the terminal.

As he moved toward me, I immediately noticed he was carrying one suitcase. It was a well-traveled old vintage model. But the size was what puzzled me. It was no larger than a carry-on bag. He was moving from Zambia to the United States—*forever*—and this was it.

Trips to Zambia and my relationship with Peter and Madalitso had brought me uncomfortably face-to-face with my own entitled Americanness.

Whether it was people walking next to speeding cars or the small, worn suitcase coming toward me, I was frequently reminded of my own naiveté and the economic advantages I took for granted.

Subtly discarding the luggage cart, I gave him a hug, and we were off.

This was my first real chance to spend one-on-one time with Madalitso. We talked in Fort Myers, but only in brief spurts as everyone focused on the tournament. In Seattle, we were constantly surrounded by other people. I wanted to get to know him as I had grown to know Peter.

Over breakfast, I was mindful that keeping an eighteen-year-old from getting bored can be a full-time job. "What would you like to do?"

He shrugged without looking up from his plate. "Whatever. Anything is fine with me."

That afternoon, we climbed the stairs at the Lincoln Memorial. "Check out this view!" I told him enthusiastically, pointing to the reflecting pool stretched out in front of us with the majestic Washington Monument towering above and the Capitol Building off in the distance.

"Yeah," he replied without a hint of interest or emotion.

John Glenn's capsule, the Wright Brothers' Flyer and Tyrannosaurus Rex. All I got was the same stony "Yeah."

Visiting the shopping mall to beef up his wardrobe produced a muted "thank you" and an awkward glance at his shoes.

I tried not to take it personally. I reminded myself that this was Mad's personality. But as the week progressed, I began wondering if anything affected him. My question was answered on a night we stayed up late and I asked him about growing up in Zambia.

He thought for a while and then said three words: "It was hard."

I stayed silent, allowing him the space to elaborate.

"It was hard seeing the homeless street kids outside my father's car. Hard seeing my classmates drop out of school because their parents couldn't afford it. And it was hard seeing the skin-and-bones bodies that were ravaged by disease. It made me appreciate my parents."

After talking for a few minutes, he suddenly caught himself and looked me in the eye. "But Zambia is a great place."

I nodded my head and smiled.

Well after midnight, we finally said our goodnights. I climbed into bed, content that I now understood Madalitso a little better. No longer would I interpret his stoicism as an inability or unwillingness to open up. Or that he simply didn't care.

Madalitso was capable of expressing himself. And was deeply impacted by his surroundings.

Just not marble statues or dinosaur fossils.

MADALITSO LOADED HIS bags into my car, and we headed to the airport for his flight to Albuquerque. During his visit we argued over rap artists, but finally managed to agree on someone we both liked: Tupac Shakur. "All Eyes on Me" filled the car as we drove.

We parked the car, made our way to the ticket counter and checked his bags.

Given Madalitso's notoriously stoic personality, I had no plans to deliver a longwinded, emotional goodbye that would make him feel awkward or obligated to reciprocate. I was going to give a short and sweet hug, followed by a quick: *Have a safe flight.*

Madalitso had something else in mind.

Boarding pass in hand, we approached the security line where we'd part. Before I could open my mouth, he turned and looked me in the eye.

"You know, for years I dreamt of going to college in America and playing NCAA golf. I wanted it so bad that every night I prayed, asking God for help. My father taught me the game and provided a life that allowed me to play. My mother kept me strong and gave me support. They stressed hard work and discipline, making me into the person I am. President Chiluba supported me and provided national exposure. But a scholarship to an American college was something that none of them could help me do. My parents, Wongani and Ivwananji knew how desperately I wanted this. All of them assured me it would happen, but none of us knew how to go about it. And so, night after night and year after year, I asked God for help.

"And then one day, God answered my prayers. He sent you."

26

"MAAAAAAD!"

Scanning the airport terminal, Madalitso finally spotted the people shouting his name: my mom and Claude. They took an earlier flight to Albuquerque to greet the newest member of our family, whom they'd only met once when he and Peter visited Seattle.

"Hi, Janet. Hi, Claude." He smiled and let out a little nervous laugh as everyone hugged.

First, they drove Madalitso to his dorm room and located some other key buildings on campus. Next was a trip to the mall for linens, towels and other necessities. Lastly, my mom purchased him a cell phone so he could reach us at all times. Her fine-tuned motherly instincts had firmly embraced the electronic age.

Their time together started by shopping and touring UNM's campus. But it quickly became something much more valuable. During a special dinner in Santa Fe one evening, Madalitso confided, "Traveling halfway around the world is hard, especially when my family is so far away. But knowing the two of you are in the United States has made me and my parents feel so much better."

My mom and Claude had one last surprise on their final day in

Albuquerque. Before leaving for the airport, they snuck into Madalitso's dorm room and installed something. When he returned later in the day, he was confused and somewhat alarmed by the loud noises coming from inside. Then, he was happy to have what he needed to become an official American:

A new color TV.

THE FIRST SEVERAL weeks were a struggle. Everything was different. Nothing was familiar. The people, the schoolwork, the way he trained for golf, even the food. Every day produced some strange new mystery that everyone understood...except him.

I was in my office one morning when the phone rang. "Jayme, something is going on!" His breathing was labored, like he just ran up a flight of stairs after seeing a ghost.

"What is it?"

"Well, I was walking to the cafeteria, and everyone around me was acting weird."

I furrowed my brow. "Acting weird? In what way?"

"Mainly it was the way they looked. They were dressed strangely."

None of this was making sense to me. "What do you mean they were dressed strangely?"

"Just what I said! They were dressed strangely! And when I got to the cafeteria, the food looked equally strange. All these weird colors! Please help me—I think I'm going crazy!"

My mind was blank until I glanced at my desk calendar. Then I chuckled to myself. "Madalitso, it's Halloween."

I explained Halloween as best I could, while restraining my laughter, mindful that he was distressed. He was still a little confused at the end, but at least I managed to convince him that the green, goblin-shaped cupcakes were, in fact, edible.

At first, it seemed like there was another culture shock every day. Standing at an intersection Madalitso saw people marching, blocking traffic and yelling. He couldn't quite see who it was or what they were saying. But since there didn't seem to be any danger, he decided to navigate his way in between the marchers.

He finally noticed the people around him. Sounding slightly bedazzled and a little bewildered, he told me, "There were women holding hands with women and shirtless men with their arms around each other." A man hollered, "Hey! Come march with us!" When he asked what they were marching for, a colorful same-sex couple told him that he'd joined a gay pride parade.

One day, a guy on the golf team passed around an adult men's magazine. At first Madalitso didn't know what was being handed to him. But after seeing naked flesh displayed lasciviously, he handed it back. "This is immoral. I want no part of it." His teammates were silent. In a culture where *Playboy* and *Penthouse* were mainstream publications on college campuses, the idea of a teenage boy thinking they were immoral shut down "locker room talk" as long as Madalitso was around.

I tried to give Mad some context for what admittedly seemed like strange and sometimes crass behavior. Particularly "Magazinegate," as I began calling it. I could hear his frustration. "Does every male college student drink, curse and act like a baboon?! I can't even take out the trash without stumbling over piles of beer bottles!"

"Unfortunately, lots of kids think that's what college is actually for in America," I explained. "I applaud you for sticking to your principles. But maybe you should pick and choose your battles. American college campuses will expose you to many things you find objectionable. I just don't want you to become ostracized. The more you can roll with the punches while staying true to yourself, the better off you'll be."

Madalitso had much to learn about his new home, like beer pong, fraternity hazing and of course, girlie magazines. But his classmates were often even *more* uninformed about the world outside their own country. His fellow students regularly asked if there were lions and elephants around his house.

"I always respond politely that Lusaka is a large city. Wildlife seen on television is only found in very rural areas. After a while, I felt like asking if these people routinely found grizzly bears and alligators in their backyards."

A few people thought that Africa is a single country. One student even asked Madalitso if Zambia was near Zamunda. If you're wondering where Zamunda is, you won't find it on a map. That's because it's the *fictional* country in the Eddie Murphy movie *Coming to America.*

American food also played games with his stomach. Bad games. The Zambian diet centers around fresh maize (corn), freshly steamed vegetables, fresh fruit, and fresh meat and fish. Operative word: "fresh." Americans are raised on artificial colors, flavors and preservatives. While healthy "organic" options can certainly be found in the United States, the mass-produced food in UNM's cafeteria didn't leave him and his stomach with many happy choices.

No one knew what he was going through. And unlike his father and brother, Mad wasn't very talkative, didn't wear his heart on his sleeve, concealed his frustrations and asked very few questions. Occasionally, I tried drawing him out. But I now knew him well enough not to press. Whenever he shared something that was bothering him, he would quickly add, "I am very lucky to be here." So Madalitso tried all by himself to gain footing in a strange new world without solid ground.

To help prevent homesickness, once a week, I hooked up a three-way phone call with me in Washington, Madalitso in New Mexico, and Peter in Zambia. Usually, Peter was nearing the end of his day in Lusaka, I was in the middle of my morning in DC and Madalitso was getting ready for school in Albuquerque.

"Were you out partying last night? You know we didn't send you all that way to drink and chase women." Of course, the idea of Madalitso as an all-night-party-animal was ludicrous. Peter simply wanted to hear his son laugh.

I offered to get off the phone and allow father and son to have private, away-at-college conversations. Peter scoffed. "Of course not, Jayme."

He never told me why I was included. No explanation was necessary. We were family now, and these calls were part of our journey together.

I was caught off guard when Peter asked to speak privately with me. Madalitso hung up.

"Jayme, I have a favor to ask. Edith and I have always pressed our children to work hard. Finish their homework. Do their assigned chores."

His tone was dead serious, so I stayed silent.

"I would greatly appreciate you staying on top of him, making sure he completes his homework, attends class and other things. This is a critical time in his life. He *must* stay on track. Madalitso is a diligent young man, so it shouldn't be a burden."

I had another silent-groan-rub-temples moment, just as when President Chiluba asked me to *help a young golfer secure a scholarship.* Yes, Madalitso was like a younger brother to me, but disciplining him? That was seriously outside my comfort zone. "Peter, I don't think that I...I mean...it's probably not my place to..."

"Jayme," he said, interrupting me. "I'm too far removed. It's impossible for me to stay on top of everything Madalitso is doing. I simply don't speak with him as often as you. Somebody *there* in the United States has to do it."

"Peter, I'm not a parent or schoolteacher. I've never been responsible for children. What if I'm too hard on him...or too soft?"

"You'll be fine, Jayme, just handle each situation as you see fit and expect of Madalitso what you would expect of yourself."

Peter had dispensed with all of my objections, except one.

"Peter, Madalitso and I have become close. If I assume this kind of role, it could jeopardize our relationship. He might resent me."

I could almost see him shaking his head. "Don't worry, Jayme. Your relationship with Madalitso won't deteriorate. He won't resent you. Besides, you have my support."

My brain frantically searched for a compelling argument to prove I was not the man for this job.

"This is important, Jayme. It would be a favor to me. Please."

I sighed. I stifled a groan. I rubbed my temples harder. Then I said the only word I could:

"Okay."

MY INTERNAL DILEMMA over how to fulfill—or avoid—Peter's request was instantly forgotten when I phoned him two days later.

"Hello." His voice was a forced whisper, hoarse and barely audible.

"Peter?"

He cleared his throat. "Yes, Jayme. How are you?"

"Uhh...Peter...are you alright?"

He cleared his throat again. "I am fine. Just a slight bout of malaria."

A *slight* bout of *malaria?!*

What the hell does that even mean? I asked myself. "My God...Peter...are you okay?! I mean...is there anything you need? Can I help?"

"No, no, Jayme." He strained to get the words out. "It's just something one has to contend with here from time to time."

My mouth hung open. Just when I thought I knew Peter and his world, I realized there was no way I could *really* know. No one gets a slight bout of malaria where I live. "Well, Peter...I have no specific reason for calling. It was just to say hello and chat a little. But maybe I should let you rest."

"Yes, Jayme. That would be better. I should be back to myself in another day or so."

"Of course." I wanted to say something that would make it better. But, of course, nothing I could say would make it better. So I ended with a variation of our usual goodbye: "Well...get better, my African dad. Okay?"

He managed a laugh, but with a harsh, gravelly tone. "Okay, my American son."

27

THE SAD NEWS WAS THAT Madalitso struggled even in the one place where he was most comfortable—the golf course. Coach Millican's training regimen included lifting weights and team runs, often culminating in sprints up the stairs at UNM's football stadium. Growing up, Madalitso ran, but only while playing soccer. Unlike American high schools, Zambia's secondary schools don't have weight rooms and giant stadiums to sprint in.

Things that he'd been doing on a golf course his whole life were suddenly wrong. During a team practice, Madalitso stood next to his ball, staring down the fairway, deep in concentration. A teammate walked over and asked what he was doing.

"I'm trying to gauge the distance from my ball to the pin."

His teammate looked at him like he was crazy. He grabbed Madalitso's arm and led him to the nearest yardage marker lining the course. Madalitso didn't grow up playing on golf courses lined with yardage markers. He always relied on his own sense of distance.

But not every unexpected twist was embarrassing. Along with their championship-caliber course, known as "South," UNM's golf facilities included a first-class driving range, a putting green and a video room to film your swings and look for technical flaws. "Everything was *really* nice," he said like a kid who couldn't believe what an AWESOME birthday present he'd just gotten.

Perhaps the highlight of his first week was walking into the huge, gleaming dressing room. He'd spent his entire competitive career as a golfer walking into dressing rooms where he didn't belong. Where he was an outsider. Like a poor distant cousin who didn't really belong in these palaces of golf.

But not now. Standing in front of his locker was a sparkling brand-new set of golf clubs inside a glossy leather bag, custom-made to fit him. No more mismatched Island-of-Misfit-Toys golf clubs for him. Now he was on the inside. He was a member of a club that wouldn't allow his father to join when he was a kid. Because he had the wrong color skin. Looking at those gorgeous clubs, Madalitso couldn't quite wrap his mind around how far he'd come. He wished his father could see these clubs. Imagined the smile that would light up Peter's face. What a joy it would be to watch Peter swing these clubs after having made his own first clubs by carving sticks.

"They were beautiful," he told me. "The nicest clubs that I had ever played with. I couldn't believe they were made specifically for me. I put them into my locker and double-checked the lock." He laughed like a young man whose dream had come true.

And then there were his teammates. Over the years, he occasionally competed against boys with professional instructors and the best equipment. Now he was living, traveling and playing with them every day.

Madalitso looked at these young men and wondered about their journeys, their families, and was struck again by how miraculous it was to be here. When he thought about it like that, it was overwhelming. The dark decades of abuse, suffering and extreme poverty endured by his grandparents. His father, the five-year-old Black boy in colonial Africa, falling in love with golf, a sport that symbolized Black exclusion and oppression, the pinnacle of White privilege in the world of sports. Scrounging for balls, grinding sticks into clubs, and searching for vacant land where a fairway could be cleared, and a hole dug. At moments like this, he couldn't quite wrap his mind around how all this had resulted in him belonging in the heart of America surrounded by all the Whiteness that had tried to grind his ancestors into the dirt.

As a newly arrived freshman, each day that Madalitso walked into the team locker room or onto UNM's immaculate, beautifully groomed championship golf course, he was filled with gratitude for his family's never-say-die determination and sacrifice. He wondered whether his University of New Mexico teammates could begin to fathom the lengths his father had gone to play something that *resembled* golf.

Madalitso was a mystery to his teammates, but they were also a mystery to him. He assumed they overflowed with confidence, buoyed by a lifetime of brand-new state-of-the-art clubs, playing on perfectly manicured courses and guided by expert coaching. But as they got comfortable with each other, walls were torn down and friendships grew. He learned that material advantages do not extinguish a player's insecurities. As it turned out, the long greenside bunker shot or the fifty-meter pitch was dreaded by all, whether you were toting a new or used wedge. Anxiety the night before a competition was universal, regardless of how much money was spent to get there.

Madalitso knew what they expected of him. Getting a near full scholarship meant that coaches, teammates, athletic department personnel and boosters demanded results. His technical knowledge lagged behind his teammates', as did his familiarity with playing golf in America. But in the end, no one really cared about any of that. He would get no mulligans. In golf or in life.

Madalitso needed to learn quickly. He could not fathom the idea of failing and being forced to return home. It was unimaginable. But as he came to know his teammates, he no longer saw his lack of training and years of poor equipment as only a weakness. In some ways, it made him stronger.

And of course, he relied on the words his grandmother passed down to his father:

If they are there and you are there, you both belong. Just focus on what you need to do.

UNM ENTERED THE 2001–2002 season with the realistic goal of winning the NCAA championship. The Lobos had an incredibly strong team anchored by Wil Collins, an All-American and winner of the 2001 Hogan award given annually to the top student athlete in college golf.

The William H. Tucker Intercollegiate was traditionally the first tournament of the year hosted by UNM. As with every event, Head Coach Millican and Assistant Coach Ryan Murphy held a competition to determine the five varsity players. The tryout for the Tucker was, in addition to his first taste of collegiate golf, Madalitso's first round of competitive golf since arriving in the United States. No matter how hard and long you practice, it's hard not to have a little rust when you haven't played in the bubbling cauldron of tournament golf regularly. Mad played okay, but not well enough to crack the top five of this elite squad. Since UNM hosted the tournament, it could field a junior varsity (JV) team. Madalitso would lead that group.

Several top golf programs participated in the three-round event, including Arizona, UNLV and Pepperdine. But they were no match for the hometown Lobos. New Mexico destroyed the visitors, trouncing the field by eleven strokes.

Madalitso was keenly aware of this moment as he walked to the first tee. Two years earlier, he looked the president of his country in the eye and said with absolute conviction that this was what he wanted. And now, here he stood. *Be careful what you wish for,* he thought to himself, wondering if he'd made the right choice. But Madalitso quickly realized he couldn't afford to get lost in what it all meant. In what-ifs. There was too much personal, family and world history at stake. He had golf to play. A tournament to try and win. Besides, this was only one stop on a long journey.

He had enough on his plate trying to negotiate wicked wind gusts and South's treacherous design over three grueling days. Of the 104-player field packed with some of the best college golfers in the world, only four players had opening round scores in the 60s. In the second round, there was only one.

Madalitso felt the brunt of South's unfriendly conditions when he teed off at the seventh hole. The long (520-yard) straight par 4 seemed a perfect chance to take advantage of his distance off the tee. Eager to start putting some low scores onto his scorecard, he pulled the driver from his bag and loosened his waist, arms and shoulders with a few full practice swings. Staring down the fairway, he eyed a desired landing spot from which he could attack the green.

Lining up over his ball he felt the wind die down...or so he thought. With his usual careful backswing and smooth follow-through, he sent his ball into the Albuquerque sky. The club wrapped completely around his body with the ball climbing higher and higher and heading straight to the area he targeted. Dead on accurate.

But as the ball reached its height, it began drifting inexplicably from left to right. *The wind!* he groaned to himself. Tacking further right on its decline, he watched it land, bounce once and come to rest in the rough on the right side. What seemed like an ideal birdie opportunity was now a fight to save par.

He wasn't alone. The next golfer, perhaps thinking the rules of Mother Nature didn't apply to him, ignored Madalitso's shot and launched one high and deep. The result was worse. Four seconds later, his ball ended up completely outside the fairway, resting in sand and surrounded by sagebrush.

The final two golfers in the group paid attention. After witnessing the bizarre flight paths of the balls hit by Madalitso and the other boy, they hit low line drives. Sacrificing distance for accuracy left them in the middle of the fairway with a long stretch of grass in between them and the green.

For his approach shot, 99.9 percent of the time Madalitso would have gone for the pin. But the erratic gusts and two bunkers that bookended the green caused him to think otherwise. An abbreviated swing and an adjustment to his stance brought a lower trajectory to the ball, which safely landed just in front of the green.

Madalitso surveyed the position of the pin in relation to his ball—about thirty feet. With pitching wedge in hand, he stood over his ball and prepared for a chip and run that might allow him to be within striking distance with his putter. Under normal conditions he would already be on the green, but the constant threat of wind forced him to lay up.

Watching the occasional gusts bend the flag back and forth, Madalitso firmly believed his ball was safer on the ground than in the air. He hit a low line drive that just cleared the lip of the green and began a long roll toward the cup. He knew immediately that the ball would stop short, but this was a round where simply avoiding disaster was a respectable goal. The ball traversed the tiered green and eventually stopped seven feet from the cup, leaving him with a makeable chance at birdie.

The line was relatively straight, just a matter of speed and direction. He stood over his ball, controlled his breathing and made contact. The ball was heading directly toward the cup and looked quite good. But ultimately, it glided just to the right, perhaps an overcompensation for what he perceived as a slight downward slant to the left. He tapped in, knelt down and picked up his ball, all while teeming with frustration that was barely detectable to the naked eye.

Of course, Madalitso knew it wasn't a single missed putt that turned this birdie into a par. It was the previous four shots where simply hitting the ball into the air was a roll of the dice.

Madalitso and others continued making adjustments throughout the day, tinkering with their swings, ball placement and club selection. Finishing their follow-throughs high and early, placing the ball further back in their stance and frequently laying up rather than going for the long ball were all done in the effort to combat the wind and challenging pin placements that dogged them all day.

Madalitso shot a respectable opening round of 73 by keeping his drives in play and avoiding the wind. Unable to drive the ball long, he needed to rely on his short game. But he struggled to find a rhythm with his chipping and putting. He followed up his first-round score with 74s in both the second and third. It was an accomplishment that he maintained consistency in a tournament where few were able to do so. A solid performance for his first college tournament, Madalitso finished twenty-fifth out of 104 players, shooting a better score than two UNM varsity golfers.

It was Madalitso's first tournament at what was now his home course. South was a highly acclaimed venue and he knew it. Madalitso was happy and grateful to be there. But it was far different from anything he had played before. The high winds, dry air, southwestern landscape, desert vegetation and elevation that was 1,200 feet higher than Lusaka all presented a myriad of new challenges to him. The 2001 William H. Tucker Invitational was a rocky start to what was going to be a long-term relationship between Madalitso and South.

More broadly, the Tucker proved to be the start of a disturbing pattern. Some days at practice, Madalitso would go toe-to-toe with UNM's best players, matching them stroke for stroke. On other days, he struggled. Mightily. His up-and-down performances on the golf course mirrored his new life in America. Some days, it would all come together brilliantly. Others, he felt lost and out of his element, like a fish flopping around out of water.

He was left off the squad for the next varsity tournament: the Adams Cup in Newport, Rhode Island. At the competition to select the varsity team, his problems went far beyond high winds and challenging pin placements. The problem was him. He couldn't seem to find a club that would make the ball do what he wanted it to. After betrayal by his irons on the first five holes, he was safely on the sixth green with two putts to save par.

The sixth hole at South has a massive 40-yard green surrounded by four bunkers. Although the cup was at the far end of the green, Madalitso was confident that his long lag putt would leave him with an easy tap-in for par. But picking the right line and speed across such a vast expanse of slick green with so many undulations proved nearly impossible. No matter how many times he walked from his ball to the hole, he couldn't see the line. Couldn't feel the speed. Eventually he had to make his best guess and leave the rest to his old friends, the golf gods.

Madalitso stepped forward and took a more upright body position, feet further apart than normal. He peered one more time across the green and took a deep backswing and follow-through, propelling his ball forward.

A few seconds into its journey, the ball vibrated and bounced. He hadn't hit it hard enough. The ball barely made it two-thirds of the way to the hole when it began to break. *Way too early.* He closed his eyes and let out a little groan as it turned, painfully slow, and stopped twenty feet from the hole.

Madalitso needed to understand how this disaster happened so he could self-correct going forward. But he was completely mystified. His next swing felt right, and the line had seemed perfect. But it was all wrong. He missed his par putt and bogeyed the sixth hole.

It was a snapshot of the whole day. His pre-shot routines, club selection, swing and every other variable seemed perfect...except the results. And his score. And his place on the team. He had failed. Worse than that, he didn't know why. Or how to fix it.

Walking off the course, he knew the fault didn't lie with the brand-new set of custom-made golf clubs that greeted him when he arrived in Albuquerque a few weeks earlier. But he still shot them a cold stare when he abruptly shut them into his locker that evening. It was the kind of day that makes any player want nothing more than to go home, crawl into bed and pray the next day brings a return to normalcy. After a round like this, Madalitso always found comfort in talking it over with his father. Now several time zones apart, it was the first time that Madalitso really felt Peter's absence.

Millican sent him and a few JV players to the Falcon-Antigua Invitational hosted by the Air Force Academy in Colorado Springs. The tournament would be played at the Eisenhower Blue Course, a Robert Trent Jones—designed venue named one of the top 100 courses in the nation.

Madalitso knew he had to step up. He'd done it so many times before when he traveled to England, when he forged his fateful victory at Fort Myers. He wanted to show his new coach and his teammates what he was really made of. He wanted to extinguish the demons in the back of his head that said, *Maybe he didn't have the right stuff after all.* Most of all, he just wanted to be himself again on the golf course, to play the best he could in this strange and beautiful new country.

After a steady opening round of 72, he arrived on day two feeling like his old self. His drives were straight, his approach shots were on target, his putts found the right line and hole after hole, the birdies piled up. "I don't know what happened in the second round. I just finally felt comfortable out there." No more comfortable than when he arrived at the sixteenth tee.

The sixteenth hole at the Eisenhower Blue Course was a behemoth—over 600 yards long and straight from start to finish. At 7,000 feet above sea level, it's a perfect opportunity for long ball hitters. Madalitso had already been playing well when he pulled out the driver and stared down the long fairway.

At the team qualifier in Albuquerque, nothing felt right. No matter where his ball was or which club he used, uncertainty and confusion plagued him on every shot.

Not today.

Madalitso was a study in controlled aggression as he nonchalantly exploded his ball through the rare air, club completely wrapping around his twisted torso, every ounce of muscle torqued into the shot. It hadn't finished its ascent when sounds of surprise and amazement blossomed all around him. "Jesus!" one guy called out. As the ball reached its crest, even Madalitso was surprised by the distance.

A sense of relief washed over him when the ball landed and rolled to its final resting place. As Madalitso walked out of the tee box, another player said to him, "That might be four hundred yards."

"Yeah," Madalitso smiled. "Maybe." It was the longest drive he could remember hitting. He collected his bag and set off down the path, finally feeling *really* good. Finally feeling like himself.

He was determined not to break his rhythm by overthinking. Two hundred yards from the flag, Mad didn't stress over the three greenside bunkers that frightened most golfers into laying up short. He didn't hit a titanic tee shot so he could baby-step onto the green. Much like his shot into the driving rain at the Henke-Berg, this wasn't a time to question his instincts or to wilt. He was in attack mode, channeling the Zulu warrior of his Zambian heritage.

Don't hesitate, he said to himself. *Just go.*

Seconds later, his ball, some sod and a few blades of grass shot upward. He knew the pin placement at the center-back of the green left little margin for error. As the ball came down, he knew that he'd either hit it too hard or it was going to be an exquisite shot.

Exquisite it was.

The ball rolled to within four feet of the hole. People from 100 yards away erupted in applause. The same guy who invoked the Lord's name after Madalitso's tee shot yelled out, "Great ball, man!" Madalitso smiled, raised his hand and glanced downward. He was looking to replace the divot he had just created, but there was also some embarrassment over the boisterous reactions.

After all the suffering he'd gone through, the disappearance of the skill that had always come so easily, it was pure joy to be playing like a champion again.

Four minutes later, he tapped in a no-brainer putt and wrote the number three into his card.

Eagle.

By the end of the round, Madalitso had crafted together a masterful 66. No one would've known it by looking at him, but Mad felt a deep satisfaction when he looked at the leaderboard and saw his name in second place.

It was his best eighteen holes since arriving in the United States. In fact, Madalitso's 66 at the 2001 Falcon-Antigua is still listed as one of the best rounds of tournament golf ever shot by a UNM player.

He shot a hard-earned, one-under 71 in his closing round, taking home second place for his new school. He was a happy Lobo.

Back in Albuquerque, Madalitso, Glen and Ryan telephoned me on speakerphone.

"I just felt good throughout the tournament. Shots were going straight, and putts were dropping. It was nothing special." He was humble and restrained as always. But I could hear a change. There was a lightness, a levity in his voice and laughter in the room with his new crew, his new peeps. I heard equal parts relief and happiness. Finally.

I breathed a sigh of happy relief myself.

Madalitso's first semester at college was easily the most unusual and difficult time in his first eighteen years on the planet. He played in four tournaments that fall and survived his freshman classes. Peter had tried to prepare his son for the rigors of college academics and golf. But nothing could simulate moving from Lusaka, Zambia, to Albuquerque, New Mexico. Everything was strange. The lingo, the dialect, the food. Seriously, how does one prepare oneself for a chalupa? How do you explain to someone who doesn't know what it is, that all you crave is bream fish or nshima (pounded white maize) with cooked vegetables?

And since when do golfers have to do sprints or run stadium stairs? Plus of course, he was away from the bedrock of his existence. His people. His home. His stuff. His brother and sister. His mom. His dad. He'd never felt more alone. Although we spoke several times a week, I was thousands of miles away in Washington, DC. His up-and-down, high-and-low performances on the golf course were a snapshot of his broader struggle to acclimate to a new universe where he was an alien with no roadmap or personal guide to support him.

And yet there were plenty of positives from his first five months away from home. It was a huge struggle, but he managed to keep up with his schoolwork. The quality and pace of instruction at his secondary school in Zambia was below that of most high schools in America. Madalitso sometimes felt like he was drowning and everything was moving way too fast. But he stayed after class and got help, meeting with classmates and/or academic advisors in the athletic department. Peter had taught him how to work hard. So, he rolled up his sleeves, gritted his teeth and slogged through it. His extra effort paid off. He passed with flying colors. By nature and nurture, he was resilient. And he knew how to put on a good face, showing few signs of homesickness—at least outwardly.

"I am happy to be at UNM," he would announce on our three-way calls. "I love school!"

Peter found great comfort in Madalitso's positive attitude. "I can hear it in his voice. My son will be fine."

But there would soon be another danger that neither father nor son knew how to overcome.

28

PETER STEWED OVER TERRIBLE NEWS. Madalitso had to drop out of school and return home.

His scholarship covered only 85 percent of his first-year tuition, books, room and board. It was December, and the University of New Mexico was asking for the first semester payment. But Peter did not have the money.

I became the communications link between UNM and the Muthiya family. "Peter...uhh...UNM called and...well...they are asking for payment of Madalitso's tuition."

"I understand."

That's all he said. No despair, nervousness or frustration. He didn't say anything about the fact that his business was barely afloat or that he was short of funds. He simply listened and promised to get back to me. We'd never had a conversation that was so short and uncomfortable.

Days passed. Pressure mounted. I heard nothing. Every morning, I telephoned Peter and sent emails. There were no replies. Not even an acknowledgment that my messages were received. For the first—and only—time in our relationship, I was mad at him. *Why isn't he at least giving me the courtesy of a simple response?*

UNM was calling with increased frequency. I was determined not to burden Madalitso in the midst of final exams. He was under enough pressure.

Finally, it finally dawned on me. Peter had been communicating with me the whole time. I wasn't listening.

My mother had become my (very willing) sounding board. Though venting ear is probably more accurate. I told Mom that I realized Peter didn't have the money. "There's only one solution," I said. "I'll cover the balance of Madalitso's tuition."

"Too late," she said flatly.

"What do you mean?"

"Claude and I discussed it. We sent a check to the university today."

When I objected, she talked right over me and shut me down as only a mom can. "Madalitso is not *your* family. He is *our* family. You take care of his airline ticket to Seattle for Christmas. We'll handle this. End of story."

Mother has spoken. Discussion over.

A million emotions washed over me. Joy, relief, gratitude, pride, euphoria. And that's just the tip of the iceberg. My mom and Claude were my inspiration. They'd welcomed Madalitso into our family without reservation, fully accepting everything it entailed. In good times and in bad.

I sent an email to Peter, telling him that my mom and Claude paid Madalitso's bill. Since our last conversation, I had done a lot of soul-searching, and my feelings had changed from anger to sympathy. *Of course* Peter wanted to pay the balance on his son's tuition. He was a proud man and came from a country and culture where the head of the family doesn't ask for help or handouts. My folks—people he had met only once—were giving him money when he had none, and it surely weighed on him. I tried to imagine how he must dread my incoming calls and emails.

"Hello, Jayme." Peter's voice was somber. It was a couple of hours since I sent the email.

"Hey, Peter."

A few seconds of silence passed before he exhaled. "You know, Jayme. They call this the third world...but I don't think that's accurate. It's more like the tenth world."

In his voice was the unbending pride that I'd come to know and love, pride that had driven him to great achievements throughout his life. But now made this situation so hard to swallow.

I offered two words that I hoped would bring this conversation to a close. "I understand."

Two weeks later, I was wrapping up some work at the office before I flew home to Seattle for the holidays when the phone rang.

"Jayme! Guess what!" My mother's voice burst with enthusiasm.

"Hi, Mom. What's going on?"

"Peter sent something from Zambia. It's a cardboard tube, the kind used to ship posters."

"Well, open it," I said, feeling excited myself.

Through the phone, I heard her wrestling with the package. "It's a painting...a painting of an African woman."

I put her on hold and dialed Peter. When he answered, my mother and I, at exactly the same time, said hello.

"Your package arrived, Peter," she said. "Thank you so much for the painting."

"Oh good, I am relieved that it found its way from Lusaka to Mukilteo." He then asked, "Do you know what it is?"

"It's a woman, a pregnant woman," my mom answered.

"Yes, but do you notice her body language?"

"She seems happy."

"That's right," Peter responded. "The artist is conveying the joy felt by a new mother. Janet, in some ways you have become a second mother to Madalitso. That is why I wanted you to have it."

Mom's voice cracked as she replied, "We are happy to have Madalitso in our lives, Peter."

"Yes, I know you are," he replied calmly. "That is why the woman reminded me of you."

29

CHRISTMAS AT CHARLES AT SMUGGLERS Cove Restaurant lasts a month. My mother's giant wreaths, glittering ornaments and bright red poinsettias bloom festively all over the English brick manor house that is home to Charles. Claude's *Bûche de Noël* is as much legend as dessert at this point. His chocolate truffles, made by hand every year, make you happy to be alive. At home, our centerpieces are the dining room table and a Christmas tree surrounded by brightly wrapped presents.

In Zambia, Christmas celebrations revolve around church, attending religious services, singing songs and sharing festive food. Exchanging gifts depends on whether a family can afford it. Most cannot.

We got Madalitso from the airport, hoping he'd feel welcome and comfortable on his first Christmas away from his home and family. An hour after touching down, Madalitso was yakking it up with the waiters at the Charles like he was born into it. He paraded right into the kitchen and greeted Claude and Brian Tvedt, our number two culinarian. He threw on an apron and, making good on his promise to learn how to cook, stood next to the oven and began asking questions. My mom and I exchanged a smile. We had nothing to worry about. He was one of us.

Welcoming comes in different forms at our house. As much as a warm hug, my mom shaking her finger at Madalitso and warmly scolding, "Whose golf clubs are these blocking the entryway?!" was a sign of acceptance.

Madalitso sprinted out from the guest room like the younger brother I never had. "Oh...they're mine! Sorry!"

"Merry Christmas!" Madalitso emerged from his bedroom on Christmas morning and exchanged a hug with my mom. He then grabbed a stool while Claude began work on a breakfast that almost put us back to sleep. The customary breakfast menu of eggs, potatoes, bacon, sausage and bread was enhanced with foie gras, smoked salmon and goat cheese. Champagne washed it all down. Madalitso opted for orange juice.

Foie gras in one hand, I used the other to call Zambia. Peter answered with a cheery "Merry Christmas" and a jolly laugh. I responded in kind, and soon we began passing around the telephone. My mom and Claude had never spoken with Edith, Wongani and Ivwananji. It was an opportunity for everyone to put names with voices. Most importantly, Madalitso got to exchange some Christmas love with his family.

After breakfast, we made our way to the living room and the Christmas tree. My mom, Claude and Madalitso each sat a few feet away as I moved in and began the important ritual of gift distribution.

Preoccupied with tearing wrapping paper, I didn't notice that Madalitso's gifts were sitting unopened in front him. As my mom nudged him to dive in, I noticed his face. He was peering downward. Not quite embarrassed, but definitely unsure.

We tried not to stare and make him feel more self-conscious. He sat for a few moments, quietly glancing at the wrapped packages in front of him. The rest of us laughed, tossing paper and ribbon in every direction, *oohing* and *ahhing* over our gifts. I kept tabs on Madalitso from the corner of my eye.

Eventually, he looked up and saw all the Christmas silliness around him. It felt to me like our antics washed away the uneasiness.

Madalitso finally picked up a gift and began opening it, slowly.

LATER, AFTER A final round of hugs, my mom and Claude left the living room. Madalitso and I decided to watch a movie. After some debate, we agreed on a James Bond film. As I fumbled with the disc, Madalitso said, "Jayme?"

"Yeah." I was still seated, facing the TV with my back to him.

"In Zambia, very few young people can receive a decent education. Most don't even finish secondary school. Right now, tens of thousands are malnourished or dying from disease."

I turned around and faced him.

"The story of Africans is a story of suffering. Of hardship. Of doing without. And yet I am in America, going to college, playing golf and now here. It's just that...I mean... I guess I don't understand. Why me?"

His face was a mix of confusion, appreciation and a touch of guilt. Despite years of hard work and tournament victories, he never projected a sense of entitlement. None of this was expected.

Why me?

He stared at me as I tried to think of an answer to his question, along with a slew of others racing through my head. Why did a five-year-old Black child in colonial Africa become entranced by a game where sticks were used to hit a little ball into a hole in the ground? Why was a six-year-old boy able to drive a golf ball 100 meters through a kitchen window? Why was he able to excel at such a technical sport with no formal training and inferior equipment? Why did the fates of a young attorney in Washington, DC, and a teenage golfer from Zambia come together?

Sitting on the floor holding a James Bond DVD, I gave the only answer I could.

"I don't know."

30

THE LOBO GOLF TEAM ENTERED the winter-spring season with seven varsity tournaments between February 4 and April 13. Madalitso only qualified for two, and his performances at both were less than memorable.

Madalitso's first winter in Albuquerque was a cold rude awakening. Below freezing temperatures from December through February made shivering the new normal for Mad. The coldest month of the year in Lusaka is June, where the average low is 47 degrees. A balmy summerlike day in ABQ winter. But the bone-rattling sting of hitting a ball in frigid weather was nothing compared to the pain of his sixth month away from his home and family. Whether it was homesickness, the weather, the lack of nshima in the school cafeteria or the million other changes he dealt with every day since leaving Zambia, life in the United States was taking a toll on Madalitso. And his golf game. He was adrift in a frozen ocean, with no oars, no compass and no land in sight.

Despite the warning signs, he was utterly unprepared for what happened at Austin Country Club, site of the Morris Williams Intercollegiate. It was Madalitso's first varsity tournament in months, but he wasn't a member of UNM's five-man team. Coach Millican decided to enter him as an individual.

Sold on Madalitso's talent, he and Coach Murphy were determined to get their prized freshman in the mix and out on the battlefield competing. They knew they needed him to break out of his funk in time for the grand prize down the road: the Mountain West Conference Championship.

Madalitso was thankful to be there. But when he arrived in the United States on a near-full scholarship, he never pictured himself as being "thankful" for simply playing with the varsity. His game had been off the rails for too long. From the first time he swung a club and sent a ball crashing through a kitchen window, he'd never endured such a long period of playing so poorly.

The first hole at Austin CC is a par 4 dogleg left, just under 400 yards. Madalitso eyed his fairway target 250 yards away and took an extra-long deep breath. *Okay,* he said. *Just this one.* Mentally going through every detail of his fundamentals, he found his grip and let her rip.

Madalitso was confident that he'd executed right technically. But it didn't *feel* right. It felt mechanical. Forced. Rigid. It was not the instinctive, natural, fluid swing that won him so many tournaments and earned him a scholarship to UNM. But it was a good enough opening drive, middle of the fairway with a clear shot at the green. Unsteady as a baby dear, he lifted his bag and trundled down the fairway.

The tournament began smoothly enough, with back-to-back pars on the first two holes. But then he arrived at the third. Some Austin Country Club employees consider it the golf course's signature hole, and when he was at his best, Madalitso would have eaten it alive. A no-nonsense par 5—perfect for long ball hitters—required a long, accurate drive. And he delivered, with a 300-yard blast straight down the fairway.

But now he was stuck with the horns of a dilemma. On the right side of the green was a series of bunkers, and on the left side was a piece of the Colorado River. Staring at the green with Pennybacker Bridge in the background, Madalitso grabbed his seven-iron. Laying up short was the safe choice. But he needed to ignite his adrenaline. To get back to playing his game. To *being himself.*

So he took dead aim at the center of the green, determined to shed the deep funk that had dogged him all morning. All winter. Madalitso settled his breath and moved into position while uttering reassurances to himself. "Come on. You've done this a thousand times before."

A textbook swing sent his ball flying at the hole. He watched, rapt, as it climbed. The distance seemed perfect and elation filled him. But then it faded right, *further* and *further* right. Wanting to avoid the risk of a watery grave on the left, he'd overcorrected. *Come on,* he pleaded. *Stop.* But the golf gods didn't listen, and his ball plummeted unceremoniously into a pot bunker on the right side.

Madalitso closed his eyes, and his shoulders sank. If he'd been his brother, he would have screamed his head off. But his muted, three-second reaction contained months' worth of confused frustration. Never one to lament for long, he gathered his golf bag, and himself, and made his way to Austin's third green.

His ball buried like a sunken treasure in the sand. Just a white tortoise shell above the surface. Trusty sand wedge in hand, he descended into the bowels of the bunker and assessed the mess he'd put himself in. The depth of the pot bunker, and the fact that his ball was submerged, meant Madalitso would have to swing hard and get well under it.

Spectators watched intently as he eyed a spot a few inches behind his ball. With the primary goal of unearthing his ball from this deep pit of despair, he drove his clubhead down hard into the sand.

The ball exploded out of the bunker. Even before the sandstorm dissipated, Madalitso knew something was terribly wrong. The height and distance were both off. Way off. Surprise turned to despair as it soared over the center of the green. He watched helpless and bewildered as his ball bounced on the far side of the green and drowned in the Colorado River.

Madalitso stood motionless in the sand as he and his ball sank. People had looked at him with awkward, strange silences many times before, of course. Usually, it was players and parents staring at his shabby clubs, shoes and clothing. Or at his black face. Their eyes had always asked the question that their mouths lacked the courage to utter. *Do you belong here?* Of course, Madalitso's performance on the course always provided an emphatic answer.

But this time, the awkward glances and the questions behind them were *because* of his play. His failure.

Madalitso double bogeyed the hole. It was one of many low points in the worst tournament of his college career. He shot 83-80-80. It was his only tournament at UNM where he failed to break 80 in a single round. It was a disaster.

Madalitso kept his composure in Austin, ever the model of sportsmanship, congratulating his teammates and fellow competitors. His seventy-sixth-place finish did not silence the questions behind the stares. But that's not what bothered him. Madalitso would never have come this far if he let people's opinions get to him. The bitterest pill to swallow was knowing his horrible performance hurt those counting on him: his teammates and coaches. He'd let down the college, and in fact his whole country.

The results were barely better at the Arizona State University Thunderbird Invite. This time, Madalitso made the five-man varsity team, inspiring hope that he was going to turn his season around.

He arrived in Tempe determined to avoid the massive blunders that had sunk him in Austin. "Caution" would be his mantra.

Madalitso stood outside the opening tee box at ASU's Karsten Golf Course, waiting to tee off. He thought about how much he'd learned since arriving in the United States. He'd always been a solo artist with no experience of "team golf." In Zambia, he registered, showed up and played. NCAA golf was completely different. The UNM golf team had over a dozen players, all of whom lived for the thrill of traveling to varsity tournaments and putting on the school colors. Failing to make UNM's travel squad so many times had made him appreciate just being able to play.

But it was a different kind of pressure than he'd ever dealt with. *Every shot has to be good. Don't screw up or you'll be taken off the varsity team.* He would've done anything to have a face-to-face conversation with his dad and soak up his advice, like the old days.

Madalitso stared down the first fairway of ASU's Karsten Golf Course, a 400-yard dogleg right. The confident high school whiz-kid prodigy who beat so many professionals at the Zambia Open and the Botswana Open would've said to himself, *Cut the dogleg. Shorten the approach shot to the green. Go for the pin!*

The self-doubting college freshman, this stranger in a strange land he'd become in America, was different. He was struggling. A different voice spoke in his head. *Play it safe, at least for now. Until you're back.*

Madalitso meticulously addressed the ball, almost as if he were making an instructional video in basic fundamentals to beginners. His swing was studious, joyless. The ball did not cut the dogleg. It landed about 250 yards away, with another 140 to the green. A good, safe shot. But not a Madalitso shot.

A few minutes later, he stood staring at the flag. Bunkers on the right side of the green, but nothing to worry about. Every instinct urged him to launch an arcing rainbow right at the flag. But he remembered his conservative game plan. *Play it safe. Play it safe.*

His ball didn't trace a graceful and arcing rainbow. It didn't give him a great shot at birdie. Instead, it landed where he aimed, in boring safety in front of the green. A chip shot and textbook putt gave him his first par of the tournament.

Madalitso's "no-risk-no-reward" approach worked for the few holes, notching three straight pars. At the fourth hole, a straightaway par 4, he began with another pedestrian, underwhelming tee shot. Lugging his bag and himself up the fairway, disappointment bit into him as he saw that his ball was much further back from the green than where it should be. He was making the game harder for himself, not easier.

Mad stood motionless behind his ball, staring at the pond to the left. The flag was also on the left, though not dangerously close to the water. Having threaded needles narrower than this, he would normally aim for the flag, or at least the center of green. But he'd been burned by water too often recently, and the ghosts of watery death for his balls haunted him.

Again, he moved gingerly, mentally double-checking everything from head to toe. He methodically hit his approach, hoping not to fail instead of daring to succeed.

Madalitso watched as the ball reached its peak and then descended. His expression was blank when it landed exactly where he planned—front right. Golfers—and most humans—are usually happy when their actions have the exact result they intended. Not Madalitso. Not today. He decided to lay up short and right because he didn't trust himself. Settling for shots like this was leaving a bitter taste. It wasn't the way of the Zulu warrior.

Moments later, he stared at forty feet of yawning green between his ball and the hole. Seeing how far away he was up close was infuriating. He had virtually no shot at a birdie. And he knew that a bold, classic Mad approach shot would have given a chance to move up the leaderboard instead of languishing at dead even. He heard his dad's voice. *It does no good stewing over the previous shot. Focus on the next shot.*

His mind scanned the terrain as he stalked back and forth, searching for the line that would get him close. Putter in hand, he knelt for one last look at the undulations. He rehearsed a few swings to get a feel for the speed, to loosen up and release the jitters. Moving into position, he focused his eyes downward. *Exhale.* The clubhead came steadily back and then briskly forward.

The ball shot straight ahead, over a ridge and down the other side. Madalitso watched closely as it moved rapidly across the green, and broke from right to left as he suspected. But it lost steam too quickly. *Come on,* he urged under his breath. *Come on.* His pleas went unanswered as the ball curved eight feet in front of the hole and stopped.

Madalitso looked down, suppressing his anger as he placed a marker down, picked up his ball and stepped aside. Trying not to let his frustration consume him, he glanced around and said a quick word to his playing partner.

When the other players holed out, Mad placed his ball down carefully. All eyes were on him. He quickly walked a circle around the 8-foot journey his ball would have to travel. Although it was a straight-ahead putt, he was now overanalyzing everything. Convinced he just needed to stroke the ball straight, he lined up and looked down at his ball. Conversations stopped.

The ball popped forward. He knew it was the right speed. As the ball got closer it moved slightly right. Madalitso leaned left attempting to influence. But once again, the universe seemed to conspire against him, sending his ball rolling past the right lip of the cup. He took a deep breath and swallowed his fury, then tapped in for bogey.

As he meditated on this hole, he didn't blame the final putt. It was his paralyzing worry over the water hazard and the decision to play it safe and lay up short. At the ASU invitational, Madalitso wasn't making the same self-destructive blunders that caused the train wreck in Austin. It was his decision to play it safe—*too* safe—that cost him.

His score of 74-75-71 landed him in sixty-third place. Four over par didn't sound bad. But this was a tournament where players were routinely shooting in the 60s. Three of New Mexico's five players finished even or under par. Madalitso had the worst score on his team.

Madalitso was devastated that failure had dragged his coaches and teammates down. UNM finished in a disappointing tenth place, twenty-one strokes behind the winner. Mad felt the weight of the crushing defeat and carried it with him all the way home.

Peter always told Madalitso the only way to answer the doubters was by being better. Better sportsman. Better driver and putter. Better behaved in victory and defeat. Because Madalitso was poor, Black and African, playing a game that originated and was always dominated by White men from wealthy countries, Peter knew the bar would be higher for his son. To be accepted, Madalitso had to meet a higher standard.

Madalitso knew it too. From the first time he competed, he had always stuck out, never able to simply blend in. His actions, good or bad, were magnified. It was why Peter spent years ingraining in Madalitso the importance of ignoring everything outside of himself. *Just focus on what you need to do.* It was the only way he could last in a world so foreign to people like him, and the only way he could endure the scrutiny when things didn't go his way. Poker face firmly in place, he went about his business with a graceful stoicism that let his game, and not his antics or the color of his skin, take center stage.

Coach Millican and Coach Murphy encouraged Madalitso in this unprecedented, for him anyway, period of frustration. They offered technical advice, strategic guidance and sometimes just a sympathetic ear whenever he felt like venting. His struggle to acclimate was obvious. They also knew Madalitso's recent struggles were not based on his talent. Since his arrival in Albuquerque, there were moments when he'd played as well as any college golfer in America. Millican and Murphy needed to bring that out. There were bigger tournaments on the horizon.

Peter and I talked more and more during this agonizing two-month stretch. I threw out theories and suggested strategies to find a solution. Peter listened politely but offered little more than an occasional "mmm-hmm."

"The only person who can dig Madalitso out of this hole is Madalitso."

When Peter said this, I was reminded how he and Edith strove above all else to instill independence in their children.

I increased the frequency of our three-way calls. Peter never changed his approach. He continued to ask open-ended questions: *"How are you?" "Are you enjoying golf?"* It was up to Madalitso to elaborate or not. If he wanted help, we were right there for him.

Wongani was a force to be reckoned with, and his temperament was very different from Peter's and mine. Now attending the University of Notre Dame in Australia, Wongani worked two jobs to afford tuition, rent and food. Combined with his classes and study time, he only got four hours of sleep a night. It was quite a pleasure to hear Wongani step up on his soapbox and give Madalitso a fiery pep talk that would make any football coach proud. "What an opportunity you have, my brother! Each day you move closer to your dream! Focus, work hard, remember who you are and where you come from!"

Madalitso seldom reacted to Wongani's impassioned speeches. But I sensed he enjoyed them. I certainly did.

Peter and Wongani provided brief moments of levity during a dark and difficult time. Eight months had passed since Peter asked me to assume a larger role in his son's life...a *cri du coeur* that I reluctantly accepted. Of course, I was comforted in knowing that Peter was there if anything serious arose.

But I couldn't help feeling like I was failing Madalitso. And Peter.

Rookie coach Glen Millican had a lot on his mind two weeks before the Mountain West Conference Championship in Bend, Oregon. Winning the conference championship in his first season would be a great achievement, propelling his career—and UNM's golf program—forward.

He and Assistant Coach Ryan Murphy pored over the team's roster, trying to piece together a five-man squad that could bring the championship to Albuquerque. Wil Collins, Michael Letzig and Scott Hailes, the three most consistent players all year, were guaranteed spots. Two spots remained. An intra-squad tournament would again decide who'd be chosen for this crucial chance to become part of UNM history.

Every day and with every shot, Madalitso improved and drew praise—*finally*. But after a string of solid practices, it was time to prove that he belonged with the varsity.

I tried to alleviate any stress during our morning call. "Just go out and have fun."

"Oh yeah, no worries." His nonchalant exterior was thin. I could hear how eager he was to break out of his slump and put the last few miserable months behind him.

Focusing on work was hard. I sent up a silent prayer at the exact moment Madalitso was scheduled to tee off, and then began *agonizingly* watching the clock.

My phone rang later that evening.

"Hey, Jayme. It's Madalitso."

"Hey, Mad. How's it going?" I tried to sound nonchalant. I failed.

"Good. We finished playing for the day."

"Ah-ha. How did you play?" I prepared to deliver a pep talk in case of bad news.

"I played okay."

His voice sounded so flat that I got ready to launch into my speech about how failure is the stepping-stone to success.

"I'm playing with the varsity in the conference championship."

"AHH...that's awesome!" Heaving a huge sigh of relief, I slumped back in my chair. From the moment Madalitso arrived, news from Albuquerque often determined whether I had a good or bad day. His pain was my pain. His joy became my joy.

For the first time, I felt responsible for another person's life.

THE CONFERENCE CHAMPIONSHIP was played at Sunriver Resort, a short distance from Bend. With Mt. Bachelor in the background, the Crosswater Golf Course looks like a picture postcard. But the beauty was also a beast. Well-placed water hazards, fast tricky undulating greens, and LONG par 4s would bring the best players in the Mountain West to their knees.

Madalitso was stoic as always when he stepped to the first tee, a straight-forward par 4. After his pre-shot routine, he took his usual three or four practice swings and moved into position, extending the club to the ball to ensure proper distance.

A smooth, rhythmic backswing and follow-through rocketed the ball down the center of the fairway. It rolled well past the other players in his group, in perfect position to reach the green. The tone was set for the rest of his round.

The course was designed to destroy golfers. Dastardly sand traps, cruel pin placements and inhuman long fairways forced prudent golfers to play it safe. Madalitso was built for this. His game was all about cautiously taking what the course gave him. And belting longer drives than anyone. All day he aimed for safety.

It wasn't spectacular. But that course, on that day, wasn't made for spectacular. Mad just kept pounding huge straight drives, pinpointing his irons so he had at least a sniff of a birdie putt and stroking the flat stick with calm alacrity.

A perfect recipe for a rock solid 72 over his first eighteenth holes. He was tied for fourth.

Day two. Early in the round, Mad heard the hero voice in his head: *Go for it! Tear this course apart!* And that voice screamed at the third, a 180-yard par 3. The green was guarded by four bunkers, *all* on the right side. Naturally, that's where the flag was. Designers were daring players to try and land their ball in this minefield. Throughout the tournament, several players were lured by their own past heroics and sense of invincibility only to find themselves getting blown up in an explosion of sand.

Madalitso read his yardage book and peered down the fairway. Grabbing his seven-iron, he considered tempting fate and daring to go straight at the pin. As he set his legs and found his grip, his muscles remembered threading similar needles almost got the best of him. Somehow, he resisted temptation. The warrior must know when to attack and when to move forward with caution.

The ball left his clubhead at a steep angle and reached a perfect arch before falling onto the middle of the green. Backspin kept his ball from rolling, leaving him with a very makeable 8-foot putt for birdie. Mad felt a void, the lack of adrenalized joy that comes when a competitor takes the safe route. But watching his peers hack their way out of the bunkers convinced him that he'd done the right thing.

He now needed to navigate a ridge with a downward slope. Remembering his pledge to avoid costly mistakes, he was mindful not to go for broke and roll past the hole. He hit his putt smoothly but with a touch of caution. The ball climbed over the ridge and down the ridge, breaking toward the hole. The line was spot on. He smelled a birdie, a breakthrough, an end perhaps to his season of torment. But it ran out of gas just in the last foot and a half, stopping six inches short. He tapped in for par.

Once again, the cautious restraint on his first putt, much like his drive off the tee, left him without a fist-pumping, hair-standing-on-the-back-of-the-neck moment. Such is the way it goes when playing smart golf. This would be his approach over the next fifteen holes, and he would grind out another solid round. Strategic accuracy and great distance off the tee, unwavering fairway, bunker and water navigation, steady-as-she-goes putting.

Methodical Madalitso worked his way around the course, playing within himself and avoiding disaster.

Seventy-one. Tied for third place with one round to go. Better than any UNM player. Ahead of other prominent collegians, including Ryan Moore, future PGA star.

Now, all he had to do was close. And Mad had always been a closer. On the par 5 sixth hole, he sat at the front of the green, needing two good shots to get a much-needed birdie, three to save par. A tabletop green stared at him, daring him to have a go at the hole. But it had a perilous slope that dropped off the back side, punishing those who overshot. Madalitso had been careful to pull back on his shots, choosing prudence over valor. But his mojo was working, and he decided to seize the day.

He clipped the ball cleanly, *too* cleanly, and watched it line drive onto the green. He held his breath and begged his ball to slow its roll. His ball did not listen. It sped past the hole and disappeared down the other side. He mentally kicked himself as he bogeyed the hole.

The par 5 twelfth hole is over 600 yards. A lake skirts the left side of the fairway, while trees loomed large on the right. After passing through this gauntlet, the green is protected by bunkers. Madalitso made it to the green with two putts to save par. The flag was at the far end of the green, but he knew that a good lag putt would see him safely home.

He guessed the distance to be around thirty feet, with a downward slope toward the cup. Navigating a slight ridge without sending his ball careening into the rough—or even worse, the lake—was his challenge.

Madalitso eyed the spot on the ridge where his ball would begin descending toward the hole. His breathing slowed, and his eyes went into deep focus. He struck it well. It cleared the ridge easily, but rather than speeding too fast, it was moving too slow. The ball started tepidly down the other side and limped to the left, stopping six feet from the cup. He shook his head, berating himself, knowing that fear had thwarted his best effort.

He needed to sink this 6-foot putt to save par. It was downhill, always the trickiest of putts. He took a deep breath, trying to prevent lingering frustration from his last shot from destroying his next one. He gripped his putter. Upon contact he knew the speed was right, direction excellent...at first. The last few inches, it strayed just to the right, caught the edge of the cup and lipped out. A groan rose from those around him. He tapped in for a dreaded three-putt bogey. He seethed a little inside. But of course, no one knew that. Except himself.

Two holes later, he was on yet another daunting green. The fourteenth at Crosswater is rated the most difficult green on the course, mainly because of a large ridge right down the middle which turns almost any putt into a stomach-churning nightmare.

Madalitso lined up a 12-foot putt to save a precious par, his ball on the opposite side of the ridge from the hole. It seemed impossible. But Mad had built his golfing career on impossible. He took one last breath before making contact. The ball cleared the ridge and headed down the other side straight toward the hole. He was filled with exhilaration; he'd hit another miracle shot.

It stopped four inches to the right of the hole. Miracle denied, he sighed and tapped in for another bogey.

After his first two rounds put him near the top of the leaderboard, the final round stuck out: 76. Never one to drone on, Madalitso summed it up this way: "Just a few missed putts I should have made." Like most golfers, he relied on visualization and "feel" for putting accuracy. And like most athletes with raw ability in a particular sport, his instincts were excellent. But after his experience on the twelfth hole, he began second-guessing his own senses. His tenth-place finish at the conference championship was a huge step in the right direction, but bittersweet considering victory was within his grasp when the day began.

"Good morning, Mukongo!" I said into the receiver. It was still early, but I couldn't wait any longer to talk to my African brother after the biggest tournament of his young collegiate career.

"Good morning, Jayme," came a voice half asleep. It took him a couple of seconds to register that I called him *Mukongo,* a Zambian tribal word for lion. He laughed.

"Way to go!" We talked about the conference championship for a minute before I said, "Lemme put you on hold. We need to reach your dad!"

"Hello." The faint, sickly gravelly voice that I'd heard once before answered the telephone.

My heart sank. I hoped that somebody else had answered the phone. Or that he just lost his voice. "Peter?"

"Yes, Jayme... How are you?"

Sadly, it was Peter. And I could hear he was ill. "I'm doing well, Peter. But you don't...you don't sound..." The words tiptoed out of my mouth. "...like yourself."

"Yes. I'm a little out of it today." His voice was so frail that I felt bad making him talk.

"What is it, Peter? Another slight bout of malaria?" I felt ridiculous asking about a *slight* bout of malaria.

"Yes, yes," he said, laboring. "Yesterday was worse. Today is a little better."

I shook my head as he spoke. Peter and Madalitso *finally* got a day to celebrate, and now this.

"I'm sorry, Peter. I have Madalitso on hold. May I connect him?"

"Of course. Go ahead." Peter was not going to let a little malaria stop him from talking to his son about a golfing triumph.

As soon as Madalitso heard his father's voice, he asked, "Are you feeling okay, Dad?"

Peter dismissed his illness like it was nothing.

I waited for Madalitso to respond, but he said nothing.

After a few seconds of silence, I jumped in. "Peter, your son has something to report. Madalitso, tell him what happened."

Madalitso was his usual understated self. "I played well. Not great but good." There was no joy, spark or color when he described his performance. He only sounded excited when he told his dad about how the Lobos came close to winning the team championship.

"Well done, son."

"Your son is too humble, Peter!" I was slightly annoyed with their modesty, so I waxed enthusiastically about Madalitso's performance. They laughed at how over-the-top I was. But otherwise, they said very little.

As the call wrapped up, Peter made a surprise announcement. "I am coming to the United States for the NCAA West Regional." It was the next tournament, and UNM was hosting the event at South.

Madalitso's voice suddenly came to life. "Really?! You are?!" His smile beamed through the phone. Ten months had passed since he left Lusaka, the last time he saw his family. And his dad.

It was killing me, but I would be away on business. Peter understood, though I could tell he was disappointed.

After we hung up, the suddenness of Peter's trip struck me as strange. We'd spoken just a few days earlier, and he said nothing about coming. I feared his illness was more serious than he was letting on. Of course, there was no way to find out the truth. Peter would always downplay the severity of his malaria...if it even *was* malaria.

I could only hope the conspiracy theorist inside my head was wrong.

MADALITSO WAS RIDING high. After two months of the worst golf in his life, he was buoyed by his performance at the Mountain West Championship *and* the fantastic practice sessions leading up to it. Ramping up for the NCAA West Regional, he was really hitting his stride. Confidence in his swing returned. Adding to his prodigious distance off the tee was increased accuracy of his approach shots. His sharp short game was turning bogeys into pars, and pars into birdies.

Quietly, I wondered whether it had to do with a certain Zambian that was on his way.

Peter was due in Albuquerque two days before the tournament. His flight descended at dusk when the city lights were on and the setting sun tossed soft pinks, reds and oranges on the dramatic desert terrain. He was impressed by the mountains and desert landscape around the city. There are parts of Albuquerque that look like Zambia. It made him feel welcome.

Madalitso waited anxiously. He was standing like he was on springs. They hadn't seen each other since saying goodbye at the airport in Lusaka. He was so mature, both emotionally and now physically, that I sometimes forgot that Mad was still a kid in some ways. But he sure acted like one now, waiting for his dad.

Peter finally emerged, and Madalitso shot through the crowd with an ear-to-ear smile. Zambians often seemed allergic to public displays of affection, but on this day, cultural norms were broken. I have no data to back this up, but I suspect it was the longest hug between two Zambians in the history of Albuquerque's airport.

Peter and Glen Millican shook hands for the first time since the Henke-Berg Tournament in Fort Myers. As before, the coach showed respect and cultural sensitivity. "Nice seeing you again, Mr. Muthiya." Glen introduced Peter to Ryan Murphy. Madalitso informed his father how well "Coach Murph" had treated him.

Peter looked both of them in the eyes and spoke with deep sincerity. "Thank you for coaching my son."

"Madalitso is respectful and polite, a welcome addition to the team and university." It was a compliment that Peter would hear over and over again during his trip.

Nothing was said, but Peter's recent illness weighed heavy on Madalitso's mind. He asked no questions, as if ignorance might somehow lead to bliss and the sickness would miraculously disappear. Besides, Mad knew his father would deflect his questions if asked. Peter would never let himself be the cause of his children's stress. Now more than ever.

During their initial embrace and in the car driving away from the airport, Madalitso carefully scanned his father for hints of physical fatigue, weakness, shortness of breath or any other troubling signs. So far, he was the same strong, outgoing, loving and comforting figure that Madalitso had always known. What a relief.

For the next few days, Peter was an honorary Lobo. He joined the team during meals and interacted with the players, like an elderly wolf joining the pack.

PETER WAS STILL on Zambia time, so he got to South way before any players, spectators or course officials on the morning of the tournament.

When the golf team finally showed up, a groundskeeper walked over. "Hey, Madalitso. There's a gray-haired man here that looks like you."

Madalitso laughed. Then he got his game face on. He was ready for business. As was the whole pack of golfing wolves. The Lobos came within two shots of winning the Mountain West Conference Championship. Preparing for the NCAA West Regional, Coach Millican reminded them over and over of the lost opportunity, a job left undone. Some pride was also at stake; South was *their* course. He asked them to picture another team flying into Albuquerque, winning the tournament and leaving the Lobos beaten in their own house. Unlike other sports, golf requires players to control their emotions and focus on form and strategy. But as much as Millican needed steady technicians, a piece of him wanted a group of hot-tempered linebackers who just heard the opposing quarterback talk smack.

Madalitso warmed up, and Peter did what he always did. He let his son do his own thing. But this was different. Nearly a year had passed since he last saw his son. He didn't come all this way to sit in the clubhouse and drink beer.

Madalitso stepped to the first tee, a par 5 540-yard dogleg left. Standing off in the shadows, Peter watched his son take his customary practice swings and eye the fairway.

One sweet smooth swing later, he launched a high arcing shot that fell within easy reach of the green. Madalitso blasted a picture-perfect tee shot. Peter watched the ball until it stopped rolling nearly 300 yards away, then turned away from the people around him. "I was trying to conceal my smile, which was probably the biggest ever to appear on my face," Peter said later.

It was a picturesque opening drive. But the hazards that were added to South for this tournament looked mean and intimidating to Madalitso and every other player. The grass was left cruelly long in the rough on both sides of the fairway and around the greens, and tricky pin placements punished players for the slightest error. In fact, sometimes they were punished even when they didn't make an error.

Madalitso arrived at the fifteenth hole already feeling the sinister power of South's makeover. The par 4 doglegged left and wrapped around a water hazard and a small forest of trees. Madalitso knew the safe play would be to land on the right side of the fairway, which would give him a clear shot to the green. But there were two problems. The longer-than-usual grass along the edges would be a bear to hit from. Plus, the bunkers on the right side of the green are *exactly* where the pin was placed to scare the bejesus out of some of the world's best collegiate golfers.

Already mired in a savage struggle to salvage anything—a hole, a par, a safe harbor on the green—Madalitso eyed the safe side of the fairway. The risk outweighed the reward in trying to cut the dogleg on the left.

Peter knew what his son was thinking. He'd been watching Madalitso analyze shots since that fateful day in 1989 when a golf ball smashed through the family's kitchen window.

In knife-slicing tense silence, Madalitso let it fly. Father and son knew in a moment that it would be on the fairway but make his approach more difficult. In most situations like this one, Madalitso would stare down danger and cut the dogleg, leaving himself a little chip and buddy of a bird. Not today.

Looking at the green, Madalitso swallowed his pride and ambition. For his next shot, he executed a careful approach that landed softly in the middle of the green, yards from the cup and the bunkers.

Two putts later, he picked his ball out of the cup, marked a par on his dance card and moved on to sixteen. But a gnawing nagging feeling of unfulfillment lingered. He knew that he could birdie fifteen at South. Heck, in practice he *had* birdied fifteen. But he also knew that today, with the stakes so high, his usual swashbuckling style was unwise, and that getting older and wiser as a golfer—and a man—was crucial to success. So he silenced his pride and quietly moved on.

Three holes later, Madalitso smiled as he walked off the course. He shook hands with the other players in his group and shared a few quick laughs with his teammates. Then he climbed into Peter's rental car, rolled down the window and closed his eyes.

For a moment, he was back in Zambia, finishing a round at a colonial-era golf course and driving away with his dad. He bathed in the comfort, security and tranquility that masked his annoyance at playing it safe all day, accepting pars when birdies were there for the taking. Especially at South. His home course.

Peter looked over and saw his son with eyes closed, deep in thought. He pulled out of the parking lot and drove in happy silence.

One hundred and forty golfers played round one. Only four registered scores in the 60s. Madalitso emerged with a hard-earned 74. His first round was more about survival than beauty. But it put him right in the mix.

That evening, I asked Peter what he thought of the round. "I know golf," he said. "I understand the difference between a good seventy-four and a bad seventy-four. This was good, or at least respectable. I walked all eighteen holes and checked the leaderboard. This course was not designed to inflate egos. It was designed to test fortitude. Afterward, Madalitso was frustrated. I reminded him that the course was a problem for everyone. The key was not to get rattled." Peter had always been a calming influence after a difficult day on the golf course. It was a comfort that Madalitso was glad to have again.

The second round was a bit of a Groundhog Day. More of the same. Golfers from nearly thirty universities grunted, trudged, cursed and hacked their way through South's eighteen demanding holes.

Madalitso realized how much he missed the calm of his father and the wisdom of his words. He kept hearing his dad's voice in his head. *The course is a problem for everyone. Just don't get rattled.* While some around him were losing their heads, he managed to keep his.

He ground out another 74. Decent. But not great.

But the Lobos were all struggling on their home turf. Their All-Americans shot uncharacteristic poor rounds of 76 and 77. Only one managed an even-par 72. With only one round left to avenge their Mountain West Conference loss, UNM stood in sixth place. Madalitso could see it on his teammates' faces—their goal was slipping away. The wolves from Albuquerque were going to have to step up and bare their teeth if they wanted to claim the trophy.

That night, rather than give more advice, Peter just listened.

Madalitso talked about painful but valuable lessons from rounds one and two. "Course management is still new to me, and it has been frustrating. While I vow to stay patient, I will pick my spots to be a little more aggressive. Perhaps do some things differently in the final round. I know I can play better," he said matter-of-factly. And that was that.

Madalitso got to South on the deciding day of the tournament with a tweak to his strategy. Driving distance had always been his calling card, and he would continue resisting the lure of the long ball in favor of accuracy, *mostly*. While going-for-broke shooting would still take a backseat to patience, he would not completely straitjacket himself.

Case in point: the seventh. A long straight 520-yard par 4. Madalitso had made his name feasting on holes like this. His length and go-for-broke mentality had rewarded him in more ways than he and his family could have imagined. But the long, punitive grass bordering the fairway and the dangerous, bunker-adjacent pin placement had him laying up the previous two rounds.

Not today. His ball roared 300 hundred yards down the fairway, center-cut. With a clear shot to the flag, it was time to throw caution to the southwestern winds. Five-iron in hand, he stared down the flag, not the safe center of the green. He knew the risk. And that his teammates and coaches needed him to step up. To be Madalitso Muthiya.

It was liberating to let his attacking instincts take over and let her fly.

He froze in his post-swing pose, watching the ball reach its peak and head pinward. But did it have enough giddy-up to get over the bunker?

He held his breath as his ball held its line and landed on the green, bounced and rolled slowly toward the hole. He let out his breath and reveled inside as it stopped four feet from the cup.

He allowed himself a polite smile as people applauded.

A few minutes later, he executed a basic putt and birdied the hole.

Madalitso kept finding the center of the fairways and the easier parts of the greens. He resisted his urge to grip-and-rip except for a few choice places where—like on the seventh hole—it felt like the right time to be a little more aggressive. Mostly he let prudence be his guide, placing the ball surgically instead of smashing the heck out of it. Parring most holes suddenly became easier and birdie opportunities were more available. And today, pars were almost like birdies in some instances. And birdies felt like eagles.

Peter followed his son from a safe distance and came to a clear conclusion. "I can see his mind processing everything. Madalitso is working his way through the problems he encountered earlier. Before my eyes, I can see his game becoming more complete. His confidence growing."

Standing with his back to the clubhouse, Peter watched his son come up the eighteenth fairway. It was a position both of them had been in countless times before. But this, he told me later, was different. "I was no longer staring at the boy that slept in the next bedroom, asking for rides to the golf course and relying on me for guidance. That boy no longer exists. Approaching me was a young man that left his family and home in pursuit of a dream, trying to figure out complex problems on his own. I looked at my son and saw myself."

Madalitso sank his final putt. He shook hands with the other players. Then he walked over to his dad and delivered the news:

Seventy-one. He'd broken par. A very good score in a tournament re-jiggered to inflict misery on golfers. When his team needed him most, Madalitso delivered like a champ. He was twenty-third out of 140 players, a few shots behind the winner, Ricky Barnes, future PGA star.

"Well done, my son," Peter said with a smile. "Well done."

"Thanks, Dad." Madalitso smiled back.

News for the Lobos was even better. Mad's teammates had delivered stellar rounds. A nicely symmetrical 70, 71, 72 and 73.

When the dust finally settled, the results were announced.

UNM took first place, tied with the University of Washington.

The victorious Lobos celebrated, high-fiving, laughing, backslapping and reliving their triumph. They shook their heads and rolled their eyes at the lumps, bumps and bruises they endured at the hands of their own cruelly modified home course.

Madalitso stepped away from his dad to engage in something that was alien to him. Rejoicing with his teammates and coaches after a huge win. While his boisterous boys talked over each other sharing their stories,

Madalitso laughed, listened and chimed in. He knew there were many things he'd never have in common with American college students, and he'd accepted that. But being able to be a real part of a team, to share all this with his teammates and coaches—in success and failure—was deeper and more meaningful than he'd ever imagined it could be to someone who had always gone it alone. It all felt so natural. Like he belonged. Finally.

The moment may have meant even more to Peter. He observed the scene with a big, broad smile on his face. When he watched with the heaviest of hearts as his son flew the Lusaka nest the previous summer, he knew it would be painful adapting to such a new, foreign environment, with different rules, food, etiquette and lifestyle. He'd felt the ups and downs of Madalitso's struggles, unable to do much of anything to help. To see his beloved son so free and easy, smiling and laughing joyfully with these happy young men, these teammates, his new tribe, was so rewarding.

Yes, it was just a bunch of young men celebrating a hard-earned victory with his son. But for years, men who looked like Madalitso's teammates had forbidden Peter from playing the game he loved at Broken Hill Golf Club. A generation later, a similar caste of young men had stared at Mad's secondhand clubs, worn out shoes and Black face, making him feel like an outsider. Like he didn't belong.

Peter thanked God that Madalitso had created, through his hard work and perseverance and innate talent, this thrilling moment. This blissful picture. His son was accepted. Of course, he knew that systemic racial equality was still far away. Whether it was being followed around a department store by a security guard or suffering a tragic encounter with a police officer, his son would face challenges these other young men could never envision. But this simple scene was proof that things were getting better. For Madalitso and the world.

Peter telephoned that evening during my business trip. "Most important in my mind," Peter recalled, "was that he confronted a number of difficult scenarios and worked through them on his own." He paused for a moment before continuing. "At this tournament, I was proud of many things more than just his final place on the leaderboard. Throughout the three-day tournament, I was approached by parents, university officials and employees of the golf course. They all wanted to tell me that Madalitso was a polite and respectful young man. It was nice to hear."

MADALITSO COULD NOW relax with an excellent ending to a very satisfying first season behind him and finally enjoy being with his dad. Now it was time for the son to teach the father. Madalitso led Peter around the university and the city. Peter learned that UNM's adobe-style buildings were synonymous with the southwestern United States. Ever the historian, Peter knew about Albuquerque changing hands between Mexico and the United States. Visiting the historic "Old Town" section of the city was on his to-do list, having read about it before his trip.

So many aspects of Albuquerque and UNM were not found in any books. Lots of young people could afford cars. And the music was so loud! "How can you study around here?" Peter asked his son. But all of Mad's teammates seemed polite and quick with a kind word about his son.

Food was another area of exploration. Peter had never eaten authentic Mexican cuisine, so Madalitso took him to a few local favorites. He had no trouble with the rice and beans, but Madalitso could not contain himself when his father used a fork and knife to cut into his hard-shell tacos. "Dad," Madalitso said in between laughs, "you just pick up the whole thing and bite into it."

Naturally, sampling the region's beer was also a priority. "I like Corona and Dos Equis," Peter said, "but I still prefer my standbys Mosi and Budweiser."

On Peter's last night in Albuquerque, Madalitso stayed in his father's hotel room. "We talked into the wee hours," Peter recalled to me later, "covering the normal father-son topics. I offered words of encouragement as any father would do. But underneath the bumps and bruises of the past year, I could tell he was adjusting to life in the United States. He was becoming a man."

Madalitso talked about being an outsider, how young Americans were much different than his friends in Zambia. Their ways of bonding, the way they used sarcasm to express friendship, annoyed him. He simply could not—and *would not*—adapt to this way of bonding through berating and belittling. And he'd had no idea that heavy drinking and partying was so much a part of American college life.

He reassured his dad that not everyone was a mocking, hard-partying windbag, but there were enough that it kept him from feeling completely accepted. It was the first time Madalitso had seen his father since leaving Zambia, so it was such a relief to unleash, unload and unburden his litany of frustrations, from the challenges of balancing school and golf to the cafeteria food.

Peter knew his son needed to vent. It made his heart happy to listen.

Madalitso paused long enough to take a deep breath and ask whether any of this made sense.

"Of course," Peter assured him. He told Mad the story of feeling like a foreigner at Munali. All the other students came from the small, upper-class Black community in Zambia. Peter's parents were poor, uneducated laborers from a shantytown. He was sure the other Munali students would never understand or accept him. Madalitso and Peter were having the same conversation that Peter had with his mother, Kaliwé, when she spoke the words that Peter gave to Madalitso so many times about playing golf. The words that had become his mantra.

If you are there and they are there, you both belong.

Madalitso stared at his father, hanging on every word. He was heartened that his father *did* understand what he was feeling. That he had been through it.

In the end, Peter assured him that people are attracted to confidence. Just be positive and proud of yourself. People will want to be your friend. And finally, Peter urged him to remember who he is and where he came from. What his grandparents went through during colonialism. He came from a lineage of fighters. Survivors. Pioneers. Ngoni Warriors. That is who Madalitso is.

A dull pain sat in Madalitso's stomach the next morning as he said goodbye to his father and watched him disappear past the security line at Albuquerque's airport.

His voice cracked when he told me, "It was so hard because I didn't know when I would see him again."

Never once did Madalitso bring up the topic that most troubled him: Peter's health. More than Americans, Africans will often avoid such in-your-face conversations, particularly from son to father. Madalitso spent their time together looking for any signs of an illness and praying he didn't see any. There was also a sense of hope that if Peter did not bring it up, it meant he was fine.

Of course, another possibility was that Peter, in wanting this trip to be sheer joy, simply avoided the topic.

31

MY FOLKS WERE OVERJOYED THAT Madalitso was spending his summer break in our home. And they considered it their happy duty to make sure his days consisted of more than just chilling on Puget Sound beaches and gorging on French food. Zambia's finest young golfer found himself opening up the restaurant with Claude in the morning, picking up fresh produce, stopping at the hardware store and scrubbing filthy dishes when he filled in for sick employees. He also got an earful if his clothes or golf clubs were found lounging around the house where they shouldn't be. Welcome to the family, Madalitso.

Peter telephoned my mother regularly to ask about the new houseguest. There was always laughter.

"Don't worry, we're puttin' him to work, Peter!"

"Now Janet," Peter said with mock gravity, "don't forget you have my permission go up Madalitso's backside if he doesn't pull his weight!"

Madalitso had no trouble keeping the rust off his game. He was in much demand at the local country clubs as everyone wanted to play with the college golf stud from Africa.

My parents noticed something strange. After these outings, Madalitso often returned with extra cash bulging in his wallet. Helping Madalitso was never something we asked our friends to do. They *wanted* to.

My mom, Claude and Madalitso spent a weekend at our good friends, the Bargreens', beachside cabin on Lopez Island in northern Puget Sound. Since my folks love to fish, they brought their poles and tackle box. During the drive, Madalitso made the terrible mistake of admitting that he'd never caught a fish—*in his life*. That's all my mom needed to hear.

Come crack of dawn the next morning, she led Mad down to the shoreline. She carried the pole; he carried the net. She introduced him to the gentle art of fishing. Where one baits a hook and begins casting into the water, while simultaneously talking about everything under the sun. School, golf, girls, friends, music, whatever else would keep him there. In the midst of my mom's gentle interrogation...

BAM!

A fish struck her lure. A big one.

"WHOA! I got one! Madalitso, come help me!"

Startled, Madalitso rushed over to her, no idea what to do next, and, for Madalitso at least, slightly panicked. "What do you mean?! Help you do what?!"

"Just come here." She handed him the pole. "Here! You take this, and I'll get the net!"

He threw his hands up, wanting no part of holding onto something with a fighting fish on the other end. "Wait a minute. Why don't *I* get the net?!"

"Just take it, please!" She shoved the pole into his hands. It looked like it was alive, bent over and jerking all over the place, as the fish fought for its life.

Filled with fear and adrenaline, Madalitso had no choice but to grab the pole and hold on for all he was worth. "But...Janet...I don't know what to do!"

My mom talked him through it. "Keep the tip of the pole up! Reel in any slack. But don't fight the fish too hard. Let him tire himself out."

The fish had no interest in being dinner that night, so an epic battle ensued. More than once, Madalitso hollered, "My arms are burning! I need a break!"

My mom had none of it. "You're an athlete. Besides, I'm a lot older than you. You can do it!"

Hearing the ruckus, Claude came over. His reaction was swift and decisive. He began laughing hysterically and cheering on the newest member of the family. "Come on, Mad, you can do it!"

Finally, Madalitso wore down the fish, as he had done with so many opponents on the golf course. My mom scooted down the rocks and wrapped the net around the catch. It was so big she needed both arms to hoist it out of the water. It was a twelve-pound cabezon. Ugly but tasty.

Madalitso dropped the pole and shook his aching arms. My mom and Claude applauded.

Claude immediately filleted and deboned the fish. Watching the knife flash with fish bones and guts flying around was a great shock to Mad's system. My folks tried to cajole him into eating the tasty fruits of his labor, but it was no use. He refused a single bite. Instead, he begged Claude to make him a steak. They reminded him that his steak was once a living breathing cow. "Yes, but I didn't kill it and put it in the supermarket."

A few days later Peter, Madalitso and I spoke as part of our usual three-way calls. Madalitso provided some highlights from the weekend. "Dad, I caught my first fish!"

"Oh, that's great," Peter replied. "How did it taste?"

Madalitso begrudgingly confessed the whole story.

After a quiet and uncomfortable silence, Peter sighed. "Aye aye aye. My son, you are a Ngoni warrior. Try and remember that."

Madalitso groaned. I laughed.

CLAUDE DROVE MADALITSO to the airport. He was about to be a sophomore in college. Standing curbside, he hugged my mom longer than she expected. "Thank you for everything," he said. "It's been a while since I've been so comfortable. This summer almost felt like being home in Zambia."

"You're welcome, honey," she replied. "We love you."

Words that are said more freely in the United States than in Zambia.

Madalitso looked surprised and a little bashful. "Me too," he said with a nervous laugh.

Claude gave him a proper European goodbye, a kiss on both cheeks. Slightly embarrassed, Madalitso enjoyed all the affection as best he could. "Now concentrate on school," Claude told him. "We're tired of your womanizing and partying every night."

My mom telephoned as she and Claude drove away. After every holiday, gift or cash advance, I thanked them for their kindness to Madalitso.

Every time I thanked them, and *every* time I got the same response as the one I got now:

"No need to thank us. He's our family too."

32

MADALITSO WAS IN A BETTER place when he started his second year at the University of New Mexico. Friendships were slowly developing. He didn't drink beer or gawk at adult magazines, but over time, he found people who enjoyed his company and respected his values. He learned how to socialize with American college students while staying true to himself. Everything his father predicted.

He moved out of the dorms and into an apartment with teammate and close friend Jeremy Kirkland, a French national. Africans and Europeans have many differences, but Madalitso and Jeremy shared the ups and downs of assimilating at a large American university.

The world no longer relentlessly dropped culture bombs on his head. His sophomore year, he laughed at the Halloween costumes, sidestepped beer bottles and inserted ear plugs when the hard-rocking neighbors kept him awake.

He even managed to use a little sarcasm. On his way to class one day, he walked by somebody he knew looking down at his cell phone, cursing loudly and causing heads to turn. "What's wrong?" Madalitso asked, thinking the guy was in trouble.

"It's my ****ing phone. I can't get any reception!"

"Ah-ha," Madalitso replied. "Well, maybe there is an international foundation that helps people with these first-world tragedies. Or perhaps we could organize a benefit concert for you."

The student just looked up at Madalitso, smiled and shook his head.

Madalitso found the firm footing that was so elusive his freshman year. He was more confident in where he was and what he was doing.

Still, challenges remained. At times, Madalitso's stoic demeanor left a sour impression. Teammates who lent him music or performed a favor often received nothing more than a perfunctory "thank you." If that. Some saw him as unappreciative, even self-centered.

I heard these stories and struggled over what role I should play. Occasionally, I told people that Zambians are less demonstrative than Americans. Outpourings of gratitude or other such displays are awkward and uncomfortable. I also reminded Madalitso how others—particularly Americans—might interpret his perceived indifference. Even as I heard Peter's voice telling me that children must learn through experience.

As Madalitso and I grew closer, I saw that the same stoicism which chafed some of his peers was also a shield from the hardships of growing up in Zambia. It helped him maintain his confidence when facing better trained and better equipped players who looked different than him. As much as his golf swing, it was this trait that helped him to succeed by following his father's advice: *Focus on what you need to do.*

MADALITSO SHOWED NO rust in UNM's first two tournaments of his sophomore year, the Tucker and the Sooner Invitational. At the Tucker, he took advantage of his familiarity with South and the altitude in Albuquerque to showcase his outstanding distance off the tee. He consistently placed the ball where he wanted, keeping himself out of danger. Out of sixty-nine players, he finished tied for twelfth with Michael Putnam, a future PGA Tour player, and neck-and-neck with a pack of other future pros. "It was," he recalled, "just a few shots here and there."

He expected to play well at the Tucker, his home course. The Sooner Invitational a few days later was a chance to test his mettle and boost his confidence away from Albuquerque early in the new season. The Tom Fazio–designed course at Stonebriar Country Club in Frisco, Texas, was completely foreign to him, the foreigner.

UNM coaches cautioned the team to keep the ball in play. Stonebriar devours balls that stray from the fairways and greens. Madalitso listened. After parring the opening hole, he came to the second, a 408-yard par 4 with a dogleg right. It was rated the toughest hole on the course. He knew the risks of cutting the dogleg: the two bunkers pinching the fairway at the corner, hungry to gobble up balls. A good performance at the Tucker and a good practice session afterward was all the convincing he needed.

He took a few practice swings to loosen his body, but his mind stayed tight. It focused on the tall trees standing guard at the bend in the fairway. If he could pull off a shot like this, it would set an early tone to the round, to the tournament. And he was determined to start strong.

The small group around the tee box stood silent. Nothing moved until Madalitso's driver slowly swung back and then accelerated down and through his ball. *THWACK!*

Anyone watching knew within milliseconds that he had taken dead aim at the bend. People locked in on his ball, none more than Madalitso. Directionally, it was right on track, but distance was the key here. Mad held his breath as it descended toward the trees and the bunkers. *Come on,* he pleaded. *Drop in.* The other players were equally curious, wondering if this might set an example for them to follow. A second later, it dropped behind the trees and onto the fairway, safely away from the bunkers.

"Wow," one player hollered. "Good ball!"

"Thanks."

It was an early morning drive that seemed to wake up and embolden the group. The next two players both tried the same thing but with very different results. One just barely cleared the trees and ended up in the rough. The other watched his ball splash into the fairway bunker. The fourth player decided to follow club management's advice and lay up just before the bend.

With its #1 handicap, the second hole leaves little time to celebrate. Mad had only 100 yards to the flag, but the giant bunker on the left side was ominous. Naturally, he chose a wedge for his second shot, but the issue wasn't distance. It was accuracy.

Mad waited patiently for other players to hit their second shots out of the sand and tall grass. *You feel good, but don't be foolish,* he cautioned himself when it was his turn to swing. With his ball slightly forward to generate loft, he eyed the green one last time. Solid grip. Breathing calm. Eyes focused down. With left arm straight, he brought his club back over his head, then powered down, through and up.

A chunk of sod accompanied his ball for the first five feet. Height and distance looked good, but he wouldn't breathe until he knew the left bunker posed no danger. As his ball soared, Mad anxiously waited for it to descend. Only then would he know if his sand wedge could remain tucked in his bag. As it began falling, he breathed a sigh of relief. A second later, he allowed himself to relax and exhale as it fell safely on the right front portion of the green, twelve feet from the hole.

"Good shot," one of the other players said, probably begrudgingly.

He had put himself in great position with two strokes to save par. His first putt was on the proper line but ran out of gas three feet short. His second was a formality. Par.

Propelled by his excellent work on the second hole, Mad went on to shoot a 68 for his first round and a 70 on day two. At six under par, he was in the top ten going into the third and final round. A great position.

But—sadly, there is a *but*—in golf, fortunes inexplicably change. His final round was defined by two holes. Or rather, two greens. After avoiding the lake along the right side of the fourteenth fairway, Mad landed his ball on the heavily tiered and sloped fourteenth green with two shots to save par. His first putt brought him to within eight feet of the cup, but a nasty slope had to be navigated.

He instantly knew the speed of his second putt was right when his ball popped off his clubhead. But it didn't break enough and rolled inches past the cup. Dreaded three-putt. Bogey.

There was no such excuse for the three-putt he suffered on hole seventeen. The green had waves, but Madalitso simply misjudged the speed and failed to get close enough with his first putt. On his second putt, a twelve-footer, he lined up with only a slight decline to navigate. The ball sprung off his clubhead with a surprising amount of force, perhaps a by-product of the weak shot he just hit. Combined with the downward angle, the ball sped past the hole. He sank a three-footer to register another bogey.

"Jeez," he said while giving his putter a stern glare.

Despite the disappointing 76 in round three, Madalitso finished in seventeenth place at the Sooner Invitational. It was his second top-twenty finish in as many outings. He returned to Albuquerque feeling pretty good. There was hope that he was turning things around. Maybe his freshman year was an aberration. Maybe he was starting to figure everything out. With three weeks of practice time before the next tournament, Mad had a positive tone in his voice, a spring in his step and a consistent smile on his face.

In these moments, the golf gods have a way of reminding how maddening the sport can be. If the Tucker and the Sooner Invitational confirmed how close he was to consistently playing with the NCAA's elite golfers, his next tournament was a lesson in how far away he still was.

In early October, the Lobos traveled to Somis, California, for the Club Glove Intercollegiate. The Saticoy Club calls itself the "premier private country club in Ventura County." By the end of this tournament, Mad would have a few other choice words to describe it.

The day began harmlessly enough with pars on his first two holes. He managed the Southern California wind well enough and, on both holes, reached the green with his second shots. The third hole seemed to be a mirror image of the first two, until he pulled the putter from his bag.

For his first putt, Madalitso faced a 30-foot downhill conundrum. Still without a good feel for the morning greens, he waited for a light to click on in his head. After several seconds of surveying the turf and watching another player execute his first putt, the epiphany he sought never arrived. Finally, he decided to just line up and let it go. He grabbed his putter and secured his footing. Perhaps because it's known as one of the most challenging greens on the course, players seemed to stop their conversations early and turn their eyes to him.

Mad lined up, settled his feet, bent over and took a couple more glances at the hole before focusing his eyes downward. A brief pause was followed by a long backswing and strong follow-through.

The ball didn't travel five feet before Madalitso knew it was *too* strong. He was already mentally tapping the brakes at the midway point. *Slow down!*

But no luck. On a hole that course management warns against aggressive downhill putts, Madalitso zoomed one past the hole and now faced a fifteen-footer to save par. There was silence from the other players and spectators. He closed his eyes, walked the much longer than expected distance, set his marker and picked up his ball.

Three minutes later, now faced with going the other direction, he placed his ball down and picked up his marker. *Okay,* he said to himself. *Let's get on with it.* After a brief analysis, he moved into position. Conversations stopped again. Bent over, he planted his feet and took a final look at the hole. The ball jumped forward to begin its uphill journey. But soon, trouble. It was simply slowing way too early. *GO!* he yelled to himself. But no luck.

The quiet lingered as Madalitso, visibly frustrated, walked to his ball. Three-putts have a way of creating an awkward silence around a green. Nobody looked at him or made a peep. With just a couple feet remaining, the other players nodded at him to hole out. Which he did. Bogey.

Madalitso knelt, picked up his ball and proceeded to the fourth hole. The speed of Saticoy's greens was a mystery he needed to solve. Quickly. But he was about to find out that the greens weren't the only challenge he'd face today.

The fourth is just a 226-yard par 3, but accuracy is required to avoid the bunkers on the right and left sides of the green. Madalitso pulled his seven-iron and mentally tried to dispatch his last hole exactly where it belonged, in the past. *Next shot.* Standing to one side, he watched the other players land their balls safely on the well-guarded green.

Stepping forward, he took a few extra practice swings, mainly to clear his mind more than anything. With the flag tucked on the right side, he thought a tee shot placed center-right would jolt things in the right direction.

As calm and focused as he would get, Mad completed his backswing and launched his ball straight into the sky. He watched it climb up and up and up, waiting anxiously for it to peak and begin its descent.

Be careful what you wish for. Right at its peak, the ball immediately started fading to the right. *Oh no,* he grimaced to himself. The news only got worse. The ball continued sailing off the green as Mad let his seven-iron drop by his side in exasperation. Helpless, he watched it plop into the sand on the right side.

Madalitso threw his bag strap over his shoulder and began walking. The only person he wanted to speak with was himself. Had he been too confident in the intervening weeks since the Tucker and Sooner Invitational? Too pleased with his performances? Had this dulled his focus and preparation? He knew such second-guessing and anxious introspection was unhelpful during a tournament, but it was hard not to scramble for answers.

What the heck is going on?! Over three days, he never found an answer.

During the final round, his approach shot on the seventh was too short. Helplessly, he watched it tumble off the green and into the rough. After a decent chip-and-roll he was left with a 6-foot putt to save par. Scraping for at least one good round, he took his time, meticulously reading what on most days was a fairly routine distance for him. Finally, he carefully stepped over his ball and closed his eyes. Calmly, he executed his backswing and sent it forward. The speed was right, and the direction seemed good. But it lipped out at the end. Another bogey.

Madalitso had no reaction by this point. He was too numb.

During a three-day stretch when nothing worked, Madalitso shot 81-77-81 at the Club Glove in Somis. His fifty-ninth place finish out of sixty-two players was the worst score on the UNM team and one of his poorest showings *ever* at a golf tournament.

I thought that Madalitso would benefit from speaking with his father, so the next week I orchestrated one of our three-way calls. It was an exchange unlike any other.

"Hey. What happened?" Although Peter's tone carried no anger, it was serious and very direct. He wanted an answer.

Madalitso sighed. "It was just one of those tournaments. I don't know."

Peter didn't like the answer. "Come on. Let's not have any more rounds of eighty-one."

"Dad," Madalitso snapped back, "do you think I'm trying to shoot those scores?! Well, I'm not!"

Knowing Peter's belief in discipline and respect, I grabbed hold of my chair and waited for Hurricane Peter to blow.

"Fine, let's just get on with the job," Peter replied in a measured tone. Madalitso said nothing.

After a few awkward seconds, Peter broke the silence. "So how is school?"

"Pretty good. Keeping me away from drugs and alcohol." Madalitso said it so dry and deadpan that everyone laughed.

Later, I asked Peter why he hadn't unleashed the big guns when trying to get through to his son. "Sometimes they are needed. Sometimes they are not," he answered. "I sensed Madalitso was sincerely disappointed in his performance. Coming down hard was unnecessary. I knew he would do everything in his power to keep it from happening again."

I suspect Peter also respected Madalitso for standing up to him. His son was becoming a man.

Two weeks after one of the worst finishes in his college career, Madalitso and the Lobos were on their way to the 2002 Barona Collegiate Cup. Located in Lakeside, just east of San Diego, the Barona Cup was the Lobos' final tournament of the fall season before the winter break and Madalitso's last chance to end 2002 on a high note.

Leading up to the tournament, he practiced angry, treating the golf course and his clubs as though he was mad at them. "One day at practice, some guys were complaining about the pin placement at a particular hole," he told me on our weekly talk. "I basically said 'screw that.' I jerked the driver out of my bag, hit the ball and birdied the hole." Madalitso wanted desperately to play well and put the Club Glove behind him. Being pissed off was his new approach.

Mad was mad. After a lackluster first round score of 74, he felt the rage burning again. So he began his second morning in Southern California by stuffing a nice breakfast into his angry belly and busting a massive drive down the left side of Barona's first fairway. He knew this 540-yard par 5 was an opportunity to explode out of the starting blocks. Still in anger-based attack mode, he strode with menace (or as much menace as Madalitso was capable of) down the fairway, jerked his seven-iron from his bag and attacked. Club management cautions players to avoid the giant oak tree looming in the middle of the fairway, but Mad aimed dead-center at the green beyond.

Grit and fury were fine, but Madalitso's temperate nature reared its head. He reminded himself that this was still golf. The warrior knows when and how to strike. He cleared his mind and controlled his breathing. He calmly saw the path to success. With over 200 yards to go, he took a robust backswing and powered through. His ball burst through a puff of grass and dirt. A green sloping toward a large fairway bunker was intended to deter players from striking at this distance. But not Madalitso. Not today.

He watched his ball tower over the oak. The only question was distance. He clenched as his ball fell. Controlling his emotions had been his trademark and carried him to countless victories. Would the new, angry Mad who had dominated recent practice sessions end up costing him? His eyes locked in on the ball. *"Come on,"* he said through clenched teeth.

His ball landed happily on the front edge of the green.

"Nice shot!" another player called out.

"Thanks," Madalitso replied, cucumber-cool from head to toe. But as he lifted his bag, he quickly glanced skyward. *Thank you.*

He arrived at the green, needing three putts for par. But Madalitso wasn't thinking par. He stared down a 40-foot slightly uphill putt with a left-to-right break. Some oomph was needed, but the giant bunker off the right side of the green brought visions of overcooked balls toppling over the side and being eaten alive by sand.

Madalitso did his usual inspection of the landscape and finally saw his line. A perfect putt from this distance was nearly impossible. But Mad knew a solid lag would bag him a birdie. Brief pause. Backswing. Strong follow-through.

The ball surged up the incline. Madalitso watched intently, still crouched.

As the ball glided forward to the left of the hole, he waited for the left-to-right break he'd seen in his read of the green. The ball slowed, and he held his breath. *Break. Break!*

This time, the ball heard him and put the brakes on, then curved right toward the hole. And the dreaded bunker. Madalitso held his breath, needing the ball to hold its speed to reach the hole, but not break the speed limit and plummet to a sandy grave.

The ball passed in front of the hole, the bunker dead ahead as Mad begged to the golf gods: *Stop! Stop!*

They heard him and stopped his ball three feet from the cup.

Applause erupted. Madalitso raised his hand, gave his little nod and grin, then tapped in.

Birdie.

He kept attacking. On nearly every hole, his approach put him in position for birdie. He navigated bunkers, trees and water hazards without breaking a sweat. His drives were long and straight. His putts were dead-on accurate.

Then he came to the par 3 sixteenth hole. Sitting at four under with three holes left would've been enough to satisfy many players. Not Madalitso. Not today. He didn't look for a safe patch of green to land on. He stared right at the flag.

He addressed the ball like a man on a mission from God. Quiet descended on the tee box.

He struck pure and true. The ball rose up toward the heavens and Mad knew it was good. The flag seemed like a magnet sucking his ball to it.

Time slowed, and Madalitso's adrenaline spiked with each fraction of a second. The excitement spread when the ball hit the green and rolled straight at the hole.

Voices rose when it became clear the ball had enough speed to reach the cup. "OHHHHH!"

WOULD THIS BE A HOLE-IN-ONE?!!

Anticipation reached a fever pitch as Madalitso leaned to the side, willing the pill to go in.

Alas, it slipped just past the left edge of the cup and stopped eighteen inches away. A collective groan erupted. Mad smiled and fell forward, mimicking a collapse. Applause and laughter. Madalitso raised his hand in appreciation.

Minutes later he tapped in for birdie, now standing at five under par. That was where he finished on day two. Of the ninety players who competed in the 2002 Barona Cup, 67 was the lowest second-round score.

That night, preparing for the final round, he scripted in his mind how he wanted it to go down. The next day, the script was written. Almost. Madalitso was putting on the fourteenth, a treacherous green with "severe sloping" according to club management. Although a mere seven feet separated him from birdie, it was a nasty downhill breaker. At least that's what his eyes told him.

After contemplating slope, distance and break, he found his stance and crouched over. Performing what he believed was a slight backswing and follow-through, the ball lurched forward. Inch by inch Madalitso watched it roll down the decline. When it was time for the break he expected, the ball curved only slightly to the left and slid just past the hole. He knew the downward slope created too much speed for the break he anticipated. He tapped in for par.

Aside from a few of these razor-thin misses, nearly every shot landed almost exactly where he wanted. The other players in his group complimented him. *This* was how he was capable of playing.

Madalitso roared back to finish the Barona Cup in ninth place, UNM's top performer. It was his second top-ten varsity finish. Tied with him on the leaderboard was Nick Watney, future PGA Tour winner.

It was a stunning comeback, considering his first-round score was the worst on the team and he was languishing in the bottom half of the field. His combined score for rounds two and three was second best in the entire tournament.

The next conversation with his dad went much better.

33

F ALL OF 2002. FOUR YEARS since the president of Zambia introduced me to Peter Muthiya. Our phone conversations were still a high point of my week. We continued to reveal the details of each other's lives, and my admiration for him grew. *"Hey, Peter, let me ask your opinion on..." "I'd like your advice on something, Peter..."* Whether it was my career, finances or relationships, he became a trusted source of advice. Hanging up the phone, I shook my head over how open and vulnerable I allowed myself to become. What seemed inconceivable for most of my life was suddenly easy, thanks to Peter Muthiya.

Peter's stories had become familiar, but never stale, as they so often offered deep personal insight:

"I was ten years old and living with my uncle in Chipata, Fort Jameson it was called then, when a European missionary in his twenties arrived to preach among the Ngoni. He had an air about him. He was arrogant—not the way for a stranger to behave if he wants to be welcomed.

"After a few days, word of his rudeness spread. He delighted in lambasting native beliefs, saving his most biting criticisms for traditional spiritual practitioners: the witch doctors. 'Ridiculous' and 'purveyors of superstition' are what he called them. People were insulted.

"Elder members of the Ngoni approached the young European to share their concerns. They explained that although a large percentage of the community was Christian, ancient African customs still held an important place. It was part of our heritage.

"The missionary listened with arms folded, bearing a scowl. When the elders finished speaking, the young man brashly dismissed their complaints: *'Rather than engage in nonsense, the witch doctors' time would be better spent plowing some unused patch of ground and planting maize.'*

"Once again, word spread.

"That night, I awoke to raised voices and pounding footsteps outside my uncle's hut. We stepped outside into a rush of people hurrying toward the missionary's quarters.

"When we arrived, I stood there with my uncle and observed a very unspectacular scene. People were gathered around a man who was on all fours digging in the soil with his bare hands. It was the missionary.

"The young European methodically churned rows of soil and planted seeds on a small plot while the witch doctors watched from a distance.

"The young missionary awoke the next day to find his shoes soiled, his clothes tattered and his hands dirty and scraped. People explained that he had spent the entire night planting a couple rows of maize. He remembered nothing. 'I thought it was a dream,' he explained.

"Over the next few days, the missionary barely spoke to anyone. He quietly packed his belongings and was gone within a week. He never returned."

I burst into laughter. "No way! Come on!"

Peter assured me it was the truth. His first name was western, he spoke a western language, practiced a western religion and wore western clothes. But he was African through and through. The young missionary was an outsider who insulted his people. The missionary was taught a lesson about respecting and honoring other people's customs and cultures, and years later Peter could barely contain his glee.

"Sooo, Jayme." His good-natured laugh and sly accusatory tone told me what was coming. "Are you getting there?"

I sighed and rubbed my temples again.

Peter just would not let this go. It was important to him, and I had no idea why. I was looking at it purely as a storyteller. In my mind, writing this book didn't require me to know every detail or all the history that Peter was constantly alluding to.

Peter viewed it differently. Writing a book was only part of the reason my knowledge and appreciation of history were important. Peter believed we had a special relationship and that anyone he allowed into his family needed a better understanding of the Muthiyas' history. Of *his* history.

It was also clear that Peter had another reason for pressing me to "get there"—he enjoyed jawing about history and ached to discuss it with me.

"I'll get *there* eventually, Peter," I promised him. "I will read a few history books, and then we can chat about it." Sometime later, when I wasn't so busy. There would be time.

No matter how long the conversation lasted, the ending was still the same.

"Goodbye, my African dad."

"Goodbye, my American son."

It no longer sounded strange, but we still laughed.

WITH HIS PERFORMANCE at the Barona Cup, Madalitso ended his up-and-down fall season on a high note. Now it was time to hunker down for final exams. He mapped out a study schedule that cut out everything except books, food and sleep. His mind was clear and ready when December 5 rolled around, and he prepared to submerge himself in his books.

The phone rang. He didn't know it, but when he answered it, his life would change.

"Dad is in the hospital!" Wongani said frantically, talking fast and breathing heavy, almost hyperventilating. Madalitso could feel his brother's despair and fear.

"What?" Madalitso asked anxiously. "Why? What is it?"

"I don't know. Pneumonia, I think. That's what Mom said."

What Peter thought was another "slight bout of malaria" was actually something more severe. He'd been diagnosed with advanced-stage pneumonia.

The two brothers talked for several more minutes with Wongani essentially repeating the same answer to Madalitso's questions:

"I don't know."

"I want to speak with Dad!" Madalitso exclaimed. "Have him call me!"

Wongani agreed, and the two brothers hung up.

And just like that, final exams were forgotten. Madalitso's heart raced as he stared at the phone. In most of the world, communication was practically instantaneous, but here, now, the waiting was excruciating. Another sad reminder of life in Africa.

After an hour that seemed like a year, his cell phone finally lit up.

DAD.

"Hello?! Dad, is that you?! How are you?! What's going on?!" Panicked, Madalitso was almost crawling through the phone to get answers.

"Oh, I'm okay." His voice was faint and rough. Clearly, he was not okay. But he was bound and determined to put his son at ease. "They say I have pneumonia. I'm in the hospital. People are looking after me."

"Dad, Wongani said you're very sick."

"I'll be fine," he whispered like a shell of himself. "It's a little rough right now, but everything will work out. I've decided to stay at the hospital for the weekend, just as a precaution. How are your final examinations coming along?"

Madalitso exhaled in frustration. "School is fine. I'm studying. But Dad—"

"That's good. Is the golf team practicing right now or taking a break?" Peter continued this dance, asking mundane questions. Anything to pretend to be normal and not admit just how sick he was.

Madalitso's frustration finally boiled over. "Dad, school is going well. Golf is going well. Look, I'm coming home!"

Peter's voice suddenly went from a whisper to a roar. "NO! Don't be ridiculous. Everything is fine, son. Worry about final exams. I'll talk with you on Monday. I'll be back at work by then." He ended the debate by exclaiming what had become a Muthiya family commandment:

Remember, focus on what you need to do!

Peter won this test of wills. Madalitso knew it. He sighed and swelled his frustration. "Will you call me later? I don't want to wait until Monday."

"Sure," Peter responded. "I will."

"I love you, Dad."

"I love you too, son."

MADALITSO.

The name on my caller ID surprised me. I knew he was trying to limit phone calls during finals week.

"Jayme, it's Madalitso." He sounded normal. But I knew that didn't mean anything.

"Well, hey, Mad. What's going on? How is—"

"Jayme, I just talked to my dad. He's really sick."

Everything became numb. "What...what is it?"

"I don't know," he fired back. "Wongani said it was pneumonia."

Suddenly relieved, I exhaled. Pneumonia is treatable. Relief became terror. Pneumonia is very treatable for me, *in the United States*, where I have access to the best doctors and the most modern, state-of-the-art medical facilities. Most Zambians have access to neither.

"Jayme," he said somberly. "I need to go home."

"Okay, Madalitso."

We mapped out a to-do list. Madalitso would speak with his professors and coaches about missing final exams, while I coordinated flights to Lusaka.

But first, I needed to talk to someone who'd cared for an ill loved one.

"Hi, Mom." My father's eighteen-month battle with cancer had made my mother an expert on shutting down emotions and figuring out a game plan while the world seemed to be crumbling.

"Hi," she replied.

"Peter Muthiya is sick," I blurted out.

"Oh, no. What is it?"

"Apparently, a severe case of pneumonia. Madalitso is very worried. He wants to fly home. I'm looking at flights."

"Of course," she replied. "He wants to see his dad, and we'll make it happen."

"Yes, but first I need to speak with Peter...to hear his voice."

"Okay," she replied. "Call me later."

As we hung up, I closed my eyes. *Dear God, please let Peter answer the phone.*

After two rings, I was connected. At first there was nothing but the muffled sounds of a phone being dragged across clothing or skin. I waited, staying silent.

"Hello?" I could barely hear Peter's voice; it was so soft and rough.

There were so many things I wanted to say. So many questions I wanted to ask. Are you really sick? Are you going to be able to get the medical help you need? Please, Peter, tell me what to do. This is what came out of my mouth:

"Hi, Peter. It's Jayme."

"Hello, Jayme...how are you?" His voice was a faint wheeze, like a ninety-year-old man on a respirator. This was no "slight bout of malaria."

"I'm fine, Peter. Look, Madalitso told me you are sick. Can you tell me what's going on? How are you?"

Long pause. "Well...not so good," he answered. "Apparently I've come down with something. But...it...it's going to be okay."

My stomach dropped. Peter Muthiya was not a complainer. For him to say "not so good" meant it was deadly serious.

"Well...Peter...what are the doctors saying?"

Another pause. "Oh, you know," he said like it was painful to talk. "I need rest. This and that." Obviously getting an accurate diagnosis from Peter was impossible. I needed to speak with somebody...*anybody* else. Now all I had to do was convince him to let me talk to somebody else.

"Peter...uh...who else is there with you?" I asked timidly.

"Edith and Ivwa are here."

"May I speak with them?"

It was a long pause where I could hear the gears in Peter's head grinding around.

Finally, he gave a one-word response that I will never forget: "Why?!"

Underneath his strained voice and labored breathing was the same direct, barbed tone that I had heard only once before—four years earlier in the Intercontinental Hotel bar. But unlike the first time, I knew what triggered this reaction. Peter resented that I was trying to go around him for information. He didn't want anyone trying to decide his fate for him. He had too much pride in his own ability to solve his problems. Asking for help was a sign of weakness where he came from. No way was he going to hand over his phone.

"Well...uh...Peter...just give Edith and Ivwa my best."

"I will, Jayme." The sharp tone had gone away. One of the things I admired about Peter was his ability to surprise you. Just when you thought you knew what he was going to do, he might just do the opposite. "Jayme, do you still know people at State House?"

My relationship with the Zambian Government ended years earlier. Frederick Chiluba was replaced by Vice President Levy Mwanawasa, a man I'd never met. "I might, Peter. I don't know. Why do you ask?"

Peter struggled to breathe, filling me with guilt over letting the conversation go on so long. "Well, I've met the President before," he said. "I know him...and...it's just...I don't think people should have to suffer like this."

My throat tightened. "No, Peter, you're right." I leaned forward, shielding my eyes.

"Jayme, I should go now," he whispered.

"Well...Peter...can I call you tomorrow?"

"Of course," he said.

"Okay then. Goodbye, my African dad." I hoped our usual lighthearted ending might help.

"Goodbye, my American son."

Nobody laughed this time.

FRIDAY, DECEMBER 6, 2002. I began looking at flights for Madalitso. My mom, Claude and I agreed to split the cost of his air ticket to Zambia. My phone rang.

"Jayme, it's Glen Millican at UNM."

Hearing Coach Millican's voice was unexpected. "Hey, Glen."

"Listen," he began, "we all know about Madalitso's father. Madalitso is pretty worried."

"Yeah. I know."

"Well, I am pretty sure we can help get him to Zambia," Glen said.

"Really? How is that?" I knew the NCAA had rules against paying for personal travel expenses.

"The Mountain West Conference has a fund for athletes that need to go home for emergencies," Glen explained. "Our athletic department is calling conference headquarters to find out if it only covers a death in the family or whether an ill parent would qualify."

"That's great. Please call when you hear something."

MADALITSO HARDLY SLEPT the night before, checking his cell phone incessantly to make sure it was turned on.

As Friday morning dragged on, he was in frequent contact with his coaches and UNM's athletic department about whether the conference would pay for his trip home. He told his professors about his situation and arranged to take his exams at a later date.

I was in constant touch with people in Albuquerque but avoided Madalitso. Every ring jarred his senses because it might be Peter or somebody else in Lusaka.

Around 11 a.m., he called, sounding more agitated than I've ever heard him. "My flight is booked, but nobody is calling me from Lusaka. I don't know what is going on!" It was a shocking outburst of fear and anger from a young man who had a preternatural ability to maintain his composure even when confronting the most extreme difficulty.

I searched for words to ease his pain. "Your dad is very strong. If anyone can shake this off, he can." I promised to call him in the morning and say a prayer for Peter and the family.

After dinner, he and Jeremy plopped down on the couch. Although Madalitso wouldn't breathe easy until he touched down in Zambia, he felt satisfied that he'd done all he could after a long day of making calls, sending emails and staring at the phone.

He went through everything he knew, searching for any bit of information suggesting his dad would be fine. He was greatly comforted by the fact that his notoriously stubborn dad had followed the advice of hospital staff and checked himself in overnight. Madalitso knew that healthcare in Zambia was woefully inadequate, but it was better than staying at home.

He also took solace in Peter's words. He'd be back at work on Monday. The idea of his dad making phone calls, sending emails and joking with people at the office gave Madalitso comfort. More than anything, his hopes were buoyed by his father's spirit, durability and indomitable strength. Battling pneumonia in the developing world was serious, but his father was the fiercest person he knew.

As he got some much-needed downtime and chilled with Jeremy on the couch, watching dumb television and talking about nothing in particular, Madalitso managed to get off his mental rollercoaster. After twenty-four hours of nothing but uncertainty and fear, sleep finally seemed possible.

Suddenly, his cell phone illuminated. His fragile calm was obliterated. Madalitso snatched the phone and glared at the caller ID, an international number. His heart pounded, and his stomach heaved. He closed his eyes and uttered a prayer before answering. "Hello?"

He heard heavy labored breathing and weeping. Finally, Wongani spoke. "Madalitso..."

Hearing his name uttered through his older brother's broken voice, Madalitso knew.

"Dad passed away."

PART III

34

"I CAN'T..." WONGANI WEPT SO hard that he could hardly talk. "I don't...believe it. Dad is gone. My God...I can't believe it."

On the other side of the world, Madalitso sat in silence, stone-faced, as Wongani went on and on. With his eyes welling up and a lump growing in his throat, he listened to every word coming out of his brother's mouth. But he barely made a sound.

After they hung up, Wongani cried for hours that night. When the tears subsided, he prayed until sunrise in Western Australia.

Dad is gone.

Nine thousand miles away, sitting on his bed in New Mexico, the words rang in Madalitso's ears. The memories flooded through him. Hours in the car on the way to Lusaka Golf Club and tournaments all over Zambia; constant reminders of "keep the left arm straight" and "eyes focused on the ball." The familiar voice in his ear, the comforting hand on his shoulder after a tournament. Sitting on the sofa to watch one of the majors. And of course, hundreds of long walks together on the golf course that were about so much more than golf. Marching up the eighteenth fairway to see his dad standing by the green.

Madalitso didn't know how many more tournaments he would play in his life, but he knew it would take a while before he stopped scanning the crowd for his father's face.

IN THE MIDDLE of the night, the phone jarred me in Washington, DC. Half awake, I let it go to voicemail.

A minute later, it rang again.

Back-to-back calls? At this hour? Suddenly alert and nervous, I reached for the phone. "Hello?"

The first thing I heard was a male voice crying. The emotion startled me. "Jayme?"

"Yes," I replied, terrified.

"It's...Wongani...calling from Australia."

My body went numb except for the dull churn of my stomach. "Yes, Wongani."

"My...father...died," he managed through deep sobs.

Words just tumbled out of my mouth. "Oh my God...I am sorry...My God, I am so sorry..."

"Thank you," he whispered.

Dazed, I asked the usual hows and whys. Wongani briefly explained what little he knew. He spoke of a cough, fever, loss of appetite and shortness of breath. Peter's discernable and commanding voice had become weak. At last, he fell asleep and was gone.

Asking Wongani how he was doing was stupid, so I didn't. "Wongani, I haven't shared with you or Madalitso how much your father meant to me. Someday I will."

"I know you and my father were close," Wongani replied.

Though I'd only met Wongani in person twice, I now shared something that was long overdue. "Hey, Wongs, I loved your dad. I love your brother. And I love you."

"Yeah," he said through his sobs. "Me too."

After we hung up, I paced back and forth in my bedroom, staring at the phone. Finally, I closed my eyes, took a deep breath and dialed Madalitso's number. My heart raced.

"Hello?" Madalitso spoke clearly, though I could tell he was crying.

"Madalitso, I am so sorry."

He paused before softly uttering, "Yeah." Madalitso did not express his emotions like his older brother, so I didn't try to draw him out. There'd be plenty of time to talk. "I'm flying to Albuquerque tomorrow. I'll call with my flight details once it's booked."

"Okay."

"I love you, Madalitso."

"Me too."

There were few flights to Albuquerque at this hour. Luckily, I found an early non-stop out of Baltimore-Washington International (BWI) Airport.

There was one last call to make.

"Mom?"

"Yes," she answered in her gravelly sleepy voice, fumbling the phone.

"Sorry to wake you," I said, and took yet another in a long series of deep breaths. "Peter Muthiya died."

It took a second to register what I'd said. "Oh...Oh my God," she gasped and moved the phone away from her mouth for a moment. "Claude, Peter Muthiya died," I heard her say. "Jayme, that is terrible." Emotion filled her voice.

"I'm sorry I woke you, but—"

"Don't be ridiculous," she said. "I would've been angry if you hadn't called."

They asked about Madalitso and the rest of the family. I shared what little I knew and told them I was flying to Albuquerque in the morning.

"Please call when you get there," she said. "And tell him we love him."

"I promise to call so you can tell him yourself." I hung up.

My mind started racing: *Where does Madalitso go from here? Will the trauma of this loss make him quit school? Quit golf? Move back to Zambia... permanently?*

I finished packing, said a prayer, climbed into bed, set my alarm and went to sleep.

That was it. No tears. They would come later.

I BARELY SLEPT that night, meandering in and out of consciousness. After I got to the airport, I made my way to the plane. The flight wasn't leaving for a while, so I sat by myself, surrounded by people I'll never know, all going somewhere.

My brain had been clenched in a fist ever since Wongani gave me the terrible news. Waiting in line over the next twenty minutes, I drifted back to the whirlwind of the night before. Suddenly, I felt the weight of the tragedy. Peter Muthiya didn't deserve this. He'd done everything right. Without bitterness or anger, he accepted being born at the bottom of the world's economic food chain. He confronted his challenges with the only tools he possessed: intelligence, work ethic and unwavering faith. Peter Muthiya prayed every day, but only to give thanks. *Never* to complain or whine or ask why. He passed every test that God dished out. This should've been Peter's time to see the rewards of his life's work.

It didn't matter that at fifty-two he lived fifteen years longer than the average Zambian male. This wasn't supposed to happen. Not to him. In the next few years, his children would receive their college degrees, and he deserved to be there. He deserved more time with his wife...to walk his daughter down the aisle...to help his older son start a business. And of course, to spend more time with his lifelong love: golf.

Peter deserved to see his youngest son play professional golf...to watch him tee off in a big tournament...to witness him make history. And now, just as all of this was on the horizon, it was taken away.

I had a blindingly clear flash of an astute-looking man standing next to a shy teenage boy in the lobby of my hotel in Lusaka. It would take me the next two years to secure his son's scholarship and enrollment in an

American university. The same amount of time it took him to change my
definition of family.

More than twenty years had passed since I was ripped apart by the tragic
and inexplicable end to such a vibrant life. Over twenty years since I gritted
my teeth and shook my head at the world. When my dad died.

The emotion came over me like a tidal wave. I looked down and covered
my eyes, which were now drenched. Feeling the stares from fellow passengers,
I tried to conceal my face and stay quiet.

Checking my boarding pass, a kind airline employee asked if I was okay.

Clearing my throat, I said, "A close relative passed away last night."

"Oh...I'm sorry," she replied, slightly embarrassed.

Walking down the Jetway, I thought of how far we'd traveled. Peter
believed that he, his son and I were companions on a mission. It was a quest
that would present each of us with unique challenges to overcome, new
opportunities to embrace and much-needed healing to happen. For Peter,
it was finding the ability to trust and welcome a young man who resembled
people that inflicted so much pain on his family while sparing his son the
frustrations caused by inept leaders who resembled him.

For Madalitso, it was seeing whether dreams really are for a kid trying to
make history by playing a game traditionally reserved for people with more
money and better stuff, who live in a world of privilege he'd never known,
and who have a different skin color.

For me, it was allowing myself once again to admire. To confide in. To
seek advice from. And to look up to. And to put aside my own life so I could
help someone else, look after someone else, take care of someone else in a
way that I never quite had before.

But there was a common goal. It was more than a college scholarship
and a career in golf. And it was here, as I slid into my window seat, that I
remembered something else: an unfulfilled promise.

Peter was convinced the three of us were brought together by someone
larger than the President of Zambia. He believed our mission was to help
Madalitso do something that somehow contradicted centuries of entrenched,
ignorant, prejudiced thinking.

I finally understood what he was driving at. People like him were poorly represented in professional golf. Not a single Black African had ever played in a major in the United States. History suggested they simply weren't good enough. And because of all this, maybe we could help Madalitso break through, do something no one else had ever done.

Fine. I knew this.

But as far as Peter was concerned, knowing that Madalitso might be the first to do something wasn't good enough for him or for me, nor was a general awareness of long-held prejudices. Many people knew these things. He had no intention of letting me off that easy. There was more to it. More details. More depth.

To truly understand our mission, I first had to know its context, its origins, and its significance. As he stressed to me in Fort Myers, "A meaningful event cannot be fully appreciated by its witnesses unless they understand how history molded the key institutions and players involved, and this includes the way that history shaped people's views."

Peter spoke with a calm, measured tone. But he emphatically made this point for a reason. Just like calling me his American son was for a reason. It was more than a humorous way to end our phone calls. Peter Muthiya loved me. He respected me. So much that he wanted me to understand the worlds in which he and his son were living and were trying to change. He wanted me to try and see it through his eyes.

I heard his voice repeating the same question: *Did you get THERE yet?*
I never did.

Countless times in our conversation, he'd give me a direct, good-natured nudge while I squirmed in my chair and made vague promises to read the history, do the research and oblige his simple yet difficult request.

I had every intention of working my way through a few books. But reading centuries of history on Africans and golf sounded more like a chore than anything remotely close to pleasure.

It was easier to put off. I was too busy with work, my travel schedule was crazy and I always had too much on my plate. It was almost as if there was a recording in my head that would repeat: *There just aren't enough hours in the day, but I will get THERE...eventually. There will be time.*

Now I realized how pathetic these excuses truly were. There was no more time.

To Peter Muthiya, the issues that I so casually brushed off were some of the most important things in his life. They were imperative to everything he was trying to help his son achieve. He didn't care what most people thought, but his feelings for me were so deep that he wanted me to know how history—at least in part—drove him. How it shaped his world and defined him. He wanted me to care enough to learn, because it was key to understanding any success that his son might achieve in this sport. And it was key to understanding his world. To understanding *him*.

Sitting on the plane, I now admitted the painful truth: for four years I simply didn't care. At least not enough. It wasn't a priority for me. I could have easily made time, but I found the whole idea too easy to dismiss. Apathy, procrastination and insensitivity kept me from reading a few books and fulfilling a promise to a person very close to me.

Turning away from the other passengers and staring out the window of the airplane, I looked back on my life and could think of no failures as disappointing as this one.

35

I WAS PHYSICALLY, SPIRITUALLY AND EMOTIONALLY exhausted when my plane touched down in Albuquerque. Madalitso met me at the airport with Glen Millican and his wife, Megan. Ryan Murphy was also there. Along with Jeremy Kirkland, these people spent the most time with Madalitso in New Mexico. Even in the depths of my grief, I was happy to see that my African brother had a great support system, good people who clearly cared deeply about him.

After I gave Madalitso a hug, I asked, "How are you?"

"Fine," he mumbled, but his red eyes said otherwise.

Glen dropped us at Madalitso's apartment. We plopped down on the couch and turned on the TV.

"Did you sleep last night?" I asked.

"A little."

"Well, don't feel obligated to entertain me. I didn't get much sleep on the plane, so a nap sounds pretty good." I knew Madalitso too well to try and draw him out. He expressed himself when he was ready—on his terms. I just wanted to be there *if* he felt a desire to talk.

He shrugged, staring at the TV. "I don't much feel like sleeping." His voice was so empty.

I kept my eyes on him but said nothing.

After a deep dark sigh, he said, "I guess I'll have lots of time to sleep on the flight home for the funeral."

The way he said "home" gave me an uncomfortable feeling. It sounded like a one-way trip. I almost launched into a *stay-and-fulfill-your-dream-as-your-father-would-have-wanted* speech. Luckily, I thought better of it.

"Your mom and sister will be happy to see you."

"Actually, it's my mom that I'm concerned about," he said, never taking his eyes off the TV.

Again, I stayed silent, giving him space, waiting for him to complete his thought.

"I don't know what she is going to do. My father was the breadwinner in the family. I haven't discussed finances with her, so I don't know if she can keep the family home and pay bills and Ivwananji's school fees."

It was the first time we discussed the nuts and bolts of Peter's death face-to-face. His first thoughts were about the welfare of his mother and sister, not himself. It didn't surprise me.

"My mother ran the home and served as the glue," he began. "My father was the engine that drove everything forward. Whether it was history, math or world affairs, he was the smartest man we knew, and he used his knowledge to benefit us. Every day he would tell a story or cite a current event to punctuate his belief in hard work, discipline and faith.

"But it wasn't just talk. My brother, sister and I knew the details of his childhood. We learned of the cruelty and degradation that colonialism and White supremacy inflicted on our grandparents. We saw the hut in Kabwé where he was born. We knew that he pulled himself out of poverty. He was an example. And now..."

Madalitso's voice was steady as a single line of tears fell from each eye. Turning away from the television, he looked straight at me.

"How do you replace a person like that in your life? How do you fill that void?"

MADALITSO CERTAINLY WASN'T alone in wiping his eyes. Over the weekend, emotions kept catching me by surprise, and I found myself weeping while trying not to. Frankly, it was a little embarrassing since *I* was supposed to be comforting *him*.

But we also laughed. Madalitso razzed me about the time Peter and I drank too much at the Cabana in Fort Myers. "Neither of you were making sense," he said. "But you both acted like you were saying the most brilliant things anyone ever said." We roared at the "Cobra Story."

Madalitso welcomed visitors all weekend. As friends, teammates and classmates filed in, it was hard to believe that just a year ago we fretted over whether this shy and soft-spoken foreigner could fit in and make friends with American college students. On Sunday morning, Coach Murph walked in with a gift: a framed photograph of Peter and Madalitso taken when Peter traveled to Albuquerque for the NCAA West Regional. Neither of us could look at the photograph for more than a few seconds without tears filling our eyes.

I kept waiting for—and dreading—the moment when Madalitso would collapse. At some point, the enormity would overwhelm him, and he would finally just break down.

It never happened. Not once.

Madalitso defined "composure" the entire weekend. He welcomed his guests, engaged them in conversation and thanked them for coming.

ON SUNDAY MORNING, we ate breakfast before my flight. It was now or never.

"Madalitso. You asked me a question the other day," I began.

He looked at me. "What was that?"

"You asked me how to replace a person like that in your life."

Looking away, he gave me a simple, "Yeah."

"You can't. Madalitso, there's no way to replace your father, a person who played such a major role in shaping you."

Madalitso listened but still would not make eye contact.

"But you can allow him to keep impacting your life," I said.

He looked up and stared at me.

"You can keep following his lessons," I continued. "Your father taught you so much. He challenged you. He told you where you came from, and he urged you to work hard and pursue your dreams. As long as you keep him in your heart and follow his example, he'll always be here. If you continue following his teachings, he will stay in your life. If you give up, then he won't. Your dad is still here, Madalitso. Whether he *stays* here is up to you."

Repeating Peter's words was easy. Honoring his memory would be the real challenge for Madalitso and others who were close to him. Including me.

Exchanging "I love you"s made him uncomfortable. So as I loaded my suitcase into the taxi, I thought of another way to give him the greatest compliment that one person can give to another. With a big beaming smile, I said:

"Hey, Madalitso. L-Bomb."

"Yeah, me too," he laughed.

THE WEEKEND WAS replaying inside my head on the flight back to DC when suddenly I thought of something else: Wongani.

Peter's older son was still pursuing his college degree in Australia, working two jobs and stretching every dollar. Could he afford a last-minute plane ticket to Zambia? Dreading the answer, I telephoned Wongani that evening.

"My mother is making funeral arrangements. She wants all of us to say a final goodbye together," he said, trying to steady his voice. "I cannot be there, and I don't know how to tell her. It's just the way things are." My stomach sank. Without knowing what to say, I tried offering a few comforting words and promised to phone the next day.

My next call was to Seattle, informing my folks that I was home. I walked my mom through the weekend, providing details that I couldn't share when Madalitso was next to me.

Then I told her about Wongani. Knowing my mother, what happened next was something I should have predicted. We spent thirty seconds lament-ing the problem before she flipped the switch. "Okay. Let's take care of this," she announced. "You, Claude and I will split the cost of Wongani's airline ticket from Australia to Zambia. Done." My mom and Claude had never met Wongani. They didn't even know what he looked like. Their only contacts were brief phone calls on Christmas morning. As much as their willingness to help a relative stranger, they appreciated the work ethic and character of a young man from an underprivileged background. It was also about their love for Madalitso. And more than anything, it was one last gift to Peter.

The next day, I telephoned Wongani and delivered the news. His reaction was predictable. "OH MY GOD! ARE YOU...OH MAN!" He thanked us profusely, over and over.

Before we hung up, I laid down one condition. "You must use the return portion of this ticket. We want you to earn your degree."

"You know, Jayme, for several hours after my father's death I thought about quitting school and moving home to Zambia," he confessed with a sigh. "Nothing made sense to me anymore. But it wore off. To accomplish my goal of starting a business, I need to finish school. Please tell your mom and Claude there is no need to worry. I will fly back to Australia after the funeral." It was a relief hearing those words. I hoped to hear them from his brother.

Before leaving for Zambia, Wongani sent a note to my mom and Claude: "Because of you I can be with my mother at the funeral and say a few words about my father in front of family and friends. Most importantly, I can say goodbye to him."

THE FIRST LEG of Madalitso's trip was to Houston where he connected with his international flight. He telephoned during his layover to discuss the long trip ahead and how much he looked forward to seeing his mother. Mostly, he just wanted to kill time before boarding—or so I thought.

"They're asking us to get in line, so I better hang up."

"Okay," I replied.

"Hey, Jayme?"

"Yeah?"

"Maybe I'm wrong, but are you concerned that I might stay in Zambia?" he asked matter-of-factly.

He caught me off guard. "Well...you just suffered a great loss, Madalitso. Sometimes people change direction or rethink their lives when they go through something like this. It's only natural."

"That's true. But I've had this dream for a long time, and my dad wanted me to pursue it." He then paused for a moment before saying rather nonchalantly, "Don't worry. I'm coming back."

It felt like a weight was lifted off my chest. "That's great, Mad." I exhaled and leaned back in my chair. "Have a safe trip. We'll see you at Christmas. L-Bomb."

"Yeah," he laughed. "L-bomb."

PETER'S FUNERAL WAS held at St. Andrews Church in Lusaka, the Muthiyas' longtime place of worship. Family members and friends spoke, including his sons, Wongani and Madalitso.

Wongani struggled to restrain his emotions as he talked to the mourners about his beloved dad. "I cannot explain the depth of my father's love...for my mom, my siblings and me. I can't explain because you had to be there. It was something you had to see each day throughout our lives. Every belief or value that I covet was influenced by him—hard work, faith, being honest with yourself and others, setting an example. He shaped who I am."

Madalitso stood and slowly walked to the front of the church. Looking over the friends and family that came to mourn his father—most of whom he'd known his entire life—Madalitso was his unique blend of calmness and sincerity. "My father had special relationships with his children, connections that each of us shared with only him. For me, it was golf. As I see it now, walking the fairways together was not about attacking a particular hole or which club to use in a specific situation. It was much bigger. He was instilling the importance of focusing on what you are doing, being careful with your decisions and striving for excellence. He was teaching me to be the best I can be—at anything. The golf course was just his classroom."

I asked Madalitso if he wrote his remarks beforehand.

"No," he replied. "I just said what was in my heart."

Pallbearers carried the coffin out of the church, while longtime friends formed two lines. Golf clubs were crossed high overhead when Peter passed beneath.

The next day I nervously dialed Edith. Like her son, I worried about her now that she was the only breadwinner in the family.

"You know," she began, "when somebody dies there are problems, some of which I have. But I've always had my own money. It's a fundamental rule of African life: never completely rely on anyone but yourself. Never. People can be taken without warning, leaving behind those who can only depend on themselves."

Unbeknownst to me, Edith owned her own home along with a separate piece of property that she rented out. She also had a farm on the outskirts of Lusaka where she grew and harvested corn and other crops, *by herself*. Altogether, it was just enough for her and Ivwananji, who was still in secondary school.

As she described her family's sudden turmoil and the safeguards she had in place, I sat with the phone pressed to my ear and a stunned smile on my face. "I don't know what to say, Edith. Good for you."

Madalitso's magical golf swing may have come from a higher power.

But his character came from Peter and Edith Muthiya.

36

MADALITSO RETURNED TO ALBUQUERQUE AND then on to
spend the holidays with my mom, Claude and me outside Seattle. None of us knew what to expect. But we were determined to let Mad
enjoy the joy and holiday festivities that always flow through our house and
restaurant around Christmas and New Year's.

Claude and my mom were here, there and everywhere. She was spending
crazy hours giving Charles at Smugglers Cove its annual holiday makeover
while Claude toiled away in the kitchen preparing for the daily diners and
the office holiday parties.

Christmas Eve was a madhouse. In the best way. I picked up Madalitso from
the airport, and after a warm reunion, we strolled into the restaurant to find
my mom hustling from one room to another, getting everything ship-shape.
The second she saw us, she put us to work. I thought Peter would've loved that.

"We need to move this table over here, these chairs over there..." And on
and on. She suddenly stopped and looked at Madalitso and winked. "Don't
you forget, your dad gave me permission to go up your backside."

"Well, I certainly don't want that," Madalitso shot back with a laugh.

It was the first time since Peter's death that mentioning him made us
smile.

THE CHRISTMAS MORNING ritual started with a bang. After good morning hugs and exchanges of "Merry Christmas," Claude whipped up a breakfast that was so big and so good, it forced all of us to renew our gym memberships. Eggs, potatoes, bacon, sausage and baguettes were supplemented with foie gras, smoked salmon and salad with goat cheese. My folks and I drank champagne. Madalitso, ever the teetotaler, again opted for orange juice.

We dialed Zambia and passed around the phone. My mom and Claude had a grand time wishing Edith a Merry Christmas. But it wasn't the same without Peter.

After breakfast, it was on to everybody's favorite part of Christmas morning. Opening presents. Wrapping paper, ribbons and bows flew as we dug into our gifts, oohing and ahhing, hugging and giving many heartfelt thanks.

I waited for an appropriate lull, then I handed Madalitso a small box. I struggled to think of a gift that had more meaning and love than a new tie or some fancy electronic gadget. Madalitso was deeply religious, and this was the first Christmas after the greatest tragedy in his life. I thought and thought, searched and searched. Finally, it came to me. Now I worried whether it would be too emotional so close to his dad's death.

Madalitso stared at the square-shaped package. Receiving gifts still made him uncomfortable. He tore off the wrapping paper to reveal a dark wood picture frame. Underneath the glass were the words Peter spoke at our press conference in Lusaka:

To Mad, my son,
The message is simple.
The road to success is often fraught with pitfalls.
It can be rough and tough.
But with the kind of discipline that you've shown,
You can achieve quite a lot.
So my message is, you cultivate between the virtues
Of self-discipline and hard work.
Both at your academics and your game.

Madalitso's eyes moved slowly from left to right, carefully reading each word. His expression remained the same.

A line of tears streamed down his face.

My mom moved over and put her arm around him. Since I hadn't told her or Claude, she leaned in to see what he was holding. Sure enough, she started tearing up, too.

Madalitso walked over to me. For the first time, it was him hugging me instead of the other way around. We hugged for longer than we ever had. Then he pulled back, took a big swallow and smiled. "Thank you. This is the best gift you could have given me."

I almost kept my voice from cracking as I said, "You're welcome."

Everyone took a deep breath. Then, Madalitso reached under the tree and handed a present to my mom. She smiled as she tore off the wrapping paper. Inside was a framed photograph of Peter and Madalitso. Attached to the frame was a handwritten card.

Meeting people like you has given me
A strong perception of what the world should really be like.
People say that home is where your heart is,
And surely being in your presence satisfies my heart.
Warmest regards from Madalitso to Claude and Janet Faure.
Merry Christmas.

The card and picture were passed around.

Along with a box of tissues that was already half empty.

37

PETER WAS THE FOUNDATION HIS children used to face every challenge in their lives. He shaped who they were. And to Madalitso, his father and golf were inseparable. It was their private bond. For him, the sport didn't exist without Peter.

As the Lobos prepared for the spring season, Madalitso's grief-steeped challenge was to begin looking at golf as a world without his dad. Peter would never again be in the clubhouse having a beer or standing beside the eighteenth green. He was not a phone call away. Madalitso's greatest test would be to excel at golf by honoring his father's edict passed down from his grandmother Kaliwé:

Focus on what you need to do.

MADALITSO TRAINED HARD for the 2003 spring season. Watching him, you would never know that the most important person in his life just died. The impact on his golf game would be revealed when practice was over and the first tournament began.

On February 3, 2003, Madalitso stood in the first tee box at the first eighteen holes of competitive golf since Peter's death. The PING Arizona

Intercollegiate at the Arizona National Country Club in Tucson was also the Lobos' first tournament of the new year. Mad had never played a round of golf without the security of knowing that his father was out there in the world ready to give comfort and advice. As he stared at the green 400 yards away, he was surrounded by players and coaches from several universities, parents, officials and casual bystanders.

And yet he felt completely alone.

Everything seemed okay as he went through the comforting pre-swing ritual. The swing felt good. But as the ball climbed higher, he saw it was off. He needed to be in the left center of the fairway, but his ball tailed to the right fairway bunkers. He prepared for an early rendezvous with his sand wedge. Luckily, the ball stayed in the short rough, just on the outer lip of the bunker. A rocky start. But it could have been much worse.

Madalitso gathered himself for the next shot, managing to place his ball just off the green.

Arizona National's first green is big and multi-tiered. He decided to chip-and-roll, hoping to get his ball on the same level as the hole. But he still didn't feel quite right. He caught the ground coming forward, slowing the clubhead and striking the ball with less force. Groaning quietly, he watched the ball land on the green with far less power than he intended. It dawdled forward and stopped before the ridge separating the tiers. Eyes closed and shoulders slumped forward with pained exasperation, Mad grabbed his putter and plodded onto the green.

He two-putted his way to a bogey on the first hole. The opposite of the start he wanted.

As much as he wanted to honor Peter by ignoring the gaping hole his dad had left inside him, Mad couldn't shake the sadness of his absence.

Madalitso played on autopilot, mostly hitting enough decent shots to stay in the round. But there were so many moments when everything seemed unfamiliar, and he felt untethered.

A 2-foot putt on the par 3 ninth hole, a gimme, was shanked.

He barely missed overshooting the green on the seventeenth, another par 3 with a massive green.

These were the same clubs and shoes he'd played with a hundred times before. But they didn't feel right. Everything was different. Stalking him around the course was an exercise in futility and uncertainty.

Madalitso's first eighteen holes of competitive golf since Peter's death was a disappointing 76. That night he knelt and prayed that it wasn't the beginning of a disastrous season. That he could pay homage to his dad by being the best golfer he could be. The best man he could be.

But Peter had trained him to be self-sufficient, to solve his own problems. On the course and off it. Now, post-Peter, he was facing his first real test.

On day two, a different man emerged from his hotel room in Tucson. Mad was eager to get back on the course, back in the game. Once again, he stared down the fairway of the 400-yard par 4. But on this new day, he was fueled more by the need for redemption, to put his first round behind him. He barely went through his pre-shot routine and just ripped his first tee shot straight down the left side of the fairway, *exactly* where he needed to be.

Hungry to keep his newfound confidence and momentum rolling, he marched briskly down the fairway, leaving everyone else behind. He grabbed his six-iron and aimed for the flag, now less than 200 yards away. With the purpose, certainty and adrenaline absent during round one, Madalitso launched his ball straight toward the center of the tiered green that had been a nightmare the day before. The ball landed on the same tier as the hole, leaving him with a 5-foot putt. Giving himself no time to overthink what was clearly a straight-ahead shot, he struck his putt. The ball seemed like it knew just what to do. It traveled five feet and fell in.

Birdie.

His group finished their putts and walked to the second hole, when another player looked him in the eye and said, "Good hole, Madalitso."

The sixth hole, a 130-yard par 3, had a green defended by hazards. Many considered it a victory to just stop their ball somewhere on the massive 37-yard green. Not Madalitso. Without hesitation, he effortlessly lashed his tee shot sky high. It landed feather soft six feet past the hole.

Ladies and gentlemen, Mad was back. And he knew his dad would've been proud.

On the par 4 tenth hole, one of the toughest holes on the course, Madalitso stood unshaken after watching another player yack his drive into the ruthless desert rough. He methodically went about his business, knowing that nailing this tee shot would launch him into the back nine and toward a round that would make himself, his school and his dad proud.

Conversations turned to whispers when he took his position in front of the ball. In a flash, Mad turned his hips and whipped his club forward. *THWACK!* All eyes locked on the ball, which never deviated. It came to rest smack dab in the middle of the fairway. He didn't even wait for it to stop rolling before he grabbed his bag and trekked toward his ball at a pace and with a posture that screamed "I am a man on a mission."

Seven-iron in hand, he eyed the flag like he already owned it. Like a man possessed, he stepped up and launched. He instantly knew it was a good shot. He had a feeling it might even be excellent.

He was right. The ball stopped three feet from the cup. All he had to do was tap in for an easy birdie. Which he did.

Madalitso shot a 69 on a tough track. The best score by any UNM player. More importantly, in the span of a few hours he proved that the death of his father could be an inspiration, not a detriment. It validated and honored all his father had taught him. Proved that his dad's training that formed the entire foundation of his life in golf—instructor, sports psychologist, role model and friend who joined him on the couch to watch the majors—had made him into a golfer, and a man, who could overcome the toughest test anyone could face.

Death.

His third and final round was similar to the second. A couple miscues stuck out: an errant drive into the heavy rough on the fifth hole that forced a bogey and a ball that lipped out of the thirteenth causing a three-putt. Otherwise, he felt good, notching a respectable 71. Good, but not great. He finished the tournament third best on the UNM team and forty-second out of the eighty-three-player field.

At the John Burns Intercollegiate in Wahiawa, Hawaii, Madalitso produced strangely similar results: 76-68-72. Again, a poor first round, followed by an outstanding second round and a decent third round. He finished in twenty-sixth place out of the one-hundred-player field.

The PING Arizona and John Burns were important. Not because they were his best performances. They weren't. It was because Madalitso overcame seemingly insurmountable odds and showed up. He laced up his golf shoes, hoisted his bag, walked out to the first tee and competed. He needed to move forward. And he did.

But from one round to the next, the peaks and valleys of these two tournaments were also a foreshadowing. Inconsistency stalked Madalitso throughout the season, becoming the hallmark of his entire collegiate career. Never was this more evident than spring of his senior year.

In March 2005, Madalitso and teammates arrived at South to play in an intra-squad tournament. The top five would be UNM's varsity team at the Southern Highlands Intercollegiate in Las Vegas. He couldn't figure out why his body and mind were so lethargic. He was in the last leg of his college career, and whether it was stress over his future, a bad case of senioritis or just the long cold lonely winter, Madalitso was sluggish. Off. His disappointing fifty-eighth-place finish at the John Burns Intercollegiate a couple weeks earlier had left him discouraged. Hardly the sharp but relaxed zone he wanted to be in at the start of any tournament. Never mind one that would determine the fate of his last few weeks of college golf.

Standing at the first tee, with downtown Albuquerque in the distance, he felt out of sorts. Sure enough, his opening drive careened inexplicably off course. Madalitso had cut this dogleg-left more times than he could remember, including two years earlier with his father standing behind him. But now he watched helplessly as his ball sailed off the fairway and into a spiteful clump of sagebrush.

He avoided eye contact as he walked off the tee box. When he saw the mess he'd gotten himself into, Madalitso hacked his ball back onto the fairway.

The first green was guarded by bunkers on the right left and rear. But its size had made it easy for Madalitso to land a putter's stroke from the hole. Not today.

His ball rocketed off his five-iron, flew the green and landed in the back bunker.

"OH, COME ON!" he yelled in an unprecedented display of frustration.

A sand wedge and two putts later, Madalitso registered a bogey on this par 5 first hole. A hole he'd dominated so many times.

Hole by hole, the whole round was like an out-of-body experience. His tee shot on the par 3 eighth hole flew past the right side of the green and nestled against a tree. Bogey.

His fifteenth hole approach hooked viciously left and died in one of the only water hazards on the course. He three-putted more times than he cared to remember. He kept swinging his clubs, but it's like the shots were hit by someone else, as if another golfer had taken over.

By the last few holes, he just wanted to be done and go home.

He didn't even look at the list of players traveling to Las Vegas for the Southern Highlands Intercollegiate. He knew he was staying home.

The day his teammates left for Las Vegas was one of Madalitso's lowest points at UNM. He was a senior on full scholarship with a solid résumé behind him but couldn't remember playing so poorly. His college career was almost over, his coaches and teammates were off to play in a Vegas tournament, and he was alone in his apartment, sulking on his bed.

Madalitso stewed over hideous rounds, shot by painful shot, visualizing his swing, the position of his feet, hands and arms. *Where were the flaws? What fundamentals were forgotten?* Every technical aspect of his game was replaying in a loop like a horror movie over and over.

Then there was endless wracking perseveration over course management and mental preparation. His dad had taught him to develop strategies for attacking golf courses. But Madalitso knew this was an area he needed to address when he arrived at UNM. Learning when to play safe and when to take chances. How to read greens, weather conditions and his own body. Had enough time been spent on these aspects of the game? As a senior in college on a golf scholarship, had enough been learned?

Madalitso dissected every aspect of his game, his character, his self, as the demons hollered in his head. They tormented him, baiting him to answer questions that had always been there, but his father conditioned him to ignore. Issues that haunted his family from when Peter was five years old and fell in love with the game at a colonial golf course where Blacks were disdained and forbidden.

Poverty, powerlessness, despair, being told they were inferior, stupid, worthless. That their lives didn't matter. These demons had haunted Madalitso's life. He saw them in demeaning stares at his equipment and clothes. He saw them in statistics showing no Black African had ever played in golf's biggest tournaments. They surfaced when people stated unequivocally that Zambia could never produce a player worthy of competing in the World Junior Championship. They were heard in the innocent exchanges among boys who talked about their brilliant coaches and proudly displayed their brand spanking new golf clubs—conversations where Madalitso was always the odd man out.

Can you really play at a high level with inferior equipment and no professional coaching? Why hasn't a Black African ever played in the U.S. Open, the Masters or the PGA Championship? Do you really belong here?

Madalitso never gave the demons the time of the day. But now they were shrieking from behind the door that his father ordered him to keep locked. Forever. They taunted him. Begged him to finally look in their eyes, to answer their questions, to prove them right.

All while he stared at the ceiling of his apartment in Albuquerque while his coaches and teammates boarded a plane a few miles away.

And then it stopped.

Madalitso sat up in bed, eyes and mouth wide open, mind breaking free, racing in a totally different direction, fueled by a rush of exhilaration. He was focused on the wrong things! It was not about technique, mechanics and course management. He had to answer the fundamental questions:

Who am I? What am I doing?

The Muthiyas were better than this. Tougher. Stronger. More resilient. His struggles had nothing to do with his grip, his clubs, a hitch in his swing or strategic mistakes on the course. It was his mindset. His attitude. His very self.

Madalitso had always succeeded because he had been taught to believe in himself and his God-given ability. These mattered more than the golf clubs his family could not afford and the professional instruction he never got.

He knew that toughness and success were in his genes, in his history. Madalitso was the son of Peter and Edith Muthiya. His father was born in a mud hut but managed through hard work and perseverance to earn a college degree and provide a life that allowed his son to play golf against the best players in the world. Madalitso was the grandson of Kaliwé and Sandikonda, who survived colonialism, having their home stolen from them and being brutalized by apartheid while *still* keeping their family intact. The Muthiyas' struggles and the poverty of his home country were not weaknesses. They had been turned into strengths. He was stronger than anyone he played against because he and his people had overcome more.

Standing in his American bedroom, he shook his head and asked: *Who am I to feel fatigued or burned out?! Especially considering where I come from and how far I've traveled.*

Of course, he experienced emotional ebbs and flows. He was human.

But no more self-pity or mental flagellation.

Enough!

This self-reflective kick in the pants was exactly what he needed. As the demons were silenced behind their locked door, his father's voice thundered. *Get on with the job!*

TWO WEEKS LATER, the University of Arizona hosted the National Invitational Tournament in Tucson. The Omni Tucson National Resort was the venue, one of the top golf resorts in America and a frequent stop on the PGA Tour. The Lobos were there. Madalitso was with them.

He could hardly remember a tournament he looked forward to more than this one. His recent poor play was a cloud hovering over his head with only one way to shake it. Play again and play better.

Eating breakfast, driving to the course and warming up all seemed to drag on as Madalitso itched to start play. Frequent glances at the clock didn't make the time go any faster.

At last, it was time to tee off. A deep breath was needed to rein in his adrenaline. There were five tournaments left in his senior season...in his college career. Gritting his teeth, he reminded himself that his focus had to be on his next shot. Nothing else. This shot.

The first hole at the Tucson National Resort was a 395-yard par 4. The small green was surrounded by bunkers and, just to make things interesting, a lake sat on the right. For the majority of golfers, parring this hole was a cause for celebration.

Madalitso eyed an area just over 300 yards away where he hoped to place his drive. Landing in the middle of the fairway with less than 100 yards to go would make his approach shot—which required pinpoint accuracy on this hole—much easier. His clubhead now extended to the ball, he took one last deep breath before beginning his backswing.

His swing and contact felt good, so good that he could have closed his eyes and knew that it was a fantastic shot. Before his ball even landed, a familiar feeling came over him. It was a sensation that everything was returning. Seconds later, there were calls of "good one" and "nice shot" as it landed and came to rest exactly where he envisioned. *Okay,* he exhaled to himself. *That's one.*

Minutes later, he stood over his ball. Grasping a wedge, he could, once again, feel the excitement. He had a great lie with less than 100 yards to the pin! Time to capitalize! LET'S GO!

"Stop," he suddenly whispered to himself. "Slow down." Taking a deep breath, he put his club back into his bag, turned away from his ball and walked a bit. At this moment more than any he could remember, he needed to rein in his adrenaline. He had hit only one shot in this tournament. That's it. One. Hardly a reason to celebrate.

During this self-correction, others finished their second shots and turned their eyes to him. He calmly steadied his breathing and completed a few practice swings while looking back and forth at the flag more times than normal, making sure he was not rushing.

Finally at ease, Madalitso lined up and uncorked a high arcing shot. His eyes closely tracked the ball, glancing briefly down to the flag. Optimism grew as it descended. *Come on.* A couple seconds later, it bounced on the front part of the green and rolled six feet closer to the flag. Any questions on the success of his approach shot were answered when other players grabbed their wedges and stepped into the sand. Two putts later, Madalitso registered a par on his first hole.

A sense of relief came over him. His good feelings before the round were confirmed, at least initially. Next hole and next shot.

If the first hole indicated that Madalitso was off to a good start, the second hole showed that he was destined for a great round. At 535 yards, this par 5 was straight but demanded accuracy. A long ball hitter, he knew this was his opportunity to score. After blasting his drive down the center of the fairway, Madalitso found himself 200 yards from a small, uneven green surrounded by bunkers. This difficult green "makes birdie a tough prospect."

Madalitso had done his homework. He knew he needed to be careful. Reaching into his bag he pulled out his six-iron. Normally, a six-iron at this distance was risky because of the dangers surrounding this particular hole, and his distance with a golf club meant he could easily fly the green. But this was not a typical day, and Madalitso was feeling much better than "normal." He was in a zone, and he wanted to capitalize.

He performed his regular pre-shot routine, a few easygoing practice swings with some glances back and forth from his ball to the flag. Trying to avoid overthinking, he stepped over his ball, planted his feet and bent his knees. Arms extended.

His careful backswing was followed by the above-average velocity through the ball that always gave him such good distance. The ball accelerated off his clubhead. He watched intently as it climbed, knowing he had taken an aggressive approach to this hole. As the ball descended, he leaned to one side to influence it with some body language.

No need. Seconds later, the ball dropped onto the green, rolled over a ridge and down the other side, eventually coming to rest ten feet from the cup. "Nice shot!" was hollered by a player several yards away. After a narrow miss with his eagle putt, he tapped in.

Birdie.

Bolstered by these first two holes, Madalitso marched through the round with his shoulders back, a purpose to his step, a sharp look in his eye and a focus on each shot. On the thirteenth, he chipped from the rough to within two feet of the hole, saving par when it seemed a bogey was almost certain. And on the 600-yard fifteenth, Madalitso hit a drive so far that another player jokingly suggested that he check the ball for damage. On a course where professionals can feel good about an even par, Madalitso notched a 70. Two under.

It was one round. Just eighteen holes. But it was his best day of tournament golf in weeks. That night at the hotel, he talked casually with his teammates and watched TV in his room, focusing his mind on other things.

The next day, Madalitso arrived at Tucson National Resort determined to avoid thinking too much. His father told him, "Anxiety to continue the previous day's good play has turned many competitive golfers into their own worst enemy. They end up generating the very outcome they hoped to avoid." Madalitso simply ate breakfast, went through his normal routine and chatted with those around him.

Although filled with less adrenaline than the first day, he still enjoyed a solid start by parring the first three holes. A decision to begin round two by playing it safe—and smart—was paying off. Loosened up, he arrived at the next tee box feeling a little more aggressive.

The fourth hole at the Tucson National Resort was a medium-length 170-yard par 3. That was the good news. The danger lay within the water that bordered the left and front of the green. Pin placement toward the edge caused most players to safely aim for the back portion of the green and then hope for a good first putt.

Not Madalitso. Not today. Removing his seven-iron, he eyed the flag, not the large grassy area to the right. Typically, a par 3 with a tricky pin placement was not the kind of hole he viewed as a birdie opportunity. But this was not a typical day; he felt good. He knew this shot would change the complexion of his round, good or bad. Settling his feet, he continued looking back and forth to the flag while taking a deep breath, making sure he was really going to do this. With his clubhead extended to the ball, he exhaled one last time before executing a relaxed, textbook swing.

The ball soared skyward. He knew almost instantly it had the right loft and backspin to prevent an unpredictable roll. But where would it land?

Madalitso didn't move, his eyes fixed on the flight of his ball with an occasional darting glance down to the green. As it descended, his stomach rose. He knew it would land on or near the part of the green with the smallest margin of error. At last, it came to earth, splashing onto the green and immediately spinning a foot or so backward and stopping. His ball was six feet from the cup. "Nice shot, Mad," one player said. Another just smiled and said, "Jeez."

Minutes later, Madalitso lined up for a straight-ahead putt. Quickly walking back and forth, he checked for any obstruction or variances in the short distance between his ball and the hole. Seeing none, he lined up, found his stance, looked at the hole one last time and made contact. Seconds later, he plucked his ball from the hole. Birdie.

Carefully choosing his moments to be aggressive, Madalitso turned in another two-under-par score at the scorer's table.

His final round was remarkably consistent with the previous two, high-lighted by his second shot on the par 3 twelfth hole. After his tee shot landed him in a greenside bunker, Madalitso estimated that thirty feet separated his ball from the hole. Facing an almost certain bogey, he tried to block out the voices questioning whether this would be the hole that knocked him down the leaderboard. Instead, he launched his ball through a cloud of sand, landing several feet into the green where it rolled to within five feet of the cup. "Great shot," one player told him.

"Thanks." Madalitso smiled in return.

He marked his ball and waited for his turn to putt. As he wiped the sand off his ball, he visualized making this right to left breaking putt.

A couple minutes later, he placed his ball back down, still noting the break. He settled his feet and found his grip, ignoring the stares of those wondering if he really could save par after his missed tee shot into the bunker. After a few practice putts, he stepped forward, hunched over, eyes glancing at the hole one last time. Calmly he completed a short backswing and made contact. It began moving from right to left toward the hole, just as he had visualized. Just when it appeared his ball would glide past the cup, the speed died down and it turned harder to the left. The ball nearly came to a complete stop as it reached the edge of the cup, but dropped in at the last moment. Par.

Once again, his fellow competitors congratulated him, and once again, he diffused the praise with a muted "thank you."

When final scores for the National Invitational Tournament were tallied, Madalitso was the only Lobo to finish in the top twelve. His three rounds of 70-70-71 were the most consistent fifty-four holes of competitive golf he had played in months, drawing praise from his coaches and teammates. It was affirmation that his hard look in the mirror—not an over-analysis of mechanics or course management—was what he needed. With a smile and an enthusiastic handshake, Coach Millican complimented him. "I can tell you are really locked in," Millican observed, "focusing on each shot. You are staying present."

But that wasn't entirely true. For deeply personal reasons, throughout the spring season, one tournament was stuck in the back of Madalitso's mind. Peter had traveled all the way from Zambia to watch his son play in the NCAA West Regional as a freshman. Not only was it the last tournament he saw his son play, but it was their last time together. Now a senior three years later, Madalitso desperately wanted his final NCAA West Regional to be his best.

Bolstering his confidence in the interim were two more top-twenty performances, finishing eighteenth at the Aggie Invitational and twelfth at the Mountain West Championship where the Lobos cruised to their third straight conference title. Madalitso celebrated with his teammates, coaches and friends but his mind was already looking ahead. At long last, the tournament he had waited for was next.

When he boarded the plane for California and the NCAA West Regional,

Madalitso briefly felt envious of players whose fathers would be there to watch. But just as quickly he brushed it away, knowing he had nothing to envy. Sure, many players would have their fathers at the golf course. But how many had fathers cheering for them in heaven?

ON MAY 19, 2005, Madalitso and his Lobo teammates walked onto a course that was ready to challenge the best collegiate golfers in the western United States. Thick, punishing rough, fast greens and ridiculously difficult pin placements made Stanford Golf Course a brutal venue. Even more, 2005 was the first year the course changed from a par 71 to a par 70. If the Lobos were going to make the NCAA Championships, this course would make them earn it.

With driver in hand, Madalitso entered the first tee box. Inserting his tee and ball into the turf, he eased through a few practice swings and settled his breathing. His personal history with this tournament and his burning desire to play well all had to be blocked out. The sole focus had to be his first shot. This moment.

The first hole at Stanford Golf Course was a 520-yard par 5. Trying to cut this dogleg left from 300 yards away was risky. Bunkers were situated on both sides of the fairway, exactly where it turned toward the hole. The safe approach was to aim for an area in the center of the fairway that would provide a straight shot to the green. But with his length, these par 5s were *his* holes. *His* opportunities.

Wanting to set an early tone for himself, Madalitso settled his feet, found his grip and extended his clubhead forward. Eyes focused on the ball, there was a brief pause before he calmly completed his backswing and propelled his clubhead forward. It was the same combination of speed, power and ease that shattered a kitchen window fifteen years earlier.

The ball exploded off Madalitso's clubhead and soared down Stanford's first fairway. With the club completely wrapped around his frame, Madalitso watched intently, hoping his first shot would establish an early rhythm. His confidence grew as the ball reached its crest and began descending. A few seconds later, it landed and stopped in an open area on the right-center of the fairway, precisely where he was aiming. At 250 yards away, he was in an ideal position to attack the green with his second shot. *Yes,* he quietly exhaled.

Turning the corner, the second half of Stanford's first hole had an odd feature. A sand trap cut into the left side of the fairway around fifty yards from the green, which was sandwiched between two large bunkers on either side. Standing 250 yards away, golfers hoping to parachute their balls into this minefield faced dangerously little margin for error.

Still too early for such boldness, Madalitso grabbed his five-iron and targeted a section of grass 200 yards away, just to the right of the fairway bunker. Knowing a good second shot would enable him to attack the hole from a favorable position, he took extra time in finding his grip and settling into his stance. Seconds later, he launched a straight ahead 200-yard arcing rainbow, an all-too-easy shot that he had hit a thousand times before on the driving range. The ball landed precisely where he intended, leaving him less than fifty yards from the pin with three shots left to go. A good chip-and-roll followed by two solid putts gave him a par on the first hole.

Madalitso breathed a sigh of relief. Possessed with such a burning desire to play well—for his team, for his dad, and for himself—it was comforting to hit a few good shots and par the first hole. To start well. To just play golf and put aside the bigger issues. His mind and game in a good place, he parred the next four holes as well, settling into a nice, almost predictable groove as he approached the sixth hole.

Then everything changed.

At 429 yards, the par 4 sixth at Stanford was a dream for long ball hitters. The hole was almost completely straight, with a small forced carry a few yards short of the green. The fairway narrowed in a few places, so accuracy was required.

Madalitso decided it was time to make a move. With driver in hand, he inserted his tee into the ground and performed a couple loose practice swings before moving into position. He knew the dangers of overthinking at a time when things were going well.

A few seconds later, he put every ounce of energy into what may have been his longest drive of the tournament. Swinging with such force always brings a risk of inaccuracy, but making par on each of the first five holes bolstered his confidence. In one of those rare moments when excellent club speed and perfect form combines with contact at the club's sweet spot, the ball blasted into the air and straight down the center of the fairway. Whether it was the force of impact or the intensity of his stare—or both—time almost froze. He held his breath as it climbed higher, hoping it stayed on its current path.

The ball soared over the first narrow portion of the fairway and began its descent. Madalitso was almost surprised by the distance of this shot, and for a moment he feared that it may travel too far. But not to worry. The ball finally landed on the fairway with less than 100 yards to the flag. "Incredible shot," one of the other players said. Madalitso later called it "one of the longest drives of my four years in college."

Madalitso knew he was in an incredible position when he arrived at his ball. He grabbed a wedge and surveyed the less-than-100 yards now separating him from the hole. Closeness to the pin and his own stretch of good play tempted him to be a little more daring in his approach, despite the tricky pin placement in the rear corner of the green next to a bunker.

Despite the intense contemplation on his face, he had already decided on a plan: loft his ball onto the rear middle of the green and attempt a roll toward the hole. On a typical day he would simply land in the front—and safe—part of the green and pursue a two-putt strategy. Not today.

Determined to ride the momentum as long as he could, Madalitso showed no hesitation in sending his ball skyward. From head to toe, his entire body was tense as he watched, knowing his margin for error was small.

As it reached its peak and began falling toward earth, he uttered to himself, "Going to be tight." Only a few feet off-target meant grabbing his sand wedge or some other club he would rather avoid. Three seconds later, now standing on his toes, Madalitso watched his ball land in the rear of the green, pause for a moment, then begin a slow roll toward the hole. Inch by inch, the news got better with each passing moment. Finally, the ball stopped a mere four feet from the cup as onlookers clapped. Madalitso grabbed his clubs and walked toward the green, looking downward to hide his glee.

With his bag resting off the green and putter in-hand, Madalitso walked behind his ball. He studied every inch of green between his ball and the hole, wondering if it could really be this straightforward. Another player gave him a nod, inviting him to go ahead and finish. Seeing no reason to believe this was anything but a simple swing of his putter, Madalitso lined up, tapped his ball and watch it fall in.

It was his first birdie of the NCAA Regional, but not his last.

On the par 5 seventh, a 536-yard dogleg left, Madalitso hit a drive long enough to clear the turn in the fairway and give himself an open shot at the green. But the most impressive shot on this hole was yet to come. Facing a green fiercely guarded at the front end by two large bunkers, most players were laying up well short and approaching the green with their third shot. It was the safer play.

But once again, Madalitso was determined to press the envelope until the golfing gods slapped his wrist. He took a deep breath and tightly gripped his four-iron, all the while questioning whether he was *really* going to attempt what he was about to attempt. It was a risk, but nailing shots like this was the only way to separate himself from such a talented field of players.

Players, parents and coaches halted their conversations and stood still. All eyes were focused on him. He was not alone in wanting to see the outcome of this shot.

Standing over his ball, in position, he peered down the fairway for one last look at the green. Three seconds later, he executed the swing that sent his ball soaring. Everyone watching immediately knew this was not a play-it-safe shot. Eyes were fixed on a ball that would either set him up for a birdie opportunity or send him digging out of a sand trap.

Time slowed as he held his club aloft and stopped breathing. The final stretch of fairway between the two bunkers was so narrow that any unintended spin on the ball or gust of wind above the trees would spell disaster. *Come on,* Madalitso said to himself as his ball climbed.

The tenseness in Madalitso's stomach slowly eased when the ball began descending. From his vantage point, he could see that it was heading toward neither of the bunkers guarding the right and left sides of the green. *Stay straight. Stay straight.*

Nervousness turned to adrenaline as his ball landed in the narrow patch of fairway splitting the two bunkers and rolled onto the fringe just off the front of the green.

Now breathing again, Madalitso nodded at the people who broke the silence with clapping hands and calls of "nice shot" and "great ball." He placed his club back into his bag and was already thinking about his next shot. But this time walking toward the green, he did not gaze downward to conceal a smile. Instead, he briefly looked toward heaven. *Thank you.*

A press release by the UNM athletic department told the story of how the hole and the day unfolded. With a photo of Madalitso above, the writer proclaimed that "Muthiya scorched the front side today with birdies on six, seven and eight to card a 32 going out. He slipped on the backside with bogeys at eleven and fifteen, but still managed to post a score in the sixties for the first time this season. It was also his best round in three trips to the NCAA Regionals."

The 69 may have been his best eighteen holes at the NCAA West Regional, but rounds two and three weren't far behind. At key moments in Palo Alto, Madalitso embraced the kind of boldness that propelled him into fifth place at the end of round one, but he also showed resilience when it mattered.

Madalitso was showing good accuracy in the second round until a drive on the par 3 eighth faded right into a greenside bunker. There were no feelings of frustration or fears of a downward slide. Rather, minutes later he calmly chipped onto the green and faced a 10-foot putt to save par. With uneven terrain on the green, he methodically paced back and forth between his ball and the hole. Finally settling into the read of his putt, he chose the line that he thought was his best option. The ball popped off his putter, moving briskly over an awkward ridge and down the other side, but Madalitso could tell it was off target. A few seconds later, it lost momentum and stopped just two feet from the cup. He tapped in for bogey.

He returned his putter to his bag, draped the strap over his shoulder and began walking the short distance to the ninth tee. Just long enough to utter a few reinforcements: "No problem. It's just one hole. Next shot."

Madalitso stood outside the ninth tee box, leaning to one side against his driver and waiting for his turn. Appearing relaxed and calm was a thin veil. He always looked that way. Inside, he was eager to move forward, glaring intently down the fairway of this par 4 dogleg right.

Finally, he placed his tee into the ground, took a few practice swings and stood over his ball. Seconds later, he smashed it straight toward the bend, some 220 yards away. It was a towering shot over a group of trees on the right, landing in the middle of the fairway with about 130 yards to the flag. It was an excellent position for attacking the green, but this next shot would determine success or failure on this hole.

Madalitso grabbed his pitching wedge and focused his eyes right at the heart of the green, all but ignoring the large bunker on the front right. With the flag positioned toward the rear, he was counting on a decent roll to put him into position for a birdie. His normal pre-shot routine was lengthened as he carefully gauged the distance to the hole and studied the terrain of the green that awaited him. *Okay. Okay,* he repeated.

Finally, he stood over his ball and took a deep breath. A careful backswing and forceful follow-through sent his ball and a chunk of sod into the air. He closely followed the flight path while maintaining a firm grip on his club. Holding his breath, he watched the ball bounce onto the green and begin rolling forward...toward the hole. It traveled further and further, a couple voices urging it on. The improbable roll finally came to rest just five feet from the cup. No doubt expressing the views of others who were there, one player exclaimed, "Shit, dude! That was nice!" Madalitso—who never cursed and was even less comfortable with compliments—just chuckled and said, "Thank you."

The eighth and ninth holes confirmed—at least at this tournament—he could absorb a setback and immediately get back on track. With every shot in Palo Alto, he was keenly aware of his body, the location of the ball and the conditions of the course. All the while, he stayed relaxed and confident.

His three-round total of 210 (69-71-70) was good for sixth place, even or better than several future PGA players. It was his highest finish at a tournament of this magnitude in his four years at UNM. The NCAA West Regional—the last tournament his father watched him play three years earlier—was a bold exclamation point of what he could do at any given moment.

"HELLO!" I EXCLAIMED, slightly out of breath after dashing upstairs to answer my phone.

"Hey, Jayme, it's Madalitso."

"Mad! How are you?"

"Good," he replied with a laidback tone. "Just boarding our return flight." The lack of exuberance did not fool me. I knew him. The levity in his voice revealed that he was happy and confident.

"I followed the tournament online," I told him. "Congratulations!"

"Thanks. It was a tough course, but I hit a few good shots."

"Yeah. I'd say more than a few."

Madalitso laughed. "Jayme, can I call you tomorrow? We are boarding the plane now, so I just wanted to say hi."

"No problem," I said. "Hey, Madalitso, we are all proud of you. I wish your father could have been there with you."

Silence came over the phone. "He was here," Madalitso said calmly. "I could feel him." He hung up and eased into his seat on the plane.

He was flying back to Albuquerque but already looking to the horizon. The NCAA West Regional was played in the memory of his father's trip to the United States and their final time together. The next—and last—tournament of Madalitso's college career would be the end of a journey where he was the lone figure.

AS A YOUNG boy in Zambia, Madalitso Muthiya turned on the television and stumbled upon a golf tournament called the NCAA Championship. It had a profound impact, eventually compelling him to ask the President of his country for help in securing an athletic scholarship to an American university. Now several years later, he and his UNM teammates arrived at Caves Valley Golf Club in Owings Mills, Maryland, to compete in the 2005 NCAA Championship.

For Madalitso, just being here was a miracle. Around 143,000 American high school boys play competitive golf every year. Only 8,500 play at the NCAA level. A mere 156 competed in the 2005 NCAA Championship. The odds of a boy making it here from Lake Road PTA School in Lusaka, Zambia, are probably incalculable.

As Madalitso prepared to tee off, he spotted a TV camera. Quietly he wondered whether somewhere in the world a child in an impoverished country was watching.

A half hour later, he was standing on the first green with putter in hand. A straight-ahead drive and a swing of his seven-iron brought him here. It was a place he had been to a thousand times before: the edge of a green with two putts to save par.

Growing up, his father always stressed the importance of putting. "Drives and approach shots can put you in good position," Peter would say. "But your ability to putt will ultimately determine your success."

With forty feet separating his ball from the hole, Madalitso knew this was a lag putt. He surveyed the undulations in the green, finally choosing a line he hoped would produce a manageable fourth shot. With bent knees, he completed a few practice strokes, rocking his shoulders. He wanted to find an early rhythm this round, but knew such thoughts had to be blocked out. *Just this shot.* A brisk swing of the putter sent his ball forward.

The early seconds of a long putt are agonizing as the player waits to see if he found the right speed and line. Halfway to the hole, Madalitso knew he hit the ball too softly, overestimating the impact of a downward slope on the green. He cringed as the ball began to curve in the proper direction, but far short of the hole. Momentum quickly died, the ball stopped and Madalitso found himself still ten feet from the cup. His putting had been so consistent over the past couple months that he was more surprised than disappointed.

Without the slightest look of distress on his face, he placed down a marker, picked up his ball and slowly walked the distance to the hole. A slight slope was the only real contour change he noted. He knew speed was key, still nagged by the image of his under-hit first putt.

Finally setting his ball down and retrieving his marker, Madalitso took one last look at the line before gripping his putter and getting into position. Shoulders hunched over and arms locked in place, he made contact and sent the ball toward what he hoped was a par-saving shot. He watched as the ball lurched off his clubhead, traveling on the upward side of the slope. As it got closer, he sensed danger and quietly uttered, "Break, break!" Alas, the speed of the ball caused it to turn late, gliding just past the rim of the cup and stopping eight inches behind. People around the green let out a collective groan. He tapped in for bogey.

Madalitso snatched his ball from the hole and walked briskly off the green. After inserting his putter into his bag, he stood alone for a moment, closing his eyes and taking a deep breath. Eventually he bent over, draped the strap over his shoulder and began walking to the second tee, trying to clear his mind. *Just one hole. Onto the next.* His last two putts—one hit too hard and one too soft—now gave rise to a level of uncertainty he hadn't felt in a while.

Later that morning, he arrived at the sixth tee after parring the second, third, fourth and fifth holes. On paper it looked like he had settled into a good flow after his bogey on one, but the scorecard didn't tell the whole story. An outstanding tee shot on the par 3 fourth put him so close to the hole that a birdie was almost a given. But his 5-foot putt lipped out.

Two holes later, he hit a 6-foot putt so hard that it nearly cruised right over the top before rattling around the bottom of the cup. He gazed skyward and let out a deep breath, almost pleading for the formula that would sync his putter with the speed and undulations of these greens.

At least the accuracy of his drives and approach shots were keeping him in good position. On the par 4 sixth, he followed course management's advice and kept his drive to the left side of the fairway, a perfect place to attack the hole with his second shot. A lofted five-iron landed him just on the right edge of the green. Once again, two putts to save par.

About twenty feet of green separated Madalitso from the hole, and he studied every inch of it. With a modest goal of just getting close, he squeezed the grip on his putter. After a slight exhale and a calm swing, his ball lurched forward. He watched intently. But the ball had only traveled ten feet when he closed his eyes and looked away, realizing it was losing speed too quickly. Three seconds later, he glanced back to see it stopping six feet from the cup. "Come on," he uttered.

He stood still for a moment, a look of exasperation on his face. With others needing to putt, he laid down his marker again, snatched his ball and moved to the side of the green where he tried to collect himself as he waited for his turn.

At South, this 6-foot putt was a gimme. Not here. *Nothing* here was a gimme. Madalitso tried to clear his head. *Carrying frustration from one shot will impact the next,* his father told him. Easier said than done.

Finally, he stepped over his ball and planted his feet. He noted the slight break to the left and chose his line. Taking one last breath, he tapped his ball toward the right side of the cup. *Break. Break! COME ON!* he mouthed. A few inches from the cup it *finally* turned leftward, but only slightly. Madalitso leaned back and gritted his teeth as the ball arrived at the rim, peered over the edge...and stopped.

"Ohhhh...OHHHH!!!" Anticipation became audible around the green as people waited for his ball to drop in. It didn't. It hung over the edge, held back by one too many short blades of grass. "You gotta be kiddin' me!" he fumed in a rare audible outburst. A player close to him awkwardly looked down rather than make eye contact. Madalitso tapped in for his second bogey on the front nine.

Struggling to decode Caves Valley's greens was the story of the first half of the tournament. Rounds one and two were an unceremonious 75 and 74. Never one to compare himself to others, Madalitso couldn't help but feel *some* relief when he checked the leaderboard. Over 150 players teed off in the 2005 NCAA Championships. A mere eighteen shot an opening round in the 60s. In round two, there were only fourteen. He wasn't as far back as he thought.

Round three had an eerily familiar beginning. A strong opening drive and well-placed second shot put him on the green with two shots to make par. Madalitso held his putter, trying to block out the frustration this club had given him the previous two days. On too many holes in rounds one and two, a strong beginning was followed by costly missed putts.

Pulling his mind back to the present, Madalitso calmly paced the thirty feet separating his ball from the cup. Determined not to second-guess his own analysis, he took a few practice strokes before stepping forward to align his clubhead with the ball. After glancing forward one last time, he completed a backswing long enough to travel the entire distance to the hole. The ball shot forward over a ridge and down the other side. *The pace seems right,* he thought to himself. Twelve feet from the hole, it began to break left, just as he had planned. Three seconds later, it stopped four feet from the cup.

Placing his marker down, he acknowledged a compliment from his playing partner and stood to the side, concealing his sense of relief over a putt that finally worked out as he envisioned. A couple minutes later, he walked back onto the green to attempt to save par. Standing over his ball, he took a deep breath, thoroughly studying the four feet between him and the hole. Carefully, he drew back his club and swung through.

Frozen, he watched the ball intently as it rolled inch by inch toward the hole. It was only four feet with just a slight break from right to left, yet how many of these putts in rounds one and two lipped out or stopped at the edge? More than he cared to remember.

Over the final few inches, as Madalitso's face winced and his breathing stopped, something different happened. It went in. Par.

While Madalitso parred several holes in the first two rounds, none came with any certainty. He never really found a rhythm. Nothing felt right.

On the first hole of round three, his two putts rolled at a pace he intended and followed the lines he chose. With a small boost of adrenaline Madalitso thrust his putter into his bag. *Okay,* he said to himself. *That's one.*

Missed opportunities in rounds one and two flashed through his mind as he walked to the second tee, ruminating over any technical changes that might have caused these two putts to go well. But he quickly stopped, realizing the futility of trying to remember differences in grip, stance and swing. For a player whose success was so overwhelmingly based on instinct and God-given ability, dissecting such details mid-tournament was futile. He just knew that today the first hole felt right. Shaking his head, he arrived at the second tee, grabbed his driver and waited his turn.

From that point forward, for reasons he could not explain, the greens began responding favorably. After a disastrous tee shot on the par 3 twelfth hole landed him in a bunker forty feet from the cup, Madalitso hit a sand wedge that lofted his ball out of the pit, onto the green and then a perfect roll to within six feet of the cup. He had no business parring that hole, but he did.

On hole seventeen, a par 4 dogleg right, his drive landed him in the rough on the left side of the fairway just past a fairway bunker. Forced to hit out of tall grass and facing several bunkers guarding the left front of the green, prudence suggested he settle for a safe part of the fairway well short of the green. But this was his final NCAA Championship and lackluster scores in rounds one and two meant he needed to take some chances. Plus, he was feeling good.

Madalitso took more time than usual, standing behind his ball and staring at the green 200 yards away. Eventually he took a deep breath, tightened his glove, gripped his five-iron and moved into position. Extending his clubhead to the ball, he knew some extra muscle was needed to cut through the surrounding grass.

The centrifugal force from his natural swing rocketed the ball skyward— along with some turf. Players and bystanders watched it soar toward the green and the five bunkers guarding the left front. His stomach rose slightly as it descended, barely clearing the deep patches of sand he hoped to avoid and onto the green where it rolled another ten feet toward the flag. "Great shot!" his playing partner hollered. Now in better harmony with his putter and the greens, he executed two manageable putts to register another par.

It wasn't a perfect round. The course was meant to challenge the nation's best college players, and it did. Nonetheless, his sudden ability to gauge the greens combined with a couple of round-saving approach shots produced a more satisfying 72.

Madalitso relaxed that evening, casually chatting over dinner with coaches and teammates. It was a much better place than the night before when the vexing greens sapped any desire to socialize. After opening scores of 75 and 74, his third round of 72 was just a two-shot improvement. But a *feel* for the course and this tournament had finally arrived. For reasons he could not fathom, it took fifty-four holes to gain comfort that he could master this course. With only eighteen holes remaining, he went to bed relaxed, confident that something good was about to happen.

An uneasy calm defined the start of Madalitso's final round, parring the first four holes with a series of safe drives, accurate approach shots and solid putts. Ho hum. But inside, he sensed the remaining script would not be so predictable.

On the fifth green, he found himself with a 6-foot putt to save par. He arrived via a familiar path. A strong drive and his iron approach shot landed him on the green. A long first putt left him with a very makeable opportunity to save par. There was nothing remarkable about the putt now facing him. The hole was slightly downhill from his ball, but the shot was straight forward. Nail the speed and another par was in the books.

He took position over the ball and completed a few practice strokes. Measuring his club to the ball, he glanced once more at the hole before focusing downward, executing a short backswing and making contact. The ball traveled the exact line he envisioned...but was rolling with more speed than he planned. Wincing slightly, he leaned back as if applying the brakes. One foot from the hole, it deviated slightly to the left, caught the edge of the cup and lipped out. With slumped shoulders and closed eyes, he quietly whispered to himself, *"What?"*

Madalitso grabbed his pencil, opened his scorecard and registered his first bogey of the day. He began having flashbacks to the missed putts that defined his first two rounds. Doubt seeped into his mind. What about the rest of today—the remaining thirteen holes of his final NCAA Championship and his college career?

But just as quickly, he shook it off. *No.* He felt good yesterday and even better this morning. Uttering "This is not going to happen. Not today," he picked up his bag and marched to the sixth tee box.

Little time was wasted. When it was his turn to tee off, he calmly but decisively inserted his tee into the ground, placed his ball on top, took one practice swing and launched a 300-yard drive down the left side of the fairway. "Good ball," another player said. Indeed, he was left with a clear shot at the green from less than 200 yards away.

Madalitso now had a decision to make. From behind his ball he peered down the remaining stretch of fairway. He knew that an easy swing of his seven-iron would place him just in front of the green—the safe play. Of course, his six-iron would allow him to reach the back of the green where the hole was located. But success required his ball to clear the large bunker protecting the left front *and* avoid flying the green. He would have to land in the front or middle of the green, a very small piece of land 200 yards away. This was the risky play.

The sixth at Caves Valley is the #1 handicap hole on the course. The most difficult. In taking a few extra moments to consider his decision, Madalitso faced an unavoidable truth. If he was going to make a move in this tournament, shots like this were needed. He reached into his golf bag and grabbed his six-iron. Moving into position, he kept looking at the flag, almost as if he was still unsure. At last, he bent his knees, found his grip and measured his clubhead to the ball. With one last deep breath, he could almost hear his father's voice before the final round of the Henke-Berg: *Go for the pin.* There was no going back.

The ball powered off the fairway. Within three seconds, Madalitso (and everyone else) knew it would either land on the green or in the left bunker. His eyes moved from the ball to the bunker and back as it reached its crest. Expressionless on the outside, inside he was imploring it further. *Come on,* he urged.

His nerves quickly eased as it descended. With a stone-cold face, a surge of adrenaline and an elated heart, he watched his ball land in the center of the green and roll to within five feet of the cup. There may have been only a dozen people who witnessed his shot, but rarely have so few made so much noise.

"Incredible shot, Mad," one player said to him.

"Thank you."

More applause erupted when Madalitso knocked in the short putt to register his first birdie of the round. He quickly retrieved his bag and marched to the next hole, pausing only for a moment to nod in appreciation. He wasn't done.

Minutes later, he stood in the seventh tee box, trying not to smile. Laid out in front of him like a red carpet was 564 yards of straightaway grass, imploring long ball hitters to test their distance. Accepting the invitation, he pulled the driver from his bag. "For players that can drive the ball, it might be the best hole on the course," Madalitso recalled.

Club in hand, Madalitso took a few extra practice swings to temper his own excitement. Loosening his shoulders, he breathed deep as he set his feet and measured his club to the ball. *Emotions, positive or negative, can cause a lapse in fundamentals,* his father told him. Focusing on every part of his body, Madalitso calmly executed his backswing and then did something that neither his father—nor anyone else—could ever teach him. He powerfully and effortlessly launched his ball into the air and down the fairway at a distance few could match. "You got all of that one," somebody said to him.

Any feelings of satisfaction were short-lived. The seventh at Caves Valley is one of the longest holes on the course *and* boasts one of the most challenging greens. Madalitso's long drive was only step one. A good score on this hole required placing his next shot close enough to reduce pressure on his short game.

Madalitso peered into his golf bag, his eyes moving back and forth between two clubs. With a five-iron he could lay up short of the greenside bunkers and chip onto the green. The safer play. But his two-iron, *if* he nailed it perfectly, would allow him to reach the green with a chance to birdie one of Caves Valley's most difficult holes. This was the riskier play. It was the final round of the NCAA Championships. Players were fighting to move up the leaderboard. He needed to press the envelope, but also be smart.

As he was weighing his decision, applause erupted on another hole. Madalitso reached into his bag and grabbed the two-iron.

Tightening the Velcro on his gloves with the club tucked firmly under his arm, Madalitso eyed the center-right section of the green. It was an area away from the left greenside bunker but close enough to have a shot at eagle. In finding his grip and taking a few practice swings, he projected a calmness that contrasted with the daring shot he was about to attempt.

Conversations turned to whispers, and eyes slowly turned in his direction as he moved over the ball and set his feet. Silence finally ensued. The next sound anyone heard was Madalitso's club slicing through the air and smacking his ball. Before the clubhead finished circling his body, he knew he had the high trajectory he wanted. He held his breath as it climbed, hearing only his inner voice. *Come on.* The ball was headed straight toward the green with distance now being the only uncertainty. Too far? Too short? Too much roll?

All questions were answered when it landed on the right portion of the green and rolled ten feet before stopping on the crest of a slope. Two dozen spectators, silenced and stone-faced just seconds earlier, now applauded with a few shouts of "nice shot!" and "way to go!" His playing partner smiled and gave a fist bump.

Golf allows little time to celebrate or lament. Another shot awaits. There is no better example than Caves Valley's seventh green. Players buoyed by a strong drive or accurate approach shot are quickly sobered when they arrive at this elevated patch of turf. Course designer Tom Fazio created a putting surface that is fast, sloped and surrounded by bunkers waiting to swallow balls that roll past their intended target. Caves Valley management has a word for the seventh green: "Treacherous."

Madalitso began walking the thirty feet between his ball and the hole, trying to find a line that made sense. The obvious break was from right to left. But how much and where? And a slight unevenness close to the hole suggested a slight break back the other way. Of course, the downhill slope meant he would have to rein in his swing. Madalitso often heard his father's voice in key situations. Some moments, it was louder than others. *You can spend hours analyzing a green like this. At some point, go with your instinct.*

People who just witnessed his approach shot now encircled the green, probably wondering if he could master this roller coaster putting surface as an encore. Settling on what seemed a likely break point, he walked back to his ball and took a few practice swings. Too soft would leave him with another challenging putt and frustrated over a blown opportunity. Too hard might be worse—reaching for his sand wedge. Any doubt that he was the center of attention was erased when silence suddenly ensued as he crouched over his ball.

A couple final looks back and forth from his ball to the break point and the hole. A final breath, a brief pause, a short backswing and a firm follow-through. The ball popped off his putter and cruised down the slope, picking up steam. Watching its brisk pace on such an unpredictable surface made his stomach churn. As it approached the break point on the slope, he held his breath. "Okay. Okay. Come on," he said through gritted teeth. The speed leveled off, and it began a gradual leftward curve toward the hole right in the area he expected.

He uncoiled from his crouched position and glared at his ball now traveling across a flat surface. The hole drew closer, the speed of his ball decreased, his adrenaline began flowing and a chorus of voices rose from all around. He raised his club and leaned back as it finally died down, cutting just in front of the hole and stopping. Just short. Madalitso's smile, closed eyes and exhale coincided with a collective groan from spectators that quickly changed to applause, shouts and whistles. The other players in his group nodded at him to finish the job, which he did from a foot and a half away. Birdie.

Madalitso lifted his ball from the hole and raised his hand to those expressing their appreciation. Rebounding from an initial bogey, he was suddenly one under par after stringing together spectacular and gutsy back-to-back shots on two of the most difficult holes on the course. Tucking his putter back inside his bag, his thoughts were calm but laser-focused.

His muscles were relaxed but in a split second could produce any amount of power, speed and agility that he asked. He was confident but knew continued success meant taking nothing for granted. Madalitso was in the zone, completely in tune with his clubs and the course. There was no second-guessing his club selection, his strategy from hole to hole or any doubt that he could hit any shot he wanted. But then he arrived at the fifteenth, and uncertainty returned.

There is no shortage of opinions on the par 3 fifteenth at Caves Valley. Club management advises players that "par will be a good score." An online source proclaimed it "the most demanding par 3" on the course, while another called it "stern" and "dramatic." Lastly, after playing Caves Valley, one course reviewer had a crasser assessment: "This hole was a bitch!"

Immediately, the ball must travel a path with little margin for error, avoiding trees pressed against a tight fairway and clearing a long stretch of wetlands. Then comes a decision: Where to land? On the right side of the narrow 40-yard green is a bunker. On the left side is an uphill embankment. The flag tucked in the rear right corner leaves golfers with a near impossible target. Perhaps the most perilous 219 yards of golf at Caves Valley, the obvious approach to the par 3 fifteenth is to land near the front of the green and hope for two good putts to save par. This is the clear decision for most players, but not for Madalitso Muthiya.

Sitting at even par, Mad was getting that feeling once again. His mind churned through a few memories as he removed the seven-iron from his bag. The first was his recollection of the fifteenth hole over the previous three rounds, specifically the ridiculously small amount of green close to the hole. Second was the hours spent working with his dad on controlling spin. Since neither Peter nor Madalitso had any technical training, they combed through books and carefully watched golf tournaments on television, listening intently to commentator analysis. Playing at UNM had bolstered Madalitso's knowledge of the game. But those early trial-and-error lessons with his dad left the largest imprint. Peter gathered enough knowledge over the years to offer a warning to his son: *Executing a backspin is fairly easy. The risk is how far it travels.*

His heartbeat accelerated as he waited for his turn to tee off, still unsure if he would go through with his plan. There was more at risk than his own score. The NCAA Championship is a team tournament. His teammates, coaches and university were counting on him to make good decisions. *Deep breath.*

It was time. Finally settled on a strategy, he inserted his tee into the ground and took a couple practice swings. Finding his grip, he stared down this gauntlet of a fairway, visualizing. Measuring his club to the ball, he paused one last time before carefully completing his backswing and driving fast, down and through—just as he was taught.

The ball shot up past the trees and over the wetlands. He watched intently as it arced toward its target. Time slowed when it reached its peak and began descending, now revealing to everyone that Madalitso did not target the front of the green. He chose the riskier path.

Except for the hair standing on his neck and the tightening muscles in his stomach, Madalitso's entire body was frozen as it sailed further behind anything considered "safe." With a jolt he could almost feel, his ball struck the rear of the green near the embankment, suddenly stopped and reversed course. His father's warning about the dangers of a backspin rang in his ears as it rolled back toward the flag, and the bunker. But Peter's voice died down while voices near the hole rose in anticipation. The ball lost momentum and stopped eight feet from the cup.

Applause and cheers followed. Madalitso just smiled, though deep down he wondered how he managed to get backspin on a ball from this distance. *Don't question,* he told himself. *Just be thankful and move on.*

So much adrenaline, anxiety and anticipation crammed into a few seconds. Madalitso took his time walking from the tee box to the green, needing every inch of the 220 yards to collect himself.

He arrived at the elevated green, eager to see what awaited. The eight feet separating his ball from the hole consisted of a modest incline with a slight leftward break. Although easier putts have been missed, Madalitso had to suppress a smile as he placed his marker down and waited for others to hit their second shots.

Putter in hand, he surveyed the terrain one last time. Convinced there were no surprises, he found his stance and gained a feel through a few practice swings. Almost as if he were playing a practice round rather than the final round of the NCAA Championships, he stepped forward, took one last look at the hole and then followed through. He remained hunched over while watching it travel the line he chose, standing upright only for the last few inches before it fell in. Birdie.

Raising his hand and smiling to those who clapped, Madalitso now stood at one under par with three holes left. And that was where he finished.

News for the Lobos got better as each group of players completed their rounds. Three UNM golfers, Spencer Levin, Jay Choi and Madalitso, all finished in the top thirty. Thirty teams competed at Caves Valley. New Mexico's fifth-place finish was the school's highest in more than a quarter century, long before Madalitso or any of his teammates were born.

Over 150 players teed off in the 2005 NCAA Championships. Madalitso ended in twenty-seventh place, one of the highest ever finishes by a UNM player. If his first two rounds equaled his last two rounds, Madalitso would have finished in fifth.

The final five tournaments of his senior season were his best stretch of golf at UNM. Playing this well for the entire year would have likely put him in consideration for All-American. That month, he was named to the Ping All Southwest Region Team.

Less than three months after failing to make the varsity team for the Southern Highlands Collegiate, Madalitso was now playing some of the best golf in his life. Equally rewarding was how he got here. This dramatic turn-around was not owed to a new set of clubs or some technical improvement to his game. It happened because Madalitso simply relied on the teachings that had always carried him to success. Faith in God. Belief in yourself. Ignore things you don't have or that lie beyond your control. Above all else, remember who you are.

Somewhere, Peter was smiling.

ROOTING FOR MADALITSO was nerve-racking. With his tournament schedule always close by, those closest to him developed their own techniques for stress management. On the mornings he teed off, I took a deep breath, uttered a silent prayer and mostly kept to myself. Tracking his tournaments in real time meant sitting on the edge of my seat, clicking the reset button on the web browser and waiting for the birdies or bogeys to pop up. It was agonizing rooting for my African brother to fulfill his potential and finally break through.

While the rest of us fretted, stewed and paced back and forth, Madalitso never let the peaks or—especially the sometimes deep—valleys stop him from being the very model of a golfing gentleman, always a paradigm of sportsmanship. No cursing. No banging his clubs. And rarely did his coaches or teammates bear the brunt of a sour mood.

Peter would have been proud.

But Peter also would've never stopped asking questions until he got answers. Like father, like son. Mad never stopped searching for the key to playing consistently enough not just to finish in the top ten, but to actually win. He watched video of his swing until his eyes glowed blurry. Morning, noon and night, he analyzed his stance in the mirror. He incessantly probed his coaches and even worked with private instructors. Theories and strategies were hashed and rehashed. But no magical formula was discovered to produce the golfer everyone knew was inside him. The one that would result in him finally holding a trophy.

If you're not a world-class golfer, you have no idea how ridiculously difficult it is to make the jump from very good college player to one of the precious few who make their living playing professional golf. This was, as it is with most serious players, Mad's ultimate goal: to be part of the select world of elite golfers that he and Peter had watched on television each week. Competing for titles all over the world. Playing in major tournaments. Like the U.S. Open.

But Madalitso faced a challenge never confronted by other players competing at this level. Apart from a few key fundamentals provided by his father, Madalitso began his collegiate career with a mechanical understanding of golf that was far behind his peers. His lack of expert technical training was bound to catch up with him as he rose with the cream to the top of the golf world. In a sport that relies on science as much as athleticism, God-given ability could only take him so far.

Madalitso's college career was all about trying to master everything on the fly.

Some days, it all came together. Others it didn't.

Even more daunting were the adjustments to life. Culture shocks, bizarre food, homesickness and loneliness plagued his freshman year. But Madalitso had beaten most of them back. In UNM's four varsity tournaments in the fall of his sophomore year, he had three top-twenty finishes. His college course load had gotten easier. He'd chosen an apartment that was close to campus but far enough to escape annoyances and late-night noise. Between grocery shopping and the school cafeteria, he'd pieced together a diet that didn't make his stomach revolt. Biting sarcasm no longer set his hair on edge, and locker room magazines had become a part of life. The world challenged Madalitso, and he was not found wanting.

But that wasn't good enough. As Madalitso overcame these obstacles and climbed out of his abyss, he was hit with a sledgehammer. Without warning, his father died. The person who formed the bedrock of his life was suddenly and tragically gone. The world cruelly rewrote the rules of the game that Mad was winning.

This was always Madalitso Muthiya's story. As much as his life was defined by his golf genius, it was also defined by the barriers designed to stop him. From the first time he competed, he had the poorest equipment, the worst clothes and the least training. And of course, he was Black in a relentlessly White world, a member of a race that had been banned from doing the very thing he was gifted to do. He fought to be part of a world that had never wanted him.

And when he finally got inside, the awkward stares, quiet whispers, social cliques and clear disadvantages let him know in loud and quiet ways that he did not belong. This happened most often during his teenage years when a child's psyche is fragile and acceptance is everything. It took his driver and a humble display of sportsmanship to warm the unwelcoming chill and quiet but clear disdain that so often greeted him. There were so many times he could have set his clubs down, gone back to his dad and said with a broken heart that he'd had enough. It was too hard. He didn't want this anymore. He wanted to do something else. Be someone else.

But he didn't. He loved golf too much. And he believed in himself too much.

From the day Peter fell in love with the game at Broken Hill Golf Club until the moment Madalitso sank his final putt at the 2005 NCAA Championship, the Muthiya family's experience with golf was a story of racism. Poverty. Tragedy. Joy. Hard work. Family. Faith. Inspiration. Unshakeable self-confidence. Triumph.

It's also a blueprint for others who faced hatred and oppression. A Black child born in one of the poorest countries on earth could earn a scholarship to a top American university playing golf and compete against the best young amateurs in America in the NCAA Championship. This seemingly impossible achievement had become a lesson for people who feel the bar is too high, the road too long or the gulf too wide.

But Mad wanted more. Back in Albuquerque, he began finishing his schoolwork, clearing out his varsity locker and saying goodbye to friends. It was hard not to look ahead and consider the possibilities. To dream big. Considering how far he'd traveled, he wanted to leave a permanent mark on the sport, and the world, to defy the odds in an even greater way.

He wanted to reach a height never achieved. To stand as a living example of beating impossible odds, fighting for justice against racial inequality and believing in one's own power. For anyone who looked in the mirror and asked whether a goal is beyond their grasp, Madalitso would be the answer.

If that happened, if he had that kind of impact, who would be more blessed with his ability to play golf and his refusal to give up along the way? Madalitso Muthiya or the rest of us?

BEFORE MADALITSO STARTED pursuing his professional golf career, one more amateur event awaited: the Pacific Coast Amateur Championship at the world-famous Bandon Dunes Golf Resort in Oregon. Many former champions have gone on to the PGA Tour, and the 2005 Amateur Championship would be more of the same. Madalitso would be going up against the best of the best, including the reigning 2005 NCAA Champion and several future PGA Tour players.

Six years earlier, I attended Madalitso's first amateur tournament in the United States, the Henke-Berg in Fort Myers. And I would be there for his last. But at the Pacific Coast Amateur, I was more than a white-knuckled spectator. I was his caddie. When he asked me, I was shocked. He knew that I was a golfing novice, so apart from shouldering his bag and handing over the clubs he asked for, I was essentially useless. It was understood that I was supposed to keep my mouth shut and stay out of his way.

It had sounded like fun. But standing over Madalitso's bag on the first tee was way more sobering and daunting than I thought it would be. Caddies are caretakers, consiglieres, psychologists, yardage givers, club selectors, gurus, cheerleaders and a second pair of eyes. I obsessively examined his bag and each clubhead for drops of moisture to dry and specks of dirt to wipe away.

But it was also exhilarating. For the first time at a golf tournament, I was part of the action. Although I'd have no direct impact on the outcome of the tournament, being inside the ropes let me see, feel, smell and hear the game from the players' perspective. I wasn't at the cinema. I was in the movie.

Meanwhile, Madalitso was preparing to cut the dogleg right on Bandon Dunes' first hole, a 390-yard par 4. He scanned the fairway, reviewed his yardage book and tossed a few blades of grass into the air to test the wind. It was fun to be up close and personal and watch him keep his mind centered on the present.

"Next shot."

This was his final amateur tournament. Ever.

"Next shot!"

Madalitso grabbed the driver from my hand with no eye contact. I'm not sure if handing somebody a golf club is an achievement, but I was proud of myself.

The morning air was still chilly as he settled in before the ball. Conversations stopped. After a deliberate disciplined backswing, Madalitso turned his hips, whipped his clubhead down and powered through the ball. Standing this close, I heard his driver cut through the air and could almost feel the *THWACK!* of his clubhead against the ball rattling my bones.

Heads turned as the small group watched his ball soar down the fairway. It landed past the bend with a clear shot at the elevated green.

I looked down at the ground to hide my smile. I still marveled at his natural, elegant, smooth, effortless yet powerful swing. It was a thing of beauty.

But as I watched now, post-Peter, more than the swing itself, I marveled at *where* the swing was created. Discovered. Every shot was a journey to Lusaka, Ndola, Kitwe and a town once called Broken Hill, far-flung golf courses in a small, landlocked, third-world country. And of course, to a house with a broken window. I was transported back to the day when a straight-faced man said there were no golf instructors in his whole country. When I believed that top-notch equipment and professional instruction outweighed perseverance, determination and God-given talent. When it didn't seem that such a thing was possible.

I also saw a whole new level of maturity. From the moment he grasped his first golf club, Madalitso could control his emotions far better than most players his age. Well, actually, than most players at *any* age. DNA, strong parenting and growing up in a harsh and unforgiving environment had shaped him. But as I watched, it was clear that his time at UNM, considering he faced everything from culture shock to the death of his dad, had made an impact. Six years after I watched the skinny kid from Zambia play in Fort Myers, I was proud to be caddying for a young man poised to enter adulthood, with all the tools he needed to succeed.

Three down, with fifteen more to go, Madalitso sat at even par when he reached Bandon Dunes' signature hole. With the Pacific Ocean ready to punish any player who let himself be mesmerized by the cliffs, beaches and waves, he teed off. Rather than risk cutting the dogleg right, Madalitso hit the ball straight at the bend in the fairway. He was rewarded when his ball landed in perfect position with 140 yards to the hole.

Grabbing his eight-iron he focused on the flag, not the bunkers in front of the green or the Pacific Ocean yawning majestically behind it. The ocean and sky above made a massive 180-degree canvas that dwarfed the green he was targeting. Standing off to the side, I got a vantage point that gave me a greater appreciation for the physical and mental skills that players possess in guiding a small ball an exact distance through a labyrinth of hypnotic distractions.

Madalitso uncorked a high shot. It was on target, but distance was another matter. It became clear that it would not fall short. But would the cliffs, beaches and ocean on the other side claim another victim? The ball bounced on the right side of the green and came to rest toward the rear. A great spot. Looking down, I again fought the urge to smile, trying my hardest to impersonate a professional caddie.

Madalitso played with his usual calm focus and steady demeanor that served him so well throughout his golf career and his life. But he couldn't quite ignore the fact that this tournament had a finality to it. The Pacific Coast Amateur would be his last amateur event before turning pro. He struggled to stay in the moment, to not get lost in memories of his amateur career, his odyssey from African tournaments no one here had ever heard of—Ndola, Kabwé, Chibuluma and Chick of the North. Each swing, each hole and each entry into his scorecard moved him closer to a future that he didn't know and couldn't control.

I had no idea this was going on at the time. From tee to green, Madalitso played like a pro's pro. On the eighteenth hole, when his second shot drifted too far right and landed in a greenside bunker, he simply took a deep breath, grabbed his sand wedge and lofted an arcing 30-foot shot that landed him in the middle of the green. No fuss, no muss. Two putts later, he had turned in an impressive 71. Three strokes off the lead. He was right there.

After notching another steady round on day two, an even-par 72, Madalitso had some bumps in the road on day three. To avoid the pot bunkers in the middle of the ninth fairway, he drove his ball too far to the left and into the rough. His shot back onto the fairway was less than ideal, still leaving him with over 200 yards to the green. On the par 4 seventeenth, he landed on the green with two shots to save par. Misjudging the speed of the green, he hit the ball too softly, and it failed to clear a ridge, causing him to three-putt. He closed with a frustrating 76. I avoided eye contact with him after his errant shots, but I could feel the disappointment.

My bird's-eye, ground-level view was further proof of the ridiculously small margin of error that separates a birdie from a double bogey. A couple of bad shots can turn raucous celebration into moaning disappointment. Of course, with Madalitso, there was no moaning or celebrating. After his shaky third round, he rebounded with a 73 to end the tournament—a nice recovery.

He finished in a tie for ninth place out of eighty-four players. A top ten at the Pacific Coast Amateur was a great finish, especially considering the quality and depth of the field.

We loaded the car and began the long trek to Seattle. Before Madalitso closed his eyes for a well-deserved nap, we marinated over the last four days. We walked side by side for seventy-two holes, ate together, shared a hotel room and talked about everything. With eyes closed but flashing a broad smile, Madalitso ribbed me about my shocking lack of caddie skills. I was completely inept at giving any club suggestions, tips on holes or even which way the wind was blowing. Laughing, he said, "I was almost concerned that you might hand me the wrong club."

"What makes you think I didn't?" I quipped. "You need to pay better attention."

He was actually fine that I gave him nothing as a caddie. Every other caddie gave valuable information on yardage, clubs and how to attack the course. Part of me felt bad that I was so far above par, pun intended, but we viewed my role as more than golf. Yes, obviously I couldn't give him strategic golf advice, but I stood behind him and helped shoulder some of the weight he carried.

And that bag was surprisingly heavy.

Before he turned over and went to sleep, I wanted to tell him that Bandon

Dunes was affirmation for how thankful I was to have him in my life and how much I missed Peter. Instead, I kept my mouth shut and let him doze off.

38

MADALITSO GRADUATED WITH A DEGREE in business economics from the University of New Mexico in the fall of 2005.

Edith, Wongani and Ivwananji couldn't travel from Zambia, but they were with him in spirit. After seeing the photo of Madalitso in his cap and gown, Ivwananji said, "You look like that photo of Dad at his graduation from the University of Zambia."

We had a celebration dinner for Mad at Charles. My mom made all the arrangements and Claude prepared a gourmet meal. We even coaxed him into wearing his cap and gown so everyone could get a picture with the graduate.

It was a night when everyone wanted a speech by the new graduate. But there was no pressure. Everyone knew Madalitso was shy. Conveying feelings was hard when he wasn't comfortable.

Luckily, he felt safe and secure that night. When everyone got a glass of wine, Madalitso stood up, glanced around the table and spoke.

"Thank you all for coming this evening. My family in Zambia can't be here, so it means a lot that you came to celebrate my graduation.

"The last four years have been very challenging. Getting my degree, playing golf and of course the loss of my father. There were moments when it was hard to get motivated to do anything. But finishing college was always a dream of mine, so I just kept moving forward.

"Along with all the people here, I especially want to thank Janet, Claude and Jayme for opening their home and making me a part of their family. If you wonder what generosity is, just look at them."

It was short but sweet. My mom and I both needed to take a deep breath.

The applause and the red wine were the only things that kept our eyes dry.

COLLEGE DEGREE IN hand, Madalitso got ready for the next phase of his life: professional golf. In February, he traveled to Chino Hills, California, to qualify for the Canadian Professional Golf Tour. Madalitso stood at the first tee of the Los Serranos South Course, a long 560-yard par 5. The course and the hole were nothing new. Neither posed any challenge he hadn't seen before.

But this was different. He didn't have his father, college coaches or teammates. His golf world that had sustained and nourished him for his whole career was gone. He was just another newbie starting a career where failure was the norm.

As Madalitso gripped his driver and loosened his shoulders, he thought of his dad working tirelessly to get him ready for this moment. Making him fly to England to play in the World Junior Open Championship *alone*. Meeting with President Chiluba *alone*. All those tournaments where Peter disappeared so Madalitso had to solve his problems *alone*. Traveling to the strange new world of America to go to college and compete in NCAA golf *alone*. It all flashed through his head as he stood ready to hit his first shot as a professional.

He put his ball on the tee and tried to convince himself that missing family and friends didn't matter. He wondered what would happen if he didn't have what it took to make money at the game he loved. What would he do? Who would he be?

So Madalitso repeated the words of his dad and his grandmother, the words he'd clung to his whole life, as he began the next chapter of his life, alone.

Just focus on what you need to do.

Thus fortified, he did what he'd worked to perfect for as long as he could remember. He picked the target. He swung the club. He hit the ball.

The ball rocketed down his first professional fairway. Madalitso needed to reach the bend in the fairway where it doglegged left without being sucked into one of the bunkers lining the far side. He realized he was holding his breath, watching, waiting with rapt intensity as the ball reached its peak and began descending. It landed safely and rolled to a stop 300 yards away. He breathed a sigh of relief. He had 250 yards of open space in front of him and a clear shot to the pin.

Maybe he could be a professional golfer after all.

Two shots later he stared down a 10-foot putt for birdie. As he paced back and forth from ball to hole, trying to surmise just how fast the greens were, he felt the adrenaline pumping through him at the prospect of bird-ieing his first professional hole. He paused and got control of it so it didn't control him. He took a deep breath and thought to himself, *No need to rush.*

He moved over his ball and calmly eyed the cup one last time. With a slow, easy backswing and smooth firm follow-through, he stroked the ball. It moved over the line he'd carefully chosen, inching closer and closer to the hole.

As it deviated ever so slightly at the end, he thought he'd missed his chance.

But no, it had just enough speed to stay the course. It grabbed the left lip of the cup and circled clockwise before dropping to the bottom with a highly satisfying plop.

Birdie.

It seemed like an omen from the golf gods. He wished his dad could see him now. Maybe, he thought, his father was smiling just a little as he looked down from heaven.

A subtle smile flashed across his face. *It doesn't matter who is here, or who is NOT here. Just focus on what you need to do. Just play golf.* Madalitso followed his own advice for the next several hours, thinking only of himself and his next shot. He would not let himself be consumed by the gravity of this being his first professional event. It was a sign of maturity and experience and a level of self-awareness that would reward him.

Making the Canadian Tour right out of the gate was a huge boost. He was living within the budget we put together and was sticking to his training regimen. In the first months after graduation, when people often struggle, Madalitso found a stable rhythm. "I'm not taking the golf world by storm," he told me during one of our check-in calls. "Success must sometimes be measured in small doses."

Madalitso was working hard at his training regimen and gaining confidence with every tournament.

Then came the day that had been circled on his calendar for months.

39

May 18, 2006. The temperature in Albuquerque was slightly above average. No rain was forecast. The front page of the *Albuquerque Journal* broke the startling news that water bills were rising by five percent. A thoroughly unspectacular day.

But not everywhere.

The 2006 U.S. Open local qualifier was being held that day at Twin Warriors Golf Club, a famous course and frequent practice venue for many PGA players. Winning a local and regional qualifier are the two steps that starry-eyed golfers must take to play in one of golf's grandest tournaments.

Unbeknownst to anyone, this golf course was about to have a day like no other in its history.

Twin Warriors has a course rating of 75, making it one of the more difficult courses in America. Trees are diabolically placed to ensure disaster at every hole. Ruthless bunkers punish anything but pinpoint accuracy. Desert landscapes buttressing each fairway warn players to keep their balls in play, or pay dearly.

Coming off a short break from the Canadian Tour, Madalitso was well rested and firing on all cylinders in practice sessions leading up to the tournament. His home course was South, but the Lobo golf team and coaches were frequent guests at Twin Warriors. So Madalitso had grown familiar with the course.

He began his round on the tenth hole, which was famous for being "the most intimidating hole on the golf course." The fairway invites maximum power off the tee. But a massively long approach shot awaits with disaster looming everywhere if the ball doesn't land in just the right spot.

It was fitting that Madalitso faced a beast of a hole first because it would set the tone for his entire round.

Madalitso stepped up and blasted his first shot on his unlikely odyssey to the U.S. Open way past everyone else in his group. Some things never change. His ability to slam the ball had always raised eyebrows and elicited kudos.

The opening drive put him as close to the pin as any player could hope to be. Now for the hard part. He had to loft the ball over a wide wash and onto an elevated green. If it weren't long enough, a bunker would devour his ball. Too far to the left or right, and he would face a very difficult par and a very easy bogey. Too long, and he'd have an impossible chip back onto the green, where there was absolutely no chance to stop the ball before it kept rolling back down the wash.

Madalitso sized up his shot and checked his yardage book and the markers on the course. The ones he hadn't even known about when he first got to America. He instinctively pulled an iron from his bag while his eyes moved back and forth from his ball to the pin. Sizing, analyzing, calculating. He took his usual two or three casual practice swings. Visualizing the shot, feeling the swing, being the ball.

Slowly, he began his backswing, then let it fly. When you have been playing as long as Mad had, you know when you hit it flush. It's one of the most satisfying things in the world. It's the thing you work and work and work for. Madalitso stuck his follow-through and watched with unexpressed glee as his shot looked better and better with each passing moment.

Since the green was elevated, he couldn't see where the ball landed, rolled and stopped. But the wild roars and applause of the gallery around the green told him.

Madalitso didn't even smile when he walked up and saw his ball sitting within two feet of the cup. On the outside anyway. Tapping in for birdie was a formality.

One hole. One birdie. One under par. On a hole where players should be "thrilled with par," Madalitso made it look easy.

It was an omen of things to come.

Shot by shot and hole by hole, the recent college graduate worked his magic on this golf course like none of the great golfers who came before him ever had.

On the par 4 seventh, Madalitso faced an approach that begged for caution. The flag was on the left atop a slope, near a menacing bunker and with some feral rough behind—many landmines to avoid. Mad grabbed his nine-iron with serenity and eyed the tiny patch of safe green to the right of the flag. This shot required so much precision that even the most accomplished pros would aim for the front of the green and accept two-putting up the slope for a pedestrian par.

But this wasn't most days. And Madalitso wasn't most pros.

He took his customary practice swings, exhorting himself not to overthink. *Just play.*

He swung, and in a flash, the ball shot upward and began its short journey to triumph or tragedy. He watched, confident yet keenly aware that one bad shot could torpedo his round against these men who were a cut above his previous competition.

Madalitso saw it fading to the right of the flag. Exactly what he wanted. It landed soft as a down pillow seven feet from the cup. It was a shot that few professionals would attempt and even fewer could execute. He heard applause and saw people typing messages into their cell phones.

He strode onto the green like a seasoned pro who'd been born with a putter in his hand, like it was part of his body. It made this basic, straight ahead, 7-foot putt seem almost unfair.

Taking nothing for granted, he scoped the turf between his ball and the hole. He took his time settling into his stance.

The ball had no choice. It went in. Another birdie.

Every club in his bag worked in perfect harmony. Applause was his companion all day, as the few who were fortunate enough to witness lavished him with adulation. His easy-peasy, laid-back demeanor made everything look simple.

Madalitso could not remember a round of tournament golf—in Zambia, the UK or the United States—where everything worked this well and he was so deep in the zone.

But his dad had trained his brain to not be seduced by success and brutalized by failure. So he refused to let himself think about the magic that was happening. Like a true pro, he kept his head down and stayed in the now. *This shot. Right now. Nothing else.*

Still, it reminded him of tournaments at Lusaka Golf Club, or Ndola, when he was a fresh-faced kid and golf was new and mystical. When he was discovering his own talents. When every round, every hole and every shot was a wonderland of discovery and revelation of things he could do with a golf club. With his life.

But this was different. Now in his early twenties, he was a far better and more seasoned player than the young teenager who went out and played without any concept of what he was doing. Four years of struggle, adjustment, tragedy and culture shock provided perspective on the masterpiece he was performing at Twin Warriors that the young teenager in Lusaka simply could not have appreciated.

Word about Madalitso's magnificent round spread, and the crowd of spectators following him got bigger and bigger. It was like when he was a teenage prodigy and onlookers gathered to watch the young phenom bring Zambia's golf courses to their knees. Despite growing curiosity, nobody asked how many shots he was below par. It was like a baseball dugout when teammates avoid a pitcher pursuing a no-hitter.

By the final few holes, birdies were anticipated and pars were a disappointment. Even the other players in his group were stunned by the explosive performance of this rookie.

Madalitso sank his final putt, shook hands and accepted the effusive congratulations of his fellow competitors, then made his way to the scorer's table. He handed over his card to the man sitting across from him. The man looked down, back up at Madalitso and back down again. He made sure this was not a case of bad math or illegible handwriting.

The final number was his actual score.

63. Nine under par. Course record. Never in the history of this nationally rated golf course had there been a round like the one posted by Madalitso Muthiya on Thursday, May 18, 2006.

Never.

He was congratulated, patted on the back and asked over and over to elaborate on how he pulled it off. Madalitso just looked down, shrugged his shoulders and kept saying:

"I just had a good day."

People probed for answers on how he pulled off this record-breaking performance. But one question lingered in the back of his mind: *Where has this been for the past four years?*

Madalitso quickly brushed it away. He knew it was pointless and unhealthy to try and answer questions that had no answers. It would only lead his mind down a rabbit hole of regret, lamenting lost opportunities and envisioning painful useless what-if scenarios.

Mad had just achieved something supremely special. He wished his dad was there to share it with him. Now was the time to focus on one priority: the sectional qualifier. The next step. Forward. Then he heard his father's voice.

Get on with the job.

Derek Gutierrez, Twin Warriors' head golf professional, walked me through what happened on May 18. "On that day, Madalitso played this course as well or better than anyone I've ever seen. Even the best PGA players that come here. People were talking about it that day and for several days after."

But when he finished heaping praise on Madalitso and his historical round, he said, "Jayme, can I tell you something else?"

"Sure."

"Lots of professional golfers practice here. They all play for free. It's a courtesy that a lot of golf courses offer."

"Okay," I replied, unsure where this was going.

"Since he started practicing here a few years ago, Madalitso is the only golfer that sends us thank you cards for allowing him to play here for free. The only one." As Derek finished, one thought came to my head:

Peter would love hearing this.

As soon as he left the course, Madalitso put his record-breaking 63 triumph at Twin Warriors in the rearview mirror and began preparing for what would be the two biggest rounds of golf in his life: when he'd attempt to qualify for the U.S. Open.

On the eve of his trip to the sectional qualifier, I took a deep breath and dialed his number. "Hey! Calling to wish you a safe flight." It was a half-truth. The waiting was finally over, and I wanted to know how he was handling the pressure of the monumental task before him. Peter had a knack for getting his son to open up by ignoring the big stuff and throwing out benign questions. I followed suit.

"Hi, Jayme," he answered. "I'm just packing." I could hear him walking back and forth and shuffling things around.

"Ah-ha, how do you feel?"

"I feel great...but I don't think it matters," he laughed.

"Hmmm," I replied, waiting for him to explain.

Madalitso stopped what he was doing, and his voice got serious. "I'd be playing in this event no matter how I felt. Whether I was sick or simply didn't want to, I don't really have a choice."

I stayed silent.

"I've always loved competing. Playing in tournaments has always been fun ever since I was little. But I can only remember two tournaments that I *had* to play...where it wasn't up to me.

"The first was the 1997 Kabwé Open. I was going to compete in that tournament whether I wanted to or not. My father made sure of that because it was too important to him. My victory and breaking the record on that colonial-era course confirmed something he spent his life trying to prove. It helped heal wounds from his childhood."

After a few seconds I asked, "What was the second tournament?"

"The one I am about to play in," he replied. "If my performance at the

Kabwé Open was his vision of what the past should have been, this qualifier is his vision for the future."

MADALITSO WAS OFF to Double Eagle Golf Club in Galena, Ohio, for his two-round U.S. Open Sectional Qualifier. Double Eagle's course rating was nearly identical to Twin Warriors. But aside from the level of difficulty, the two venues had little in common. Double Eagle had fairways lined with ash and oak trees. The rough was a mix of wildflowers, prickly bushes, fescue and other nasty native species. And Double Eagle is closer to sea level, so the ball did not travel as far.

For Madalitso, one similarity stuck out right away: his first hole was the most challenging. At Twin Warriors, it was the tenth. At Double Eagle, it was the first. Both were lengthy par 4s.

Like a slap in the face, Double Eagle's first hole jars your senses. Locals have long complained it's cruel to have an opening hole that's basically a guaranteed bogey. Players have to hit their opening drive to the right at a massive set of bunkers and trees. It seems a foolish and terrifying strategy. Except that hitting left is far worse. A long, well-placed drive along the right fairway—which is ridiculously difficult—is the *only* way to have a shot at the green.

And what a shot it has to be! The green is guarded by a ravine that promises catastrophe to all who enter. So you can't be sure. But if the ball goes too long, it'll end up buried in a treacherous bunker that loves nothing more than eating golf balls. Madalitso stood in the tee box and thought, *This is a pretty hole, but it won't be fun.*

The 63 at Twin Warriors was now a memory. None of his hungry fellow competitors cared. The USGA officials managing the U.S. Open certainly didn't care. All that mattered was this. Nothing else. He channeled his dad: *Get on with the job.*

Madalitso pulled his driver from his bag and minutely inspected the fairway, searching for the spot, the target, the goal. A few casual practice swings later, he moved into position. He realized that for a hole that causes so much anguish and agony to so many, it was actually a short warm-up hole if you played it just right.

The dozen or so people who bothered to show up that morning and chose to watch this young unknown pro stopped talking and watched the ball explode off his clubhead, roaring into the morning sky.

The second his driver smacked his ball, he knew it was a long drive. As its flight path became clear, a calmness came over him. The ball landed precisely where he commanded it to. There was a small smattering of enthusiastic applause. Mad heard someone say:

"Man. *That* was a long drive."

Yes, it was, Madalitso thought to himself, feeling both relieved and exhilarated. *Now don't revel in that shot or overthink the next one. Just keep going.*

Madalitso approached his second shot knowing there was zero margin for error. He needed to stick his ball on the green. After a couple of easy practice swings, he took position. Taking a deep breath, he launched a smooth, sweet approach. It felt as good as it looked. And the closer it got, the better it looked. The ball landed nice and soft. It rolled straight and true. It stopped eighteen inches from the cup.

Birdie.

It was déjà vu all over again. Just like at Twin Warriors, he stared down the beast of his first hole and tamed it. Again, it set the stage for the rest of his round.

Madalitso barely knew Double Eagle, but he put on a golfing clinic for the second time in as many outings. His putter found the right lines and the speed of the slick, tricky greens. When the course required strategic, pinpoint accuracy, he supplied it. And when the course gave him a chance to let out some shaft, he blasted drives that made the gallery go nuts.

Madalitso approached the eighteenth and final tee box. The green was reachable in two shots, but only to the long and strong, the brave of heart, the dragon slayer. Only a titanic first drive would make it over the water where so many balls have gone to die. All self-doubt must be eviscerated.

But Mad was deep in the zone and looking to stay there, so he made sure not to think as he pinpointed a spot where he would *command* his ball to land. Then, all he had to do was get out of his own way. Play loose and free like the little kid who swung with the swing God gave him and blasted a ball further than any child his size had a right to straight though his own window.

Mad immediately knew it was massive. So did the ever-increasing members of Mad's army, many of whom stuck with him all morning. The ball cleared the water without even breaking a sweat.

He had brought the monster to its knees and turned it into a chew toy. A lollipop second shot had him dancing a few feet from the cup, well within striking distance.

He had to fight the urge to reflect on the spectacular round of golf he was about to finish.

Focus on this shot, he barked at himself. *Nothing else matters.*

It was a straightforward putt. All he had to do was get it there. He breathed, he executed. The ball shot over across the slick grass, right at the hole. As the ball slowed, Madalitso wasn't sure it had the legs. His body gave the ball all the English it could muster, trying to will it further home. The throng of spectators that had grown all day rose, waiting to scream in glee one more time for the phenom from nowhere who was becoming a legend right before their eyes.

"Ahhhh!" A groan rose from the fans when the ball stopped six inches from the cup.

He easily tapped in for birdie, and waves of applause broke over him.

Sixty-five. That was Madalitso's score after his blistering, jaw-dropping first round. He could not remember stringing back-to-back rounds like this one and the 63 he produced at Twin Warriors in Albuquerque. But thanks to his effortless swing, lack of theatrical celebrations and the quiet no-nonsense way he carried himself, the whole thing had a ho-hum feel to it.

Players rested, milled around and refueled in between rounds. There was lots of chatter about the 65. Naturally, Madalitso paid little attention. In fact, he never checked the leaderboard. Bad karma. There was so much golf left to play, and he knew from hard-won experience that an opening round, no matter how scintillating, offered no guarantees of victory.

Madalitso's gallery doubled after the break. A 65 at such an important event has a funny way of drawing attention. People wondered whether the soft-spoken young stranger could keep it going.

As he stepped up to the daunting first tee box again, it didn't matter to Madalitso that there was plenty of golf left to play and one mistake could completely change the leaderboard. He ignored the ever-growing fans and spectators following him around. He didn't pay attention to the other players, any of whom might suddenly get hot and surge ahead. And lastly, he didn't care that history was there for the making. As he later said to a reporter with the *Toledo Blade*: "That's why I am here, to play well and try not to be consumed by what's going on around me."

Despite the physical and mental fatigue that comes from playing eighteen holes of golf, Mad hadn't lost the adrenaline-filled spring in his step or the razor-sharp look in his eye. But he knew round two would not be easy. On the fifth hole, he pulled his drive way left of his target. He closed his eyes and quietly groaned. Without talking to his caddie or making eye contact with anyone, he trudged up the fairway, trying to calm his mind and right his ship.

His ball was deep in a gnarly tangle of rough. *Oh God, will this be the unraveling?* he asked himself. Was this a sign of what was to come? Would this impossible journey end over the next thirteen holes, under a barrage of pulled drives, fat-hit irons and missed putts?

Standing over his ball, Madalitso shook his head, took a deep breath and uttered to himself, "This shot, that is all that matters right now. Not the next shot, not the next hole. This shot."

After carefully, studiously calculating where he needed to strike the ball to escape the thick morass, he launched it back into the center of the fairway along with a hunk of earth.

After a nice approach, he was left with a knee-knocking fifteen-footer to save par.

Madalitso mentally dissected every inch of green and detected a slight downward slope from left to right. He slowly walked back and forth across the green, that separated his ball from the hole. Gripping his putter, he stood over his ball and selected a spot where he expected it to eventually break toward the hole. Last breath before his backswing and firm follow-through. The ball cruised up the green to his left just as he had planned. It slowed and began breaking downhill to the right, a little earlier than he expected. He screamed at his ball to hurry. His ball didn't listen. It cut just in front of the hole.

Bogey.

Madalitso ignored the applause as he walked up the path to the sixth hole.

He started sinking into himself, rage clouding his vision as he peered down the fairway of the next hole, a 500-yard par 5.

He caught himself and replaced self-doubt and anger with his dad's mantra:

Next shot!

Double Eagle's sixth hole doglegs left with a green surrounded by rude bunkers waiting to destroy lives. Precious little margin for error. Opening drives have to do a fly-over to escape a painfully long patch of appalling rough to reach the comfort of the fairway. Then the hole turns radically left, so too much distance lands you in the tall grass, or the taller woods.

Madalitso stood in the tee box and weighed his options. Safety dictated that he land on the fairway that he could see, just past the rough. Risk whispered to shorten the hole by zooming over the trees and cutting the dogleg. But of course, if he didn't clear the trees, he'd end up in the dark forest. Disaster.

These are the choices in life that determine who you want to be. And who you are.

Madalitso knew he didn't make it here from the hinterlands of Zambia by playing it safe. By listening to conventional wisdom. That's not who he was or wanted to be. But he didn't make it by being rash, reckless and stupid either. He'd been down that road and knew it would lead to ruin. He got here by studying the game, believing in himself and ignoring the naysayers.

Ignoring the Zambia Golf Union when it told him and his peers that no Zambian boys could compete at the World Junior Open Championship in England. Ignoring "common sense" that players without coaching or good equipment could never earn a Division I College scholarship. Ignoring history that proclaimed players with his heritage of poverty, his background of exclusion and the skin color that denied him so many rights and opportunities simply do not play in the U.S. Open.

He eyed the trees separating him from his target. Then he swung his swing and took his shot.

It was a satisfying blast, arcing majestically, easily high enough to clear the trees. The only question was distance. Would it clear the bushes or tall grass just past the trees? Or go *too* far and disappear into the prison of woods on the other side?

Madalitso watched, breath bated, as his ball disappeared on the other side of the trees.

Madalitso walked briskly to find out whether the golf gods had rewarded or punished him. He turned left as the fairway bent toward the green.

Hallelujah! His ball was sitting pretty with a perfect line to the green. *Sigh.*

His tee shot wasn't a reckless role of the dice. Madalitso had studied the shot scrupulously and carefully considered his own ability. He'd believed in himself. Like he was taught to do by his mentor, his coach, his confidant, the man who had made him into the man he was.

His dad.

An easy nine-iron put him twelve feet from the cup.

The scent of eagle was in the air.

The putt was straightforward with a slight decline. As with any downhill putt, the key was to not hit the ball too hard and have it motor past the hole. The legendary Sam Snead captured it best when he said, "The three things I fear most in golf are lightning, Ben Hogan and a downhill putt."

Madalitso wanted the eagle—but not at the expense of the birdie.

He surveyed the putt from every angle imaginable, factoring in the green speed, which had gotten faster all day. The gallery went silent when he moved over into position, and like a pendulum of a clock that kept perfect time, his putter struck his ball.

The line was right. But that wasn't the issue. The ball picked up speed as it proceeded downhill. Madalitso urged it to slow down with all of his mental energy and body language shouting: *STOP!*

The ball briefly dipped into the hole. He'd done it. *Eagle!* he exclaimed to himself.

Then it caught the left edge of the cup and lipped back out, stopping inches away.

His own sorrowful exhale mirrored the collective gasps from the crowd.

He tapped in for birdie.

Madalitso's bogey on the fifth hole and his birdie on the sixth pretty much summed up his second round of the U.S. Open Sectional Qualifier at Double Eagle. Every shot was a master class in maintaining focus. Nothing could be taken for granted. Time and again, he dug himself out of a self-imposed jam where his next shot had to save him from his last one. He was playing well, but whereas his morning round of 65 was flowing in the zone, every aspect of his game clicking, at one with the golf gods, the afternoon round was all grind and struggle.

By the last hole, Madalitso was mentally and physically spent. It had been an exhausting day of golf on an unfamiliar course, and he had run out of gas. But it was a good tired. He didn't know how others had played, but that was never a concern when he competed. Madalitso knew that he had played as well as he could and left it all out on the course, and that was all that mattered.

He again walloped a mammoth drive off the par 5 eighteenth tee that carried over the water and left him with a simple shot to the green. His second shot landed on the green and rolled into the short rough, avoiding the bunkers on both sides. With fifteen yards to the hole, he had three shots to save par. But he wanted more.

Madalitso saw it would be a classic chip-and-roll with subtle unevenness in the green. He blocked out the fact that these were the final shots in his U.S. Open Sectional Qualifier.

Just this shot. Nothing else. This shot.

The ball jumped off his clubhead, bounced on the green and began its roll to the hole. One last time, Madalitso steered and pushed the ball with his eyes as it cruised toward its destination. Noise rose from the crowd that had grown bigger all day. The crowd was ready to let loose when the ball plunged victoriously into the hole.

Three feet short of the cup, it finally ran out of steam, stopping twelve inches short.

After a collective groan, the gallery burst into raucous applause.

Mad walked toward his ball, raised his hand in appreciation and tapped in for birdie.

69.

Madalitso shook hands with his caddie and fellow players, humbly accepting their congratulations.

A tournament official rushed over excitedly and asked, "Do you know where you finished?"

"No," Madalitso replied. "I haven't been checking other scores."

"You won!" The official beamed. "Congratulations." They shook hands, and the man walked away.

Madalitso stood alone on the eighteenth green at Double Eagle. Like any young athlete fresh off a career-making triumph, he was elated.

But for Madalitso Muthiya, there was a depth to this victory that was too much to process. His whole golfing life, he'd been told that Zambia couldn't possibly produce a world-class golfer who could hold his own on the sport's biggest stages.

And he knew why. For centuries, Zambians had endured slavery, poverty, dislocation, mismanagement, subjugation and systematic abuse. While many ancient cultures within Zambia have much to be proud of, by any measure, the lives of Zambian men, women and children have been inhumane and brutal. In a country where the average person survives on less than a dollar a day, the basic requirements to excel at golf—good equipment, professional instruction, travel expenses—were unthinkable. How could Zambia produce a top-level golfer when there is not a single professional golf coach in the *entire country*?

For as long as Madalitso could remember, people have recited all the reasons why he would fail. As he grew up, his father challenged him, putting him in uncomfortable difficult situations so that he would be ready for the worst. At the beginning, he'd been shocked, intimidated and distracted. But over time, he overcame his fears and the negativity slung at him—of swinging the worst clubs, wearing the worst clothes, having no coaching, being the only Black player in tournaments. There were stumbles and setbacks, but with each hurdle surmounted, he got stronger, more resistant to the weight he was forced to carry, more resilient, more determined to define himself and *not* be limited or defined by the doubters, the haters or history. When adversity reared its ugly head, he simply did what he'd been told to do by the man who made and shaped him, the man who continued to be an invisible presence with him on the golf course and in life. His father. The dad who drilled into him the need to focus on the job right in front of him with tough love.

This ball, this club, this hole, this shot.

Adherence to this simple yet maddeningly difficult-to-follow mindset meant that one man was about to be the first Zambian—*the first Black African*—to play in one of the world's premier sporting events. A game that was invented, played and ruled by White royalty, the architects of the slave trade and colonialism, the rich and only those who could afford it. Of the billions of Black Africans who ever walked the earth, none had ever done it.

But Mad couldn't let himself be consumed by the fact that he had smashed centuries of historical prejudice and precedent or that he'd rewritten the world's definition of who could play in golf's grandest tournaments. There was no time to ponder any of this. More urgent priorities demanded his attention.

Madalitso Muthiya was playing in the U.S. Open.

JUNE 5, 2006, may have been the most productive day of my career. I submitted four memos, took a ten-minute lunch break and was probably the most antisocial person in the office. Burying myself in work kept my mind focused on anything other than the U.S. Open Sectional Qualifier taking place in Galena, Ohio. My plan was to work late and then finish the day with a marathon workout at the gym. Madalitso would call me when he felt like it. I wasn't going to call him.

I left the office and headed toward the underground metro station. After swiping my card and proceeding through the turnstile, I walked down the escalators to the train platform. A few people were waiting alongside me.

A couple of minutes passed when my cell phone began vibrating. It was Madalitso. *Oh God.*

Hoping for the best and trying not to expect the worst, I closed my eyes, took a deep breath and exhaled.

"Hey, Mad," I said in my best nonchalant voice.

"Hey, Jayme." I couldn't tell from his mellow, upbeat tone whether he'd finished last or first. I have never met a person who masks their emotions better than Madalitso Muthiya. "How is it going?" he asked. I heard him take a drink of something.

"Good," I responded flatly. "Heading home from work. How are you?"

"Good. Just having some water. It was a warm day, especially when you're playing thirty-six holes."

I couldn't take it anymore. I had to ask. "Madalitso, how'd it go today?"

"Good," he said nonchalantly as he took another drink.

If I heard the word "good" one more time, I was going to throw my phone onto the train tracks.

"I won."

"WHAT!?" I thought maybe I'd just heard what I wanted to hear. My brain told my mouth to make sure that my ears heard right. "Did you just say that you won the sectional qualifier?!"

"Yes," he said flatly, like I'd asked him if he had a nice lunch.

"You really won?" I could hear how incredulous I sounded.

"I am the medalist."

"So...you're going to play in the U.S. Open?!" I needed him to verbally connect the dots.

"Yes, Jayme," he laughed. "I won the sectional qualifier, so I will play in the U.S. Open."

"YEEEAAHHH!!! YEEAA HAAAHHH!!!" I dropped my bag and began jumping up and down, pumping my fist in the air.

Everyone around me snapped their heads around to see who was yelling and carrying on like a lunatic as Madalitso laughed again.

As I came back to earth, I asked, "Oh my God, Madalitso! What were your scores?!"

He had another swallow of water and said, "I shot a sixty-five in the first round and a sixty-nine in the second round. I won by four strokes."

Exhilaration turned to numbness. One hand held the phone firmly to my ear while the other pressed against my forehead. "Madalitso, congratulations! What a feat! I'm so proud of you!"

"Thank you," he said bashfully.

I paused for a moment before asking him, "Do you know what this means? DO YOU?! This is big, Mad. THIS. IS. BIG!"

"Yeah, I know." He didn't sound like he did.

It was hard to imagine anyone fully grasping what Madalitso had just accomplished. That would come later. Now, there were only next steps.

"Jayme, I need to take care of a few things here, some paperwork. Can I call you later?"

Congratulations and *I'm proud of you* seemed a woefully inadequate way to end the conversation. So instead I said:

"L-Bomb, little brother."

"Yeah...L-Bomb." Then he laughed.

At least three trains passed by during our conversation. Maybe four. I don't remember. Boarding was out of the question because my reception could've been cut.

When our call ended, it was impossible to process the enormity of what had just happened.

Madalitso Muthiya was playing in the U.S. Open.

Later, I telephoned Double Eagle Golf Club to get additional perspective from those who witnessed Madalitso's victory. An enthusiastic Chris

Abernathy, Double Eagle's head golf pro, remembered Madalitso vividly from that June day in 2006 and shared some additional perspective.

"I was there that morning when the quiet guy with the unusual name stepped into the first tee box. Madalitso had an incredible day. But more impressive than what he shot was the way he treated his opponents and the employees of Double Eagle. When he finished his first round, he didn't close himself off or ignore people. He answered questions from the staff. They were curious about him. Where he was from. He just sat there and talked to them. He gave them all the time they wanted.

"That's what I remember most—his attitude and how he treated everyone around him. That night, I went to dinner with the guy who was my boss at the time, Chris Shimko. We talked about Madalitso while we were eating. Chris looked up from his plate and said to me, 'Whether or not he succeeds in golf, that young man will succeed somewhere in life.'"

40

WHERE IS PETER? WHY ISN'T he here?
Those questions repeated inside my head as our SUV cruised along Boston Post Road from Rye to Mamaroneck. It was Thursday, June 15, the opening round of the U.S. Open. As the miles passed, I heard echoes of a conversation eight years earlier at a hotel bar in Lusaka, Zambia.

You mean that no Black golfer from any African country has ever played in a major on U.S. soil?

No.

Not the U.S. Open, PGA Championship or the Masters?

No.

None of them?!

No.

Peter's final "no" came with frustration, clearly from being asked the same question. Not once, not twice, but three times.

No. No. No.

Golf is well documented. Its players, records, statistics and facts are catalogued meticulously. To this day, I have never met a person—other than Peter and Madalitso—who knew that no Black African had ever played in a major on U.S. soil.

Every United States Golf Association (USGA) official, news reporter or fan had the same surprised reaction that I gave to Peter in Lusaka: "Really? Never?"

Africa has produced generations of world-class athletes capable of mastering golf and earning the right to play in the U.S. Open, the Masters or the PGA Championship. The reasons they hadn't up to this point had nothing to do with ability. It had to do with money, power, colonialism, exploitation, greed and shameful inequality.

Madalitso Muthiya was the most unlikely man to be the first. His father was not a wealthy head-of-state or oil minister who could pay for private golf lessons, travel expenses or first-rate equipment. Madalitso did not come from South Africa or Zimbabwe, two countries where golf was far more advanced than in Zambia.

And he had none of the bravado, swagger or larger-than-life persona that so often seems to accompany people who make history. He was an introvert, so humble that he would've been perfectly content to compete at the U.S. Open like anybody else, distinguished only by an unusual name next to a national flag that had never been on the leaderboard. If nobody knew that history was being made that year at Winged Foot, Madalitso would have been fine with that.

But I wouldn't. People *needed* to learn about Madalitso and Peter Muthiya.

And those men deserved to have their stories told.

So I decided to bend the ear of anyone who'd listen. I told everybody about five-year-old Peter grinding sticks into clubs and scrounging for balls at Broken Hill Golf Club. About a father who applied his love of science and math to teach basic golf fundamentals to himself, then his sons. About a broken window at home and broken records at once-segregated colonial golf courses. About television being a substitute for professional instruction. About a miracle shot in a torrential thunderstorm in Fort Myers that produced a college scholarship. About the tragic death of a father. About the fulfillment of a dream that history could be changed by a son.

When I told the USGA, a press conference for Madalitso was immediately scheduled for June 13, two days before tee-off. Every news organization covering the tournament was invited.

Madalitso was led into a vast tent and escorted onto a stage. He sat behind a table overlooking a sea of reporters, newspaper columnists, sports radio personalities and television cameras that would watch, take notes, record and videotape every word. This was intimidation personified, even for those experienced being in the spotlight.

Madalitso was no stranger to media. Over the years, he'd grown used to seeing his name in the paper. But usually, he had face-to-face conversations with one or two reporters. This was different. Dozens of reporters from the top to the bottom of the news food chain around the world were waiting to interrogate him and send his answers from there to Zambia and back.

Madalitso sat on stage and responded the only way he knew how: by being himself. Soft-spoken, honest, unpretentious.

The interviewer, Rand Jerris with the USGA, began by asking Madalitso to "start us off with some comments about what it means to you to be representing your country in the U.S. Open."

"It's very exciting for me. A lot of people have been congratulating me and acknowledging what I've accomplished so far." The slight quiver in his voice, a little fidgeting and rubbing his hands together were all tells of how shy and nervous he was. But this only endeared him to fans and the media accustomed to the blustering braggadocios of many modern-day athletes.

Jerris then asked Madalitso to "talk to us a little bit about golf in Zambia and your childhood growing up."

Madalitso smiled: "It all started when I was stealing clubs from my father's bedroom, my brother and I...happened to break a window, so he happened to find out that we were stealing clubs and hitting golf balls. He got us started playing golf, and that's how I got started."

"Who were your coaches in Zambia? Who helped you develop your swing?" Jerris continued.

"I never had a lesson until I got to college," Madalitso replied matter-of-factly. "I was basically self-taught, and it was through watching TV and reading magazines and just trying through trial and error—and also observing what the pros do."

Surprise and disbelief filled the faces of the hardened journalists. No one could quite believe it.

"How do you compare Zambian golf courses with those in the United States?"

Mad's eyes opened wide. "It [Lusaka Golf Club] was one of the best courses there, but it's nowhere in comparison to the golf courses here in terms of infrastructure or technology. The way the fairways are manicured, the greens, how many grounds staff there are. I'm amazed by that—how many people actually take care of the golf course. When I was actually young and watching golf on TV, I wondered how you could ever hit a bad shot or miss a putt with such good greens. These greens are actually very tough so you can miss putts, but it makes it a lot easier for you to strike a putt, I think."

"Is it an inspiration that the two top money winners in the history of this game are men of color, Tiger Woods and Vijay Singh?"

"I'd like to start by saying that I've been inspired by a lot of golfers regardless of, I guess, their race, I would say. I grew up watching Nick Faldo and Tom Watson, learning by watching them on tape."

"You mentioned the passing of your father while you were in college. Was it unexpected? Just describe what happened."

Madalitso faltered, thrown for a loop, and looked down to collect himself. His voice shook when he said, "I guess we spoke to him about two weeks prior, and he said he wasn't feeling well. And then like two, three days before, he had gone to the hospital...and they told him that he should spend the night there. So he did. At the end, he was gasping for breath."

Sad silence hung over the press tent as Madalitso stopped again, clearly battling deep sorrow and grief. "It's...hard because I keep on remembering."

I was so used to Madalitso never showing anything that I was also suddenly choked up.

"How did you end up at the University of New Mexico?"

Madalitso told the story of his conversation with President Chiluba, the day he and his father met me in Lusaka and the miracle of the Nolan Henke/Patty Berg Junior Masters.

Reporters typed on their computers, scribbled on their notepads and made sure their tape recorders and cameras were recording every word. I looked around and saw smiles, surprise and admiration. I was so happy to see that people were *finally* getting to hear the improbable and inspiring story of this special young man and his father. It was a harbinger of the media storm about to rain down on the world.

My cell phone blew up. ABC, NBC and CBS all did stories. *Golfweek* and *Golf Digest* profiled him. The Golf Channel aired Madalitso's press conference and replayed clips over the next several days. ESPN conducted a long television interview.

Austin Murphy, one of the best and most well-known sportswriters in the world, talked to Madalitso several times for *Sports Illustrated*. *SI* was so taken with Mad's journey that they sent a photographer to Zambia to take pictures of the Muthiya family.

People all over the world turned on their TVs and opened their morning newspapers to find the unlikely story of a young Zambian becoming the first Black African to play in one of golf's grandest tournaments.

Dirt poor beginnings. Tragic setbacks. Hard work. Doubt. Belief. Fortitude. Struggle. Persistence. Triumph.

This timeless and universal story spread from Albuquerque, New Mexico, to Fort Myers, Florida, to Washington, DC. Then it went international, from Canada to the UK, Spain to China, India to Singapore and all the way back to the source: Africa.

In Zambia, Madalitso could've been elected the youngest President in history.

Yes, all the attention was flattering. But Madalitso Muthiya never yearned for the spotlight. He didn't measure himself or his worth by how many times he saw his name in the newspaper or heard it on TV. Publicity was fun from time to time, but it never drove him.

Madalitso believed there was value in fame and being the center of attention. But that value was never self-aggrandizement.

Steve Elling of CBS Sports wrote a piece on Madalitso. Inevitably, he got around to the topic of race. Of Black and White. Elling mentioned Tiger Woods, the absence of "the next Black player of impact" and how Woods "represents the hopes and dreams of millions." Elling then asked Madalitso how his own extraordinary life story might someday impact the lives of others.

Madalitso's answer was instantaneous and heartfelt.

"For me, it's not only about being Black; it's being underprivileged. It could be a kid from Asia or Europe or America. I am coming from a poor environment and trying to make an opportunity out of nothing.

"So I am trying to inspire any person who wants to be inspired, rich or poor."

Where is Peter? Why isn't he here?

MAD WAS SUPPOSED to play Tuesday's practice round with Tiger Woods and Tommy Armour III. But a last-minute scheduling issue paired him with Vijay Singh. Initially, of course, it was disappointing not to play with arguably the greatest man ever to swing the club, Tiger Woods. But it turned out that the golf gods were once again smiling on Madalitso Muthiya.

Madalitso didn't know what to expect when "The Big Fijian" sauntered up to the tee box. His laidback, carefree walk was unmistakable—one of the most unique on the PGA Tour. He looked like a man strolling from his couch to the refrigerator to get another beer. It was an amusing contrast to the high-pressure surroundings he found himself in at work every week.

The World Golf Hall of Famer broke the ice immediately, cracking a broad smile and extending his hand to Madalitso. "Hey, how are you?"

"I'm good, Mr. Singh," Madalitso said with a slightly nervous laugh. "How are you?" Singh's warm, generous friendliness washed away all of Mad's jitters.

As they worked their way around the famous Winged Foot track, Singh peppered Mad with questions:

"What do you think about this hole?" "Where is the best place for your ball to land here?" "What's the best spot to land on the green?"

While using those eighteen holes to familiarize himself with the course, Singh also took a younger and much less experienced player under his wing. Aside from course management and golf strategy, he talked with Mad about life strategy. How to manage constantly being on the road, how to battle through the endless grind, how to make dreams come true in the face of failure. Over the course of the afternoon, a kinship developed, and the world-famous legend assumed the role of friend and mentor.

Madalitso was slightly overwhelmed to go from slogging through qualifiers to suddenly being at the U.S. Open talking strategy with Vijay Singh. It's easy to imagine a raw rookie being distracted from his own preparation. But Singh's carefree demeanor, his open warmth and his genuine interest made it easy for Madalitso to forget that he was receiving a private tutorial from one of the world's greatest.

As much as the professional advice, what Madalitso remembered most was Singh's sense of humor. A quick story or one-liner would make Madalitso burst into laughter. On one hole, Singh suggested a seven-iron instead of the eight-iron Mad had in his hand. Madalitso respectfully replied, "Well, my caddie recommends something different."

Singh gave Madalitso a sly grin. "Hey, ignore the caddie. Listen to big daddy."

Mad cracked up. It was a great lesson in how to stay loose and have fun. A reminder that this pressure-packed profession was a game that he played as a child because it made him happy.

After the round, Singh shook Madalitso's hand and looked him in the eye. "Listen, you've got the game to be out here. Just play the lower tours, go to Q School, be patient and get it done. Do that and you'll make it."

Mad couldn't stop his usually blank stoic face from breaking out into a big wide grin as he profusely (for him anyway) thanked the giant champion for such a wonderful afternoon of golf.

Later, Singh complimented Madalitso in the press, calling his swing "very good."

A rare and very special stamp of approval that would put any aspiring golfer on Cloud Nine.

And of course, Madalitso was full of praise for his playing partner. "Mr. Singh is a very serious individual, and he gave me a lot of helpful tips. But he's also a jovial person. The public doesn't see that side of him. He's honest about his opinions, and if you ask him what he thinks, he'll tell you like it is. He was a funny guy, enjoyable to be around, and he said a lot of encouraging things to me. That is what I remember about him."

Where is Peter? Why isn't he here?

OUR SUV GLIDED up the long tree-lined driveway and into the parking area. Madalitso's caddie retrieved his clubs, and we made our way to Winged Foot's clubhouse. Madalitso strode inside and up the stairs to the players' locker room like it was no big deal, like he'd been competing in the U.S. Open his whole life. Thanks to the "Manager" pass hanging around my neck, I followed him past security, feeling that I really had no business being among these golf superstars. Everywhere I looked, the world's best golfers were getting dressed and chatting with each other.

I averted my eyes to avoid gawking at Sergio Garcia lacing up his shoes. At the fact that Colin Montgomerie was taller than I thought. But not as tall as the gigantic Ernie Els chatting with Pádraig Harrington.

I watched Madalitso closely but clandestinely for any reaction. Any change of expression. Nothing. He knew exactly whose shoulders he was rubbing up against. Whose voices he was hearing just a few feet away. He'd admired them for years. But just as with Mohammed Zulu, Kevin Phiri and the other adult players he bested as an adolescent, he was there to compete. Not to get autographs.

And there were calluses that had hardened his emotions over the years. Madalitso had seen death and disease up close. He personally knew children forced to drop out of school because their parents died of AIDS. His cool composure was another example of a young man whose eyes had seen the tragedy that life could dole out. After staring down everything from his people dying too young and too often to navigating flesh-eating ants while trying to hit a five-iron, walking through a bunch of international superstars was a walk in the park.

But even more fundamentally, there was something else. If Peter belonged at Munali Secondary School, then his son firmly believed that he belonged at Winged Foot. Madalitso walked through the locker room and passed the other players as if he'd done it a thousand times before. We set his clubs next to his locker, and he said with utter nonchalance, "I'm going to the restroom."

"Okay, I'll wait here."

Not three seconds after he walked away, I saw a shining behemoth of a golf bag with this sewn into its leather:

"Phil Mickelson."

Before anyone noticed, I put Madalitso's bag next to Mickelson's and took a picture. Before Mad got back, I returned his bag to his locker. It was a memento he wouldn't see until after the tournament.

Today, the photo brings two thoughts to mind. First, the golf bags standing side by side were identical—same height, same weight. The only difference was the players' names. Second, for a brief moment I let myself be a giddy golf fan.

And now it was time for Madalitso to be left alone. "Do you need anything?"

He smiled. "No, I'm fine."

One last hug before I maneuvered through the sport's greatest players and exited Winged Foot's storied locker room. Standing at the door I stopped to take one last look around.

Where is Peter? Why isn't he here?

I'D GOTTEN A box of polo shirts from our family friend Howie Bargreen with "Team Muthiya" sewn into one sleeve and the Zambian flag on the other. I was sporting one. It was exciting to see our hosts Ryan and Karen

Lake wearing theirs in the bleachers with all the other buzzing fans. We nervously chatted for a few minutes, waiting for our man to appear.

Eventually, Madalitso made his way toward the throngs of autograph-seekers lining the pathway from clubhouse to the driving range. Kids reached over the makeshift barriers with their pens and paper, hoping their heroes would stop long enough for a signature.

Many players were so busy mentally preparing to compete in one of the world's biggest sporting events that they marched right past their disappointed fans.

Not Madalitso. After the media blitz of the past week, he was recognized far and wide. He heard a steady drumbeat of shouts:

"Madalitso!" "Over here, Madalitso!" "Madalitso, please sign my program!"

He couldn't ignore a nine-year-old who wanted an autograph. If one of his fundamental motivations really was to reach and inspire young people, how could he say no?

After doling out a bunch of handwritten souvenirs, Madalitso knew he needed to warm up before his walk into history and *actually apologized* for having to leave. As he turned toward the driving range, he promised the kids and their parents that he'd sign more autographs later. His humble politeness was in stark contrast to the self-involved celebrity of so many contemporary athletes.

Madalitso methodically went through his pre-tournament ritual like he was back on his home course in Lusaka. Photographers, TV cameras, journalists, hundreds of onlookers and world-famous players he'd watched on TV for years were everywhere. It looked like the only person who was oblivious to the madness was Madalitso Muthiya.

Of course, he knew that Winged Foot was now the center of the sporting world and that all eyes were on the 156 players fortunate enough to be there. Including, miraculously, him. His heart pounded and his mind raced as he remembered Broken Hill Golf Club, the Whites-only course where his father was forbidden to play. It seemed like a galaxy far, far away from where he now stood.

Deep, deep breath. He paused to clear all that away. He loosened his muscles. Madalitso would not let himself be consumed by this moment. He had a tournament to play. By now, he was a master at blocking everything out, thanks to years of loving life lessons from his father. Some tournaments were more distracting than others, but Peter made no such exceptions.

Not even for the U.S. Open.

Just focus on what you need to do.

From the bleachers, Madalitso was a model of composure. A professional. We watched him display his fluid, effortless golf swing. No matter how many times I saw it, I still smiled and shook my head. So little exertion. So much power. Ball after ball launched into the far reaches of Winged Foot's driving range. A couple of rows behind us, I heard a man say, "Hey, that's the guy from Africa. The guy in today's paper."

I stared down at the empty seat on my right.

Where is Peter? Why isn't he here?

MADALITSO PROCEEDED DOWN the foot path, casually striding toward the first tee as if walking in slow motion to that monumental first shot. Recalling his practice round, he mentally went through his strategy, visualizing where his ball needed to land. He wanted to play well. He wanted to win. Like he did every time he teed up. Every ball in the rough and every missed putt would be a disappointment.

But in the grand scheme of things, what he shot that day wasn't important. These final steps to the first tee were what really mattered. They were the culmination, the final leg of a journey that began fifty years ago when an African boy in Broken Hill, Northern Rhodesia, fell in love with a sport that he wasn't allowed to play and couldn't afford to play.

Naturally, if Peter were here, he would say that Broken Hill Golf Club in the 1950s was *not* the starting point. Not to him. Madalitso was the period at the end of a sentence that began centuries ago, before the White man came in and conquered, took away the Muthiyas' ancestral land, culture, language and life. It began when golf was ordained as the game of Scottish and English royalty and Black Africans were designated as the race of slaves.

And all it would take was one swing of his driver. That's all that was needed. One shot. It didn't matter if he drove the ball 400 yards or if it trickled off the tee. As soon as his club struck the ball, golf's historical records would show Madalitso Muthiya as the first Black African in history to play in a major on U.S. soil.

But at that moment, he looked nothing like a man preparing to make history. He stood relaxed and leaning to one side with his hand on his hip, waiting patiently outside the ropes for the threesome before him to finish teeing off. He casually chatted with his caddie like they were in line at a grocery store.

Madalitso finally stepped inside the ropes. His adrenaline flowed as he walked forward, but his face stayed calm as a summer pond. He took a deep breath. The picture was a mass of contradictions. A young golfer was about to do something that had never been achieved. Yet the entire setting, including him, appeared so unremarkable. So ordinary. Just another golf shot in a seemingly endless series of golf shots stretching back from when the game was invented in Scotland, transported into Zambia and was now here in New York at the 2006 U.S. Open.

Suddenly, the announcer turned on the microphone. The hum silenced the buzz of the crowd. Over the loudspeaker, it boomed loud and clear:

"Next up, from Lusaka, Zambia, Madalitso Muthiya."

The fifty or so spectators clapped their hands enthusiastically and turned their attention to the young man in front of them. Amidst the applause there were calls of:

"Yeah!" "Go, Madalitso!" "Go Zambia!"

Not every important moment in sports history—or history *period*—is caught on camera. Landmark achievements aren't always witnessed by millions of people. They don't necessarily involve Green Jackets, Super Bowl trophies or Olympic Gold Medals. Sometimes it's a single golf shot that takes place in front of fifty people, most of whom are completely unaware of the history they're witnessing.

Madalitso pulled the driver out. Walked into the box. Stuck his tee into the ground. Carefully placed his ball on top. He stepped back. Took a couple of easy swings while staring down the fairway.

The spattering of applause died down. Conversations ceased. Silence.

For a split second, I looked toward the sky, closed my eyes and took another deep breath.

Where is Peter? Why isn't he here?

Suddenly my anxiety washed away and everything became clear.

Don't worry. He's here.

Madalitso set his feet and extended his club to ensure the proper distance from the ball. Like he always did. He bent his knees and paused for a second before beginning his backswing.

When the clubhead was all the way back to parallel, he let it go. In a perfect display of his God-given swing, he launched a titanic blast. Up and up and up again, disappearing for a moment.

The silence gave no clue whether it was headed down the fairway toward glory or toward the punishing rough for disaster.

Finally, after a few seconds that seemed like a few days...applause.

"Nice shot!" "Good ball!" "Way to go, Madalitso!" "Go Zambia!"

The ball had rocketed well over 300 yards down the center of Winged Foot's first fairway. It landed, rolled and stopped right in the middle. Exactly where he needed to be. He had a fantastic lie with the pin in clear sight.

I snapped my head back to look for any reaction. For a brief second, he looked in my direction. As we made eye contact, a slight smile came over his face. Otherwise, no emotion. He took it in stride. As always.

I, on the other hand, did not. My exhilarated grin stretched from ear to ear. My fists clenched in celebration. The hair on the back of my neck stood at attention.

Of all the phenomenal golf shots that Madalitso had made in his life, three stood out.

The first broke a window in his parents' house.

The next clinched a scholarship as thunder boomed through the heavens.

But this one changed history.

It was perfect.

41

MADALITSO BATTLED FIERCE, FAMED WINGED Foot and enjoyed some real success.

From the day he first held a golf club as a young boy, he had an uncanny ability to drive the ball. The 2006 U.S. Open would be no different. After day one, against arguably the best 156 players in the world, Madalitso Muthiya was tied for ninth in driving distance, with an average of over 310 yards per drive. On day two, he was tied for twenty-fourth with an average distance of over 302 yards.

He parred five of his first seven holes—no easy feat at a golf course that was tailored to make low scores almost impossible. At certain points, Madalitso was playing so well that he got facetime on ESPN. Famed commentator Chris Berman spoke kindly about him.

But like so many players before and after him, Madalitso ultimately fell prey to Winged Foot's treachery. On the fourth hole, Madalitso stood over a very makeable putt, not much different from hundreds of others he routinely sank over the years.

After surgically selecting his line and determining speed, he sweetly and rhythmically stroked the putt. He knew the speed was perfect. As the ball arrived at its intended destination, the crowd came alive, waiting for it to break toward the hole.

It never did. It just kept sailing past. Cameras focused on him, groans could be heard from New York and Lusaka, where his family was watching. Whether it was the well-publicized depression in the middle of the green or the golf gods simply not answering everyone's prayers, the fourth hole was Madalitso's first bogey of the U.S. Open. It would not be his last.

The eighteenth hole was its own dubious subplot to this tournament. Winged Foot's website proclaims it became "the nemesis of Phil Mickelson, Colin Montgomerie and Jim Furyk at the 2006 U.S. Open."

It was soon to become the nemesis of Madalitso Muthiya.

He stepped into the tee box, ready to attack all 460 yards of the par 4 in front of him. He lined up knowing the safe play was to the right center. But the ball careened left—and stayed left. A classic pull.

Madalitso thrust his club into the arms of his caddie as if to say, *Here, get this thing out of my sight.* Every step down the fairway confirmed his worst fears.

His caddie joined him in a hunt that lasted seconds but felt like an eternity. Finally, his ball was found resting miserably in the tallest rough he'd ever seen. It was a position that had become all too familiar since his historical tee shot thirty-six hours earlier. Like any golfer left with no good options, he shook his head and hacked back onto the fairway.

Approaching the green felt like passing through the last stage of a bloody bruising gauntlet. The end was near, but with each step, he felt the accumulated physical, mental and emotional punishment of the last few days.

When he finally got to the green, he was greeted by a long, deeply unpleasant putt that required his ball to travel over angled rises and slopes that claimed more victims with each group that traipsed through. He tried in vain to see a line that would lead him to the promised land. But later he said it was like driving through a thick fog on a treacherous road you'd never been on and trying to guess the next curve.

Finally, Madalitso stepped over his ball and set his feet. He tried to avoid wondering whether this putt might be a positive end to an otherwise frustrating two days. He tried to avoid wondering anything.

One last big breath before he struck the ball with the flat stick. Optimism filled the air as it looked like he had the right line.

It was close. But no cigar. The ball stopped inches from the cup. He looked toward the heavens and closed his eyes. He tapped in his final putt and the last entry on his scorecard was made at the U.S. Open.

Double bogey.

Madalitso Muthiya failed to make the cut at the 2006 U.S. Open. But at least he was in good company. So did some of golf's greatest names, including Corey Pavin, Justin Leonard, Davis Love III and Tiger Woods—all winners of Major Championships. In fact, the 2006 U.S. Open was the first time that Woods missed the cut in a major as a professional. Sadly, his dad had just recently passed away. Madalitso could relate.

Not that any of this was consolation to Madalitso. Peter had taught him early never to measure himself by the success or failure of others, so the performance of Tiger Woods, Vijay Singh or any other player was irrelevant. His singular focus was to play the golf course to the best of his ability. Madalitso knew he didn't do that at Winged Foot. To him, that was all that mattered.

His unbelievable streak of fantastic performances that began with the local qualifier at Twin Warriors had suddenly and inexplicably come to an end. As the late PGA professional George Archer, a former Masters Champion, once said:

"One thing about golf is you don't know why you play bad and why you play good."

MADALITSO DIDN'T STORM off the course in a huff after his final putt. He didn't retreat to the locker room. He didn't sulk, curse or hang his head. Instead, Mad made his dad proud.

He put on his best smile and kept his promise to the young autograph seekers. He walked over to where a group of children were pressed against the rope, clutching pens and paper in their little hands.

"Hey! How are you guys doing?" he asked. "Did you all enjoy the tournament today?!" After his bitter disappointment, pleasantly talking, smiling and writing his name over and over was far down on the list of things he wanted to do. He did it anyway. Madalitso signed every autograph they requested. He even thanked them for waiting so patiently. That's how he was raised.

After saying goodbyes, we made our way to the parking lot. A couple of times, I glanced back over my shoulder to see Winged Foot's majestic A-framed clubhouse growing smaller behind us. I wanted to soak it all in, not sure when or if I'd ever return.

Madalitso walked in front of me. He never turned around. Not once.

We pulled into Ryan and Karen Lake's driveway. A few of us decided to stay outside on the front lawn. Madalitso walked over to me, and we peeled off from the others.

"How are you?" I asked.

"Good." His response was firm and calm. "It's just that...I didn't do what I came here to do. There is unfinished business."

"I know," I replied. Madalitso was, and is, a competitor. The last thing he wanted was a pat on the back and a lame just-be-happy-you-made-it-here speech. So, I gave him my honest opinion. "You can play much better than you did. You could've made the weekend cut...even more. I know that. But that shouldn't take away from what you achieved—something that *nobody* has ever done. You have a lot to be proud of."

"This experience only makes me hungrier," he declared. "I have a long way to go. My goals are not even close to being achieved." He emphasized this last point for me. And for himself.

"You know, Madalitso. Maybe in some way the struggles you had out there today are a good thing. The road ahead is going to be long. It's the nature of the sport. Of life. Maybe this will help you handle setbacks and obstacles...to get back here."

"Setbacks and obstacles?" Madalitso said with a hint of American sarcasm. "I think I've already had some of those."

I cracked a smile and lowered my voice. "I was just doing my best Peter Muthiya impression. You know, the road with pitfalls being rough and tough."

Madalitso let out a slight laugh and looked down at his feet.

"Speaking of him," I continued. "Your goals are still out there, but your father achieved his."

"Yeah. He told me at the airport when I left Zambia to begin college. He wanted to give my siblings and me opportunities he never had. Putting me on that plane and sending me away was one of the hardest things he ever did."

It was a beautiful June evening in suburban New York. I remembered this was Peter's favorite time of day to play golf as a boy in Eastern Province. *The time when the sun set and the sky changed colors.*

We couldn't have asked for a more fitting backdrop since golf's image had truly changed that day, if ever so slightly. Glancing up at the mix of blue, orange, pink and red, I wondered if somewhere Peter Muthiya had orchestrated it.

We were relaxed, standing in the grass, as Madalitso asked, "What about you? How are you doing?"

I thought for a few seconds. "Well, let's just say I have something to do...a promise to keep." After all this time, I was unsure if Madalitso knew about the tug-of-war that Peter and I waged throughout our relationship. His father may never have told him, so I left it vague. "It's a place I need to go."

Madalitso suddenly flashed a broad smile. "There?"

"Yes," I laughed. "There."

Acknowledgments

THE COMPLETION OF THIS BOOK is owed to strangers who welcomed me into their lives and to longtime friends and family who encouraged me across the finish line.

My wife, Stacey, and our children, Aveline and John, are my reason for being. Stacey's hard work and perseverance throughout her life are an inspiration and a lesson in fortitude. As my stepfather, Claude Faure, was slowly consumed by cancer, Stacey planned nights out and dinners in. And on those days when fun distractions were impossible, she held my hand as I cursed the sky. Intelligent and insightful, I have always valued her opinion. When I eventually summoned the courage to let her read my manuscript, her positive feedback was a timely and needed shot of adrenaline. As any father can understand, witnessing Aveline's birth was the most beautiful and moving experience of my life. Every day, Stacey, Aveline and John inspire me to be a better husband and father, and each night, I cannot wait to see what tomorrow brings for our family.

My mom, Janet, has always been my hero. Looking back, I cannot imagine a parent making me feel more loved, cherished and supported. Born into a poor family with five children, her most valuable assets were grit and determination. By age twelve, she was buying her own school clothes. In her twenties, she helped create and grow her first successful business.

"There is no magic to this life, Jayme," she would say. "You wake up, work hard and have a plan." It was a formula that saw her persevere and succeed through the death of her mother when she was eleven years old, the death of her first husband (my father) when she was thirty-one, and the death of Claude when she was only sixty-five. Despite enduring more than her share of tragedy, she managed to pay both my college and law school tuition. My mom provided me with opportunities that as a young girl she could never imagine. Although life could have easily hardened her, there has never been an absence of affection or a conversation that ended without her saying, "I love you."

My father, Lyle James Roth, died when I was just ten years old. It took a couple years for cancer to destroy his strong body and claim his life. My memories of him before the illness are a mix of his love for my mother and me, his tireless work ethic and a tough fiery temperament that fueled a drive to be more than average. His courage to start a construction business with my mother left a deep impression on me. That piece of family history convinced me that having the backbone to take an unconventional path with my own life, including writing this book, was in my DNA. The moments of my life that I wanted to share with him are too many to remember, including the completion of this book.

At eighteen, I *begrudgingly* welcomed a new person into my life, Claude Faure. We barely knew each other at first, and he probably sensed that I preferred keeping it that way. By the time he became my stepfather, my feigned indifference toward him was worn away by his kindness, patience and generosity. And his love of travel, his unmatched abilities as a chef and his courage in moving to the United States as a young man inspired my willingness to think outside the box, to accept and appreciate people of different cultures. For me, Claude became the benchmark for how to enjoy life and treat others. When he passed away, my passion and drive for completing this book died with him. I stopped writing for over a year. But while his death sapped my motivation, remembering his life eventually brought me back. Claude Faure was the best man I have ever known.

Family and friends have read and provided critical comments to many drafts over the years, and I am grateful for their time and thoughtful input. In chronological order (as best as I can recall), they are Janet Faure, Claude Faure, Rich Pederson, Andrew Stewart, Ross Guberman, Karl Reinke, Nancy Arnold, Kristen Hardy, Dina Martinez Grimstead, Jim Layton, Dave Williams, Chris Berta, David Robinson, Tim Layton, Beverly Roulst and Kim Kaufman.

Over the past few years, I worked closely on the final draft with David Henry Sterry and Arielle Eckstut. An accomplished writer with a sharp wit, David helped me to look critically at my own work. He unapologetically identified areas of my manuscript that needed extra attention. His timely and well-placed edits made a significant contribution.

James Levine was my literary agent. Having represented several famous and best-selling authors, working with James was a pleasure. His enjoyment of this book and his passion for the story were very much appreciated.

Four other experienced professionals in the literary industry offered critical analysis and constructive feedback throughout the course of this project: Melinda Bargreen, Beth Davies, Greg Jordan and Rosemary Mackin.

Along with being a good family friend, Melinda Bargreen is a seasoned writer. In reviewing this book, she brought her more than three decades of experience writing for the *Seattle Times* and the lessons learned from authoring her own book, *Classical Seattle*.

Beth Davies served as my literary agent for an earlier version of this work. She was the first stranger to read the manuscript and be emotionally moved. Her enthusiasm and never-say-die attitude was welcome affirmation as I began sharing my work with a wider audience.

A writer of his own compelling sports biography, *Safe at Home*, Greg Jordan forced me to make some difficult choices early on. Greg pulled no punches in telling me what he thought was essential and what was "extraneous" material that belonged on the cutting room floor. Greg was also the first person who stressed that my own triumphs, setbacks and emotions were essential to this story—that I needed to be completely open in sharing the personal details of my life.

Rosemary Mackin was equally helpful as I sought to shorten my original draft. As much as anyone, her aggressive redlining challenged me to look critically at my own writing, to closely examine nearly every page for sections that were too verbose or unnecessary.

At the time of the U.S. Open in 2006, I was working on Capitol Hill for Senator Evan Bayh. The general rule for staff is that no vacations are taken while the Senate is in session. The Senate Floor and Committees are too busy, the demands of preparing the Senator for his meetings are too great and requests from constituents are too numerous. Regardless, Senator Bayh assured me that my attendance at the U.S. Open was one of "those moments" that justified bending the rules. His encouragement and support in taking time off during a busy week in Congress are one of many reasons I respected him as a boss and now appreciate him as a friend. Thanks also goes to Charlie Salem and Tom Sugar, the senior leaders on Senator Bayh's staff in 2006 who equally supported my time away.

Special thanks to the Library of Congress in Washington, DC. Completing the research for this book and the history Peter wanted me to learn was only possible because of the library's vast resources and dedicated staff.

Life as a professional golfer is expensive. Airline tickets to tournaments, hotels, rental cars, food and countless incidentals run well into the thousands. For a player who dedicates himself to golf full-time, which is almost a requirement considering the travel schedule and training regimen, there is the added cost of paying rent and other daily living expenses. In the months between Madalitso's college graduation and his appearance at the U.S. Open, a few generous people stepped forward to provide him with critical financial support. It is only fitting that they be mentioned here:

Janet and Claude Faure of Mukilteo, Washington. For years, my folks joined me in making family investments. Throughout his college years and immediately afterward, they assisted Madalitso with clothing, travel expenses, tuition and even medical needs. More importantly, they cheered during his good times and grieved during his bad times. Their willingness to welcome and support new members of our family has been an inspiration and lesson to me.

Howie, Melinda and Owen Bargreen of Everett, Washington. The

Bargreens were our first friends to meet Madalitso. Not surprisingly, they liked him right away. During each ensuing holiday and summer vacation, Howie, Melinda and Owen made a point of spending time with Madalitso. Every year, they came to our home for Claude's Christmas dinner. Some of our closest friends, the Bargreens never asked if they could help Madalitso. They insisted.

Don and Lori Armstrong of Beaverton, Oregon. Don and Lori took an interest in Madalitso from the moment they first met him in our home. Madalitso was a regular guest at their golf club, Bear Creek, and they actively followed his collegiate career. Over the years, they have been frequent holiday guests and cherished members of the extended family that we have built. People are lucky if they have friends like Don and Lori Armstrong.

Ryan and Karen Lake of Rye, New York. When Ryan and Karen welcomed a young stranger into their home in June of 2004, their generosity could have ended there. It didn't. Like so many others, the Lakes were drawn to this soft-spoken and polite Zambian. As a result, they joined his growing fan club. There was no hesitation when they were asked to support his fledgling golf career. Ryan and Karen Lake are proof that lifelong friendships can begin at any moment.

Steve Fidel of Albuquerque, New Mexico. Steve was a booster of UNM's golf program. Along with his generous assistance to amateur athletics, Steve is also a successful businessman and avid golfer. He came to know Madalitso through his support of the Lobos. Like most entrepreneurs, Steve has an eye for hard work and determination, qualities he saw in Madalitso. The two developed a good rapport during Madalitso's time on the golf team. Steve was all too happy to assist when we asked.

Jeff, Patti and John Anderson of Boynton Beach, Florida. Madalitso was not the first amateur athlete to receive assistance from the Andersons. For years, part of their family's mission has included helping aspiring young people from less-privileged backgrounds. Jeff knew about Madalitso's life story, and he made it clear that help was available. All we had to do was ask. Madalitso is one of a growing handful of young people to be aided by this generous family.

Mike and Jody Petrie of Carmel, Indiana. Mike Petrie is the only donor on this list to never have met Madalitso face-to-face, which made his gift all the more gracious. But this is not surprising, since much of Mike's lifework has been spent aiding men, women and children he doesn't know, mainly through his efforts to combat homelessness and provide housing to low-income families. Mike is an avid golfer, so assisting Madalitso was an outgrowth of his passion for the game and for helping people.

John and Karen DeCarolis of Bloomfield Hills, Michigan. Dr. John DeCarolis and his wife, Karen, welcomed Madalitso into their home when he competed in the 2002 U.S. Amateur Championship. Within hours, it was clear that a friendship was developing between the DeCarolis family and their well-mannered and courteous houseguest. John's thriving dental practice is only one of many ways this kind family gives back to their community. Like the others, the DeCarolis family didn't bat an eye when asked to help Madalitso pursue his dream of becoming a professional golfer.

Thanks to Glen Millican and Ryan Murphy, Madalitso's coaches at the University of New Mexico, and to Ms. Janice Ruggiero in UNM's athletic department. From the time of his recruitment until he donned his cap and gown, these and other members of the UNM family went beyond their job descriptions to support Madalitso through some very difficult times.

Heartfelt appreciation is given to the people of Zambia. In my three trips to the country, my most enduring memories of Lusaka and the smaller towns I was fortunate to visit are the warm smiles, engaging sense of humor and gracious hospitality of the men, women and children I met.

Expressing my love and appreciation for Peter, Madalitso and the Muthiya family is best left to the pages of this book.

Made in the USA
Coppell, TX
19 November 2021

66026143R10232